Export-Import Financing

WILEY FRONTIERS IN FINANCE SERIES

STYLE INVESTING: UNIQUE INSIGHT INTO ASSET MANAGEMENT
Richard Bernstein

VALUATION: MEASURING AND MANAGING THE VALUE OF COMPANIES, SECOND EDITION
Tom Copeland, Tim Koller, and Jack Murrin

DAMODARAN ON VALUATION: SECURITY ANALYSIS FOR INVESTMENT AND CORPORATE FINANCE
Aswath Damodaran

INVESTMENT VALUATION: TOOLS AND TECHNIQUES FOR VALUING *ANY* ASSET
Aswath Damodaran

FINANCIAL STATEMENT ANALYSIS: A PRACTITIONER'S GUIDE, SECOND EDITION
Martin S. Fridson

OPTION VALUATION AND HEDGING: A TRADING PERSPECTIVE
Marti G. Subrahmanyam and Sanjiv Das

FIXED INCOME SECURITIES: TOOLS FOR TODAY'S MARKETS
Bruce Tuckman

Export-Import Financing

Fourth Edition

HARRY M. VENEDIKIAN
GERALD A. WARFIELD

JOHN WILEY & SONS, INC.

New York • Chichester • Brisbane • Toronto • Singapore

This text is printed on acid-free paper.

This publication is designed to provide accurate and authoritative
information in regard to the subject matter covered. It is sold
with the understanding that the publisher is not engaged in
rendering legal, accounting, or other professional services. If
legal advice or other expert assistance is required, the services
of a competent professional person should be sought. *From a
Declaration of Principles Jointly Adopted by a Committee of the
American Bar Association and a Committee of Publishers.*

Library of Congress Cataloging-in-Publication Data

ISBN 0-471-12105-3

Printed in the United States of America

10 9 8 7 6 5 4 3 2

In memory of Manouk and Zepur Venedikian

Preface to the Fourth Edition

When Gerhard Schneider's *Export-Import Financing* first appeared in 1974, it immediately became the industry standard. Not since William Shaterian's *Export-Import Banking*, published in 1947, had any book attempted such complete and detailed coverage of all aspects of foreign trade financing. In the second edition, much of Schneider's original explanations and examples were preserved. Subjects first introduced in that edition included International Banking Facilities (IBFs), permitted by the Federal Reserve in 1981, and Export Trading Companies (ETCs) permitted by the U.S. Export Trading Companies Act of 1982. Other new material included sections on computerized customs clearance, reinsurance, and international trademarks. Some existing sections requiring revision were letters of credit, bills of lading, certificates of origin, foreign exchange, commercial bank lending, factoring, and foreign export-import bank facilities.

By 1991 changes in market conditions and regulations—not to mention the political upheavals within Central Europe—rendered portions of the second edition obsolete. With this, the third edition addressed these changes with discussions of the European community market, ECU currency, international banks custody operations, banking deregulation trends, bank involvement in insurance, and changes in the maritime industry. Chapter 15, "Recent Innovations," was another added feature.

This fourth edition brings with it a myriad of changes. Professionals and students alike should be referred to a new section in Chapter 14 entitled "Documentary Letter of Credit Examination Procedures." Enormous amounts of time and money would be saved (guaranteed) if the documentary section of a bank's letter of credit department used these procedures regularly. Other recent developments include the latest risks of collection services and the risks associated with red clause credits. Also see the specifications for the new ECU currency basket and recent currency fluctuations permitted by the EMS. Other areas of interest include air cargo updates, revised U.S. foreign trade definitions, bank guarantees for advanced payments, the loosening of the McFadden Act, and risk management in financing goods stored in warehouses.

The information contained in this book has been compiled from a wide variety of sources and some of it is subject to differences of opinion and interpretation. Furthermore, time, expediency, and common sense somewhat limited the amount of detail that could be presented. While every effort has been made to ensure accuracy and sufficient comprehensiveness, no responsibility can be assumed by the authors or the publishers for errors, omissions, or misinterpretations.

For ease in reading, masculine pronouns have been used throughout. This in no way implies that women are not included in the field of export-import financing.

HARRY M. VENEDIKIAN
GERALD A. WARFIELD

New York, New York
January 1996

Preface to the First Edition

This book is directed to the problems of those concerned with financing and otherwise facilitating U.S. exports and imports. As such, it is designed to provide guidance and orientation to international traders, corporate officers, bankers, and students of foreign commerce and banking.

Throughout I have attempted to emphasize the practical. Theoretical discussion is brought in only when it is useful in generalizing and clarifying practices and procedures. Much of the material is descriptive in that it endeavors to portray the functioning of institutions, vehicles, and processes in the movement of cross-border trade. Where appropriate I have also made a special attempt to bring in analytical discussion as an aid to evaluating risks and benefits as well as advantages and disadvantages of different approaches.

Most of the financial and technical services discussed are relatively timeless in their usefulness to internatinal traders and bankers. Such instruments as letters of credit, bankers' acceptances, and trust receipts have been with us for many years and have demonstrated repeatedly their usefulness in foreign trade financing. Many of these instruments have also been adapted to new uses. Thus, while commercial letters of credit are still as important as always in international trade, increasing use is being made of the letter of credit for special, noncommercial transactions. Similarly, bankers' acceptances are being used not only for financing U.S. exports and imports, but also for financing third country trade. At all times, I have tried to demonstrate the adaptability of timeless vehicles to modern financing needs.

In preparing this text, I have received valuable assistance from a number of institutions and individuals. Gratitude goes to The Chase Manhattan Bank for the invaluable experience I have gained in the art of international banking. Thanks are also due to my colleagues for their useful suggestions and for permission to reproduce a number of the bank's forms. Several officials of the First National City Bank of New York also have been most helpful in answering specific questions, reviewing portions of the manuscript, and permitting the use of illustrative material.

I am also greatly indebted to Shapiro Factors, the Foreign Credit Insurance

Association, the Export-Import Bank, the American Institute of Marine Underwriters, the Green Coffee Association and the Home Insurance Company for assistance of various kinds. Special gratitude goes to Professor Harold Kellar of Baruch College, City University of New York, and to Mr. Howard Miller for their counsel and advice. However, despite the assistance I have received, the views expressed in the book are my own and should not be attributed to any of the mentioned individuals or institutions.

Very special gratitude is finally reserved for my wife, not only for typing many drafts of the manuscript, but also for patiently and understandingly enduring my use of weekends, evenings, and vacations for the writing of this book.

GERHARD W. SCHNEIDER

New York, New York
April 1974

Contents

List of Figures

Export-Import Financing

PART 1

Facilities, Institutions, and Services

The financing of trade requires enormous amounts of capital in the form of various types of loans and advances as well as other financial services, such as guarantees and letters of credit. Also needed are a host of specialized or technical services for making international payments, finding new markets, determining the reputation and financial strength of potential suppliers and customers, and so forth.

The vast resources required—both financial and human—can be found in a variety of institutions that specialize in supplying the types of services needed. To marshal capital for the financing of trade requires organizations that have sufficient strength and repute so that depositors and investors are willing to entrust their money to them. The technical skills of financing trade also require many highly trained and experienced people.

A knowledge of the institutions that make important contributions to the financing of trade and related services is vital for international merchants and investors. Part 1 gives an overview of the most important organizations that exist and summarizes the services they offer.

Chapter 1 is devoted to tracing some of the past and present trends in world trade and investment flows and evaluating the impact that these have on financial institutions and vehicles. Recent developments such as export trading companies and international banking facilities are introduced.

The most important institutions that provide services for international trade and investment are commercial banks. The larger ones, especially, have the financial and human resources required to get the job done. Smaller banks can also offer valuable services through a network of correspondent relationships. Chapter 2 is entirely devoted to outlining the organization and services of commercial banks.

Even though banks enjoy a central position in the financing of trade, they cannot do everything. A small, rapidly growing company with much enthusiasm and potential but little capital may not qualify for bank credit. It would, therefore, turn to other institutions that specialize in secured lending, such as factors and finance companies. Moreover, most banks rely primarily on short-term demand and time deposits for their funding. Consequently, they have a decided preference for making short- and medium-term loans. When longer terms are required, such as to finance the export of airplanes or whole industrial plants, other specialized institutions may be needed. To reduce some of the risks inherent in foreign trade, exporters may wish to insure the payment of their foreign accounts receivable through the Foreign Credit Insurance Association. Such insurance also may make bank financing easier to obtain.

Chapter 3 describes the most important private nonbank institutions that may be of financial assistance to exporters and importers.

Sometimes private industry is not willing or able to take specialized risks associated with export financing. In a drive to increase U.S. exports, the Export-Import Bank has become an aggressive and useful vehicle in helping the exporter. Other U.S. government agencies may also help. Eximbank and other governmental and international agencies such as the International Monetary Fund (IMF) are discussed in Chapter 4.

Just as the United States has the Foreign Credit Insurance Association (FCIA) and the Eximbank, many other countries have set up private and/or governmental agencies to help their exporters by providing guarantees and/or financing. Such private and governmental assistance, available in many European and Asian countries, is briefly described in Chapter 5.

CHAPTER 1

The World of International Financing and Banking

Current trends toward financial deregulation in the United States and massive increases in the need for trade-related credit and financing worldwide have created export-import markets of unprecedented depth and complexity. Large financial institutions that traditionally provide high-quality banking are finding their services increasingly in demand, even though growing numbers of smaller banks, in an effort to expand their bases of operations, have also begun to engage in export-import services. In turn, banks both great and small, recognizing a growing source of fees and service revenues, have begun to market their export-import services far more aggressively than was the industry norm only a few years ago. It comes as no surprise, therefore, that risk managers and those who specialize in the multitude of support services required by international trade are finding greater demand for their skills from banking and nonbanking institutions and corporations alike.

The present state of export-import financing has evolved (and continues to do so) in response to a number of general forces. These include underlying economic conditions, applicable government regulations, and the structures of financial institutions designed to implement international trade. The extent to which governments and private institutions are sensitive to the needs of both domestic and international trade is one of the most important factors influencing the health of a nation's exports and imports.

PATTERNS OF UNITED STATES AND WORLD TRADE

According to the IMF, world exports and imports, after an allowance for inflation, increased 14-fold from 1950–1980. Following a slowdown in the early 1980s, the former pace was restored by mid-decade, and by 1991, with higher oil consumption and industrial growth worldwide, international trade had experienced six years of unprecedented expansion and development. After 1991, however, expansion was brought to an abrupt halt, first by a mini-recession, then by a full-scale recession and high unemployment worldwide. Signs of a recovery did not reappear until the end of 1994 and then with only modest growth coupled with lower unemployment.

Most economists agree that over the long term international trade remains at a fairly constant percentage of the gross world product. There are year-to-year variations, of course, and in periods of economic prosperity, the tendency is for trade to increase faster than production. This, in fact, has been the case in most of the years since World War II.

From our perspective, however, it is not the absolute level of world trade that is important, but the U.S. portion of that trade. From 1957 to 1977, U.S. exports generally lost ground against those of the rest of the world and have only begun to recover since 1983. Imports, from 1957, fluctuated between 12.5% and 15.5% before they, too, began a steady climb in 1982. Perhaps the most significant year was 1971 when total U.S. exports dropped below imports, remaining there every year since except for 1975. As a result, in the second quarter of 1985 the United States became a debtor nation on recorded transactions for the first time since 1914. Also in 1985, however, the depreciation of the U.S. dollar in relation to other major currencies enhanced the competitiveness of U.S. goods on world markets and strengthened the growth of U.S. exports that was begun in 1983. In 1988, according to the IMF, world trade expanded by more than 9%, the highest rate of growth since 1976. That same year the United States experienced real export growth of 23% thereby recovering most of the share of world merchandise exports that it had lost between 1980 and 1985. By the end of 1993, according to the Commerce Department, U.S. exports had increased by 14% due primarily to the rapid and unusual appreciation of the Japanese yen, which softened the value of the U.S. dollar and made U.S. goods and services more competitive abroad.

Traditional Patterns. Before the present levels of industrialization, much trade was in agricultural commodities and raw materials—while there was somewhat less activity in manufactured goods. It is well known that even today the United Kingdom traditionally imports raw materials and a substantial proportion of its foodstuffs. In turn, it exports manufactured goods produced in its capital-intensive economy. On the other hand, the United States, rich in land, has always been an important exporter of agricultural commodities. Beyond an historical—and expected—growth in the volume of those exports there have been changes in the nature of the goods traded. The United States, for example, has become a major exporter of high technology and services.

Comparative Growth Rates. Broadly speaking, traditional trading patterns still exist, but on a greatly expanded scale. However, there have been significant changes in emphasis that make today's trade flows quite different from what they were before or just after World War II. World exports of chemicals, machinery, other manufactured products, and fuels have grown significantly faster than average. In contrast, export growth in food products and raw materials exclusive of fuels has grown substantially less than average.

Specific Growth Areas. Taking the previously mentioned trends as a point of reference, it may be useful to look at some specific growth areas of the past that might continue to manifest themselves in the future. The implications that these trends have from a financing point of view will then be discussed in Chapters 2 and 3.

Luxury Goods. As individual economies were rebuilt in the post-World War II era, they became more self-sufficient in basic consumer goods as well as in some agricultural commodities that previously had to be imported. The obtaining of self-sufficiency in some areas freed funds for the importation of new types of goods. As per-capita income increased and trade and exchange restrictions were liberalized, individuals were able to buy imported luxuries that had not been affordable in the past.

High Technology Capital Goods. In addition to luxury consumer goods, advanced industrial economies also generate a need for a myriad of sophisticated equipment, replacement parts, computers, electronic devices, and so on, for which, in simpler times, no market existed. Countries wishing to expedite their industrial development have frequently resorted to the importation of entire factories.

Raw Materials. Developed nations need more than machinery and equipment for the operation of industrial plants. There is also a demand for an enormous quantity of raw materials. Keeping machines running requires increasing quantities of petroleum, uranium, coal, and other fuels.

For many years, demand for raw materials was the major growth area for most third-world nations. Recently, however, overproduction has caused a glut on many markets and a concomitant drop in commodity prices. This has been particularly true in oil and copper. Many countries have recently discovered that a balance of payments deficit cannot be rectified by means of the ever-increasing production of raw materials. Unless world demand increases substantially, raw materials will no longer be among the major growth areas of world economies.

Oil. Sharp rises in the price of oil brought profound changes to the balance of trade and the payments of many nations. In the aftermath of the October War among Egypt, Syria, and Israel, the 1973 oil embargo caused the price of crude oil to skyrocket on world markets. In September 1973 the average price of a barrel of crude was $4; by 1978 it had risen to $22, and in 1980 it had reached a peak of $44. Since World War II, probably no other single factor has wreaked such havoc on the world economy and has had such a profound effect on international trade. Eventually, massive exploration and overproduction, triggered by these price levels, produced an oversupply, pushing prices back to $22 a barrel for some grades. Then on August 2, 1990 Iraqi forces entered Kuwait and a new wave of price escalations began. The oil well fires left in the wake of this war served to keep prices at these new levels until 1992 when a world recession and the depreciation of the U.S. dollar brought the price of a barrel to $14, a level not seen since the mid-seventies. By the beginning of 1995, with a modest growth in world economies, the price had risen to $17.

Know-How. Know-how may be sold as part of a larger project, such as a turnkey plant or the export of management and technical talents that takes place when companies set up foreign subsidiaries. Know-how may, however, also be sold in its own right. In this case, the buyer receives patent rights, blueprints, and specifications. Buying the necessary machinery and equipment and assembling it into a viable factory is then the responsibility of the buyer. In recent years, basic know-how has been part of or responsible for more and more international trade. The buyer receives something that would take several years and enormous expenditure to develop. The seller, on the other hand, has marketed something (usually at an attractive price) with very little out-of-pocket expenditure.

Services. Technically, service differs from know-how in that it involves the employment of skilled personnel. Many high-technology consulting firms have developed a steady export of the skills of their staffs to those countries in need of technicians for the development of their industries. It should be noted that the export of services does not include the sale of machinery or tools, but may involve the *use* of such equipment, as in the shipping and airlines industries.

Service is a vast area that can include anything from running a fertilizer plant to planning a communications system. U.S. banks, for example, earn sizable fees by managing overseas banks, especially those with complex international operations. Another example is U.S. oil drilling and exploration, which conducts a multimillion dollar industry abroad, assisting oil-producing countries in their day-to-day operations.

Direction of Trade

Trade can never be a one-way street for a prolonged period of time. Imbalances may exist for several years and can be counterbalanced by drawing down reserves and borrowing abroad. Sooner or later, however, these imbalances have to be corrected. Following World War II, the United States was clearly the world's principal exporter. Countries requiring U.S. goods first used up their gold supplies. Then their imports were aided by a series of grants and credits primarily extended by the U.S. government and some international organizations like the World Bank.

As economies recovered, the picture gradually began to shift. The U.S. trade surplus narrowed and then became negative. Most dramatic, probably, is the case of Japan, which moved from being a net importer to a substantial exporter.

The softening of the U.S. dollar has currently given new life to U.S. exports. Nevertheless, export levels have remained far below those of imports and a negative balance of trade has thus persisted into the nineties. At the same time, Japan, with technological know-how and good management, has emerged as one of the strongest exporters in the world—serious need for oil being almost its only problem. As mentioned before, high oil prices seriously altered the import patterns of most countries. The developing countries that needed oil often found that they could afford little else; and later, when oil prices began to fall, countries, like Mexico, which had come to depend on high oil revenues, found themselves with serious problems.

Future Trends

What trade patterns might we see in the future? Unless governments impose a round of new trade restrictions, we can be fairly certain that world trade will continue to increase at a faster rate than gross national product. Less developed countries, following the lead of the major trading nations, will export those products which they can produce most efficiently and will import others.

The pulling down of the Berlin Wall in December 1989 was a graphic representation of the growing independence of Eastern Bloc countries. As this trend continues it will enliven prospects for future trade and investment, although it is still too early to predict the economic relationship of those countries to the rest of the world whether in a new context of limited capitalism or an extension of world socialism. Whatever their course, economic self-sufficiency, for so long the goal of the former Soviet Union, is a thing of the past. At the same time, in China the appearance of equity exchanges and the anticipated annexation of Hong Kong may herald a turning point in China's policy of economic isolationism.

It is probable that the future will also see substantially increased production and trade in consumer and high-technology goods. More of these products will be produced in low-labor-cost countries for export to regional and world markets. This, in turn, will give developing countries more exchange to buy needed industrial machinery, consumer goods, and, perhaps, also some luxuries. Instead of exporting all raw materials directly to western markets, developing countries will probably endeavor to carry them through at least initial stages of processing. These raw materials will thus be exported only after they have had some value added, that is, in the form of semifinished or finished goods.

BALANCE OF PAYMENTS

As a background to our study of export-import financing we will take a brief look at the economic relationship of the United States to the rest of the world, as expressed in the U.S. balance of payments.[1] For any country, the balance of payments consists of a systematic record of its receipts from, or payments to, other countries. Note that it is not the shipment of the commodity or the performance of the service that affects the balance of payments; it is the transfer of the payment (thus the name, balance of "payments"). Each payment is categorized as to commodity, service, and so forth, and recorded as a debit (if the funds are leaving the country) or a credit (if the funds are entering the country).

The primary accounts of the balance of payments are the current account, capital account, and official settlement. While the rest of this book is concerned with transactions affecting the balance of goods and services (a subcategory of the current account), an understanding of the total balance of payments can be helpful. Not only can an overall picture of the economic health of a country be obtained, but certain specific risks can be more carefully evaluated, such as tariffs, quotas, and exchange rate movements. We now consider each of the major accounts that make up the balance of payments.

Current Account

The current account consists of payments or receipts within one of the following categories:

1 Goods and services
2 Foreign aid

The data for goods and services is broken down into its obvious components:

(a) Merchandise trade: Known as "visible" trade, this consists of tangibles, such as raw materials, manufactured goods, foodstuffs, equipment, and so on. References in the media to the balance of trade generally refer to the balance of merchandise trade unless otherwise specified.[2]

(b) Services: Known as "invisible" trade, these consist of intangibles, such as interest and dividends on securities (but not payments for the

[1]Balance of payments data for the United States and other countries may be found in the *Balance of Payment Yearbook*, IMF, Washington, D.C. Quarterly U.S. data may be found in the periodical *Survey of Current Business* (March, June, September, and December issues) published by the U.S. Department of Commerce.

[2]Merchandise trade statistics for most western countries may be found in the *Monthly Bulletin of Statistics*, Statistical Office of the United Nations. For only United States data, see the Department of Commerce Reports FT110 and FT410 for imports and exports, respectively.

securities themselves), international shipping expenses, technology transfers, and transfers of the salaries of migrant workers to their countries of origin. An example of a technology transfer would be know-how (as mentioned before), such as the purchase of a patent or the acquisition of rights to a manufacturing process.

The other major subdivision of the current account is foreign aid. This is made up of economic assistance to friendly foreign governments by, for instance, the Agency for International Development. The reimbursement of such aid by the receiving country is assumed to be made on a long-term credit facility. A minor component of this account is personal gifts donated to friends and relatives overseas by individuals. These are one-way transactions and not two-way transactions like shipments and payments.

Capital Account

The capital account records all long- or short-term capital transfers into and out of a country. It is broken down into two subcategories:

1. Private investment: This includes all purchases of securities as well as major holdings in companies, factories, and so forth.
2. Transactions of central banks: These are mostly international securities transactions, foreign exchange covers, and government-to-government settlements.

When the net result of both the current and capital account yield more credits than debits, the country is said to have a surplus in its balance of payments. When there are more debits than credits, the country is said to have a deficit in the balance of payments; the net balance, therefore, represents either the deficit or surplus, as the case may be.

Official Settlement

It is in the third account, official settlement, that the deficits are offset by official liabilities of the government or that surpluses are retained as U.S. official-reserve assets. When the United States was on the gold standard, deficits could be offset by demands on its gold reserves. Today, deficits are offset by currency transfer transactions and obligations of official foreign bodies such as central banks. Sometimes, settlements may be made in Special Drawing Rights (SDR) dollars.

Summary

There are different ways of condensing specific accounts of the balance of payments, but a complete picture, as has been described previously, would be as follows:

Balance of Payments

I. Current account
   A. Goods and services
      1. Merchandise trade
      2. Services
   B. Foreign aid

II. Capital account
   A. Private investments
   B. Transactions of central banks

III. Official settlement

It is interesting to note that the flow of funds worldwide, in the categories that make up the current account, is one-tenth or less than that of the capital account. At this time, the total world trade in goods and services is about $15 trillion a year while the capital flow is from $53 trillion to $63 trillion. By comparison, about $90 trillion is traded in currencies each year by banks.

EXPORT INCENTIVES

The political and economic advantages of exports are recognized worldwide and, as a result, most countries offer a variety of export incentives. Some nations, through various agencies, pay exporters up to 30% bonuses in the form of subsidies or entitlement bonuses. At one time, industrialized nations even offered low-cost export financing. Today, most offer at least market rates for export financing and provide various guarantees against political risks associated with exporting. Even loans and foreign aid may be used to support exports if the recipients of such loans or aid are required to use the funds to purchase goods or services from the donor country. Most of these programs are discussed in subsequent chapters.

Developing countries also have a wide variety of special incentives at their disposal for encouraging domestic or foreign investors to develop export-intensive industries within their borders. For example, the governments of some countries rebate value-added tax. This is an incentive now offered by countries of the European Common Market. Some countries waive duties on imported materials or equipment vital to the export industry. Sometimes, the host country even undertakes to finance and to build needed facilities or infrastructures.

In the United States, financing and guarantee programs are available through the Eximbank, Private Export Funding Corporation (PEFCO), and the Foreign Credit Insurance Association. Also, valuable information for companies who wish to develop foreign markets is made available through the U.S. Department of Commerce. So far, however, the major incentive has been the establishment of foreign sales corporations.

Foreign Sales Corporation

The Revenue Act of 1971 established Domestic International Sales Corporations (DISCs). The act was designed, in particular, to encourage small companies to develop export operations, although large companies frequently benefited from its provisions, as well. Under the act, companies were permitted to set up wholly owned subsidiaries for the purpose of exporting U.S. goods and services. Such subsidiaries had the option of deferring the payment of U.S. corporate income tax on as much as one-half of their net earnings. For 13 years, DISCs constituted the U.S. government's primary tax incentive for exporting U.S. goods and services.

The Tax Reform Act of 1984 replaced DISCs with Foreign Sales Corporations (FSCs). It is required that an FSC be incorporated in, and maintain an office in, a foreign country or a possession of the United States that has an IRS-approved exchange of tax information program with the United States. The following criteria must also be met:

1. There can be no more than 25 shareholders.
2. No preferred stock may be issued.
3. A complete set of permanent books of account must be kept at an office of an IRS-approved country.
4. Certain tax and accounting records must be maintained at some location in the United States.
5. At least one member of the board of directors must not be a U.S. resident.
6. The FSC must not be a member of a controlled group of corporations that has a DISC as a member.
7. A proposal to be treated as an FSC must be passed in a corporate election, and the election itself must be agreed to by all shareholders.

For purposes of both incorporation and office location, possessions of the United States include American Samoa, the Commonwealth of Northern Mariana Islands, Guam, and the U.S. Virgin Islands. Puerto Rico is excluded in that it is considered a part of the United States. As such, goods manufactured there are eligible for FSC benefits.

If the FSC is to be located in another country it is necessary that that country either have an income tax treaty with the United States that includes an exchange of information provision or that there be an independent exchange of information agreement. Such an agreement would be subject to IRS approval. Domestic laws restricting access to records in the home office of the FSC would be grounds for nonapproval.

Foreign trading gross receipts (FTGRs) must be generated by FSCs. These receipts typically include receipts from sale of export property, exchange of export property, lease or rental of export property as long as its use is outside the United States, performance of services related to such sales or leases, and the performance of managerial services for unrelated FSCs, as long as 50% or more of the FSC's gross receipts are derived from the activities mentioned. Engineering and architectural services on sites located outside the United States may qualify.

For the purposes of FSCs, "export property" includes property that is manufactured, produced, grown, or extracted in the United States by an entity other than the FSC itself. However, up to 50% of the fair market value of the property may be attributable to imported materials.

Foreign trading gross receipts of an FSC do not include receipts from export property used in the United States, services ultimately used in the United States, transactions financed by U.S. government subsidy, sales to another FSC that is a member of the same controlled group, half of all receipts from the sales of military property, or investment income and carrying charges.

Export property does not include property that is leased by the FSC to, or for the use of, an affiliate of the FSC. Also excluded are oil and gas, oil and gas products, products the export of which is prohibited by the Export Administration Act, or products found to be in short supply in the United States. Intangibles, such as patents, inventions, copyrights, trademarks, and franchises, are also excluded.

Destination and ultimate use tests for FSCs are similar to those for the former DISCs. Foreign presence and foreign management requirements are, however, more stringent. The latter requires that all meetings of the board of directors and the shareholders be held outside the United States. The principal bank account of the FSC must also be outside the United States. Dividends, legal and accounting fees, and salaries of officers and members of the board must be paid from bank accounts not located within the United States.

DIRECT INVESTMENT

A direct investment differs from an ordinary portfolio investment in that the former is an equity holding substantial enough to bring with it a degree of control in the company. Obviously, the outright purchase of more than 50% of a foreign company is a direct investment. However, in practical terms, there is no exact percentage that normally constitutes effective or partial control. In most countries it varies from industry to industry, as it does in the United States. Of course, there are many cases where holdings substantial enough to bring with them a degree of control are treated like portfolio investments, that is, they are held primarily for income or capital gains.

It may be surprising to some that direct investment in foreign industries can actually stimulate foreign trade and vice versa. For example, investments in production facilities abroad can create new trade in capital equipment, replacement parts, and raw materials that will be needed by such industries. Similarly, the expansion of an export market for a particular product line can lead to the establishment of a foreign plant, so as to bring production closer to the intended market.

The increased production capabilities and other competitive advantages of established local firms within their own market areas is obvious. The concern for U.S. companies is that their export potential can be substantially impaired by local domestic firms—particularly if they have modern efficient plants and relatively low labor costs. Direct investment, besides solving the problems of local competition, also, of course, has the advantage of participation in rapidly growing local economies.

United States Investment Abroad

After World War II, most European nations offered liberal incentives to attract U.S. investment. The desperately needed dollars initially provided through the Marshall Plan had to be eventually replaced by dollars generated through free-market export operations. Thus, U.S. firms wishing to establish overseas branches and subsidiaries were granted various tax, financing, or regulatory concessions. In a few cases, outright government grants were used to induce companies to locate plants in their countries.

By the 1960s, however, the balance of power gradually shifted the other way. New and recovering European countries became increasingly concerned about the large-scale U.S. presence. While foreign investment was still considered beneficial, incentives were removed and some restrictions began to appear. Feelings were particularly strong against the practices of some U.S. companies who borrowed in the Eurocurrencies markets for the purpose of foreign investment rather than remitting the money from the United States. Instead of the needed influx of U.S. dollars, Europeans sometimes found that direct investment in Europe was being financed by borrowed European money.

In recent years a strong dollar and high interest rates attracted massive amounts of foreign investment to the United States. Even after the weakening of the currency in 1985 and a concomitant drop in interest rates the perception of that country as a "safe haven" kept a great deal of foreign capital invested there.

Restrictions and Nationalization

In reaction to the unparalleled growth of U.S. direct investments abroad, some nations began to protect domestic companies or industry sectors from foreign ownership. Among the first restrictions were limitations on the amount of a company's stock that could be held by nonresidents. As in the case of Japan, this sometimes took the form of outright quotas on the percentage of foreign ownership that could be recorded in a company's books. It was possible for these limitations to be exceeded, but only with the direct permission from the government.

Sometimes, as in the cases of Switzerland and Sweden, two types of securities were issued, such as voting and nonvoting shares, or registered and bearer form shares. Foreign investors, being restricted to nonvoting or bearer shares, were then automatically limited to the equity represented by that particular issue or class of stock.

Japan, one of the most protectionist of all free countries, has the requirement that foreign shareholders must appoint proxies in Japan to hold their voting rights. These roles are usually filled by Japanese brokers who then have absolute discretion in exercising these rights.

Another step taken by foreign governments to protect ailing companies from foreign takeovers is nationalization. Usually, this is invoked only in the case of large companies or companies within industries that are considered to be central to national security, such as utilities or banks. The likelihood of nationalization is, of course, much affected by the political ideologies of the political party in power. Naturally, a socialist government is more prone to nationalization than a capitalist government.

With the exception of France, the trend is away from both ownership quotas and nationalization. Japan, for instance, is loosening its percentage restrictions on foreign ownership for a group of companies (mostly oil companies) considered central to the country's security. The United Kingdom, as another example, has begun divesting itself of industries nationalized by the former Labour Party. In 1984, the sale of British Telecommunication, the U.K. telephone company, constituted the largest single offering of stock in the world. France, as mentioned before, has been the major exception with the nationalization of several industries, most notably, banks.

Direct Investment in the United States

A variety of reasons make the United States attractive to investment from abroad. Periods of high interest rates make dollar-denominated debt securities popular with foreign investors and, thereby, tend to result in upward pressure on the dollar. Equity instruments and real estate are also in demand because of the size of U.S. markets, perception of safety in that country, and advantage of favorable exchange rates.

Law of Comparative Advantage

The law of comparative advantage clearly demonstrates the advantage of concentration on those industries within a country that can produce most efficiently even though another country may hold an absolute advantage in the same industry. Although beyond the scope of this book, it is mentioned here because, to a considerable extent, it has guided U.S. direct investments abroad, domestic investment, and the direct investments of other countries.

Impact of Direct Investing on World Trade

The consequences of direct investment on foreign trade are sometimes not fully appreciated. Obviously, goods and services produced abroad compete with U.S. exports in local and third-world markets. Moreover, goods and services produced abroad, as a result of direct investment, are often imported to the United States and compete on domestic markets.

The overall picture, however, is more complicated. It has been shown that an average of 25% of direct foreign investment returns almost at once to the United States in the form of orders for capital goods. Not only is capital equipment needed, but continual orders are generated for replacement parts, raw materials, and additional machinery. Many of these orders will, of course, be satisfied on local or other foreign markets, but many will also be filled in the United States and thereby will stimulate foreign trade and create jobs in that country.

MULTINATIONAL COMPANIES

Striving for profits through large-scale purchasing, manufacturing, and marketing led inevitably to the creation of the modern multinational company. Although overseas offices and plants of U.S. companies were initially run by Americans, many managers today are commonly nationals of the country where the subsidiary is located. Gradually, foreign subsidiaries and plants have become more international in their operations, managements, and, inevitably, in their general philosophies. Additionally, more and more senior positions at U.S. headquarters have also been filled by foreign nationals.

Even the ownership of many companies has become multinational. Shares in U.S. corporations are owned not only by Americans, but also by nationals of many countries. These shares are increasingly traded on European stock exchanges. Some exchanges, such as the Amsterdam Stock Exchange, have created special equity instruments to facilitate the trading of American shares on their own exchanges.

Multinationality, of course, is no longer just an American phenomenon. European companies, such as Philips, Unilever, Royal Dutch Shell, ICI, Olivette, and so on, have worldwide operations. Major Japanese companies have also evolved into multinationals. Hitachi and Matsushita Electric, for example, have plants in 16 and 25 countries, respectively.

Advantages of Multinationals

There are many advantages to multinational operations. The most obvious, perhaps, are the economies of large-scale production and distribution that can be achieved by worldwide integration of facilities. For instance, the engines of an automobile can be produced in one country, transmissions in another, and remaining parts can come from various third countries. All parts can then be shipped to one or more assembly plants in the proximity of the consumer market.

Similar to worldwide integration, vertical integration on a worldwide basis can also be advantageous. In this situation, a subsidiary's product in one country is shipped to a subsidiary in another country for further processing or assembly, then to another, and so forth. Goods may move along a rather lengthy manufacturing/distribution process, from one country to the next until they ultimately reach their intended market.

Locating production facilities in a variety of countries gives companies substantial sourcing advantages. A particular market can be supplied either from one or another country, depending on the availability of goods, shipping costs, tax considerations, and other factors.

Research and development may often benefit from multinational operations. An innovation discovered by one subsidiary may also be usable in other parts of the world. Cross-fertilization of technological know-how and new ideas in production management, distribution, and finance can benefit an entire company as well as the consumer.

In the financial area, there is the possibility of moving funds to where they are most needed through judicious intercompany pricing, deferring or accelerating payment of intercompany receivables, and centralized cash management. It can also be more convenient to borrow in markets where the company has established subsidiaries and where funds may be cheaper or more readily available. Minimization of taxes is also a major consideration in cash management of multinationals.

IMPLICATIONS FOR BANKING

Before discussing the implications for banking, we will summarize a few of the key trade and investment conditions so far considered.

First, large-scale investments continue to stimulate world trade in capital goods. While it is true that the initial act of investment abroad is in terms of money, a modern plant ultimately requires a large amount of machinery, equipment, and know-how. Much of this will be imported from the original capital-supply country and from other countries as well.

Second, exports of capital goods are often not of a "once only" nature. Machines break down and require the importation of spare parts. Old pieces of equipment wear out or become obsolete and must be replaced. Plants become too small and have to be expanded to meet growing markets. Hence, after an initial capital investment, chances are that there will be follow-up demands for parts, replacements, and additions.

Third, foreign-capital investment stimulates trade in basic raw materials, fuels, and commodities used in the production of industrial goods. Often the cheapest and most efficient source of raw materials and subassembled products is the parent company or other firms within the home country. Thus, capital investment leads directly to an expansion of trade in order to keep the new plants supplied with required inputs. It should be pointed out that, of course, much of this additional trade tends to be intercompany, that is, parent or affiliated companies act as suppliers for newly formed subsidiaries.

It should also be mentioned that foreign capital investments, over a number of years, may add substantially to the local standard of living. Whenever there is a significant increase in individual purchasing power, a large proportion of the increase tends to be spent on imported luxury items. An indirect but still significant effect of foreign capital investment, therefore, has been an increase in trade of nonessential consumer goods.

What implications do these conditions in world trade and investment have on the financing and banking needs of individual companies? Basically, the implications are as follows:

The need for traditional short-term financing of raw materials, fuels, commodities, and manufactured consumer goods is generally strong in keeping up with growth in merchandise trade that requires such financing. Disruptions do occur, however, such as those caused by rising (and falling) oil prices and other essential commodities.

Large-scale investment in infrastructures, manufacturing, and extractive industries creates an enormous demand for financial resources. A good part of these resources is, in turn, used to buy imports of machinery, equipment, and industrial plants.

Since a great deal of capital is necessary to buy machinery and equipment, today's and tomorrow's needs are greatest for medium- and long-term funds. The short-term credit that banks have traditionally been willing to grant, while still necessary, is not adequate for the longer-term needs of capital investment.

Companies that sell and invest overseas often need more than money. They may be unfamiliar with local marketing as well as regulatory, financial, employment, and supply conditions. Hence, the emphasis in banking has been not only the supplying of financial resources, but also the offering of services. It can be invaluable to a company expanding in a particular country to have bankers furnish it with detailed information on considerations, such as where it might be most advantageous to locate a new plant, what the required government formalities might be in getting the new plant established, what the local employment conditions are like, and countless other useful questions.

INTERNATIONAL BANKING FUNCTIONS TODAY

Classical Financing Functions

The traditional purpose of international banking has been to finance foreign trade, and a large part of that trade is in items, such as raw materials, foods, fuels, and similar commodities. The need for the financing of such items is of a short-term nature, that is, up to six months or, perhaps, a maximum of one year by foreign bankers. This is because goods such as raw materials, grains, foods, and other consumer items are generally "used up" within weeks or months after having arrived at their destinations. The payout in this type of situation comes from the ultimate consumer in a relatively short period of time. In the United States, the Federal Reserve Bank allows financing up to the time of consumation of the goods.

Banks have always been eager to provide financing for this kind of trade. It is attractive because banks know exactly where the payback of loans will come from—sales to the ultimate consumers. In the meantime, especially in the case of commodities, the bank has, as collateral, some readily marketable goods that can be sold at short notice should anything go wrong with the borrower. Additionally, since repayment can be expected in the relatively short time of six months to one year, the bank does not tie up its capital for a long period of time. It makes a loan, gets repaid, and soon has money available again for new lending.

Capital Goods Financing

Capital goods require longer-term financing than traditional commodities. This is because the amount of time it takes industrial machinery to pay for itself is considerably longer for capital goods than it is for raw materials, grains, foodstuffs, and so on. This amount of time, known as the capital-goods cycle, extends into years. First, the machine must be shipped overseas and installed. Even after it is on line, however, it may take considerable time before enough goods can be produced for it to pay for itself. This is true not only for industrial machinery, but also for such capital goods as ships, airplanes, trucks, or anything else that has to operate for a number of years in order to pay for itself.

Risks. When financing capital goods, a banker has to be prepared to have funds tied up for a much longer period of time. Moreover, there must be some assurance that there will still be a ready market for the new capital-goods items when they are finally produced. The party making the investment has to have sufficient engineering expertise to make the equipment work efficiently and profitably. It must also have sufficient marketing ability to predict or create adequate consumer demand for the end product at a price high enough to pay for all direct inputs, recover the initial investment,and, hopefully, make a profit. Thus, a banker who makes a loan financing the exportation or importation of capital goods must take substantially greater risks. Not only will funds be tied up for several years, but there must be some certainty that the underlying project is sound and that the loan can ultimately be repaid.

Financing Institutions. Although banks are willing to finance the export and import of capital goods, in many instances the term and risk go beyond the willingness of one bank to carry so that several banks may act as a syndicate in financing large-item exports or projects requiring longer terms. There are also specialized institutions that have been formed to engage primarily in long-term financing of trade and investments. In addition, most industrialized countries have some government-sponsored assistance in financing or guaranteeing the financing of capital-goods exports.

Local Currency Financing

Banks in the United States have traditionally supplied domestic companies with seasonal working capital. Banks are also willing to make substantial term loans and revolving credit available in order to finance the purchase of machinery and construction of new plants. As U.S. banks have expanded abroad, they have offered the same type of financing in local foreign currencies or Eurocurrencies that may be exchanged for local currency. While this type of facility is not directly related to foreign trade financing, it represents an important added dimension to servicing the financial needs of multinational as well as local companies.

Financial Services

Banks offer a host of services that, next to short-and medium-term financing, greatly facilitate the movement of international trade. Some of these, like letters of credit and financing of foreign accounts receivable, are part of the traditional function of banks as providers of short-term trade financing. Other services, such as assistance in finding new markets or new sources of supply, financial consulting services, rapid money transfers, and letters of introduction for businessmen traveling abroad, can also be of substantial help in furthering the volume and efficiency of international trade.

Creation of International Banking Facilities

Rapid growth in international trade, financing, and investing has prompted the central banks of most nations to review their regulation of trade-related banking. In the United States, the Federal Reserve Board amended its regulation regarding reserve requirements and interest rates on deposits in order to permit the establishment of International Banking Facilities (IBFs). In that this is the most current major regulatory change, it will be considered here in some detail. The following press release from the Federal Reserve Board, excerpted almost in its entirety, announces the changes and applicable limitations:

> FEDERAL RESERVE Press Release: June 18, 1981
>
> IBFs may be established, subject to conditions specified by the [Federal Reserve] Board, by United States depository institutions, by Edge and

Agreement Corporations,[3] and by United States branches and agencies of foreign banks.

In general, under the rules adopted by the Board, an IBF may accept deposits from and extend credit to foreign residents or other IBFs. All such funds will be exempt from reserve requirements of Regulation D[4] and from interest rate limitations of Regulation Q. The Board believes that establishment of IBFs at U.S. banking offices will enhance the international competitive position of banking institutions in the United States.

In amending its regulations respecting reserve requirements and interest rate ceilings to permit the establishment of IBFs, the Board made a general statement of policy regarding the use of IBF deposits and IBF loans.
The policy statement to the Board's action said in part:

The Board expects that, with respect to nonbank customers located outside the United States, IBFs will accept only deposits that support the customer's operations outside the United States and will extend credit only to finance the customer's non-U.S. operations. Deposits should not be used as a means of circumventing interest rate restrictions or reserve requirements . . .

This policy, the Board specified, must be communicated in writing to all IBF nonbank customers when a credit or deposit relationship is first established, and the Board supplied a model statement that could be used for this purpose. In addition, IBFs are required to obtain acknowledgement of receipt of such notice from nonbank customers that are foreign affiliates of United States residents whenever a deposit or credit relationship is first established with an IBF. The Board also supplied a model statement for their acknowledgement.

Under the rules established by the Board, IBFs may, free of Federal reserve requirements or interest rate limitations:

1. Offer to foreign nonbank residents time deposits with a minimum maturity, or required notice period prior to withdrawal, of two business days. Such deposit accounts require minimum deposits and withdrawal of $100,000.

2. Offer time deposits to foreign offices of United States depository institutions for foreign banks, to other IBFs, or to the parent institution of an IBF with a minimum one day (overnight) maturity.

3. Extend credit to foreign residents (including banks), to other IBFs, or to the parent institutions of an IBF.

[3]Domestically chartered corporations authorized to engage in international or foreign banking, or other international or foreign operations.
[4]This regulation requires that all depository institutions, whether members of the Federal Reserve System or not, hold reserves against their demand deposits, time and savings deposits, and borrowings from foreign banks or branches abroad. The amount, set by the Federal Reserve Board, is specified as various percentages of the totals within each of these categories. The requirement is satisfied by holding vault cash or by holding deposits in one of the regional Federal Reserve Banks. Such deposits do not earn interest.

IBF loans and deposits may be denominated either in United States dollars or in foreign currencies.

Advances by an IBF to United States offices of its parent institution will be subject to the reserve requirement on Eurocurrency liabilities of the United States office in the same manner as advances from a foreign office to its United States office.

IBFs will be subject to the same examination and supervisory procedures as apply to other operations of its parent institution. The Board may require special reports from IBFs for monitoring monetary and credit conditions and for other purposes.

BANKING STRUCTURE

Thus far, we have seen that world trade and investment continues to require, along with greater bank services, much more capital in absolute amounts and for longer periods of time. This has been a major challenge to the banking system and has brought about changes, some of which are still taking place.

Expansion Overseas

The original impetus for overseas expansion was defensive: As U.S. domestic companies expanded through branches, subsidiaries, and joint ventures overseas, U.S. banks had to follow so as not to lose their international and domestic business. It did not take a crystal ball for bankers to see that if a competing local bank had a branch in West Germany, through which it could offer a company's West German subsidiary foreign as well as international banking services, that there was a great possibility such a competitor would be in a strong position to get the business at home as well. Thus, there was a scramble by U.S. banks to establish themselves, one way or the other, in every major country. Today the largest U.S. banks are present, through one vehicle or another, in practically every country where it is legally possible. Even medium-sized banks are expanding in major money market centers through branches, association, or representative offices.

Branches. The actual vehicle for establishing a presence in a foreign country depends on the market, local conditions, regulations, and a bank's own preferences. One of the main advantages to branching is direct control over the branch's operations. A U.S. bank's branches abroad are in a position to extend credit facilities and other services to a company's local subsidiary based not only on local profitability, but on the profitability of the total banking relationship with that company worldwide, be it through other overseas branches or through the bank's head office in the United States.

Another advantage of direct branching is that the overseas branch is legally part of the parent bank with all its capital resources. This gives the overseas branch the same kind of credit standing and stature as the parent institution. The ability to gather required funds and otherwise offer banking services to customers is thereby greatly enhanced.

On the negative side, foreign branches sometimes are unable to attract the local currency deposits necessary to satisfy all actual and potential customers' requirements. After all, a foreign branch is competitive with well-established local banks, some of which may have hundreds of offices all over the particular foreign country. Those offices are capable of gathering local currency funds in the form of checking accounts, savings deposits, and so on. A branch of a U.S. bank with only one or a few offices in a country is more limited in this respect. It must concentrate on borrowing its required funds from corporations, through the interbank market, or by swapping Eurocurrencies into local currencies. While the stature of the branch's parent bank will certainly assist in its money buying operations, "bought" money is expensive when compared to funds obtained through savings and checking accounts. In many financial markets, the supply of money which can be bought is sometimes limited and subject to extreme fluctuations, depending on whether money conditions are tight or easy. Regulations of the host country can tie up deposits earmarked for foreign exchange, and, moreover, bank liability varies widely. Thus, if primary reliance is placed on purchased local currency, it may be difficult for the branch to build up a large-scale lending operation.

Associations. It is partly to overcome the problem of gathering local currency funds that a number of banks have established themselves by buying an equity interest (which may be a majority or a minority interest) in a local bank. Such a course of action may be politically preferable in some geographic regions, because as it is sometimes argued, the image of economic imperialism is reduced. It is also the case that direct branching is not permitted in some areas, so that association with local interests is the only alternative.

Banks forming associations lose some of the advantages of direct and complete control—particularly in the case of a minority holdings. On the other hand, an existing local bank will generally have a broader branch network and, therefore, a deposit base which, coupled with aggressiveness in marketing and credit that the U.S. partner contributes, can often go far in meeting the banking needs of multinational corporations.

Representative Offices. Some U.S. banks have established a local presence through a representative office when branch banking or teaming up with a local partner is not permitted or when the market is not big enough to warrant direct participation. Such a representative is not allowed to engage in the gathering of deposits, financing, or other banking activities. Representatives, however, sometimes can be useful to bank clients in supplying information about local conditions and in making needed introductions to local banks and key government officials.

Conflicts of Interest. The overseas expansion of a number of U.S. banks has brought with it problems of conflicting interests. For many years, international banking has been accommodated through close correspondent relationships that are mutually profitable. For example, a foreign bank may keep an account with its U.S. correspondent (generally one of the big city banks) who profits from the demand balances kept. The U.S. bank, in turn, is able to route lucrative letters of credit, collections, and remittances to its foreign correspondent. Moreover, if a U.S. customer needed banking services in a country before its U.S. bank had a direct branch or affiliate there; the U.S. bank would introduce the company to its best local correspondents. Thus, if a U.S. company wanted to set up a subsidiary in a foreign country, its American bank would be able to offer services indirectly by introducing it to a local bank. The latter, in turn, could reciprocate by keeping increased demand balances with the U.S. bank's head office.

This scenario changed when U.S. banks began to increase substantially their branches and associates abroad. Obviously, U.S. banks have strong incentives for sending customers to their own branches or associates. As far as the traditional business (letters of credit, collections, and remittances) is concerned, most banks have worked out a compromise: Some of the business continues to go to good correspondents even though the U.S. bank may have its own presence in that particular country. However, new customers who need local bank services are almost always sent to the bank's own branch or affiliate. Only if the affiliate branch cannot offer all the required services does the bank call in the help of a correspondent. In the latter case, the banking business that develops from the introduction is often shared by the correspondent bank on one side and the branch or affiliate of the U.S. bank on the other.

Most companies that set up an overseas subsidiary (as distinguished from a branch) will need at least two banks: (1) a local domestic bank for purely local needs, such as payroll accounts and local currency financing and (2) a branch or affiliate of a U.S. bank to provide limited local currency funding, and more importantly, to offer any Eurocurrency financing that may be required and to take care of other international needs that the subsidiary may have. It is possible, in some cases, for local banks to obtain Eurocurrency financing, but such banks must have a staff that is knowledgeable in foreign markets.

Edge Act and Agreement Corporations

A 1919 amendment to the Federal Reserve Act permitted commercial banks to establish federally chartered corporations for the purpose of engaging in international banking. These entities are commonly referred to as Edge Act subsidiaries after the senator who sponsored the amendment.

Three years earlier, in 1916, another amendment to the Federal Reserve Act had permitted national banks to invest in state-chartered corporations engaged in international banking activities. The powers of each corporation were to be delineated in separate agreements with the Federal Reserve. For this reason they were called agreement corporations.

Edge Act and agreement corporations have expanded rapidly in various money centers in the United States. Most operate as trade-center units in order to market and service priority customers involved in international trade. Basically, they are used for three types of international banking activities:

1 *Holding Companies.* Many Edge Act and agreement corporations are used as holding companies for equity investments in banking and near banking entities abroad. Often banks that have expanded overseas, via partly owned banking associations, have found an Edge Act entity to be a useful vehicle for owning the shares of stock. Similarly, shares in foreign development banks, private investment banks, finance companies, factors, leasing companies, and management consulting companies are often held by Edge Act or agreement corporations.

2 *Equity and Loan Financing.* It may be difficult for the parent bank to extend certain high-risk loans to overseas borrowers, especially for large industrial development projects or certain types of real estate whose complete financing package may also require an equity participation. Since banks are not allowed to make equity investments directly, Edge Act and agreement corporation subsidiaries are used as vehicles. In a typical transaction of this nature, an Edge Act subsidiary or its parent bank may extend a large loan to build a new industrial plant in a developing country. At the same time, the Edge Act company will take a small equity participation in the project. The idea is that after a few years, when the new plant is operating profitably, the equity interest can be sold at a profit.

   This type of loan/equity investment combination once appeared to be a promising growth area, but the volume of financing currently done on this basis is modest. Multinational companies investing overseas usually choose the route of fully owned subsidiaries and do not offer equity interest in Edge Act subsidiaries of commercial banks.

3 *Additional International Banking Offices.* Many U.S. banks have set up Edge Act subsidiaries in other U.S. cities for offering international banking services. In particular, U.S. banks headquartered on the West Coast and other parts of the United States have found it useful to open Edge Act subsidiaries in New York, since a substantial proportion of international trade financing moves through this financial center. In turn, New York–based banks have set up Edge Acts on the West Coast, in the South, and other parts of the country.

Edge Act subsidiaries may not engage in any domestic banking business. They may, however, offer a full range of international banking services including letters of credit, remittances, collections, deposits connected with foreign business, acceptance and loan financing of foreign trade, and similar international activities. The setting up of subsidiaries in other parts of the United States represents a welcome expansion of a bank's international activities where direct branching would be prohibited. The financial requirements of regional exporters and importers may thus be more effectively served by Edge Act subsidiaries of major international banks.

Multinational Services

Major U.S. banks have just about blanketed the free world with branches and affiliates. One advantage to this kind of banking is the acquisition of a great degree of multinational expertise. A bank with locations all over the world is in a perfect position to advise customers on foreign items, such as local laws, tax structure, customs, markets, ways of doing business, and so on. In a real sense, banks are no longer just sources of money, but have also become "knowledge" banks.

Another advantage of such multiple locations is their practical ability to offer one-stop banking. U.S. companies generally expand not only into one, but several foreign countries. A bank that can offer financing and knowledge in several such locations—all coordinated at a central point in its head office or regional headquarters—enjoys a tremendous advantage over its competitors.

Multinational Banking Groups

Tremendous growth in world trade and investment has created unprecedented capital requirements and longer lending terms, often beyond the scope of any one bank to supply. Partly to meet these requirements, there has been another significant development in international banking, namely the establishment of joint banking ventures and groupings. One form such cooperation can take is for a number of banks of different countries to join forces in establishing a new bank. It is then hoped that the new bank can marshal resources and take financing risks that would have been difficult or impossible for any of the owners to do alone. Over the past few years, dozens of such joint ventures, semimergers, and other multinational bank groupings have been formed. To illustrate their purpose, range, and the financial services they offer, it is useful to describe two of them.

European-American Banking Corporation. This is a consortium formed by Midland Bank, Amsterdam-Rotterdam Bank, Deutsche Bank, Societe-General de Banque, Creditanstalt Bankverein, and Societe Generale, all of which joined forces in establishing the European-American Banking Corporation. Its purpose is to tap the U.S. banking market, in particular serving subsidiaries of European companies located or about to locate in the United States.

Other Institutions

More is said about the following institutions in later chapters. For now, it is enough to emphasize that most of these organizations have been either formed or reactivated in recent years specifically in order to meet the increasing needs of financing world trade.

Factors and Finance Companies

Banks are the major institutions that provide for international financing, but they are by no means the only ones. To meet constantly growing financing needs, many banks have established factoring and/or finance company subsidiaries. Citibank N.A. (formerly the First National City Bank of New York), for instance, joined with a U.K. insurance company to form a new factoring subsidiary in the United Kingdom. The First National Bank of Boston has a factoring concern that is active in international trade. Also Citibank N.A. has bought or has established local finance companies in different parts of the world. Currently, there are factors and finance companies not yet affiliated with major banks, but they are nevertheless actively engaged in financing international trade.

Medium-Term Lenders

The need for medium-term funds (five to eight years) has given impetus to institutions that specialize in this segment of the market. Important among them is the Private Export Funding Corporation (PEFCO), which was originally established to help provide export financing for large projects requiring long terms. Other institutions have specialized in medium-term nonrecourse financing for exports to areas of the world that commercial banks may find too risky.

Credit Insurance

Finally, as far as private organizations are concerned, the Foreign Credit Insurance Association (FCIA) was established in 1962 in order to provide commercial and political risk guarantees to U.S. exporters. Unfortunately, the debt crisis of 1982 has raised questions as to whether the FCIA could withstand massive international defaults.

The FCIA cooperates closely with the Eximbank of the United States, which, in fact, underwrites FCIA's political risk coverage. The Eximbank also has been active and innovative in assisting U.S. exporters by either providing appropriate guarantees or actually putting up some of the required financing.

FINANCING VEHICLES

A number of innovative financing vehicles have been developed. As with the structural changes described earlier, their purpose is to meet the demands for short- and medium-term financing.

Financing Innovations

Foremost among financing innovations is the market in offshore currencies, particularly in Eurodollars. This market offers a new source of financing for international trade and investment. If a company needs short- or long-term funds, say for up to seven years, it can borrow Eurodollars from its bank (or a banking consortium or syndicate), sell the dollars in exchange for local currency, and use the proceeds to buy inventory, expand its plant, and so on. If money is needed for a longer period of time, there is also the option of raising it in the Eurobond market—either in the form of straight debt or convertible debentures—because in many instances the Eurodollar financing rates are lower than those available in local markets.

Borrowers in the Eurocurrency market have a myriad of vehicles available to them. Short-term loans, term loans, revolving credits, floating-rate loans, and, occasionally, fixed-rate loans can readily be obtained by borrowers with good credit standing. Additionally, some banks have been willing to make available multiple currency credit/deposit facilities. Under such an arrangement, a company may borrow in one or a combination of Eurocurrencies depending on its needs. Loans are available for periods of from one day up to one year. Conversely, should a company have a temporary excess of funds in any one of the currencies, it may deposit this excess with its bank at the going market rates. Hence, these multiple currency lines make cash available immediately when needed and allow any excess cash to be immediately productive in earning interest.

Many more financing services can be provided by use of offshore markets. These are discussed further in Chapter 11.

Parent Guarantees

Sometimes the overseas subsidiary of a domestic company, being a new venture, will not have sufficient financial strength to borrow from banks or in the Eurobond market on its own. On the other hand, the parent back in the home country may enjoy an excellent financial reputation. To enable an overseas subsidiary to borrow on it parent's strength, banks frequently lend to the subsidiary under a parent guarantee. Similarly, bonds issued in Eurocurrencies, while in the name of the overseas subsidiary, may also carry the guarantee of the parent company. Sometimes such a guarantee is channeled through a bank that issues a performance letter of credit. (See Chapter 14.)

By means of guarantees or performance letters of credit, the borrowing capacity of a newly formed overseas subsidiary can be substantially increased, enabling it to make greater capital investments than would otherwise be the case.

Syndications

The financial needs of a company will sometimes be so great that it is impossible for only one bank to meet them. To solve this problem, one bank may take a leading position in making part of the credit, while syndicating the remainder to other interested financial institutions. Usually, the leading bank acts as an agent for the others and gets a special fee for these services. Each bank that participates in the loan, up to a set percentage, does so for its own credit risk and, of course, also gets an appropriate return in terms of interest rate and commitment fee. It is important to note that, by acting as a syndicate, banks can both spread the risk associated with the loan and at the same time marshal greater resources than any one bank could, or would want to do, by itself. Critics maintain, however, that the spreading of risk in international lending is largely illusory.

Syndicated loans have been commonplace domestically for a long time. Their extensive use in international money markets, however, is somewhat more recent.

Cash Management

The scarcity and high cost of money has forced many companies to reexamine the efficiency of their treasury. To stimulate more efficient use of cash resources, several companies have centralized their financial operations. This has often reduced costs and has allowed for the rapid movement of funds to where they are most needed.

Cash resources have also been more effectively preserved through tighter inventory control and more extensive use of trade credit. Often, after studying their worldwide cash resources and needs, companies have found that while there have been pockets of available cash in some countries, subsidiaries in other countries have, at the same time, been borrowing at high rates. Once these problem areas have been discovered, they can usually be eliminated through centralized management. Banks have been of substantial assistance in offering cash management services either on a fee basis or, in the case of good customers, for free. The following examples are typical of services currently offered by banks.

Cash Management Services. These services are designed to meet the needs of corporations, banks, and credit unions to manage their inflows and outflows of cash. Each day in the normal course of running its business, a company takes in and pays out money. At any time, there may be a pool of cash from incoming receipts that has not yet been paid out to meet expenses. Most companies want to invest these excess funds to earn an interest return for the period until the funds need to be paid out. To make the most of investment opportunities, a company must obtain incoming funds as quickly as possible, control the flow of outgoing payments, and have information on its cash position at any time.

Collection and Concentration. These products help customers achieve the fastest availability of their receipts. When a company collects payments by check from customers or others, there can be considerable delays before the money becomes available as cash. Checks must first be received and processed, and, once a check is deposited, it can take from one to five days or more for it to clear. Delays can be extended even further if payments received and deposited in various branch office locations must be transferred to a central account for consolidated management. Collection and concentration products can be used to provide more efficient collection and deposit of these receipts, leading to faster availability of funds and improved operating efficiencies.

Payment Products. These products help customers control their outgoing payments and increase efficiency. When a company makes a payment by check, it generally deposits money immediately into its account to cover the check. However, the check may not actually be presented for payment for several days or even weeks depending on how long it takes the payee to receive and deposit it, and on the time it takes to be collected through the banking system. Meanwhile, as long as the company's money is tied up in the account waiting for checks to be presented for payment, the company forgoes the opportunity to invest it or put it to other use.

Post Office Lockbox Service. A company that receives a high volume of checks from its customers may spend significant time and money processing deposits and waiting for them to clear through the bank. The company wants the fastest availability of funds from its incoming checks, with transactions processed accurately in a cost-effective manner. With a post office lockbox, the bank processes and deposits all payments the day they are received at a special post office box. It reports deposits to the company each day and sends the supporting information to the company for updating of its accounts receivable. Lockbox services must be tailored to meet the customer's specific operating and reporting requirements. Because receipts are deposited the same day they are received, the lockbox customer has more immediate use of the funds. Lockbox also reduces the customer's internal clerical activity and costs, and simplifies accounting.

EXPORT TRADING COMPANIES

The U.S. Export Trading Companies Act of 1982 was the first legislation in more than a decade to aid U.S. exporters in effectively penetrating and expanding into foreign markets. (This act is somewhat similar to the Edge Act of 1919, which permitted U.S. commercial banks to set up federally chartered corporations for engaging in international banking activities.) The stated aim of the act was to increase the export trade of U.S. businesses, and, in particular, to encourage small- and medium-sized firms to enter into exporting for the first time. (When the act was written, only about 10% of U.S. manufacturing firms engaged in exporting.) Since this is the most recent major legislation, we consider it in some detail. The act itself is reprinted in its entirety in Appendix 1.

The Export Trading Companies Act allows any U.S. business to enter international export activities regardless of its size, and it allows producers of goods and services, exporters, freight forwarders, shipping companies, and insurers to form corporations with banks in order to establish themselves in foreign markets.

Background and Reasons

The need for Export Trading Companies (ETCs) was debated in hearings in 1978 by a subcommittee of the Senate Committee on Banking, Housing, and Urban Affairs. During later discussions, examples of major trading countries that fostered similar companies were considered. These were mostly European and Japanese companies that for several years had successfully combined banking and exporting. A great deal of scrutiny was given to the U.S. Antitrust Laws, which hampered the formation of such export trading companies. The Reagan administration, after careful consideration and evaluation, concluded that the legislation offered important potential for increasing U.S. exports and encouraged passage of the bill.

Functions

The act defines an ETC as a company

> Which is exclusively engaged in activities related to international trade, and which is organized and operated principally for the purposes of exporting goods or services produced in the United States or for the purposes of facilitating the exportation of goods or services by unrelated companies.

Export Trading Companies are permitted to engage in a broad range of export services including, among others, financing, foreign exchange, international market research, consulting, insurance (with limitations), transportation (including trade documentation and freight forwarding), warehousing, and, under certain circumstances, taking title to goods.

Various combinations of banks and companies engaged in export or export-related services form ETCs. One of the key aspects of the legislation is to open greater access to financing by permitting bank holding companies and some other financial institutions to invest in them. In the past, banks have been prohibited from mixing lending activities with commercial activities. Thus, they have been prohibited from directly investing in the equity of export companies. In this act, bank holding companies (including banks owned by banks) may invest up to 5% of their consolidated capital and surplus in ETC equity. In addition, Edge Act and agreement corporations that are subsidiaries of bank holding companies may also invest up to 25% of their consolidated capital and surplus if they are not engaged in banking; for those in banking, however, the limit is 5%.

Crucial among the incentives for ETCs are the exemptions from antitrust laws for certain export activities. Other important benefits are the availability of the Eximbank to assist in establishing guarantees, under certain conditions, for loans to export trading companies. Also important is the raising of the limits on the amount of banker's acceptances that a bank that is a member of the Federal Reserve System may use to finance exports. From a former ceiling of 50%, under certain circumstances, the limit is up to 150% and even 200%.

The single most important characteristic of the export Trading Companies Act is the relaxing of the rule that banks must separate banking activities from commerce. As a result, export companies, especially small- and medium-sized companies, can more easily obtain essential funding without violation of antitrust laws.

SUMMARY

It is obvious that the demand for traditional services to facilitate and finance world trade is increasing. However, the changing structure of world trade and investment has also placed much more exacting demands on the innovative ingenuity of international bankers. Not only is an increasing amount of financing requested, but bankers are being asked for longer terms than they have been willing or able to grant in the past. To meet these challenges, banks have expanded overseas and have formed affiliations, joint ventures, consortiums, and syndicates. In this process, they have also tapped new sources of funds, such as Eurodollars and other Eurocurrencies. At the same time, they have made financing possible by encouraging the use of such vehicles as the parent guarantee and the performance letter of credit. To make long-term export credits more accessible, organizations, such as PEFCO, have been formed, and relatively established institutions, such as the Eximbank and FCIA, have been substantially strengthened by the introduction of new and more liberal programs. Finally, new possibilities for financial support of export and export-related businesses have been made possible through the formation of ETCs.

Certainly, the future will hold many additional challenges for international banking. The groundwork seems to have been laid for marshaling the resources needed to finance expected growth and change in world trade and investments. Commercial banks, together with other government and private financial institutions, appear to be well-positioned to provide the amounts and terms of financing and related services required.

CHAPTER 2

Commercial Banks in the United States and Abroad

Commercial banks, both in the United States and abroad, finance the vast bulk of international trade. Their size, long tradition of trade financing, and experienced personnel make them entirely suitable for this activity. Banks have the financial resources to extend international credit and most have business networks and human resources that enable them to offer companies an entire gamut of finance-related services without which international trade would be difficult, if not impossible.

Unfortunately, in many countries the job of obtaining the necessary foreign exchange for the importation of basics, such as foodstuffs and raw material has been made much more difficult because of the additional burden of continual rescheduling of international debt maturities. The resulting pressure on local currencies has made foreign currencies, especially U.S. dollars, increasingly expensive.

It is the purpose of this chapter to outline those functions of commercial banks that involve the financing of foreign trade and related services. Some services, such as the collection of foreign trade, bills, letters of credit, and foreign exchange, are detailed in later chapters; therefore, only a brief mention is made of them here. First, we discuss the functions and services of larger banks, and later in the chapter we consider those of medium- and small-sized banks.

BASIC BANKING FUNCTIONS ABROAD

Commercial banks have four functions:

Gather deposits
Make loans and other investments
Offer finance-related services
Act for others in a trust or fiduciary capacity

Deposits

Commercial banks obtain deposits through current (demand) accounts maintained by individuals and companies, savings accounts, money market accounts, time deposits, and the sale of such instruments as certificates of deposit, bankers' acceptances, and capital notes. The gathering of deposits is more or less routine. A merchant may need a safe place to store funds until they are needed, for instance, to pay for imports. In such a case, money would probably be kept in a time deposit or invested in certificates of deposit or bankers' acceptances timed to mature at or slightly before the anticipated need for the funds.

International banks with overseas branches, affiliates, or correspondents can also arrange for deposits in local currencies of different countries. A trading firm may be selling to, as well as buying from, the same country. Instead of converting the proceeds from sales denominated in local currencies into dollars, a trading firm may wish to keep them on deposit abroad until they are needed to pay for purchases that are denominated in the same currency, thereby saving the fee for foreign exchange.

Loans

As banks gather financial resources from depositors and other investors, finding a safe and profitable use for the money becomes important. This leads us to the second vital banking function, namely, the making of loans and investments. A merchant or manufacturer with a sound credit rating, who needs money to carry inventory, finance accounts receivables, purchase equipment, or build a new plant, can find a ready source of funds from a commercial banker. Although the majority of commercial loans go to finance domestic businesses or consumers' needs, a large number are made to finance international trade. An exporter may have an immediate need to purchase goods or raw materials in the domestic market but may have to wait several weeks or months to be paid by an overseas buyer. Conversely, an importer may have to pay a foreign supplier before being able to sell imported goods and receive payment. In either case, a commercial banker may be able to help in the interim with an appropriate loan. Branches, affiliates, or correspondent banks can also make loans available in foreign currencies, as they may be needed by foreign traders and investors.

It should be mentioned that risk managers are playing an increasingly important role in the financing of international trade. Obviously, the risks inherent in granting loans to less healthy borrowers, particularly those located in countries experiencing difficulties in meeting loan repayment schedules, must be evaluated carefully.

During recent years, many international and domestic loans made by money-center banks (commercial banks) have been severely criticized. Circumstantial events have drastically affected the soundness of these loans.

Formerly, preliminary credit evaluations were made on the assumption that the price of crude oil would continue to escalate. When these loans were approved, the price of crude oil was about $42 per barrel worldwide.

The subsequent drop in oil prices made the job of keeping some banks solvent a very difficult one, as many had loaned heavily to oil- and energy-related industries. In 1984, there were several failures among financial institutions and a number of runs by large depositors on various savings and loans associations. Furthermore, the federal loans made to Continental Illinois Bank concerned some legislators, regulators, and bankers because of the financial burden such rescues might impose on the government, should they be expected to continue on a steady basis in the future.

Investments

Banks usually invest funds that are not needed for customer lending in money-market instruments, such as U.S. Treasury bills, municipal securities, and bankers' acceptances. Such instruments have the advantage of providing liquidity should there be an unexpected increase in loan demand or decline in deposits. Here, as with loans, risk managers must examine those areas of investment appropriate for the bank and must warn against use of bank funds in instruments or ventures that have an unacceptably high degree of risk.

Services

In addition to gathering and lending resources, banks also serve as important financial intermediaries in making domestic and international payments, lending their names to importers that are not internationally known, bringing buyers and sellers together, and offering a host of related services. Without many of these intermediary functions, domestic and international commerce would be impossible to conduct at its present scale and level of development.

Trust and Fiduciary Functions

Finally, banks frequently act as trustees for pension funds, investment advisors for individuals or mutual funds, executors, paying agents, and so on. All these activities may be classed under trust and fiduciary functions. Although some pension funds have begun to invest heavily in foreign securities, the trust and fiduciary responsibilities of a bank are largely domestic operations and, as such, nothing more will be said about them for our purposes.

LENDING

The principal function of commercial banks is to make carefully considered loans. Such loans should be self-liquidating at maturity and should not impede the normal flow of interest return. Obviously, the performance of such loans should be free of the threat of moratoriums or government interventions.

Credit and loan decisions are at the heart of banking, and most of a bank's income derives from interest on loans. Therefore, banks must be particularly careful about the creditworthiness of its customers. In addition, loans must not be made that are beyond the banks' resources, that is, adequate primary and secondary reserves on remaining available balances must be maintained. Whether the lending is domestic or international, banks must be certain that its officers make the right lending decisions and consult the appropriate risk managers before finalizing any decisions.

Lending Departments

A good portion of a bank's managerial personnel is concentrated in the lending department. Customers' requests for credit are constantly received and must be analyzed in terms of the financial soundness of these borrowers and their ability to repay their loans.

Lending Officers. Close contact with customers and a knowledge of their businesses are essential for making sound credit decisions. Therefore, a commercial banking department consists primarily of lending officers who are highly trained in credit principles and finance, so that they can make sound judgments with the bank's money and can act as financial advisors to business clients. Additionally, lending officers must function somewhat as salespeople. They must be well aware of the services a bank has to offer and, of course, try to sell as many as possible.

Organization. Banks organize their lending activities in a variety of ways. Large- and medium-sized banks (to which the comments in this section generally apply) traditionally break down their lending geographically into three major departments: metropolitan, national, and international.

Metropolitan. The metropolitan department makes and services loans to customers in the same metropolitan area as the one in which the bank has its head office and branches. An importer or exporter located in New York, for instance, would most conveniently obtain financing at the branch office located closest to his or her place of business.

National. The national department serves lending customers anywhere in the United States where the particular bank has no offices. Since it has been illegal in this country for a bank to have branches outside its home state, such business is done by the national department. (Note that banks may set up Edge Act banking subsidiaries in other states, but these subsidiaries are restricted to international banking activities.) Lending officers in the national department spend a great deal of time traveling to their customers' places of business. Next to personal visits, national banking is conducted by computers, mail, telegram, and telephone.

International. The international loan department conducts business outside the United States through overseas branches, associates, joint ventures, representatives, and correspondent banks. Lending officers frequently travel to overseas territories for which they are responsible. During these trips, they call on and try to cultivate new overseas customers. At the same time, they also gather useful information about business, economic, financial, and cultural conditions. They can, therefore, be valuable in advising domestic bank customers who invest in or trade with foreign countries. Domestic lending officers in the metropolitan and national departments of a bank (along with their customers) frequently consult with international officers and risk managers on the domestic ramifications of any foreign transactions in which they may be engaged.

Trends in International Organization. While the traditional organization of lending areas is geographic as previously outlined, there is also a trend toward functional specialization. Some banks, for instance, have organized their lending areas along industry lines. In this case, there might be a group of officers who service only the chemical industry all over the United States or even worldwide. This has the advantage of allowing the customer to do business with a banker who knows the industry intimately. Also, it is sometimes easier for lending decisions to be made by bank officers who are industry specialists. This type of organization, however, has a potential disadvantage. One industry may use management or financing methods that could be useful for a company in a completely different field. A bank officer who serves customers in all branches of industry will often have a broader knowledge of all methods available and may, therefore, be a more useful consultant to the customer than a banker who is an industry specialist. To get the best of both worlds, some large banks continue to organize geographically but have a separate department with industry specialists who can be called on for consultation as needed.

Another functional division is among large corporate clients, small businesses, and correspondent banks. Each of these customer segments has some financial requirements and problems that are unique. Consequently, setting up a special department to serve each group on a national or even an international level can be practical.

Analyzing and Making Loans

Since a major part of a bank's earnings comes from interest on loans, and an excessive amount of loan losses may be disastrous, considerable attention must be devoted to the making of lending decisions.

Credit Department. All banks have established credit departments for the analysis of loan proposals. When customers request loans, they are asked to furnish full details on the purpose of the loan, their financial position as stated in audited financial reports, the exact nature and function of business, sources from which the loan will be repaid, and a list of available collateral that may be available. A credit analyst takes all this information and conducts an in-depth study with the purpose of arriving at a recommendation as to whether the requested loans should or should not be granted. After the study is completed, the credit analyst makes written or oral presentations of the findings and conclusions to one or more lending officers.

Loan Decision. The lending officers determine whether or not to grant the credit requests and under what conditions, based on the credit analyst's study, any additional information, and experience with other loans. The actual decision may be made by one lending officer alone or by several acting as a committee. Very large loans relative to the bank's own capital may even be referred to the board of directors for approval or review.

Credit Factors. The criteria on which the lending officer makes credit decisions are complex. Therefore, we highlight only the major factors.

Reputation. The first prerequisite for a loan must be a good character and reputation on the part of the borrower. If the borrower is known to have engaged in unscrupulous business practices or if there have been former attempts to avoid payment obligations, then a bank extending a loan to such a party is only looking for trouble.

Purpose. A good reputation, however, is only a beginning. The bank must be convinced of the borrower's ability to repay the loan when due, and the purpose of the loan must be a legitimate one that will directly or indirectly generate the funds for repayment. Basically, the bank looks for two financial factors that should be present in a sound loan proposition—cash flow and asset protection.

Cash Flow. In this context, cash flow means that as a result of the loan funds will be generated for repayment. A typical short-term cash-flow loan is the financing of commodity imports or exports, such as an exporter with a firm order for a specific quantity of wheat that can be sold abroad. This exporter not only needs bank financing to buy and ship the wheat (if properly insured), but also terms that will make enough time (e.g., 60 days) to sell the wheat and obtain payment from the importer. It is clear that the successful completion of such a transaction depends not only on the exporter, but also on the reputation and financial strength of the importer. If the latter is a solid company, everything should go well and the transaction will be, in fact, self-liquidating. The exporter expects payment for the wheat within the time specified and, in turn, will pay the bank.

The export financing of machinery or, indeed, a whole plant can also be viewed from a cash flow point of view. In this case, the exporter usually wishes to be paid on delivery and financing is for the account of the importer. When the machinery is set up, it is expected to turn out a product with a ready market that will allow the manufacturer/importer to sell at a profit. If the manufacturer's homework has been done properly, a complete feasibility study will have been done on the cost of the machine, direct inputs, labor, overhead, and expected selling price of and demand for the product. The manufacturer and banker will, therefore, know approximately how long it will take to repay the money that has been borrowed to import the machine. Accordingly, the repayment schedule can be tailored to fit the actual inflow of cash from operating the machine or industrial plant.

Asset Protection. To minimize risk, the banker generally looks not only to cash flow but also to some asset protection. The calculation of projected cash flow always involves some uncertainty that expectations may not be fully realized. The importer of wheat, for instance, may refuse to accept the shipment because there was a big drop in the market price while it was in transit. Similarly, the machine may become prematurely obsolete and, therefore, may not generate either a profit or enough money to pay for itself. In such cases, the banker expects the borrower to have sufficient capital to repay the loan even if the expected cash flow from a particular transaction does not materialize.

The best asset protection is a strong balance sheet with a high net worth relative to borrowings and substantial current assets that can easily be turned into cash. If a borrower's balance sheet is not strong enough to warrant unsecured credit, the bank may request collateral in the form of marketable securities, accounts receivable, inventory, or a mortgage on the plant. Sometimes, the guarantee of a financially strong person or company can also be accepted as sufficient asset protection.

Types of Credit

Since the needs of different borrowers vary, bankers grant different types of loans tailored to satisfy individual needs. We illustrate some of the most common types, with special emphasis on those used by firms engaged in exporting and importing.

Unsecured Line. This is a credit facility for short-term borrowings of up to one year. The bank sets a maximum amount up to which the customer may borrow at any one time. Under this type of facility, the bank usually requires a total cleanup for at least 30 to 60 days annually. This means that for a 30- to 60-day period each year no borrowings are allowed to be outstanding. Since the line of credit is unsecured, it is given only to borrowers with very strong financial positions. Additionally, the bank generally wishes to know that the money is being used for short-term, self-liquidating, legitimate business purposes.

Line for Opening Letters of Credit. This type of short-term facility is granted to importers who need the bank to open letters of credit on their behalf. The importer borrows no actual money. The bank, however, warrants that it will make payment under the letter of credit, which is usually in favor of (i.e., made out to) a foreign exporter, regardless of whether the importer is able to pay or not. Thus, the bank lends its good name and credit to the importer and for this it receives a commission.

Letters-of-credit lines may be unsecured for importers of strong financial standing. In other cases, banks may require various kinds of collateral and possibly even cash deposits for full amounts of credit.

Refinancing Sight Payments. When a bank, under a letter of credit, is required to make payment on behalf of an importer, it looks for immediate reimbursement. The importer, on the other hand, may wish to wait until the goods have been sold before paying the bank. To accommodate him, the bank may be willing to extend credit until the goods are sold, a period of time usually no more than 180 days for each transaction. Financing may be extended by means of a direct loan or through creation of a banker's acceptance. Rather than requesting immediate reimbursement from the importer, the bank is thus refinancing a sight payment that it is obligated to make to the importer under the letter of credit.

This type of credit facility may be unsecured. However, the bank will frequently turn over documents that give the importer title to the goods against either a trust receipt or a negotiable or nonnegotiable warehouse receipt. Thus, a security interest is maintained in the goods until the importer makes final payment. Trust and warehouse receipts are discussed in greater detail in Chapter 10.

Financing Foreign Receivables. This is a secured facility (i.e., line of credit) that may be available to exporters who ship abroad on a documents-against-payment basis, thus creating accounts receivable from overseas importers. Using these receivables as collateral, exporters may be able to get financing up to an agreed-on percentage of the total receivables outstanding at any one time. The exporter assigns the accounts receivable to the bank so that when payment for foreign receivables is obtained, proceeds come directly to the bank and are used to liquidate the exporter's loan.

Purchasing Foreign Currency Drafts. Exporters sometimes draw on foreign buyers with a draft denominated in a foreign currency. To convert the foreign currency account receivable into the domestic currency of the exporter's country, the exchange, that is, the export bill of exchange, may be sold to the bank. Such a sale is almost always done with recourse to the exporter should the purchasing bank for some reason not be able to collect from the drawee.

Foreign Exchange Futures Contracts. Exporters and importers may wish to sell and buy foreign currencies for future delivery. A seller of future exchange is obligated to deliver the exchange sold to the bank at a specified date. The bank, therefore, runs the risk that the seller will not be able to deliver the exchange when promised. Likewise, a buyer of forward exchange is obligated to take delivery and pay the counter-value in dollars at a specified date. The bank, consequently, takes the risk of a buyer's unwillingness to take the delivery of exchange bought and make the corresponding dollar payment.

When agreeing to write a foreign exchange futures contract, a bank must make a credit evaluation of its customer. A line of credit for a future exchange contract is usually established, based on a customer's needs and credit standing.

The risks a bank takes when writing foreign exchange futures contracts are generally less than when extending money-using credit facilities. Should a customer default in meeting a future exchange contract obligation, a bank's loss will usually be limited to any adverse currency changes that may have occurred between the time the contract was written and the time of default. For this reason, banks are generally willing to make higher limits available for future exchange contracts than they would when extending a money-using credit facility to the same customer.

Term Loan for Financing Trade. As the name implies, this type of credit is for periods in excess of one year for the purpose of exporting or importing capital goods. It may be secured or unsecured. Generally, the borrower agrees to repay the loan in equal, annual, semiannual, or quarterly installments over several years. If an export from the United States is financed for a foreign importer, the loan may be made jointly with or under the guarantee of the Eximbank.

Revolving Credit. The financial needs of a rapidly growing company may increase over a period of years for the purpose of carrying domestic and foreign accounts receivable and inventory. To meet this need, banks are sometimes willing to grant a credit that is available for several years and may be used or repaid, as required by the borrower, but is eventually amortized like a term loan. As with a term loan, all particulars of a revolving credit account are spelled out in a loan agreement between the bank and the borrower. The rate of interest, usually tied to the bank's prime rate, is specified. The bank also usually charges a commitment fee of from ½ of 1% to 1% per annum on any used portion of the credit. This fee is in recognition of the fact that the bank legally obligates itself to make money available any time the borrower desires. As with a term loan, a revolving credit agreement will usually contain a number of covenants that attempt to ensure that the borrower continues to be a viable, profitable company over the life of the loan. Such covenants often require maintenance of a minimum working capital, limitation on other borrowings, limitation on dividend payments, prohibition of certain mergers that may endanger the health of the company, and so on.

These illustrations of credit facilities are by no means exhaustive. Depending on the needs of the customer, there may be other types of facilities or combinations. A bank may, for instance, give an importer an overall credit line of $1 million of which $250,000 may be used for opening letters of credit, $250,000 for unsecured loans, and $500,000 for refinancing sight payments made under letters of credit against trust receipts for a maximum of 90 days. Indeed, the variety of lines of credit that can be made available is limited only by the needs and financial strength of the customer and imagination and willingness of his or her banker.

INTERNATIONAL OPERATIONS

All banking institutions are engaged in the execution of financial transactions, from the simplest transfers to the most intricate financing of syndication loans. The bulk of these various transactions is routed through a bank's operations department. Typically, operations are broken down into two sections—domestic and international. The domestic department has the function, among others, of clearing the many checks that flow through a bank each day. Accounts have to be debited when checks are drawn against them and credited when deposits are made. At large banks, millions of transactions are processed every day.

A bank's international operations department is of primary importance to us here because of the many banking functions essential to foreign trade, such as international payments. Generally, international operations is broken down into a number of departments, some of which, especially in very large banks, may have several hundred employees compartmentalized to perform assigned functions. At smaller banks, the same variety of functions may be performed by a more limited number of departments and employees. Indeed, at very small banks, the entire international department may consist of only one clerk, albeit a very versatile one.

Since 1970, banks have been engaged in the automation of the various operational departments. In particular, rapid execution of unwinding bookkeeping entries (the distribution of book entries to the various accounts) by computer has resulted in far fewer errors than was the case with manual execution. Also, by the early 1980s, the various operating units of foreign branches of the same bank were on line and could instantaneously transmit instruction to their home office or other branches.

International Payments

Before describing how international payments are made, we have to show how banks maintain foreign currency accounts with one another.

Nostro Accounts. A large U.S. bank will periodically have a demand for the major free currencies of the world. To keep itself supplied with an inventory of such foreign monies, it can, of course, always keep a reserve of the respective bank notes in its vaults. Indeed, many banks do keep a small supply of foreign bank notes primarily to sell to tourists who are about to travel abroad. For larger foreign currency transactions, however, it is impractical, even impossible to keep all the cash on hand. For this reason, major banks maintain a number of foreign currency accounts with banks abroad. Thus, a major U.S. bank may maintain accounts in German marks, French francs, Dutch guilders, Japanese yen, and other currencies with commercial banks in these respective countries. Through these so-called *nostro* accounts (meaning "our" account with other banks), a bank, in fact, has an inventory of foreign currencies for its use. Note that in the first case, we were obviously talking about the physical objects (i.e., the bank notes themselves), whereas in the second, we were referring only to credit balances—the usual form of bank accounts.

Vostro Accounts. By the same token, most banks abroad find it useful to maintain dollar accounts with U.S. banks. These so-called *vostro* accounts ("your" account with us) represent an inventory of dollar exchange held by foreign banks with banks in the United States.

Dollar Payments. Since the U.S. dollar has become the world's major currency, a large bulk of international payments are carried out in dollars. Often both the payer or his bank and the recipient or his bank have an account at a U.S. bank. If both have their accounts at the same bank, the payment becomes very simple. When the U.S. bank receives properly authenticated instructions, it merely debits one account and credits the other. When the accounts are at different U.S. banks, the procedure may become somewhat more complicated. We may broadly differentiate between two possible situations as follows:

The paying and receiving U.S. banks maintain a current account relationship.

Neither the paying nor the receiving U.S. bank maintains an account with the other.

Let us assume that the bank that is instructed to pay has on its books an account from the bank that is to receive the funds. To effect payment, the paying bank merely credits the account of the receiving bank, and, at the same time, sends an advice giving the full name and address of the ultimate beneficiary. The receiving bank's balance in the account it maintains with the paying bank is thus increased. The receiving bank then merely credits the account of the ultimate beneficiary on its books.

In the past, if the two banks did not maintain an account relationship, the bank having the account to be debited usually wrote a check and sent it to the bank possessing the account to be credited. Appropriate entries were made on the books of each bank and the paying bank's check was sent through the daily clearing system to reach ultimate settlement through the Federal Reserve System. Today, much of this process, called a "street transfer," is accomplished interbank through computer hookups.

International dollar payments at large banks are made by an international paying and receiving department. Thousands of transactions are handled each day, many in large amounts of millions of dollars. Therefore, both speed and accuracy are essential. If a large payment is delayed for only a day, there will be a substantial loss in interest. On the other hand, even greater losses might result if a payment is made without proper authority or to the wrong person.

Foreign Currencies. In addition to U.S. dollar transactions, a number of international payments are made each day that involve foreign currencies. A U.S. resident may, for instance, be the lucky recipient of a remittance in a foreign currency. Since one cannot buy anything in the United States with foreign money, it first has to be converted into dollars in order to be credited to an account or before a check can be made out for its use. A similar situation prevails with outgoing remittances to foreign countries. If the remitter pays dollars, these have to be converted into the desired foreign money.

Some Examples. Let us look at some typical illustrations depicting how international payments can be made by using the services of commercial banks.

A foreign company that imports from the United States has to make a payment in dollars to its supplier: If the foreign company has a dollar account in New York, it merely writes a check on the account or instructs the bank by letter or tested cable (see "Testing Arrangements," which follows) to make payment to the U.S. exporter. If the foreign company has no dollar account, it must buy the needed exchange from a local bank that does have an account in New York. The local bank will then instruct its New York correspondent to make payment to the debit of its dollar account.

A foreign company that imports from the United States has agreed with the exporter to make payment in its own local currency: In this case, the company merely instructs its local bank to pay the foreign exporter. Having made local currency available to the exporter, the importer's responsibility is fulfilled. The U.S. exporter now has a balance in its favor at a foreign bank. To convert this into dollars, the exporter sells the local currency to a U.S. bank that is prepared to buy it at a given rate of exchange. The foreign bank is instructed to debit the account of the exporter and credit the *nostro* account of the buying bank with the amount of foreign exchange in question. The U.S. bank, having received the equivalent in foreign currency, is now willing to pay the amount in dollars to the exporter.

A U.S. importer has to make payment in foreign currency. To illustrate the international payment mechanism, let us look at the various ways (some more advisable than others) through which such payment can be effected:

1 The importer buys foreign bank notes (i.e., the physical objects) in the amount needed and mails these to the foreign exporter in payment. This method is clearly not very desirable because:

- **a.** There is the danger of theft in the mail.
- **b.** Insurance protection to cover theft is expensive or may not be obtainable at all.
- **c.** The shipment of currency is cumbersome.
- **d.** The exact amount of currency needed may not be readily available in the United States.

2 The U.S. importer buys a foreign currency draft with dollars from a U.S. bank. This is merely a check denominated in the particular foreign currency needed and drawn on the *nostro* account that the U.S. bank maintains at a bank in the foreign exporter's country. The importer then mails the newly acquired foreign currency draft to the exporter. The exporter deposits this draft with a local bank, the same as any other check. Eventually, the draft will be cleared and the U.S. bank's *nostro* account debited.

3 The U.S. importer pays the dollar equivalent of the foreign currency needed to his local bank and instructs the bank to remit the amount due to the foreign exporter. The U.S. bank then writes or telexes a foreign correspondent bank in the exporter's country with which it maintains a local currency *nostro* account authorizing a debit to the account and a corresponding payment to the beneficiary. This is probably the most efficient means of making the payment. When large amounts are involved, time becomes especially important. Also, if the U.S. bank telexes its foreign correspondent, the required funds can be in the hands of the beneficiary within one day. Note that the final result, under this method, is the same as when the importer buys a foreign currency draft. Ultimately, the *nostro* account, which a U.S. bank maintains with one of its overseas correspondents, is debited with the amount of the payment.

A German coffee roaster buys green coffee from a Brazilian exporter with payment to be effected in U.S. dollars: The latter then authorizes its New York correspondent to debit its dollar account with the amount in question with a corresponding credit to a named Brazilian bank for the account of the exporter. Let us assume that the Brazilian bank has a dollar account at the same New York bank. The transfer then becomes a simple one, from one account to the other, on the latter bank's books. The Brazilian bank's dollar account is thereby increased and, as a result, the bank is willing to pay the equivalent amount in cruzeiros to the Brazilian exporter.

Telegraphic Services and Computerized Message Services

For many years, telegraphic services were the nerve center of both domestic and international operations. As late as 1979, incoming telegrams were routed through telegraphic services where they were tested and then sent on to relevant departments by means of pneumatic tubes or messengers. Outgoing telegrams were also routed through this telegraphic service.

However, in the early 1980s, with the bulk of messages rapidly increasing, it was becoming impossible for several money-center banks to direct and receive messages fast enough. On heavy trading and calendar days, a single bank might send and receive more than 15,000 messages. With this volume a single telegraphic service within a bank quickly became a bottleneck and further automation and decentralization was necessary.

Gradually, each service center, such as money transfer, collections, letters of credit, demand deposit accounts, and bank's inquiry and adjustment, received its own messages via computer with the necessary testing arrangements for the bank's institutional, corporate, and government customers. This process greatly reduced both the bank's overhead and the time necessary to send and receive messages.

Testing Arrangements. To verify that the person giving payment instructions is properly authorized, a special system of authenticating incoming messages is used: Each telex or computer communication containing instructions to pay out money must include a special code called a "test key." This authentication code serves the same function as the signature on a check. Of course, outgoing messages containing payment instructions to branches or other banks abroad must be similarly coded and authenticated.

Occasionally, the system of authenticating messages between banks can be useful to customers even when no payment of money is involved. A U.S. company may wish to pass a signed cable or telex message to one of its overseas customers or affiliates. It can, of course, wire or telex directly via one of the wire services or send the message by computer over the telephone lines. However, unless it has specifically set up testing arrangements with the overseas party, the authenticity of the message cannot be fully established. To make use of the bank's already established authentication system, the U.S. company merely sends the message to be transmitted to its U.S. bank. The latter, checking its signature files to make sure the person signing for the company is authorized, transmits the message to a correspondent bank with the appropriate test key. The receiving correspondent then merely passes the authenticated message to the party for which it is intended.

Volume Handled. It should be obvious that the sheer volume of thousands of telex and computer messages handled by large banks each day is no simple task, especially in view of the fact that any message sent by wire or computer telephone lines is important and requires immediate attention. Added to this are the exacting security requirements that are necessary because large amounts of money are involved. The misuse of a test key by only one department employee could cost a bank a great deal of money. All banks, therefore, take strict security precautions and actual defalcations are rare.

Other International Operations

Most important for the international trader are letters of credit and outward and inward collections. Since separate chapters are devoted to these activities, no further comment is necessary here.

Usually, large banks also have a department called international mail tellers. As the name implies, these departments receive deposits that are to be credited to accounts maintained on the books of the international department. It is not uncommon for the international mail tellers of large money-center banks to receive up to 100,000 checks a day.

Foreign Exchange Trading

This department is neither a part of international lending nor of operations, although it is heavily relied on by both. It consists of a number of foreign exchange traders whose main job is to buy and sell foreign currencies. Many transactions are done on behalf of exporters who have foreign currency receipts that they would like to sell for dollars and importers who need foreign exchange to pay their overseas suppliers. The bank acts as a middleman, selling and buying different currencies as required. For its trading services, the bank does not charge a commission but, instead, retains the difference (called the "spread") between the bid and asked price on each currency.

OTHER BANK SERVICES

In the process of sketching out the functions of some of the major departments, we have already outlined a number of bank services, concentrating, for our purposes, on international operations. It is the purpose of this section to complete the picture by briefly describing some of the other services useful to the foreign trader that are not described in greater detail in later chapters.

Trade Development

A number of banks have set up trade development departments with the objective of bringing together buyers and sellers wishing to export and import. The procedure is very simple. If a U.S. exporter, for instance, wishes to sell a specific product abroad, and if his bank makes available a trade development service, he merely gives the bank complete specifications about the product, such as the price, quality, and quantity that can be delivered; descriptive flyers and brochures giving illustrations of the products may also be helpful. The bank then sends the information to some of its branches or correspondent banks in countries where the product could most likely be sold. In turn, these branches and correspondents contact some of their customers and others who might be interested in the product.

After the initial contact between the buyer and the seller has been established, the two negotiate directly and the banks may eventually finance the transaction through letters of credit. Usually, this trade development service is offered free to existing customers and correspondent banks. Of course, whenever a sale is made, the banks will also benefit because the buyer and the seller will need the banks' financial services for completing the transaction.

Publications

Most large banks issue periodic and special publications concerning domestic and international economic, business, and financial conditions. Analytical summaries are given of new government or central bank regulations, taxes, developments in the foreign exchange markets, interest rate trends, and similar topics. This section works closely with the risk managers in a bank's various sections in order to give an accurate picture of economic, political, or social conditions that might affect international trade.

Some banks also distribute detailed country-by-country fact sheets on local exchange and trade regulations. Usually, this is a loose-leaf service with individual pages being replaced whenever there is a change in a country's regulations. This service is extremely useful for exporters who must be up-to-date on the latest regulations in the countries to which they ship, especially those countries whose currencies are not easily convertible.

Some banks bring out other specialized publications. Booklets on individual countries that a bank wishes to highlight are sometimes available. These usually contain detailed information about a country's economic and political system, business conditions, how to go about setting up a local labor subsidiary, government investment incentives that may be available, local labor availability, wages, and so forth. Other booklets may give useful, general information for foreign traders, such as a guide to exporters and importers that describes the general procedure to be followed in opening letters of credit, sending out foreign collections, and obtaining financing.

Publications of this kind are sometimes sent free of charge to customers of the bank and sometimes to others, such as educators, who ask to be put on the mailing list. Frequently, however, there is an annual fee for these publications—even to customers.

Credit Information

Next to its analytical function mentioned earlier, the credit department also furnishes customers with needed credit information on buyers and suppliers, such information, of course, without engagement or responsibility on the bank supplying the information.

Information on Importers. When exporters receive orders from foreign buyers whom they do not know, they must decide under what terms to ship: If the importer is a large, reputable company, it may be necessary to quote open account terms (i.e., on consignment and payable within 30 to 90 days) for competitive reasons. If the buyer is less well known and not as financially strong, shipment on a foreign collection or even confirmed irrevocable letter-of-credit basis may be advisable. (See Chapters 12 and 13.)

To find out the size, reputation, and financial strength of a foreign buyer, an exporter can check with its bank. The bank may already be familiar with the company, either because it has an account relationship or because it has had previous inquiries from other exporters. If the bank is not familiar with the company, it will generally write or telex one of its overseas branches or correspondents for a complete credit report. A bank may also consult credit agencies for additional information.

Information on Exporters. While most credit inquiries are made by sellers to determine the ability and willingness of buyers to pay for the product, it is sometimes useful for a buyer to investigate the honesty and reputation of a seller. If a buyer pays for goods in the expectation of getting a certain grade or quality and then gets something inferior, he may not be able to sell to the anticipated market. Hence, it may be advisable to investigate a seller's ability and record in delivering the exact product advertised.

Preparing an Inquiry. When asking a bank to conduct a credit check, it is beneficial for the inquirer to inform the bank of its reason for seeking this information and to give an approximate idea of how much money is involved. Knowing the reason for the inquiry and amount of money needed will enable the bank to reply specifically to the needs of the inquirer. A small but reputable company may, for instance, be perfectly acceptable for open-account credit up to $50,000, while $250,000 may be totally unacceptable—not because it is disreputable, but because the amount is too high in relation to the company's size. If the banker knows how much money is involved, he can relate this to the size of the company and amounts of credit it usually enjoys from other suppliers and banks.

Mergers and Acquisitions

A few large banks have departments that help bring together buyers and sellers of companies. If a U.S. company wants to buy a subsidiary in Europe, merge with an existing company, or set up a joint venture, it may give the exact specifications of what's it's looking for to a bank with a foreign mergers and acquisitions capability. The bank will then use its overseas branches, correspondent banking relationships, and other connections to see if a suitable partner can be found. Of course, the same procedure operates in reverse if an overseas company is looking for a partner or an acquisition in the United States.

Introductions

It has been frequently said that no businessman should travel abroad without a series of letters of introduction from his banker. Banks, by virtue of their business, have many excellent connections with foreign banks, businesses, government agencies, and central banks. It is often easy for a banker to write a letter of introduction to exactly those persons the customer has to see. If, for instance, a businessman is traveling abroad to investigate the possibility of establishing a subsidiary, he will have to talk to various government agencies about required permits, licenses, investment incentives, taxes, and so forth. It will also be necessary to talk to local banks about financing the new venture and he may finally wish to talk to the local chamber of commerce about the hiring of workers, local labor laws, market conditions, and similar topics. Letters of introduction that will open the appropriate doors can usually be obtained by a customer through an international banker.

Money Mobilization

Idle money that sits in bank accounts around the world and earns little or no interest can be expensive to multinational businesses. A company's funds might be unused in one country, while the same company has to borrow at a high rate of interest in another. Even transfers from one country to another may take several days and even weeks. Again, this ties up money that could be working for the business.

To help companies realize the maximum potential from their money, some banks have set up money mobilization plans. The goal of these plans is to keep idle cash balances to an absolute minimum. And international bank with many foreign branches can frequently effect very rapid transfers of funds from one country to another. After all, a transfer from a bank's branch in one country to a branch in another country is basically a bookkeeping entry that can sometimes be effected the same day. Any funds that have to be idle for a few weeks or months can be concentrated in one account (such as a Eurocurrency deposit with the bank's London branch) where the bank can pay a high rate of interest.

When offering money mobilization to a customer, a bank generally makes a detailed study of all the intercountry money flows that must take place to conduct the company's normal business and the remittance of profits and/or dividends. After the bank has an accurate picture of the currency flows, it can generally come up with a more efficient plan to do the same thing, sometimes saving the company several hundred thousand dollars yearly in interest and transfer expenses.

Some banks perform money mobilization studies free of charge in the hope that the company will use the bank's branches and affiliated banks throughout the world. Other banks may charge for the service, possibly basing the fee on the estimated annual savings that the company realizes as a result of the new procedures.

BANK BRANCHING

As the current trend toward deregulation in U.S. banking continues to unfold, serious disagreements have developed among bankers and legislators as to the extent to which commercial banking in the United States may continue to expand into new areas, services, and markets. For now, the major federal acts that define the limits of banking in the United States are as follows:

1. The McFadden Act of 1927 restricted national or state chartered banks from branching into other states.
2. The Glass-Steagall Act of 1933, adopted in the aftermath of the Wall Street crash, separates commercial banking from most of the securities industry.
3. The Bank Holding Act of 1956 allowed commercial banks to enter into other banking activities; however, the Douglas Amendment to this law prevents corporations that own banking institutions from setting up banking subsidiaries in other states unless such banks obtain prior approval from local authorities.

Loosening of the Glass-Steagall Act

In September 1990, the Federal Reserve Board granted J. P. Morgan & Company, a major U.S. bank, the right to trade and underwrite corporate stocks. Corporate bond trading had already been approved a year earlier. In granting this right the Federal Reserve Board made use of a provision in the Glass-Steagall Act that allowed the existence of a securities unit within a bank holding company so long as that unit was not principally engaged in securities activities forbidden by the Act. Among those activities not forbidden were dealing in Treasury or municipal bonds and private placement (the selling of stocks from a single issue to a handful of institutions).

When Congress created the Federal Deposit Insurance Corporation (FDIC) it prohibited banks, through the Glass-Steagall Act, from using the newly insured deposits to finance stock market speculation, a type of financing common prior to 1933. In accordance with this intention, the recent Federal Reserve Board ruling limited the revenues from stock and bond trading of a securities unit to 10% or less of the total revenues of the parent bank holding company.

Loosening of the McFadden Act of 1927

After years of failed attempts by previous lawmakers, the U.S. Senate, on September 13, 1994 approved landmark legislation abolishing decades-old barriers restricting banks from operating branches across state lines. Entitled "Interstate Banking and Branching" (Number HR.38.41), the bill cleared the way for coast-to-coast banking. Customers would be allowed to deposit checks or get loans anywhere in the United States where their hometown bank had a branch. The lifting of these legal barriers, dating from the McFadden Act of 1927, virtually assured an acceleration of acquisitions in the banking industry that had already seen its ranks shrink by more than 3,500 institutions over the past decade.

Domestic Branches

Because of the previously described regulations, many of the lending and deposit-gathering functions are performed by the network of branches that a bank has in a city and, where permitted, in the state within which it operates. Important also for our purposes is the fact that many international transactions may have their start and finish at a domestic branch.

Services. Companies that export and/or import frequently do not wish to do business with the distant head office of a bank. Rather, they prefer to work with the branch that is just around the corner from the company's plant or head office. Thus, the company maintains its deposit account at the branch, gets its loans from the branch, and if it needs bank services in any area, including international, it looks primarily to the branch officers whom it knows and who know the company, its personnel, operations, and problems.

International Transactions. When exporters need a line of credit to finance foreign accounts receivable (i.e., outward collections), they are likely to apply to an account officer at local branches. Similarly, when importers need the bank to open letters of credit, they will again apply and receive credit lines for that purpose at local branches. On the operational side, if branch customers have foreign remittances to make, documentary drafts to send out for collection, or applications for letters of credit to submit, they will not wish to make a long trip across town to a bank's international department at its head office. Clients will generally submit these papers to the international clerk at the branch which, after a cursory check for accuracy, will promptly forward the items by interoffice mail to international remittances, outward collection, letters of credit, or whichever other head-office department has prime responsibility for handling the items in question.

International Questions. Often customers will ask account officers at the branch a specialized question to which the latter may not know the answer. All that is then necessary is for the account officer to know which of the bank's specialized departments must be consulted in order to get the answer. A telephone call to the right person at the head office will get an immediate answer or at least put the customer in direct contact with an expert with whom the question can be discussed in detail.

National Department. A similar situation tends to prevail in relations with customers of the national department. Of course, a customer located in another state does not have the advantage of a branch "around the corner." Deposits, collections, letters of credit, and similar transactions can, however, be done through the mail. Moreover, a long-distance telephone call will put the customer into contact with any expert in the international department. For more difficult problems, a personal visit may be appropriate. When calling on a customer, the account officer may take along a needed specialist or may consult the risk manager. Conversely, the treasurer or some other official may visit the bank's head office in order to consult with various experts.

Foreign Branches

Unlike the domestic branch, the foreign branch is too distant to depend on the head office to perform its operating functions. Even with excellent communications, time zones would often make such arrangements impractical. Thus, most foreign branches tend to be almost self-contained banks in their own right (although on a much smaller scale), complete with domestic and international operating departments.

Originally, foreign branches of U.S. banks primarily served local subsidiaries of U.S. companies. Now they are often capable of serving indigenous companies of all sizes.

CORRESPONDENT BANKING

So far, we have only considered the organization and foreign banking capabilities of a large bank, which may be described as one with a full-scale international department that includes overseas branches and a sophisticated department for international operations. A medium-sized bank will have a full-scale international department with full operations but few or no branches overseas. A small bank, on the other hand, may have no or only limited international capabilities. Its entire international department may be no more than one officer or clerk who works only part of the time on international banking transactions.

Importance of International Business to Small Banks

Although most of their revenues may come from domestic business, small banks cannot ignore international banking. Chances are that they have several customers who, in addition to their domestic business, also do some exporting and importing. A manufacturer may have to import some raw materials or sell some finished products abroad. Other manufacturers, while never having sold abroad, may wish to get into the exporting business, especially in times when domestic demand is slack. These customers will be looking to their bank for assistance and, if such assistance is not forthcoming, they may turn elsewhere not only for their international business but for their domestic banking needs as well. It is therefore advisable for a small bank to develop enough international expertise to satisfy the needs of these customers. Indeed, an aggressive, small bank will bring the opportunities of world marketing to the attention of local manufacturers, be they actual or only potential customers.

Domestic Correspondent Banking

Luckily, through correspondent banking relationships, a small bank can offer its customers almost the same services as larger city banks. To make this kind of arrangement attractive to both banks, the small one keeps a demand deposit account with the big bank. In appreciation for the balances kept in the account, the large bank is willing to make its international department services available to the small bank and its customers.

Letters of Credit. It is impossible for a small bank to open a letter of credit on behalf of its customers. The bank, no matter how good it is, in terms of financial strength and reputation in its own local market, will not be recognized internationally. Since the whole purpose of a letter of credit is to put the name of a well-known financially strong bank behind a not so well-known importer, a small bank that is unknown internationally cannot do the job. To solve this problem, the small bank may ask its large city correspondent to open the letter of credit on its behalf.

Generally, large banks supply their correspondents with an application blank which is, in fact, a two-part form. The first part, to be addressed to the local bank by the importer, requests the opening of a letter of credit. There is a place for the customer's signature by which the customer agrees to reimburse the bank when drawings are made. The second part is a letter to the large bank, to be signed by the local bank, requesting the latter act as its agent in opening the credit.

The local bank takes the full risk, and the large bank, while it actually issues the letter of credit in its own name, looks to the local bank for eventual reimbursement. The credit of a large, well-known bank is thereby substituted for that of the unknown local bank. This arrangement is usually a satisfactory way to assure payment for the exporter's goods.

Outward Collections. The large bank can also be of assistance with collecting drafts payable abroad (outward collections). Again, the small bank will not have an outward collections department, that is, familiar with all the intricacies of collection work, nor will it have the required capability for follow up when a collection remains unpaid. Large banks supply foreign collection letter forms with the name of the addressee bank left blank. The small bank can fill in its own name as the addressee and can give the form to its customers for their use. This enables clients to address collection letters to their own local banks, which will immediately forward them to the outward collection department of its large city correspondent for further processing and eventual collection from the overseas importer.

Remittances. Another illustration of how the correspondent relationship functions can be drawn from the area of foreign remittances is when a small bank, on behalf of one of its customers, has to make a remittance abroad. It is allowed by the large bank to draw foreign currency drafts directly on the latter's *nostro* accounts with overseas branches or correspondents. Again, to execute the transaction, the large bank furnishes the local bank with special draft forms. The first copy of the multiple form is the actual draft on which the name of the local bank has already been printed. It is given to the customer, who can mail it to the beneficiary. The second and third copies are receipts for the customer and issuing bank, respectively. The fourth copy is sent immediately by the local bank to the city bank to alert it to the fact that the draft has been drawn and that it must make funds available to its foreign branch or correspondent where the draft is payable.

Other Services. We have illustrated some of the formalized services available between domestic correspondent banks. There are, in addition, many other areas where cooperation is possible on a less formalized basis. The small bank may have a customer who is planning to build a new plant overseas and who needs some advice from the large bank's area officer. A telephone call of introduction from the small town bank to its city bank account officer will get the former's customer the same treatment as if he or she had an account at the city bank itself. It must be remembered that the reasons the city bank is willing to make its services available is because the local bank maintains an account with it that has demand balances that can be profitably employed.

International Correspondent Banking

Just as domestic banks of various sizes are interconnected through a network of correspondent relationships, so foreign banks often keep accounts with one another because it is to their mutual benefit. Practically all foreign banks, for instance, maintain dollar accounts with one or more of the large U.S. banks. This enables the former to take advantage of the services their U.S. correspondents can offer, such as the confirmation of letters of credit, the making of international payments, and the granting of various kinds of credit facilities, particularly U.S. dollar loans and acceptance financing. Most services of U.S. banks that have been outlined are, of course, also available for foreign correspondent banks and their respective customers.

Large- and medium-sized U.S. banks also frequently maintain foreign currency accounts abroad with the most important banks of each country. Again, this has the advantage of making international payments possible that must be made in foreign currencies (e.g., the foreign currency remittances discussed earlier). Also, many large U.S. banks are active in foreign exchange dealing. Accounts maintained in foreign currencies with banks abroad (*nostro* accounts) represent an inventory for foreign exchange trades that are active in selling and buying these currencies each day.

Disadvantage of Correspondent Banking

We have pointed out a number of advantages of correspondent banking. There are, however, also a few shortcomings worth mentioning. When a large city bank assists a local bank's customer, it sometimes takes a bit of restraint not to also solicit that customer's account. It is true that most large banks, as a matter of policy, do not solicit their correspondents' customers. On the other hand, once the customer sees the greater international capabilities of the large bank, he or she may request to open an account. It is partly to counter this kind of competition by the large banks that Allied Bank International, mentioned in Chapter 1, was formed.

On the foreign side, some U.S. banks that decided to open branches abroad did so only after their clients, who set up local subsidiaries, were unable to get adequate service from some of the foreign correspondents.

Despite the few previously mentioned disadvantages, correspondent banking still flourishes. This indicates that its advantages far outweigh its shortcomings. Banking is a specialized industry requiring knowledge of local economic, political, and financial conditions. The scope of knowledge and expertise is too broad for one bank to be able to completely master. Therefore, it remains convenient for all concerned—the banks as well as their customers—to have a close network of correspondent relationships that can be depended on when assistance is required.

CHAPTER 3

Other Private Institutions

We have already outlined, in the first chapter, the greater need for short- and medium-term financing of trade due to the continuing surge in international trade. These substantial needs, as well as the greater prevalence of open-account shipments, have prompted the formation or involvement of a number of specialized financial institutions. Factors and commercial finance companies, for instance, whose concerns were once primarily with domestic needs, have now increasingly entered the international field through short-term financing of trade. A greater need for medium-term funds has also given rise to a number of institutions that specialize in financing capital exports and/or discounting of medium-term trade paper without recourse. Finally, the FCIA has revamped its programs to make them more competitive with those of institutions in other countries offering similar facilities. Therefore, it is the purpose of this chapter to describe some nonbank, private financial institutions that may be of help to exporters and importers.

FACTORING

Factors are in the business of buying accounts receivable without recourse to the seller (i.e., they accept the responsibility for making collections and absorb any credit losses). The primary services offered are credit investigation, credit approval, assumption of credit risk, accounts receivable bookkeeping, and collection of matured accounts. Note that a factor is not itself a bank (although it may be a division of a commercial bank) and extension of financing is not necessarily a part of the arrangement between the factor and the client. If only credit, bookkeeping, and collection services are required (i.e., the accounts are not actually purchased), the factor remits funds to the client at the average maturity date of the accounts in wholesale transactions or when collected in retail transactions. The distinction is due to the fact that mills, manufacturers, and other wholesale customers will accept interest charges when they pay after due dates, whereas retail stores, for the most part, will not.

If financing is also desired, the factor is usually willing to advance funds as soon as the sale is made and a receivable is created. In this case, there will also be a finance (interest) charge calculated from the date of the advance to the normal average maturity date (for wholesale) or until the receivable is to be paid (for retail).

At one time, factoring was generally confined to domestic operations, but factors have now moved aggressively into the international field. A number of them have set up affiliations or cooperation agreements with foreign factors. This, in turn, has enabled the U.S. factor to overcome the major obstacle to export factoring, that is, the unavailability of adequate credit information on overseas buyers. On the import side, factors have been of increasing assistance to U.S. importers who require the opening of letters of credit and financing of their accounts receivable. Capitalizing on their thorough knowledge of the creditworthiness of U.S. firms, factors also offer their services to foreign companies that sell in the United States through agents or subsidiaries.

Export Factoring

Export factoring is a service by which an export company delivers all copies of shipping documents and assigns all accounts receivables to a factoring company, often without recourse.

Method of Operation. Before finalizing an export contract, the client checks with his factor to get credit approval. After approval has been obtained, the exporter ships in the usual manner, sells the account receivable to the factor, and lets the latter worry about all bookkeeping and collection work. Once having approved a particular sale, the factor assumes all commercial credit and political risks. Proceeds are remitted to the client when received by the factor or on the average maturity date. If needed, financing can also be arranged. In cases of default or delayed payments, the factor is covered by a release or disclaimer required of the client.

Credit Approval. The big challenge facing export factors is their ability to give rapid credit approval when asked to do so by a client. Usually, their international credit files are not as extensive as their domestic ones and delays may result if they write or telex overseas for credit information on a proposed importer. To overcome this problem, U.S. factors have teamed up with similar organizations abroad, either by establishing foreign offices, buying equity interests in existing concerns, or setting up correspondent relationships. Cooperative arrangements with overseas factors often provide for the latter to handle sales of U.S. factors' clients in their own countries. Reciprocally, U.S. factors handle sales of foreign factors' clients in the United States. Some U.S. factors have also set up overseas branch offices to handle credit approvals and collections. The overseas branches, affiliates, or correspondents will usually have extensive files on local importers and can, therefore, telex credit evaluations and recommended decisions rapidly. Factors that are, in fact, divisions of commercial banks can also draw on the banks' worldwide branch networks for rapid credit information.

Growth of Export Factoring. Export factoring has grown rapidly in the past few years. It offers the client some unique and valuable services. By assuming all credit and political risks, factors free exporters to put all their talents to work in building international sales and entering new markets. Factors also save exporters the expense of running bookkeeping sections for foreign receivables.

The timely approval of foreign sales, however, still represents a major problem for those factors who neither have overseas locations nor extensive cooperative relationships. More and more factors have established international ties to give them the extensive credit information needed.

Advantages of Factoring for an Exporter. Among advantages of factoring to domestic exporters are the following:

1. All delinquent account receivable risks are eliminated for the exporter and assumed by the factoring company.
2. Administrative and accounting expenses are reduced.
3. The exporting company is free to concentrate on international sales and development of new markets because the factoring company has assumed responsibility for sales accounting and collection of funds.
4. Exchange risks are eliminated.
5. Open account agreements with the buyer, guaranteed by the factor, are made possible. That is, the factor guarantees the credit risk of the foreign buyer.

The financial arrangements between the factor and the commercial corporation may be varied, based on whether the commercial institution needs the funds immediately or at the actual or average maturity dates of the accounts receivable and whether the anticipation payments before the maturity dates will be with or without recourse to the drawer (which, in this case, is the commercial entity). Consequently, if the risk for collecting the funds increases, the fees and the rate for financing the accounts receivable increases based on the degree of risk exposure.

Import Factoring for Domestic Clients

An importer often requires the opening of a letter of credit in favor of a foreign seller. Once the documents arrive they have to be paid for and the goods must be cleared through customs. (In many factoring arrangements the importer has already arranged for a final buyer of the merchandise. This is often insisted on by the factor in order to reduce risks and costs.) An account receivable, which again has to be carried until final payment is received, is then created. Since importers frequently operate on limited capital compared to their sales volume, they are often ineligible for adequate unsecured bank credit. The intermediary service of a factor or finance company may, therefore, be most useful.

Procedure. When financing imports, factors have a particular advantage in that they can maintain possession of both the underlying merchandise and subsequent accounts receivable throughout the transaction.

Opening Letter of Credit. To help the importer in making a purchase overseas, factors arrange for the opening of letters of credit through domestic commercial banks in favor of the overseas supplier. Factors, by serving as intermediaries between their clients and the bank, substitute their own credit for that of the client. In fact, since factors guarantee letter of credit applications, the bank is willing to open the credit, whereas it might not have done so for the importer directly.

Releasing of Documents. Once shipment has been made, the title documents are either consigned or endorsed over to the factor. In turn, the factor releases the documents to the importer against either a trust or warehouse receipt. In the case of a trust receipt, the importer receives physical possession of all the goods but agrees to hold them in trust for the factor. All proceeds from sales (including accounts receivable and cash) must be immediately turned over to the factor. In the case of a warehouse receipt, the goods are stored in an independent warehouse for the account of the factor. Once a final sale has been arranged, the factor issues a delivery order allowing release from the warehouse of a specified quantity of goods for sale to the final customer. In either case, factors always carry their client's inventory.

Accounts Receivable. Once a final sale has been made to a customer whose credit was previously approved by a factor, an account receivable is created. According to the agreement with the client, the factor buys this receivable without recourse. The factor, therefore, takes all credit risks and assumes the work of collecting the account.

Financing Arrangements. As soon as a commercial bank receives shipping documents from a foreign bank, they are turned over to a factor. Some arrangements then have to be made to settle the obligation to pay under a sight letter of credit. Factors may use their own funds to pay the bank immediately and clear the goods through customs. In this case, the bank has actually extended an advance to the client. This advance is finally liquidated on the average or final maturity date on the account receivable that the factor has bought from the client without recourse.

Time letters of credit (issued by order of a factor for the account of a client) are paid to the bank by the factor at their maturity dates and the resulting acceptances are charged to the clients' accounts for payment to the factor when due. Advances required from the factor for the payment of acceptances prior to the maturity dates of the underlying accounts receivable are subject to interest charges in accordance with the factoring agreement.

Often, instead of making immediate payment under a sight letter of credit, factors will want to make use of their own credit lines with commercial banks. Factors may, therefore, borrow the funds needed, either by asking banks to create banker's acceptances on a refinance basis or by charging their own loan accounts. (Factors use their own credit lines to obtain the additional financing—usually not exceeding 180 days.) In either case, factors become obligated to pay the bank at the maturity of all loans or acceptances. These maturities will usually be timed to coincide as much as possible with the expected payments of the accounts receivable by the ultimate customers.

Control over Goods and Proceeds. As can be seen by the example just given, the factor retains almost complete control over the import transaction from its inception to the final payment. The factor is secured throughout, first, through possession of the title documents, then by a trust or warehouse receipt covering the actual merchandise, and finally, through possession of the account receivable.

In contrast to a factor, a commercial bank relies less on the value of underlying collateral and more on the general credit strength of the borrower. An importer with limited capital can thus obtain substantially more financing through a factor than through a bank.

Factoring Charges. Since factors are usually willing to accept higher levels of risk than banks, one expects the finance charges to be higher. Also, there are the additional services provided by the factor, such as bookkeeping and collection of accounts. If an importer of adequate financial strength has a choice of using either a factor or a commercial bank, the importer has to weigh these services against the additional cost.

Import Factoring for Foreign Clients

Some foreign companies have a substantial sales volume of exports to the United States. As was previously pointed out, the main strength of domestic factors is their extensive knowledge (credit files) of U.S. companies. Consequently, it is natural for U.S. factors to offer their services to foreign firms that export to this country. Before concluding a sales contract, the foreign seller or his U.S.-based agent obtains credit approval from the factor. Once approval is obtained and the shipment has been made, the factor buys the account receivable without recourse in the usual manner. The foreign exporter receives the proceeds of sales at the average maturity date or when collected. All credit risk, bookkeeping, and collection work is assumed by the factor.

If the foreign client requires financing, some arrangement can usually be made.

COMMERCIAL FINANCE COMPANIES

For purposes of exposition, we will differentiate between factors and commercial finance companies. In real life, the two are more often than not separate divisions of the same corporate entity. While factoring refers specifically to the buying of accounts receivable without recourse, commercial finance companies make other types of loans that are secured by various kinds of collateral. Such loans may generally be thought of as being too risky or, for some other reason, undesirable for commercial banks. In domestic trade, commercial finance companies finance a myriad of different transactions including the carrying of inventory and accounts receivable, purchase of machinery and equipment, floor-plan financing, acquisition of real estate, and so on. In international trade, the activities of commercial finance companies can again be conveniently broken down into the financing of exports and imports.

Exports

Situations arise when a business has the opportunity for a sizable export but cannot obtain commercial bank financing.

Back-to-Back Letters of Credit. An exporter may, for instance, have a firm order from an overseas buyer covered by an irrevocable letter of credit. The exporter, however, has to buy the goods from an inland manufacturer. If the exporter's financial condition is not strong, the manufacturer may insist on a letter of credit in his favor. Unfortunately, commercial banks are generally unwilling to open letters of credit for financially weak exporters. By putting the finance company between the exporter and the commercial bank, the needed letter of credit can be opened and the sale finalized.

The most practical mechanism under back-to-back letters of credit is to assign the total amount of the credit to the finance company, which in turn opens a domestic letter of credit in favor of the inland manufacturer. The usual procedure is for the exporter to send a form, called an "Assignment of Proceeds," to the advising (U.S.) bank for the letter of credit. The exporter's local bank certifies the authenticity of his signature (to the advising bank) and pays a fee, which is usually ¼% flat on the amount of the assignment. In this process, the advising bank (discussed in Chapter 13) is the U.S. bank that has received the request from its foreign correspondent to advise the foreign bank's credit to the U.S. exporter.

Confirmed Order. Sometimes an exporter, while not the beneficiary of a letter of credit, will have a contractual order from an overseas buyer. Again, the exporter might need the services of a finance company to prefinance the domestic purchase of the necessary goods or even finance the manufacturing process. To maintain control throughout the transaction, the finance company may wish the goods to be stored in an independent warehouse prior to shipment. It may also require that the underlying sales contract and resulting account receivable be assigned to itself so that all proceeds will come directly to the finance company.

When deciding whether or not to prefinance a confirmed order, a finance company will look carefully at the foreign buyer who has executed the sales contract. It is important that the overseas importer is a reputable and financially strong company that will not renege on its obligation. Also important, of course, is the technical ability of the U.S. exporter or manufacturer to deliver the desired goods in compliance with the contract requirements.

Financing Export Accounts Receivable. While a factor actually buys an exporter's accounts receivable, a finance company may be willing to make advances with the accounts as collateral. In this case, it retains recourse to the exporter if the foreign buyer refuses to pay. Alternatively, the finance company may also be willing to provide credit directly to the foreign importer without recourse to the exporter.

Financing Company versus Bank Credit. Why can a commercial finance company do what a bank cannot? The finance company, for one thing, is very experienced in secured (collateralized) lending. While it induces the commercial bank to open a back-to-back credit under its own line of credit, it also ensures that it has control of the underlying merchandise throughout the transaction. In the case of a back-to-back credit, for instance, the finance company will request that the proceeds of the primary letter of credit (the one in favor of the exporter) be assigned to itself. Moreover, in addition to the usual collateral promissory note, the finance company will also often request the personal guarantee of the exporter to back up the transaction. Finally, as mentioned before, the finance company's interest charges are usually a bit higher than those of commercial banks to compensate for the higher degree of risk it is willing to take.

In summary, a finance company can be of substantial help, either by helping the exporter buy merchandise from the manufacturer (for which a firm order from abroad has already been received), financing the actual production of goods prior to export, or granting advances against the exporter's foreign receivables. In the latter case, the finance company makes ready cash available which can be used by the exporter in entering into a new trade transaction.

Imports

Commercial finance companies can be of help to importers in ways similar to those already described under export financing. An importer may have a confirmed order from a domestic buyer, but needs a letter of credit opened in favor of a foreign seller. The finance company may be able to arrange the needed letter of credit by adding its own financial strength to that of the importer. Again, the finance company will try to maintain control over the merchandise until final payment is received. It may also insist on assignment (to itself) of the domestic buyer's confirmed order and the importer's accounts receivable.

Sometimes, an importer has ordered goods shipped on a documents-against-payment basis. (See Chapter 12.) The goods and documents may arrive in due course, but the importer may have a cash-flow problem and not be able to pay for them. A finance company may be willing to grant a loan to pay for the goods. At the same time, it will maintain control over the underlying merchandise by means of either a trust or warehouse receipt. Any accounts receivable that are created when the goods are sold may again be assigned to a finance company until receipt of the final proceeds.

It should be clear that in some of the transactions previously described, the finance company may be taking substantial risks. For instance, the goods imported that serve as collateral may be of inferior quality and not cleared through food and drug inspection or other regulatory agencies. The domestic buyer who has executed a firm order may default on the contract. Alternatively, if no firm order exists, goods may not be salable at the previously expected price, due to poor quality or a general deterioration of the market. While a finance company always retains recourse to the importer, the latter's low net worth may make such recourse of limited value. A finance company's interest charges will usually reflect such a higher degree of risk.

Lastly, it must be stressed that finance companies have no monopoly over secured lending. Most of the activities of commercial finance companies can also be performed by commercial banks, provided their overall policy, experience in secured lending, and interest-rate structure permit it.

MEDIUM-TERM FINANCING INSTITUTIONS

To finance an increasing trade volume in machinery, airplanes, ships, industrial plants, and similar capital goods, a number of specialized institutions have been created. Factors and commercial finance companies may also provide medium-term financing; their main business, however, is in the short-term area, since their resource structures preclude any very large commitments to longer-term credit.

The setting up of special, private institutions to finance trade resulted from a need for services not offered by commercial banks and other financial intermediaries. In periods of limited capital availability, it became necessary to set up separate institutions to tap new sources of funds and channel them into international trade financing. We give brief descriptions of a few organizations that specialize in medium-term financing of foreign trade; the list, however, is not all inclusive.

Private Export Funding Corporation

The Private Export Funding Corporation (PEFCO) was organized in April 1970, by a group of fifty-five U.S. commercial banks and seven prominent U.S. industrial companies. Its basic purpose is to mobilize private capital to help finance U.S. exports. It derives funds primarily from the issuance of its own securities both in the United States and abroad.

Cooperation with Eximbank. To make these securities more attractive and lower the interest cost, they are collateralized by promissory notes of foreign importers to whom PEFCO grants financing. The obligation of foreign importers to PEFCO are, in turn, guaranteed by the Eximbank of the United States. To obtain Eximbank's guarantee on the obligations of foreign importers, PEFCO pays a guarantee fee. Eximbank also guarantees the payment of interest on PEFCO's own debt obligations that Eximbank approves for issuance. The fact that PEFCO cooperates closely with Eximbank and Eximbank indirectly stands behind PEFCO's debt adds greatly to the latter's ability to raise substantial amounts of capital in private markets.

Lending Activities. On the lending side, PEFCO was set up to help U.S. exporters sell large-ticket items such as wide-bodied jet aircraft and power plants, by providing the needed financing packages. For large-ticket exports, the financing required to make a sale will often be in excess of ten years. While Eximbank is usually willing to finance the late maturities and a commercial bank the early ones, PEFCO has tended to pick up those maturities that are in the middle. Also, since its inception, PEFCO has financed some medium-sized exports in addition to the larger projects for which it was designed.

PEFCO endeavors to match the maturity of its own notes to the maturity of pledged, guaranteed notes of foreign importers. Hence, its sources and uses of funds are fairly closely matched as far as maturities are concerned. PEFCO can quote borrowers a fixed or floating interest rate for its portion of the financing. Even if a borrower initially accepts a floating rate, he may have the option of later converting it to a fixed-rate loan at PEFCO's lending rate at the time of conversion. Borrowers often prefer fixed to floating rates, since fixed rates allow them to determine exactly the amount of future interest payments.

Typical Loan Transaction. A typical transaction to finance a power plant might be brought to PEFCO by a commercial bank. The financing would be arranged between the lending institutions and the foreign buyer. Typically, repayment might occur over 15 years in 30 semiannual installments. The commercial bank might finance those installments due in the first five years, while PEFCO might take those installments due in the middle five years. The entire portion financed through private sources (i.e., the first ten years) would be guaranteed by Eximbank, for which the commercial bank and

PEFCO pay Eximbank a guarantee fee. This guarantee fee is, of course, added to the financing charges that would have to be paid by the foreign buyer.

Discount of Trade Paper

There are a host of institutions, both in the United States and abroad, that specialize in discounting medium-term trade paper without recourse to the exporter. Some of these institutions are willing to finance any transaction that comes along and presents a good credit risk. Others specialize in certain markets, such as the financing of sales to emerging markets of the former communist countries of Eastern Europe.

Usually, the actual financing transaction is simple. The importer executes a number of serially maturing promissory notes payable to the exporter. If the importer is in an Eastern European country, the guarantee or endorsement of the exporter's central bank or government-owned foreign trade bank is usually required. In other cases, when the importer is not well known and/or financially strong, the guarantee or endorsement of a prime commercial bank may be required. Once the importer has received the notes, they are offered to the financial institution. The latter will discount the notes without recourse at current market rates for the particular currency and risk involved. Net proceeds are remitted to the exporter. At the same time, the importer is notified to pay all installments and interest directly to the financing institution rather than to the exporter.

One thing the exporter should realize is that the interest paid by the importer is not necessarily equal to the market rate at which the paper can be discounted. If, for instance, the importer is willing to pay interest at 6% per annum on the financed portion, but the exporter has to pay 8% per annum discount charges, the latter loses 2% on the financial part of the transaction. This differential has to be anticipated and to be built into the exporter's price.

Often an exporter wishes to have assurances that financing will be available before entering into a sales contract. To meet this need, financing institutions are usually willing to extend an advance commitment to discount the notes without recourse when they are finally issued. This is called a "silent" or "blind" confirmation. Depending on the need and risk involved, such advance commitments may be outstanding from a few weeks to up to one year or beyond. A commitment fee ranging from .5% to 2% per annum is usually charged.

Leasing

Specialized leasing companies, as well as commercial banks, have entered into the international leasing of capital goods. The vehicle is, in all cases, a finance lease. The bank or leasing company, in fact, buys the equipment to the specifications of the ultimate user (i.e., the importer). Since the financing institution is the actual owner of the equipment, it can take advantage of available tax benefits, such as accelerated depreciation or investment tax credits. Since the lessee might not be able to take advantage of accelerated depreciation or investment tax credits, this represents one of the main advantages of leasing.

Monthly, quarterly, or semiannual lease payments over the period are calculated to recover the entire cost of the equipment plus the desired finance charges for the leasor.

FOREIGN CREDIT INSURANCE ASSOCIATION

Export Credit Insurance, available through the FCIA, is discussed in this section, but first it is useful to say a few general words about some of the risks inherent in exporting, as well as some of the benefits that may make exporting profitable despite the risks.

Benefits of Exporting

The most obvious advantage of exporting is, of course, the additional sales and profits that are generated. Not as readily apparent is the fact that exports are often marginal sales that can make use of a plant's excess capacity. Hence, certain fixed costs, like depreciation and overhead, are incurred automatically and are, therefore, not increased due to export sales. To the extent that export sales absorb excess capacity, they may be even more profitable than regular domestic sales.

Exports may also be used to help smooth out cyclical business fluctuations. In past domestic recessions, many exporters have discovered that offshore sales may increase at the same time that domestic sales decline. Those manufacturers and commercial firms whose businesses are very cyclical may be able to introduce a degree of stability into their operations by entering export markets.

The U.S. government has initiated various tax programs to stimulate exports, such as the Western Hemisphere Trading Corporations and, more recently, FSCs. Through setting up an FSC, an exporter may be able to defer taxes on 50% of the income derived from exports.

Businesses looking for sales growth that is substantially faster than the economy may also find exporting a useful tool. Over long periods of time, exports have grown considerably faster than the economy as a whole. Although the exceptionally strong dollar of the 1980s reduced U.S. exports greatly, it is now expected that growth in U.S. exports will once again outstrip growth in the economy.

The financing of exports is relatively easy to obtain. Banker's acceptances are also particularly easy to arrange for exports and imports, and bankers are generally more willing to finance readily identifiable trade transactions. Additionally, the FCIA and Eximbank have substantially revamped their programs to be of greater financial assistance to exporters.

Risks of Exporting

While there are many advantages to exporting, it is not without risk. Indeed, there are often factors present in international markets that make foreign sales substantially more risky than domestic ones, including the credit risks of nonpayment or nonacceptance of the merchandise by the buyer. For international sales, these risks are far more pronounced than they are domestically. Often credit information on the importer is not available or, at best, sketchy. It is much harder to judge the financial strength, reputation, and integrity of a buyer who is thousands of miles away and belongs to a different culture. Moreover, many importers may have good reputations in their own environment, based on the local value system; they may, nevertheless, engage in some surprising business practices when judged by a different set of standards.

If an importer refuses to accept a shipment, or if an importer refuses payment, settlement of the dispute usually becomes much more difficult than in domestic commerce. A case of domestic nonacceptance or nonpayment can often be cleared up with a simple telephone call. If the merchandise is unacceptable for reasons of quality, it can generally be returned to the seller. Alternatively (and, again, domestically) a price concession to induce the buyer to accept the goods can often be arranged by telephone or a personal visit. If a domestic buyer refuses to pay, the seller has immediate recourse to a legal system similar to his own and, if the seller has a valid case, judgment against the buyer can be obtained.

For international sales, the problem of settling disputes becomes much more difficult. If an importer refuses to accept delivery, the merchandise remains in a foreign port incurring heavy demurrage charges (pier, warehouse storage charges, and insurance). Shipment back to the exporter's country is usually so expensive as not to be worthwhile. In the local market alternative buyers can probably be found only by allowing heavy discounts. In case of nonpayment, collection through the courts will invariably be difficult, time consuming, and expensive. Moreover, the legal system of the importer's country may make a judgment in favor of the exporter difficult to obtain.

In some cases, exporters may also incur a preshipment risk. If a U.S. company receives a foreign order for a piece of equipment that has to be specially manufactured, it runs a real risk if the order is canceled before shipment and receipt of payment. The equipment, being specialized for one use only, cannot usually be sold to an alternative buyer if the original order is canceled.

In addition to the credit and commercial risks we have outlined, international transactions take on a whole new dimension of political risk. The importer may be willing and able to pay for the goods, but the local central bank may refuse to make foreign exchange available. A previously approved import license may be canceled by the government, making it impossible for the importer to accept the shipment. Inadvertent infractions of required packing, shipping, marking, and other import regulations may make the shipment subject to confiscation by the local government or a heavy fine may have to be paid. War, strikes, insurrections, and similar disturbances in the importer's country may make acceptance of the shipment or payment impossible. All these risks are usually not present in domestic shipments but must certainly be taken into account by exporters. If shipments are well diversified (i.e., to many different countries) the political risks may be acceptable. If, on the other hand, shipments are concentrated in a few politically unstable countries, an exporter to these areas may be taking an unacceptably high degree of risk.

In addition to commercial and political contingencies, there are other risks unique to exporting operations. The most common is damage to goods while they are in ocean transit, a risk usually covered by marine insurance. In this section, we deal only with commercial and political risks that can be covered through the FCIA.

Origin of the FCIA

In 1962 the FCIA was formed by a group of insurance companies. It is a private organization through which the member companies and Eximbank insure exporters against commercial and political risks. The FCIA cooperates very closely with the Eximbank. The latter institution underwrites all political risk coverage and reinsures part of the commercial risk.

The FCIA was set up primarily to help U.S. exporters compete with the credit terms offered by foreign competitors that had their governments' support. Many foreign countries have similar export insurance schemes to help the sale of their products throughout the world. Before the establishment of the FCIA, U.S. exporters often found themselves at a disadvantage on the payment terms they could offer to foreign buyers. Risks inherent in exporting were assumed by both government-sponsored and -supported insurance programs in countries abroad, while U.S. exporters had to assume all these risks themselves.

The FCIA has introduced several new programs; the promotion programs have been stepped up, and the FCIA is planning to establish a total of twelve regional offices to bring information and support closer to exporters. So far, ten of these offices have been established.

Insurance from the FCIA is normally sold through insurance brokers and agents. Many large insurance brokerage houses have a FCIA specialist on their staff who can underwrite insurance and be of general assistance to exporters. While policies may also be obtained through one of FCIA's offices, there are certain advantages to using a broker or agent as an intermediary. Brokers and agents can advise exporters as to the type of insurance coverage they should take for their particular needs. They can also help exporters to prepare required documentation. Moreover, if there are any insurance claims, a broker or agent can be of assistance in processing the claims and obtaining prompt FCIA reimbursement.

In addition to insurance brokers and agents, a great deal of business is brought to the FCIA via commercial banks. The latter sometimes recommend FCIA insurance to exporters who wish bank financing.

Risks Covered

Depending on the exporter's needs, FCIA offers comprehensive coverage (commercial and political) or political coverage only.

Credit Risks. Commercial credit risks for which coverage is available include:

1. Insolvency (bankruptcy) of the foreign buyer.
2. Protracted default, that is, failure of the buyer to pay the insured within six months after the payment date for goods delivered to and accepted by the buyer.

Political Risks. Political risk coverage includes losses resulting from any of the following:

1. Transfer risk, that is, inability to convert the buyer's currency into U.S. dollars due to local exchange restrictions.
2. Nonpayment due to war, hostilities, civil war, insurrection, or similar disturbances.
3. Cancellation after the date of shipment of a previously issued export license.
4. Cancellation after the date of shipment of a previously issued and valid import license by the country of destination.
5. Expropriation, confiscation, or intervention in the business of the buyer by a government authority.
6. Transport and insurance charges incurred after shipment due to an interruption or diversion of the voyage because of political reasons.

Special Endorsements. The basic policy insures against the political or comprehensive risks previously outlined. Preshipment risks, consignments, nonacceptance, and sales invoiced in foreign currencies are not covered by the basic policy. These risks may, however, be insured by policy endorsements (i.e., by riders appended to the basic policy document).

Preshipment Coverage. Normally, insurance coverage commencing with the date of shipment is sufficient. Sometimes, however, a manufacturer of specially fabricated equipment may need protection against insolvency of the buyer and political contingencies during the manufacturing period. This can be done by a special endorsement to the basic policy.

If the basic policy includes coverage against commercial credit risks (i.e., comprehensive policy), the preshipment endorsement protects the exporter not only against political risks but also against insolvency of the foreign importer prior to shipment. Not covered, however, is the importer's unwillingness to accept the goods or a unilateral cancellation of the sales contract. In these cases, an exporter would presumably find redress through the courts.

Preshipment coverage against political risks (available under comprehensive or political-risks-only policies) includes losses caused by the following:

1. Cancellation of a valid export or import license *prior to* the shipment date.
2. War, revolution, and expropriation occurring *prior to* shipment.

Preshipment coverage may be available for periods up to 365 days, depending on the nature of the goods and length of the manufacturing period.

Nonacceptance Coverage. The basic policy does not insure against nonacceptance by the buyer of shipments that comply with the underlying sales contract. A special nonacceptance endorsement is available partly to protect against this risk. The endorsement for short-term policies provides that the insured has to bear the first loss up to 40%, while the insurers bear the last 60% of authorized buyer credit limit, whichever is less. The endorsement for the medium-term policy also provides for the insured to bear the first loss up to a specified percentage (usually 25%).

No insurance is available if nonacceptance by the buyer results from a fault or omission of the insured.

Coverage in a Foreign Currency. Most U.S. exports are invoiced in dollars. Therefore, standard FCIA policies are denominated in the same currency. Exporters who invoice in foreign currencies can obtain a foreign currency endorsement appended to their policies. This provides that the insurers may pay a valid claim either in the currency of invoicing or in U.S. dollars at the prevailing exchange rate.

Usually the foreign currency endorsement is available only for short-term policies; under certain circumstances, the FCIA may also be willing to make it available under a medium-term policy. Whenever a foreign currency endorsement is in effect, there cannot be any exchange risk coverage.

Consignment Coverage. Exporters shipping goods overseas on a consignment basis retain actual ownership until a final sale from consigned stocks is made. Since the inventory is stored in a foreign country, the exporter may wish to get coverage against political risks, such as war, requisition, confiscation, cancellation of import or export license, prohibition against reexport of consigned stock, and so on. This coverage is available through a special consignment endorsement to an existing policy.

The maximum period of consignment coverage is 180 days. This can then be renewed for another 180 days.

Exclusion and Limitations. It is important for the exporter to know which risks are not covered by FCIA insurance.

Generally, risks that can be insured through other means are not assumed by the FCIA. Hence, the usual ocean marine risks are not covered. Losses resulting from exchange fluctuations, devaluations or revaluations of currencies can usually be covered by other means and are therefore not included under FCIA insurance.

The exporter is expected to live up to all stipulations of the policy. Any excesses over the specified discretionary credit limit, special buyer credit limit, or aggregate credit limit are not covered for commercial risks. Excesses over specified limits may, however, be covered against political risks on shipments to certain markets that are defined by the FCIA (as well as Eximbank) as "A," "B," or "C," markets. Shipments to these markets are deemed subject to only moderate political risks. Any excess over established limits on shipments to so-called D markets (the most risky ones) are not covered.

In some instances, the policy or the FCIA's country limitations schedule requires the opening of a letter of credit. Consequently, insurance does not become effective unless such a credit has been issued.

Advantages

Aside from eliminating political and commercial risks, FCIA insurance may give the exporter other advantages. Proper insurance may, for instance, allow the exporter to enter new markets and perform larger-size transactions that would otherwise present too high a degree of risk. If an exporter's foreign credit and political risks are insured, it may also be easier to obtain financing at a more favorable rate of interest.

Policies set by the FCIA can be used as collateral for bank loans, as is described at the end of this chapter. Today many capital goods can only be sold if the exporter, at the same time, can also arrange for prolonged payment terms. Such medium-term financing of exports becomes easier to arrange if the shipment is insured against political and credit risks.

The FCIA can furnish credit information on foreign buyers. Over the years, it has accumulated files on more than 50,000 buyers that can be consulted for making a rapid decision on whether or not to ship. For 20,000 selected foreign buyers, the FCIA has preestablished credit limits up to which it is willing to be exposed. This prequalification of foreign buyers allows the FCIA to respond quickly to requests for insurance coverage on individual medium-term sales.

It is often advantageous for exporters to obtain an advance commitment of insurance coverage from the FCIA prior to receipt of a firm order. This greatly enhances the chances of closing a successful sale, since financing can be negotiated in advance.

In addition to this advantage, there are also some limitations. Medium-term insurance set by the FCIA sharply limits the percentage of non-U.S. content covered, and FCIA short-term insurance is available only for exports that have 50% or more of their value added in the United States. Also, for certain high-risk markets, FCIA and Eximbank have established upper limits on the total amount of political risk they are willing to underwrite. Hence, each exporter must participate to a varying degree in the risk of extending credit abroad. Unfortunately, the percentage of coverage is usually lowest for the most risky markets (i.e., so-called D markets), thus imposing coverage limitations where insurance is needed most. Premium rates also vary, depending on the country, with high-risk areas naturally being more expensive. Both of these factors are also generally present in insurance schemes of the countries of competitive exporters.

While FCIA insurance is useful, in many instances, for both protection and financing, for some U.S. exporters coverage may not be necessary. Large companies shipping to a diversified set of countries may, for instance, be perfectly capable of assuming all risks themselves. But, even here, an exporter of capital goods may wish to insure a shipment to a specific buyer or country by one of the FCIA's medium-term policies.

If an exporter primarily ships to politically stable countries with strong currencies and to importers in those countries considered to be prime credit risks, no insurance may be needed. Moreover, it would be redundant to insure sales that are paid by cash-in-advance or covered by irrevocable letters of credit opened or confirmed by prime banks. However, if a letter of credit is not confirmed by a prime U.S. bank and is opened by a bank in a country whose reserves of foreign exchange are inadequate to meet current requirements, insurance covering transfer risks could be desirable. In other cases, when shipments are made on an open account, consignment, documents against payment, or documents-against-acceptance basis, FCIA coverage may also be worthwhile.

Traditional Policies

While the FCIA has recently initiated several new programs that may eventually replace traditional policies, the latter are still actively used at the present time. There may be situations when coverage most suitable for the needs of a specific exporter will be found among the traditional rather than new policies. We, therefore briefly describe the five basic types of coverage made available since the FCIA's inception. Newer programs and their advantages are discussed in the next section.

Short-Term Comprehensive Policy. This policy is meant for shipments usually sold on payment terms up to 180 days.

Types of Goods Insured. Items frequently insured include commodities, raw materials, consumer software, parts, and other goods that are "used up" in a relatively short period of time.

Insurance Coverage. The term "comprehensive" refers to the fact that the policy covers both commercial and political risks. Commercial credit risks are insured up to 90% and political risks up to 100%. The small remaining risk is carried by the exporter. In the case of bulk agricultural commodities, the exporter is required to retain only 2% of the risk. This is in recognition of the low margin markup usual in the sale of such commodities.

A small retention of risk is a good insurance principle, since it prevents the exporter from making sales recklessly to foreign importers who obviously are in no position to pay for them.

Permitted Exclusions. The short-term policy covers all of the insured's exports for a period of one year. Underwriters prefer to cover every export, since they don't want to end up insuring only those shipments that are the most risky. Certain shipments may, however, be excluded from coverage, at the option of the exporter, if what remains still provides the insurers with a reasonable spread of risk. It is, for instance, acceptable to exclude all shipments to Canada as well as those covered by irrevocable letters of credit. No cash down payment by the importer is required under this policy, since full payment must be made, in any case, within 180 days. Exceptionally insured shipments (e.g., agricultural commodities) may be sold on terms up to one year.

Discretionary Limit. For commercial risk coverage, exporters are given discretionary credit limits within which they may ship to individual buyers and be covered automatically without first consulting the FCIA, provided they have obtained certain basic credit information about the buyer and such information is not adverse. For amounts above the discretionary limit, the exporter has to request FCIA approval. Once such approval has been obtained for any specific buyer, a special credit limit is established that can then be used on a revolving basis as long as the underlying policy remains in force.

Short-Term Political Risk Policy. While the comprehensive policy covers both commercial and political risk, this policy covers political risk only. Up to 100% of the political risk is assumed by the underwriter, that is, by Eximbank, with any remainder retained by the exporter. Other features of this coverage are similar to the previously outlined comprehensive policy. Both the comprehensive policy and the political-risk-only policy cover the exporter's sales for a period of one year.

Shipments under short-term policies are usually reported monthly to the FCIA together with appropriate premium payments.

Medium-Term Comprehensive Policy. The sales of capital goods and quasi-capital equipment often requires the granting of credit terms up to and even beyond five years. Goods sold on such payment terms may be insured against commercial credit and political risk by use of the medium-term comprehensive policy. The importer is usually required to make a cash payment of 15% on or before delivery with the remainder payable over a period of no longer than five years in equal semiannual, quarterly, or monthly installments. Up to 90% of commercial and 100% of political risk is covered by the FCIA with any remainder being retained by the exporter.

Medium-term insurance is generally arranged on an individual-transaction basis. It is, however, also possible to cover all sales to a specified buyer up to a maximum amount. The exporter has to support the application for a comprehensive medium-term policy with credit and financial information of the foreign importer.

Medium-Term Political Risk Policy. This is basically the same as the medium-term comprehensive policy except that only political risks are covered up to 100%, with the remainder being retained by the exporter. Goods covered by a medium-term comprehensive or political risk only policy must be essentially of U.S. origin. Transactions involving goods with some foreign-component content may be considered on a case-by-case basis.

Combined Short-Term and Medium-Term Comprehensive Policy. This policy combines short- and medium-term coverage on sales of capital and quasi-capital goods and related parts to foreign distributors and dealers. During the time the goods are kept in inventory with the dealer or distributor, short-term coverage applies and no cash payment has to be made. Once the products have been sold by the dealer on deferred payment terms, the short-term may be converted to medium-term coverage. In this case, the dealer has to pay the usual 15% cash and execute a promissory note for the remainder of the amount due. Payment may then be made over a period up to five years in the usual manner. Such a policy is particularly useful when capital goods are sold through dealers or distributors, since normal medium-term repayment requirements may be deferred up to 270 days. This allows time for the middleman to resell the product to the final user.

The FCIA also allows U.S. exporters to extend repayment terms up to one full year to new overseas dealers and distributors for the initial stocking of parts, accessories, and other shelf items. The usual term for such goods is 180 days when no new dealer or distributorship is involved.

New Policies

Recently, three new policies have been introduced with the objective of providing substantially automatic coverage under a "master policy" for all of an exporter's sales on terms ranging up to five years. To keep premium costs and paperwork down to a minimum, a deductible feature has been made part of the master policies.

Master Comprehensive Policy. This policy provides commercial and political risks coverage for all of an exporter's eligible short-term, as well as medium-term (up to five years), deferred payment sales. Hence, only a single policy is required to cover all foreign sales of an exporter, whether short- or medium-term. Various types of foreign buyers and different repayment terms are handled by special endorsements to the master policy. As with the more traditional policies, the exporter is expected to retain some, that is, at least 10%, of commercial risks.

Deductible Feature. A most interesting aspect of this policy is the deductible feature, whereby "first losses" up to a stated maximum amount are for account of the exporter. The amount of the deductible limit is set individually for each exporter. It is based on such factors as total past and expected sales volume terms, previous and projected loss experience, geographic spread of risk, and the seller's profit margin on exports. The deductible feature applies only to losses from credit risks, not to losses from political risks. If the deductible feature is also applied to political risks, further reductions in premium rates are possible.

Discretionary Limit. One advantage of the deductive feature is the lower premium that has to be paid by the exporter. Also important, in many cases, is the fact that the exporter is given considerable latitude in making credit decisions up to a maximum limit. This greatly reduces paperwork and speeds the exporter's ability to conclude deals with foreign buyers. When setting this discretionary credit limit, the FCIA usually tries to make it large enough so that most of the exporter's foreign sales are covered.

Three Variables. Generally, there are three variables that may be combined in different ways to meet the individual needs of the exporter:

1. Premium rate
2. Size of the deductible
3. Extent of the discretionary limit

By accepting a large deductible, exporters can obtain very low premiums. Moreover, the larger the deductible, the larger the discretionary credit limits within which exporters may act without first going to the FCIA. Conversely, if exporters wish a small deductible, they must be willing to pay larger premium rates. The important feature here is the substantial degree of flexibility offered by the master comprehensive policy to meet individual needs.

Master Political Risk Policy. Also called "Catastrophe Policy," this program provides coverage of losses from political risks up to a certain percentage individually specified in each policy, depending on the exporter's needs. All of an exporter's eligible credit sales on terms up to five years may be covered. Since the exporter is, in fact, coinsurer for a certain percentage, premium rates for the catastrophe policy are substantially lower than the traditional short- and medium-term political coverage.

Unlike the traditional policies, claims arising out of inability to convert local currencies into dollars (transfer risk claims) are not eligible for indemnification until one year after the maturity date or after the date on which a local currency deposit was made, whichever is later. In most cases, this last feature recognizes that when there is a transfer delay, the importer merely goes on a government waiting list until exchange becomes available. Exchange is then allocated on a first-come, first-served basis. Since the required delay period is usually less than one year, the FCIA's one year provision, in fact, makes indemnification unnecessary in most cases. Again, this saves much paperwork, which is reflected in lower premium rates.

As the name implies, catastrophe policies are particularly suited for exporters who feel they can assume normal commercial risks, but wish to be covered in case of unforeseen, serious political contingencies. This type of policy is especially suited for businesses doing a high volume, low-profit-margin type of business and exporting primarily on secured payment terms, such as release of title documents to the importer against payment.

In special cases, a business insured under a master political risk policy may apply for comprehensive coverage on a specific buyer or group of buyers. This provision may be especially attractive for established exporters who need only political coverage for their regular markets. The ability to obtain comprehensive coverage for certain groups of countries and/or customers may enable exporters to aggressively penetrate new markets on a large-volume basis.

The FCIA coverage is usually given only for arm's-length business transactions between independent buyers and sellers. Sales to overseas subsidiaries may also be insured, but only against political risks. In such cases, as when the overseas subsidiary is not wholly owned and controlled, some limited coverage may also be available for commercial risks.

Small Business Policy. This policy is meant to be an introduction to credit insurance for businessmen who are new in export trade or for exporters with modest sales volumes. Coverage is available for short- and medium-term sales to all buyers or for any sales to such buyers as the exporter may designate. However, if the exporter decides to cover only a portion of sales, the greater risk that this implies to the underwriters (the insurers) is usually reflected in a higher premium rate. The small business policy is comprehensive in that both commercial credit and political risk are insured. As with other policies, 10% of the commercial risk is retained by the exporter. A deductible may also be required, depending on the risk evaluation made by the FCIA.

To be eligible for the small business policy, a company's average annual export volume over the past three years may not exceed $200,000. Once granted, the policy remains in force for two years or until the exporter has insured an aggregate export volume of $500,000, whichever comes earlier.

After exporters become ineligible for small business coverage, they must sign up for one of the other standard, small business policies if they wish to retain FCIA insurance.

One of the advantages of the small business policy is that exporters may request the FCIA to obtain information showing the creditworthiness of foreign buyers, instead of having to obtain this information themselves. Another advantage is that it allows the exporter to insure only certain foreign buyers rather than being required to offer all accounts for coverage.

FCIA Coverage As a Financing Tool. One of the advantages of FCIA insurance is that it can be used as a means of obtaining credit to finance exports from banks and other financial institutions. To obtain financing for foreign receivables, an exporter may assign the proceeds of FCIA insurance to the institution providing the financing. Two types of assignments are possible: the simple notice of assignment and the special assignment agreement.

Simple Notice Assignment. In the simple notice of assignment, the exporter and exporter's bank merely notify the FCIA that they wish the proceeds of the particular policy to be assigned to a specific financial institution. Under this assignment, the financing institution obtains all the rights to make claims under the policy. Should nonpayment by the importer occur due to the fault of the exporter, however, no collection from FCIA can be made. In such a situation, the financing institution retains recourse to the exporter. When the exporter is financially strong, the need to take recourse, if the FCIA does not pay a claim, is probably satisfactory to a commercial bank. Sometimes, however, an exporter may not be strong enough financially to induce banks to rely solely on recourse. This is a tangible shortcoming that can be overcome by a special assignment agreement.

Special Assignment. The special assignment provides the FCIA's unconditional guarantee to the financing institution. Under such a "hold harmless" assignment, the FCIA agrees to repay the financing institution, even though it can be shown that the policy did not cover the risk that led to default on the part of the importer. While the FCIA unconditionally reimburses the financing institution for any losses, it retains recourse to the exporter if the loss was not due to a risk covered by the policy, such as noncompliance or failure of the exporter to fulfill the terms of the sales contract or obligations under the policy.

Assigned Transactions. Policy assignments, whether simple or special, may be done on an overall basis, buyer-by-buyer, even obligation-by-obligation. Assignments of policy proceeds could be on a buyer-by-buyer or obligation-by-obligation basis if different assignee financial institutions are involved.

Policies for Financing Institutions. Banks and other financial institutions may use the FCIA for obtaining policies in their own names. Factors, for instance, who buy all of a company's foreign accounts receivable, may insure them under one of the FCIA's policies. To date, about 50 commercial banks have also taken out policies in their own names to cover their accounts receivable financing activities. Banks may sometimes offer financing to overseas buyers who purchase from one or several U.S. exporters. These credits are also insurable through the FCIA, provided a reasonable spread risk is offered. Moreover, a number of banks have signed up for medium-term policies covering their financing of capital-goods exports for up to five years.

Adjustment of Claims

Insured exporters who have a claim can file it with their insurance agent, broker, or any FCIA office. Once the exporter has been paid, the FCIA assumes the burden of collecting from the buyer. If any recoveries are received, the FCIA first deducts its collection expenses. Of the remainder, the FCIA returns to the insured the percentage of the total risk that was retained at the time of the loss. The FCIA's collecting services may be another valuable asset to insured exporters.

CHAPTER 4

U.S. Government and International Financial Institutions

INTERNATIONAL MONETARY FUND

The deepest recession to restrict the economies of the free world since World War II ended in 1982–1983. However, substantial questions remain concerning the durability of the recovery and the ability of developing countries to honor their financial commitments, that is, to meet the repayment schedules of debts incurred before and during the recession. The fact that economic order has prevailed and major international bankruptcies have been avoided is probably due to the International Monetary Fund (IMF) more than to any other national or international body.

Historical Background

Headquartered in Washington, D.C., the IMF has grown from its original membership of 44 countries in 1944 to a total of 176 countries as of 1995. Each member contributes to the capital of the IMF, and the accumulated moneys are employed in financing IMF lending operations.

When new countries join the IMF, they are assigned a quota to contribute toward the IMF's capital formation. All member countries then enjoy both voting rights and special drawing rights in proportion to their respective contributions. The primary objective is to provide refinancing to those member nations experiencing financial difficulties in their foreign trade and balance of payments.

International monetary assistance can be crucial to developing nations. However, a country's financial difficulties can obviously extend to its commitment to the fund itself, and the more developing countries admitted, the more assistance may be needed from the remaining members.

Politicians in the United States frequently take a dim view of requests to increase our own subscription to the IMF's capital. Indeed, it can be demonstrated that the austerity programs designed to "rectify" a debt-ridden country's problems can, in the short run, impact negatively on the developed countries that support the fund. For instance, austerity measures required of receiver nations usually include a reduction in imports. However, a large percentage of those imports invariably come from developed nations, such as the United States. Another not infrequent result of enforced austerity, in return for IMF aid, is increased illegal border crossings. This kind of illegal immigration to more affluent countries has the potential to create enormous social problems.

It is necessary, therefore, for the IMF to balance fiscally responsible policies within the confines of a developing country with the export needs of developed countries. Also, in assessing the financial problems of developing countries, the IMF must be careful to distinquish between normal deficits incurred by a developing country and those deficits that are the result of inflationary policies.

Due to the widespread problems of international debt, in 1982 the United States was asked to increase its quota by $8.5 billion. At that time, failure by Congress to approve such an additional quota would have been interpreted by the international community as an unwillingness on the part of the United States to assist further in resolving the debt problems of developing nations. After considerable debate, Congress ratified the increase.

Lending Activities

When the IMF was established at the Bretton Woods Conference in 1944, its purpose was to assist countries through transient financial hardships. When these difficulties were resolved, it was expected that normal trading operations would resume. Today, the resources of the IMF are also committed to large-scale problems of a much longer term, such as avoiding international defaults.

During the 1970s, the sharp price increase in crude oil inflicted severe strains on the economies of many nations, and the governments of those countries, if they were members, applied to the IMF for additional refinancing. To enable the IMF to meet its members' increased demands for new loans, which continue to the present, the IMF has been compelled periodically to call on its members for increases in their capital subscriptions.

Financial Problems

In order to gain a better understanding of financial difficulties currently surrounding the IMF, one has to examine the roots of the problem. In the mid-1970s, when U.S. commercial banks were considering ways to recycle petro-dollars (on deposit from countries receiving oil revenues), they stimulated borrowing on the part of developing nations as a means of promoting domestic growth and coping with unemployment and internal social problems.

Credit managers of banking institutions viewed these loans as secured, since the borrowers were countries and not corporations. It was felt that a country, unlike a business, could not go broke. Unfortunately, lenders seriously underestimated the risk of default and the possibility of unilaterally declared moratoriums. During subsequent years, many of those loans turned sour, as borrowing nations were unable to meet their repayment schedules.

One of the most significant programs of the IMF to benefit developing nations has been the Oil Facility Subsidy Account created in 1975. It assists those IMF members most seriously affected by crude oil price increases by calculating subsidies as a percentage per annum of their average daily balances.

Buffer Stocks

Buffer stocks, also known as reserve stocks or safety stocks, are quantities of commodities set aside, usually under national or international programs, for the purpose of guarding against excessive price fluctuations resulting from unpredictable shortages or exceptional demand.

The IMF's buffer stock financing facility (BSFF) was established in 1969 to provide balance of payments assistance to eligible member countries in connection with the financing of their compulsory contributions to buffer stock agreements that meet the Fund's criteria. Drawings under the BSFF may be made up to 45% of a member's quota, and members using the facility are expected to cooperate with the Fund in an effort to find solutions to their balance of payments difficulties. Drawings are to be repurchased within three to five years or earlier if contributions to the buffer stock are refunded or the borrowing country's balance of payments situation improves. Drawings under the BSFF are subject to the Fund's normal rate of charge.

Further extension of the program occurred in 1990 with respect to the 1987 International Natural Rubber Agreement (INRA). After examining the terms of the agreement, the IMF decided that its BSFF could be used for the financing of eligible members' compulsory contributions to the buffer stock of the INRA. The INRA entered into force in April 1989 and provided for an international buffer stock of 550,000 tons of rubber to stabilize world rubber prices within an agreed price range. Since then, the agreement has received automatic extensions every two years.

Since the establishment of the BSFF, the Fund has assisted members under the Fourth, Fifth, and Sixth International Tin Agreements, and the 1977 International Sugar Agreement; it also stands ready to assist members under the 1972 International Cocoa Agreement, under which no drawings have been made. By mid-1990 the BSFF had been used by 18 countries with total drawings amounting to SDR 557.7 million (U.S.$725 million).

Use of Buffer Stocks. Price instability for primary commodities is historically well documented. Bumper crops, for example, can impact negatively on revenues if the price fall is not compensated for by an increase in volume. In the past, countries have attempted to protect farmers through guaranteed prices or deficiency payments linked to preestablished parity levels. It is also possible to stabilize commodity prices—to a limited degree—by buffer stocks. However, if prices continue to fall as the limits of funding for a buffer program are approached, then the avoidance of further price deterioration may require export quotas. This would result in a short-term accumulation of buffer stocks and, in the long term, a limit in investment and production.

Export quotas may alleviate a surplus—at least in the initial phases of stabilization—but buffer stocks may still be more effective in maintaining stable market prices. Members of the IMF that are able to demonstrate need in terms of balance of payments may participate in buffer stock schemes by contributing to buffer stock facilities established by international commodity agreements. The goal of buffer stock programs is to break the cycle of production surpluses and shortages in exporting countries and, over the long run, to reduce competition from opportunistic substitutes, which proliferate during periods of high demand.

Future Outlook

The IMF has raised $30 billion to rescue debt-ridden countries and enable them either to meet the repayment schedules of loans granted by private bankers or, at least, to honor the interest payments. By doing so the IMF retained the confidence of its major subscribers, particularly the United States.

As the international debt crisis has deepened, fears of major financial collapse have repeatedly arisen. Obviously, solutions beyond the rescheduling of loans is necessary. Nevertheless, the making of new loans to already nonperforming debtors has become a harsh reality to many bankers. All too frequently, bankers have had to return to their respective boards for approval of new loans, solely to inject new funds into the economies of debt-ridden countries, and without even guarantees as to the uses of these monies to make up payments in arrears.

Many affected countries have agreed to cut their public sector deficits. However, internal political pressures have sometimes not permitted them to keep those promises. The projected rescue operation, in many circumstances, depends on the recovery of industrial nations themselves, which will, in turn, increase their share of imported goods from debtor countries. Even an increase in tourism would significantly aid the economies of many of these countries.

It is of some comfort that the IMF possesses about 103 million ounces of gold which, at current market value, could bring more than $49 billion. Thus, the IMF has some tangible assets with which it can, at least partially, back its programs.

EXPORT-IMPORT BANK OF THE UNITED STATES

Although the roots of the Eximbank date back to 1934, it was not established as an independent U.S. government agency until 11 years later by the Export-Import Bank Act of 1945. In the immediate postwar period, Eximbank embarked on a program of large-scale reconstruction lending. It made loans available in Europe and Asia so that purchases of U.S. equipment could be financed, thus contributing substantially to the surge of world trade and rebuilding of devastated economies after World War II. With the establishment of the Marshall Plan, in 1948, however, Eximbank's efforts were redirected to help finance projects in developing countries.

Among the amendments of the Export-Import Act of 1945 was the Export Expansion Finance Act of 1971. This act substantially increased the overall amount of export loans, insurance, and guarantees that could be extended by Eximbank. The act excludes receipts and disbursements of Eximbank from the unified budget of the U.S. government. This exempts the bank from the annual expenditure and net lending limitations imposed by the budget on the government. Other significant provisions of the Export-Import Bank Act, as amended, include the following:

> Eximbank is directed to provide export financing with rates, terms, and other conditions that are competitive with government-sponsored export financing available in major foreign countries.
>
> Eximbank is directed to accord equal opportunity to small firms such as export agents, independent export firms, and small commercial banks in the formulation and implementation of its policies.

Current Functions

Eximbank's main function today is to give U.S. exporters the necessary financial backup to compete in other countries. This is done through a variety of different export financing and guarantee programs to meet specific needs. All are designed to be in direct support of U.S. exports, whether the eventual recipient of the loans or guarantees are foreign or domestic concerns. These programs can be categorized into four basic types:

Direct loans
Discount loans
Guarantees
Export credit insurance

It is important to stress that Eximbank does not compete with private sources of funds. Its sole purpose is to step in where private credit is not available in sufficiently large amounts, low rates, or long terms to allow U.S. exporters to compete. Often Eximbank cooperates with private lenders, encouraging them to extend part of the export credit with the agreement that Eximbank will take the commercially less desirable portions.

After outlining some of Eximbank's basic programs, we illustrate how it cooperates with commercial banks and other financial institutions to put together attractive export financing packages. Appendix 4 contains a chart of all Eximbank programs. Included for each program are eligible products, eligible applicants, coverage limitations, repayment periods, fees, and any special features.

Advantages

To the U.S. exporter and commercial banker, Eximbank offers many benefits. Today, international competition for sales does not only revolve around price, quality, and ability to deliver. Availability of credit for sufficiently long terms and at competitive rates is also a major factor. Eximbank, by guaranteeing against risks that exporters or commercial banks would not be willing to take, helps the exporter tap private sources of export financing. Moreover, benefiting from an Eximbank guarantee, lenders are often willing to extend credit at substantially lower rates.

A former advantage to participation by Eximbank was exemption from the Interest Equalization Tax (IET). The purpose of this tax was to strengthen the dollar by restricting certain types of capital outflows. Obviously, it was to the advantage of the U.S. economy and dollar to exempt loans to foreign exporters who were buying U.S. goods and services. However, the tax was reduced to zero in early 1974 and the law authorizing it expired a few months later.

Limitations

Eximbank is prohibited from extending credit to a communist country or any other country if the product financed is principally for use in a communist country. This prohibition may, however, be waived if the president of the United States determines it to be in the national interest. In this case, the president must make a complete report to Congress within 30 days of making such a determination. So far, specific sales to the former Yugoslavia and Romania, as well as to the Republic of Russia, Poland and Hungary have been exempted from the prohibition. Further exemptions are likely, depending on various considerations—including the future of global relations with the United States.

Eximbank is also prohibited from extending or guaranteeing credits to any developing country for the purchase of military equipment or services. Such defense products and services, however, have the option of obtaining financing or guaranteed bank credits through programs of the Defense Department.

Whenever Eximbank finances all or part of an export transaction, the goods have to be carried exclusively on U.S. vessels, unless a waiver is obtained from the U.S. Maritime Commission. The latter generally allows the vessels of importing nations to share up to 50% in the carriage of Eximbank-financed goods. There is no requirement concerning U.S. vessels when the Eximbank merely extends its guarantee but grants no direct financing.

Major Programs

Eximbank offers many different programs to meet the various needs of U.S. exporters and foreign importers. The fact that Eximbank provides export credit insurance in cooperation with FCIA is discussed in Chapter 3. We Now describe the major direct loans, discount loans, and guarantee programs available. (See also Appendix 4.)

Direct Loans. To help finance large purchases of U.S. goods, especially capital goods requiring extended terms, Eximbank makes direct loans to foreign importers. Loans are granted in dollars and disbursements are made directly to U.S. suppliers of goods and services. The borrowers, that is, the overseas importers, have to repay the loans plus interest over a stipulated number of years. Availability of the direct loan program allows U.S. suppliers of major items of capital equipment to provide financing terms that are competitive with those offered by government-sponsored export financing institutions of other countries. Direct loans are made for large projects, such as nuclear power plants, importation of wide-bodied jet aircrafts, and similar large-ticket items requiring long-term financing.

Private financial participation is required for any transaction seeking Eximbank direct lending. If necessary, Eximbank may extend its financial guarantee to assure repayment of the private loan. Eximbank is also prepared, when necessary, to finance, through its direct lending, the later maturities of the total credit. This allows the private lender to obtain repayment of its loan in a shorter period of time.

Application for Loan. An application for a direct loan may only be made by the prospective borrower. It should be in letter form, together with schedules and enough details to enable Eximbank to evaluate fully the technical, economic, and financial aspects of the transaction. When considering an application, Eximbank makes its evaluations on the basis of the following:

1 The borrower should have sufficient financial strength to provide Eximbank with reasonable assurance of repayment. The guarantee of a reputable local commercial bank or even the central bank may be required.

2 The project should be financially self-supporting. It must be economically, financially, and technically sound.

3 The project may not adversely affect the economies of either the United States or the country in which it is located.

Procedures. When granting a direct loan, Eximbank negotiates a loan agreement with the foreign buyer in which all stipulations of the credit are spelled out. The rate of interest depends on market conditions at the time. The importer acknowledges the obligation by signing a loan agreement and by issuing a promissory note or other negotiable debt obligation to Eximbank. Terms of repayment usually vary between five and fifteen years, depending on the nature of the capital goods sold and the amount involved. Regardless of the term, repayment of principal is generally made in equal, semiannual installments starting six months after delivery of the equipment purchased or completion of the financed project. After Eximbank makes a formal commitment to finance a particular transaction, the borrower is required to pay a commitment fee of ½ of 1% per annum on any unused balance of the approved loan.

Agricultural Exports. In addition to financing exports of capital equipment, Eximbank also makes credits available to help foreign importers buy U.S. agricultural products. Terms of repayment may range up to one year. (For relevant insurance programs see Chapters 5 and 9.)

Among the early direct credits authorized by Eximbank in the financing of agricultural products were those for exports of cotton to Asia. For these transactions, foreign buyers of cotton asked their local banks to seek a credit line from Eximbank. Such a line is made available for use over a 12-month period. The foreign banks then arranged for the opening of a letter of credit with a U.S. bank in favor of the exporter. The latter, after making a shipment, submitted the required documents to the U.S. bank. If everything was in order, the U.S. bank promptly paid the exporter and reimbursed itself from Eximbank. Eximbank, in turn, debited the loan account of the foreign bank that had the approved credit facility. Repayment of the loan was made by the foreign commercial bank and ultimately by the importer, according to the previously arranged credit arrangement.

Guarantees for U.S. Financial Institutions. Frequently, U.S. banks are prepared to make direct loans to foreign purchasers of U.S. goods and services. Sometimes, the bank is willing to assume the full risk of making the loan to the foreign obligor. For exports to certain high-risk areas or to specific borrowers, however, banks are only willing to make loans if they are backed by the full credit of the U.S. government through an Eximbank financial guarantee. To promote U.S. exports, Eximbank is prepared to unconditionally guarantee repayment by the borrowers of up to 100% of loans granted to it, assuming there is no competition from other export credit agencies. Refer to Appendix 4 for specifics of available programs including PEFCO.

Application for Guarantees. A letter of application for a guarantee may be submitted by the borrower, exporter, or U.S. financial institution. As with the direct loan program and all other applications to Eximbank, it must include sufficient information to allow an evaluation of the technical, economic, and financial aspects of the proposed project.

Procedure. To evidence the borrower's financial obligation to the U.S. commercial bank, there has to be an underlying loan agreement. The agreement must provide for repayment of principal and interest no less frequently than semiannually. The total term of the credit should not be longer than what is customary in the particular industry. Frequently, the obligation of the borrower has to be guaranteed by a local institution satisfactory to Eximbank, such as the central bank or a prime commercial bank in the country of the importer. In all other respects, the loan agreement between the borrower and the U.S. commercial bank must be acceptable to Eximbank.

Default. If a guaranteed loan is in default for 30 days, Eximbank will, on application by the commercial bank, pay the amount in default. Eximbank may then also, at its options, prepay the entire amount of the guarantee and, in fact, take over the loan.

Guarantees for Non-U.S. Financial Institutions. Eximbank is generally willing to extend its financial guarantee to non-U.S. financial institutions only if private U.S. sources of funds are unwilling or unable to finance the transaction at reasonable terms. If U.S. funds are not available, the guarantee program helps U.S. businesses by increasing the sources of funds available for financing their exports. Considered as "non-U.S. financial institutions" are foreign branches of U.S. banks, foreign offices of U.S. trading companies, and other U.S. financial institutions, as well as non-U.S. commercial, investment, and development banks. When money in the United States is tight, these foreign-based institutions may be able to raise needed funds, perhaps in the Eurocurrencies market.

Normally, loans made by non-U.S. financial institutions are associated with projects in which Eximbank also participates with a direct loan and/or in which U.S. financial institutions also participate. Loans made by non-U.S. financial institutions may also cover the U.S. portion of consortium projects in which suppliers of other countries are also involved.

Procedurally, Eximbank guarantees to non-U.S. financial institutions are handled in the same manner as those for U.S. institutions. The interest charged (and therefore guaranteed) has to be at a rate satisfactory to Eximbank.

Commercial Bank Exporter Guarantees. The Eximbank guarantees so far considered all apply to credits given directly to importers. An alternate way of financing is for the exporter to extend credit to the foreign customer. The latter then incurs an obligation to pay the exporter over a number of years. This obligation is evidenced by one or several serially maturing promissory notes or drafts.

Exporters are usually not in a position to carry long-term receivables of this nature. They need the proceeds of their sales right away for the continuous conduct of their businesses. To obtain the needed cash, exporters may be able to sell the debts due them to commercial banks or other financial institutions. The sale of the debt obligation may be with or without recourse to the exporter. If it is with recourse, the financing institution may collect from the exporter if the importer does not pay on time. If it is without recourse, the exporter is free of all obligations; if the importer does not pay at maturity, the financing institution suffers the loss.

To induce commercial banks to buy foreign importers' debt obligations without recourse to U.S. exporters, Eximbank is willing to extend its guarantee. Usually the guarantee covers all the political risk and everything but 10% of the commercial credit risk. If the original credit period is three years or longer, if the first half of the loan is repaid promptly, and if the private, foreign importer remains in good financial condition, Eximbank provides, on request, a comprehensive guarantee for the remainder of the commercial bank's 10% credit risk as well as for the remainder of the exporter's participation.

For acceptable government and government-related buyers, Eximbank offers a guarantee that covers, from the outset, all of the political and credit risk of the commercial bank's export loan.

Credit Evaluation. Since commercial banks assume part of the credit risk on sales to private buyers, they have to make a credit evaluation of the foreign importer. With large banks that are experienced in international financing, Eximbank relies heavily on these banks' own credit evaluation. Many U.S. banks have been given discretionary limits up to which they may commit Eximbank as long as they themselves are satisfied with the credit risk.

Procedure. Upon receipt of an overseas order or inquiry, the exporter should discuss the availability and cost of financing with his bank. Once the latter has itself made a positive decision on the foreign credit risk, it will contact Eximbank for its approval of the guarantee. Those banks that have discretionary authority do not have to get prior Eximbank approval if the amount is within the authorized limit. The bank, of course, still has to inform Eximbank. Once shipment is made, the commercial bank purchases the buyer's promissory note from the exporter without recourse. On proper notification of such purchase, Eximbank promptly issues its guarantee in favor of the commercial bank.

Terms. General requirements for exporter guarantees are similar to other Eximbank programs: Credit terms may not exceed terms commercially customary for the particular type of goods. The maximum term limit is usually five years, although in special circumstances Eximbank may be willing to extend the limit as far as eight years. Credit terms on sales to distributors for resale to local users are limited to three years for most products—except passenger cars for which the limit is only two years.

Down Payment and Exporter Retention. The exporter has to receive from the importer a cash payment of at least 15%, making the financed portion 85% of the invoice amount. Of this financed portion, the exporter must retain at least 10% of the risk. Hence, under normal circumstances, the amount financed by the commercial bank and guaranteed by Eximbank represents 75% of the invoice amount. An exception, however, is made for agricultural commodities, which only require 2% exporter retention.

Guarantee Fee and Limitation. Guarantee charges vary, depending on the term of the credit and the importing country. Eximbank has divided the countries of the world into four classifications according to economic and political conditions. Those in the most economically sound and politically stable category enjoy the lowest guarantee rates.

Procedure. As usual, a minimum 15% down payment is required from the importer, making the financed portion 85% of the invoice amount. Eximbank charges interest to the cooperating institution at the usual rate of 7% per annum. Hence, the maximum rate to the importer on the 50% financed by Eximbank is 9½% per annum. The cooperating institution assumes all political and commercial risks for the entire financed amount. In some cases, for sales to importers in countries other than the location of the cooperating institution, Eximbank is prepared to insure the convertibility risk on the entire financed amount.

The maximum term available under a cooperative financing facility is five years, although exceptions to this rule are possible if the underlying transaction warrants it. Selected cooperating institutions may have a discretionary limit within which they may make decisions without first consulting Eximbank.

Funding. Sometimes, a cooperating institution requires funding from another financial institution for its 50% of the financing. In this case, Eximbank may extend to the funding institution (called the participating financial institution) a financial guarantee covering both political and commercial risk. In other cases, that is, for funds supplied by itself, the cooperating institution may charge interest at its usual commercial rate.

The cooperative financing facility has been an effective tool for providing financing to small- and medium-sized importers of U.S. goods and services. Presently, Eximbank cooperative facilities have been extended to almost 300 non-U.S. financial institutions.

Relending Credits to Non-U.S. Financial Institutions. As a further facility to help medium- and small-sized foreign companies buy U.S. goods and services, Eximbank has established relending credit lines to selected non-U.S. financial institutions. On the basis of this credit line, the non-U.S. financial institution makes subloans to local concerns to finance their U.S. imports. These relending credits are made available, however, only for a selected list of products in a limited number of countries and only when private sources of funds are not available. Part of the purpose of the relending facility is to create more extensive foreign markets for selected U.S. products which, in Eximbank's opinion, have substantial unrealized export potential.

Guarantees of Leases. In recognition of the fact that more and more exports are consummated in the form of financial leases, Eximbank is prepared to extend to lessors its guarantee of payment by the lessee. Of course, to be eligible under the program, the underlying lease agreement must result in the export of U.S. equipment. (For specifics see Appendix 4.)

Lessors have the option of a comprehensive guarantee that covers both political and commercial credit risks or a guarantee that covers only political and transfer risks.

Assignments. Lease payments, as well as Eximbank's guarantee, may be assigned by the lessor to a third party. This makes it possible for the lessor to offer security for any financing required to carry the lease. Before assigning the lease payments and Eximbank's guarantee, the lessor must obtain Eximbank's written permission.

Credit. Before Eximbank guarantees a lease, it must, of course, be satisfied with the creditworthiness of the lessee. Often the guarantee of a prime financial institution is required.

Application for Guarantees. Applications for lease guarantees should be in the form of a letter to Eximbank with the following information:

1. A copy of the proposed lease agreement.
2. A detailed description of the lease transaction.
3. A description of the equipment, including a statement as to whether it is new or used.
4. The estimated dollar inflow to the United States as a result of the lease transaction (the Eximbank guarantee is never greater than this estimated dollar inflow).
5. Detailed credit information on the lessee, lessor, and guarantor.
6. Whether the lessor desires a comprehensive or a political-risks-only guarantee.
7. The use to be made of the equipment.
8. Any other pertinent information, especially regarding any other agreements that relate to the specific lease transaction.

Default. If a lessee defaults, the lessor has to notify Eximbank within 30 days. Subsequently, a demand for payment must be filed by the lessor. In this demand, the lessor must include evidence indicating that every reasonable effort was made to repossess and dispose of the leased equipment and that all other necessary actions were taken to minimize loss. Eximbank will make payment within 30 days of receipt of the formal demand. It may also, at its option, continue to make regular lease payments to the lessor, in lieu of the total payment required under the guarantee.

Short-Term Discount Program. This program was initiated in early 1972 to make available an additional financing source for exports being sold on payment terms of 365 days or less. While short-term financing from private sources is more readily available than medium-term loans, certain gaps still exist when compared with competitive facilities offered in other countries.

As with other Eximbank programs, short-term discounting of export paper is meant to supplement, not compete with private sources. Hence, each applicant must certify to Eximbank that a discount loan is necessary to complete the transaction and that it cannot be financed in the bankers' acceptance market. Indeed, since bankers' acceptances are limited to 180 days, while maturities under the short-term discount program may go up to 364 days, an important new financing dimension is added.

Procedure. Banks wishing to take advantage of the discount loan program should first apply for an advance commitment from Eximbank. Such an application has to be made before actual shipment of the goods or services being financed. If Eximbank approves, it will issue a commitment to finance the full amount of the specific transaction. This commitment is valid for the entire term of the specific export debt obligation. Hence, if a commercial bank initially has sufficient funds to carry the transaction itself, it may do so. If funds are needed at a later date, the debt obligation may then be discounted at Eximbank. Banks may also prepay discount loans at any time they desire.

When Eximbank discounts an export debt obligation, it does so with full recourse to the U.S. commercial bank. The latter thereby takes on itself the full credit and political risk of the foreign obligor. Alternatively, eligible export debt obligations may be insured through a master insurance policy issued by FCIA. They may also be covered under a separate Eximbank guarantee.

Obtaining a Preliminary Commitment. It will often be required that exporters negotiating a transaction present a financing plan to the potential buyer. Similarly, foreign buyers find it useful to have an indication of the terms and conditions under which financing or leasing of a major import item or project will be available. In these cases, it is most useful to get from Eximbank a preliminary estimate concerning the amount and term of any direct credits and/or guarantees it is willing to make available. As soon as Eximbank has sufficient information to reach a favorable judgment, it is usually willing to give, without charge, a preliminary commitment stating the following:

1 The amounts, interest rate, terms of repayment, and any other conditions under which it might make available direct loans.
2 The amounts, terms, and conditions under which Eximbank is willing to guarantee loans made available from other sources.
3 Amounts of financing required from other sources and requirements concerning terms and conditions on these loans.
4 The requirements for a guarantor (such as a prime financial institution in the country of the importer) or other alternatives satisfactory to Eximbank.

5 A schedule of information and assurances required before final approval will be made.
6 The expiration date of the preliminary commitment.
7 Any other conditions that have to be fulfilled before Eximbank will issue its formal commitment.

Applications. Applications for direct loans, guarantees, and preliminary commitments may be made to Eximbank by letter. While there is no standard form, the application should provide sufficient information to allow Eximbank to evaluate the economic, technical, and financial feasibility of the project, as well as on the creditworthiness of the primary obligor and guarantor. Usually the following details are needed:

1 Name, address, and nature of business of borrower.
2 Ownership and brief history of borrower.
3 Financing required for total project, including total amount of financing required and different currency components.
4 Documents, including financial statements, which describe the financial responsibility of the borrower.
5 On applications relating to projects of a comprehensive nature and involving more than one supplier, additional information must be furnished, when applicable, that is:
   a. A description of the items to be purchased and, if identified, the names and addresses of suppliers as well as particulars on any agreements already made with the suppliers.
   b. Sources and availability of raw materials that may be required for the project.
   c. A description of markets to be supplied, likely competition, and other market information that may be available.
   d. Detailed information demonstrating the viability of the project.
   e. A proposed time schedule toward completion of the project with phases, such as planning, designing, construction, equipping, delivery, start-up, and marketing.
   f. A description of the management plan for the project from an engineering and operational point of view.
   g. A description of measures the host government intends to take in assuring the viability of the project, such as tariff or quota protection, tax benefits, and so on.
6 Description of items to be purchased and how they will be used.
7 Identification of any guarantor of the import debt obligation—if the guarantor is a private company or bank, recent financial information should also be furnished.
8 The amount and purpose of any local-cost financing that may be needed,

as well as the name of the host-country entity that would guarantee repayment of local cost advances. Evidence of foreign competition also offering publicly assisted local-cost financing must be furnished.

9 An estimated schedule of when an Eximbank response to the applications is needed and final approval of the financing arrangement will be required.

10 A description of efforts to obtain dollar financing from other sources and the results thereof.

Other Programs and Services. We have so far outlined Eximbank's major financing, guarantee, and insurance programs. There are, in addition, several other services that U.S. exporters or commercial banks may find useful in the solution of specific problems.

Local Cost Financing. To meet competitive programs offered by export promotion schemes in other countries, Eximbank occasionally offers to assist exporters in obtaining local-cost financing for up to 15% of the cost of goods and services exported from the United States. It will usually do this by offering its financial guarantee to cover loans made by non-U.S. financial institutions.

To qualify for help with local-cost financing, the exporter must clearly demonstrate that it is necessary for consummation of the U.S. export. Local costs may include expenses for engineering services, public utility connections, local construction materials, equipment installation, and so on.

Financing of Special Studies. Export sales of goods and services tend to follow the nationality of the firm making the feasibility study. In view of this tendency, Eximbank is willing to finance the preparation by U.S. firms of engineering, planning, and feasibility studies of large capital projects for overseas clients.

If funding of the study is done by the U.S. contractor, Eximbank provides a Commercial Bank Exporter Guarantee, allowing the contractor to sell the foreign debt obligation to a commercial bank without recourse. If the overseas importer supplies the funding, Eximbank's assistance is given in the form of a financial guarantee. The term of Eximbank assistance usually permits one year's grace after the feasibility study contract is signed. Thereafter, two to three years are allowed for repayment in semiannual installments. Eximbank normally requires a financial participation in the study by both the U.S. contractor and overseas client.

Before extending a guarantee, Eximbank requires an unconditional debt obligation executed by the foreign client. Hence, Eximbank will be paid, regardless of whether the feasibility study is completed in proper fashion or not. To protect the overseas client against nonperformance by the contractor, a guarantee from a bonding company or performance letter of credit from a bank is often required.

Credit Information for Commercial Banks. As a result of its extensive experience with lending abroad, Eximbank has accumulated a substantial knowledge of countries in general, as well as individual files on commercial firms abroad. Eximbank is willing to make nonconfidential information available to U.S. banks that are studying individual projects for possible financing. This service is particularly valuable to smaller banks that do not have extensive economic research departments or international credit files. An indication of the payment record of foreign buyers or the ability of specific governments to provide dollar exchange may be especially helpful to banks that are considering a lending decision.

Counseling. Eximbank provides a counseling service for exporters, banks, and other financial institutions to help solve problems of financing U.S. exports. Information can be given on financial resources and services available in the United States and abroad. Eximbank is, of course, also prepared to give counseling on any of its own programs that may meet the needs of exporters or financial institutions. Those exporters who have encountered difficulty in obtaining financing for their sales should certainly contact Eximbank for assistance.

Training. Eximbank holds periodic seminars and training sessions for U.S. businesses as well as commercial banks. One-day training sessions for businesspeople are particularly geared toward explaining the various Eximbank programs available. The seminars for commercial banks are designed to help them explain export financing techniques to their customers. These seminars are held in the bank's local community; business customers, as well as the bank's account officers, are invited. The agenda varies depending on local needs, but usually includes a review of export financing techniques, as well as an explanation of pertinent Eximbank programs.

Eximbank also makes available a six-month training program for employees of commercial banks who have been nominated by their managements. The program is an on-the-job training experience that brings the trainee into contact with all major phases of Eximbank's operations.

Financing Packages

Eximbank's many programs are meant primarily to supplement private sources of export credit. Hence, there are many occasions when commercial banks and other suppliers of funds work closely with Eximbank to come up with a total package.

Since commercial banks and other private lenders wish to keep their loan portfolios as liquid as possible, they tend to shy away from loans with long maturities. The maximum term for a commercial bank is usually five years. Occasionally, especially in the Eurodollar market, banks are willing to go out as far as seven years on a floating-rate basis. To consummate exports of heavy capital equipment, power plants, industrial plants, and large commercial aircraft, terms well in excess of seven years are usually required. Moreover, due to foreign competition, the interest rate often has to be lower than what is available from commercial sources. For these reasons, it has become typical for Eximbank to finance the later maturities of an export loan, while a commercial bank finances the early maturities. If the total term is ten years, for instance, a commercial bank might take the first five years, while Eximbank would take the last five years. Since repayment of such loans occurs in equal semiannual installments, with the first one usually six months after shipment, the commercial bank's portion is liquid. Indeed, average maturity is only about three years. Eximbank's portion of the loan, on the other hand, is outstanding for the full amount until the middle of the sixth year when repayment commences; its average maturity is therefore about eight years.

The portion financed by the commercial bank may or may not be covered by Eximbank's financial guarantee. If the political and/or commercial risk appears too high, it is usually easy to arrange for an appropriate guarantee for the commercial bank's portion.

If loans to finance exports are required for shorter maturities and U.S. commercial lending rates are competitive with those offered under subsidized programs available in other countries, a commercial bank may be able to do the entire transaction by itself or in cooperation with other private sources of funds, such as PEFCO. In these cases, Eximbank can still make a significant contribution to the package by adding its guarantee. The fee for the guarantee is modest when compared to the impact it has in reducing the risk to private financing institutions.

WORKING CAPITAL GUARANTEE PROGRAM

The Working Capital Guarantee Program seeks to expand U.S. exports by encouraging lenders to make working capital loans to U.S. businesses for various export-related production and marketing activities. Lack of working capital financing is one of the biggest barriers small and medium-sized companies face when trying to export. Despite their creditworthiness, potential exporters sometimes find lenders reluctant to offer them such financing. Some companies have already reached the borrowing limits set by their banks; others do not have the type or amount of collateral their banks require. The Working Capital Guarantee Program encourages lenders to extend working capital financing by significantly reducing the risk associated with these loans. The potential exporter applies for the program through an eligible lender.

Program Description

Under the Working Capital Guarantee Program, Eximbank provides repayment guarantees to lenders on secured, short-term working capital loans to qualified exporters. The guarantee can apply either to a single export-related loan or to a revolving line of credit that covers repetitive sales to one or more buyers. If the exporter defaults on the loan, Eximbank covers 90% of the principal of the loan and interest up to the date of claim payment at the stated rate on the loan or 1% over the U.S. Treasury borrowing rate, whichever is lower.

A word of caution: This program protects the bank only from default by the exporter. It does not cover the exporter if the buyer defaults. The lender and exporter should together determine whether they need credit risk protection on foreign receivables. Eximbank's guarantees and FCIA insurance are available for this purpose.

Eligible Exporters

The program is designed to facilitate the expansion of U.S. exports that would not have occurred without Eximbank's guarantee. Eximbank envisions the program helping small and medium-sized firms, minority businesses, and agricultural concerns that have exporting potential but need funds to produce or market goods for sale overseas. It may be used to cover working capital loans to any U.S. business if the lender certifies that the loan would not be made without Eximbank's guarantee and Eximbank determines that the exporter is creditworthy.

Eligible Lenders

Any commercial bank, provider of commercial credit, or other public or private creditor can participate in the Working Capital Guarantee Program. The lender must have the ability and resources to service the loan. Experience in providing business loans, perfecting required security through Uniform Commercial Code (UCC) filings, and collecting loans normally constitute adequate ability.

Eligible Uses of Loan Proceeds

The exporter can use the financing secured under the program to purchase finished products, or to purchase materials, products, services, and labor to produce goods and services for current or future export sales; and to market products, participate in trade fairs, or conduct other promotional activities aimed at developing new overseas business. The lender must state clearly the purpose of the loan in its application.

There are restrictions. Proceeds of the loan may not be used to pay off an exporter's existing debt. Military goods or goods destined for military use are not eligible for Eximbank support; nor are products to be exported or reexported to countries that are not eligible for Eximbank financing.

Eximbank's charter also places some restrictions on Eximbank support of exports to South Africa.

Security

Amount. The amount of each loan cannot exceed 90% of the value of the collateral. Goods purchased with the proceeds of the guaranteed working capital loan may be used as collateral, as can accounts receivable resulting from transactions generated by the loan. While exportable inventory and export accounts receivable are acceptable collateral, Eximbank will accept requests for its guarantee with other suitable types of collateral. Lenders must provide an adequate description of the security and the rationale used for its valuation.

Inventory as Collateral. For inventory used as collateral, at least 50% must be U.S. content, which would include U.S. labor, materials, and services but exclude the U.S. exporter's profit or markup. Exportable inventory should normally be valued at either cost or market value, whichever is lower. However, given the potentially large variety of inventory that may be given as security, lenders should be aware that the liquidation value of the security may be less than cost or market value, especially in the case of specialized products or equipment. For other than "shelf items" or commodities that can be easily liquidated at a readily identifiable value, lenders should provide Eximbank with an analysis of net liquidation value.

Accounts Receivable As Collateral. Lenders proposing export accounts receivable as security must also analyze whether or not those receivables can be collected. While no specific criteria can be given for this evaluation, lenders should consider the following:

1. Receivables more than 60 days past due are not eligible security.
2. Export credit insurance may improve the ability of the lender or exporter to collect on some receivables. This insurance is available through several private companies as well as FCIA.
3. Receivables on terms of an irrevocable letter of credit confirmed by a U.S. bank do not require export credit insurance. Unconfirmed irrevocable letters of credit opened by banks in developed countries also generally do not require coverage.

There are restrictions. Collateral in the form of inventory destined for military use abroad and receivables from military buyers are not acceptable security under this program. Eximbank's charter also precludes certain markets. Receivables from some communist countries are not eligible security. Eximbank's charter also has some restrictions related to the support of transactions with South Africa.

Guarantee

Coverage. Eximbank's guarantee covers 90% of the principal amount of the loan, and interest up to the date of claim payment at the stated rate on the loan or 1% over the U.S. Treasury borrowing rate for comparable maturities, whichever is lower. The lenders must retain the risk on 10% of the loan amount, on interest in excess of the guaranteed rate, and on any late interest. If the lender obtains any security for its risk retention, it shares this security with Eximbank in the same ratio as it shares the risk on the loan amount.

Availability Date. Each guarantee commitment has a 90-day availability period. The lender must forward the appropriate fee to Eximbank within 90 days of Eximbank's authorization. Guarantee commitments automatically expire at the end of this period if the fee has not been paid in full. Partial payments of fees and installment payments are not allowed; no refunds are given. Any loan funds disbursed to the exporter prior to Eximbank's receiving the full guarantee fee are not eligible to be covered by the guarantee.

Extensions. Once the fee is received, Eximbank's guarantee is in force for the guarantee period stated in the request for guarantee. If the lender desires to extend the guarantee, one six-month extension is available with payment of an additional fee. If the lender desires to continue the guarantee beyond the maximum period allowed, it must submit a new application with updated attachments and a new request for guarantee to Eximbank. The new application must include updated financial statements and the lender's experience under the existing guarantee (including high credit, repayment terms, and record of collection activity).

Guarantee Fees

Eximbank's guarantee fees are calculated on the loan amount and vary with the guarantee period. In the case of revolving lines of credit, the loan amount is the highest credit the lender is willing to make available under the Eximbank guarantee. For loans with terms up to six months, the fee is 1% of the loan amount. For loans with terms of six months to one year, the fee is 1.5% of the loan amount.

Guarantees are usually available for one year. However, one six-month extension is possible. The fee for such an extension is 0.5% of the loan amount. Fees are payable as a one-time, up-front sum. The guarantee is not in effect until the correct fee is paid in full.

Lender Interest Rates and Fees. Eximbank imposes no interest rate ceilings or maximum fee limitations in its Working Capital Guarantee Program. However, Eximbank monitors the rates and fees charged under the program. Lenders should take into account that most of their risks are covered by an agency of the U.S. government and price their funds accordingly.

Application Procedures. Upon application Eximbank decides whether a request meets the program guidelines and offers a reasonable assurance of repayment. Lenders are required to submit their own credit analysis and to describe how they will control disbursement, application of funds, and payment procedures. The more complete the application and attachments, the more promptly Eximbank decides on the request. The documents required are the application for working capital guarantee, the attachments to the application, and the request for guarantee.

Upon approval, the guarantee agreement and the request for guarantee are signed by an officer of Eximbank, thereby constituting the guarantee. A guarantee of the principals must be obtained for borrowers that are closely held, and the borrower must have a positive net worth or the borrower's principals must show adequate resources. For loans of $1 million or more, the borrower's financial statements must be audited. Principals or senior management of the firm must have at least two years' export experience.

The application will request the following information:

1. Name, address, and type of exporter.
2. Relationship of borrower to lender.
3. Type of loan, terms, and security offered (including methods of valuation).
4. Export markets of the exporter.
5. Reasons the exporter applied for the loan and the reasons the lender is requesting an Eximbank guarantee.
6. Type of insurance coverage for the transaction, if applicable.

Attachments. The lender must also attach to the application for working capital guarantee the following:

1. Brief history of the borrower and guarantor, if any, including the date organized, legal status, and a description of its operations and major shareholders.
2. Borrower's and guarantor's signed or audited financial statements for the past three years (if available), including the aging of receivables and a breakdown of sales by domestic and foreign sales.
3. Projected financial statements for the period that the loan will be outstanding, showing the borrower's ability to service the additional guaranteed debt.
4. Three recent credit reports or references.
5. A short biography of principal owners and senior management.
6. Signed personal financial statements of principal owners.
7. Additional information the lender feels is relevant.

Request for Guarantee. The request for guarantee must be completed and submitted simultaneously with the application and attachments. This form is brief, requiring the lender to fill in the name and address of the borrower and guarantor, value of collateral, the amount of the guaranteed and nonguaranteed portions of the loan, fees, interest rate, and the guarantee period.

Guarantee Agreement. The guarantee agreement sets forth the general terms and conditions of Eximbank's guarantee to the lender. Eximbank will execute the agreement and the request for guarantee, and send two copies of it to the lender. The lender must then sign both copies of the agreement, including the request for guarantee, and return one copy with the guarantee fee to Eximbank.

Disbursement Notification. Within ten days of the expiration date of the Eximbank guarantee, the lender must submit a disbursement notification (called "Annex A") to Eximbank. This notice details the date and amount of disbursements made to the borrower under the loan agreement.

Nonpayment

Delinquencies. The lender is required by the guarantee agreement to notify Eximbank in writing of any delinquencies of guaranteed loans within 30 days after a delinquency has occurred and to report the status of such delinquencies on a monthly basis thereafter. Even if a delinquency has yet to occur, Eximbank should be promptly notified of any information that might indicate a possible loss. The lender must not disburse any additional funds until the delinquency is rectified.

Claims. The lender has 120 days after a default (failure to pay principal or interest as scheduled in the loan agreement for more than 30 days) has occurred in which to make a claim. The claim must describe what actions the lender has taken to minimize the loss, including demand on guarantors. Lenders must give Eximbank copies of the UCC filings on the collateral.

A lender may request an extension of the claim filing date from Eximbank in writing if it believes that, by doing so, the account may be brought current or the loss may be mitigated in some way (such as by liquidation of the security at a higher value). Reasons for such a belief must be detailed in the request.

Rescheduling. No rescheduling is permitted without Eximbank's written consent. Any request for rescheduling must be accompanied by the lender's analysis and cash flow forecasts that indicate that the borrower can pay back the rescheduled debt.

COMMODITY CREDIT CORPORATION

The Commodity Credit Corporation (CCC) is an agency of the U.S. government that functions within the Department of Agriculture. Its objectives include the providing of assistance in the production and marketing of U.S. agricultural commodities, administration of agricultural commodities, and related functions. As part of its overall responsibility, the CCC is also charged with the development of foreign markets for U.S. agricultural commodities. It is in connection with this last responsibility that the CCC provides assistance for the sale abroad of surplus agricultural commodities. Four different programs are offered:

Dollar financing up to 36 months.
Sale of surplus agricultural commodities against local currencies.
Sale of surplus commodities under long-term supply contracts.
Barter transactions.

Financing

Exporters of agricultural commodities usually operate on a low-markup, high-turnover basis. Since they have limited capital, they cannot grant credit to foreign buyers in excess of terms they themselves receive from suppliers. Moreover, since agricultural commodities are consumed in a relatively short period of time, it is not considered to be prudent banking to extend export credits in excess of 180 days. To overcome this limitation in the availability of private credit, the CCC has initiated a program that makes financing available up to 36 months.

There are some exceptions to this rule, however. Some countries import feed grains that are used to raise livestock, such as hogs. Once the hogs reach maturity, they are slaughtered and turned into canned hams. These are then sold for local consumption or reexport. This whole production cycle takes about two years and, therefore, two-year financing might be considered legitimate banking terms.

In connection with the granting of three-year credit by the CCC for the financing of agricultural exports, it is worth noting that this, in fact, violates one of the basic tenets of sound banking. Agricultural goods are generally in the hands of the consumer and eaten up within six months; hence, three-year credits to finance them make little sense and are, in fact, slightly disguised foreign assistance or subsidies for U.S. agricultural exports.

Eligible Commodities. Goods eligible for financing under the program must come from private stocks of surplus agricultural commodities. The list of commodities eligible for financing varies according to availability and is announced by the CCC on a monthly basis. While commodities financed come from surplus stock, all sales under the program are made through private U.S. exports.

Sales Contract. To initiate a specific transaction, the foreign importer will probably approach several U.S. exporters to look for the best terms. The chosen exporter and the importer will then enter into a tentative sales contract, subject to obtaining credit approval from the CCC.

In all applications to the CCC, exporters must include a description of the commodity, country of destination, value of the commodity, and credit period requested.

Financing Period. Financing is generally available for up to 12 months. If longer credit periods are requested, a special justification has to be included in the application. Terms of up to 36 months may be available under any of the following justifications:

1. To permit the U.S. exporter to meet credit terms offered by competitors in other free-world countries.
2. To prevent loss or decline of established U.S. commercial export sales caused by noncommunist factors.
3. To permit U.S. exporters to establish or retain U.S. markets in the face of penetration by communist suppliers.
4. To substitute commercial dollar sales for local currency sales or for barter transactions.
5. To stimulate new use of an agricultural commodity in the importing country.
6. To permit expanded consumption of the agricultural commodity in the importing country.

Performance Credit. Once CCC approval has been obtained, the importer and exporter will finalize their sales contract. The foreign importer then asks a local bank to open an irrevocable letter of credit in favor of CCC to guarantee eventual payment. This credit must be advised (referred) to the CCC by a U.S. bank. Moreover, a U.S. bank must add its confirmation covering the commercial risk of the transaction for at least 10% of the credit. The political risk is assumed by the CCC.

For the part of the financing that is covered by the portion of the performance letter of credit confirmed by a U.S. bank, the CCC charges a rate of interest 1% below the rate it charges without such a confirmation. For this reason, foreign importers find it desirable to get confirmation for 100% of the credit amount, even though only 10% is required. The importer is usually also required to furnish the CCC with a promissory note or some other evidence of debt obligation.

Payment. After the appropriate letter of credit has been opened and advised, the exporter ships the commodities in accordance with the sales contract. Evidence of shipment, such as a copy of the bill of lading, commercial invoice, and other documents, must then be submitted. If everything is in order, the CCC pays the exporter without recourse. Thereafter, it will look to the foreign importer and the opener/confirmer of the performance letter of credit for ultimate payment.

It should be mentioned that CCC financing is limited to U.S. port invoice value only. It does not include the cost of ocean transportation.

Sales for Local Currencies

Unlike the financing program discussed in the previous section, the sale of surplus agricultural commodities for local currencies does not involve the granting of deferred payment terms. Payment must be made in local currencies after the commodities arrive at the importing country.

Application and Letter of Credit. Sales of commodities under the program are made directly to the governments of importing countries. Normally, the importing country submits an application to the Department of Agriculture for authorization to purchase commodities for local currency. In its application, the importing country will give the name of the U.S. commercial bank that is to receive the Department of Agriculture's letter of commitment when issued.

Next, the importing country opens an irrevocable commercial letter of credit through a foreign bank that has been approved by the Department of Agriculture. This letter of credit is in favor of the U.S. exporter and will be advised and/or confirmed by a U.S. bank.

Reimbursement. After the exporter has shipped the commodities in accordance with the letter of credit, documents must be submitted to the U.S. bank for payment. If everything is found to be in order, the U.S. bank promptly pays the exporter the amount due. The bank then sends title documents to the overseas importer and, at the same time, applies at the Federal Reserve for reimbursement.

Once the importing country has received title documents needed to take ownership of the commodities, it arranges for a local-currency deposit in favor of the U.S. government.

Long-Term Supply Contracts

Under this program, the CCC finances the sale of agricultural commodities on credit under long-term supply contracts. The objective is to sell U.S. surplus agricultural commodities on long-term credit. At the same time, the program is designed to promote economic development; funds generated from the sale of commodities have to be used for private development projects.

Agreement with Private Trade Entity. To start, the CCC enters into an agreement with a private individual or organization (private trade entity) for the supply and financing of surplus agricultural commodities. This private trade entity is usually a commercial firm located in the importing country. It buys the commodities from U.S. exporters on long-term credit from the CCC and resells them locally. The private trade entity agrees to use the proceeds from the sale of the commodities for one or more of the following purposes:

1 Expansion of dollar exports of additional U.S. surplus agricultural commodities.
2 Development of foreign markets for U.S. agricultural commodities.
3 Assistance in the economic development of friendly nations.

Delivery Period. The delivery period for agricultural commodities, under this program, generally lasts up to three years. If the private development project requires more time, however, the delivery period may be extended as long as ten years.

The maximum term of credit extension is also related to the completion of the project. The private trade entity may have up to 20 years to repay the CCC for credit extended under the supply contract.

Procedure. The actual shipping procedure is similar to the one used in the sale of commodities for local currencies, except that the CCC deals with a private trade entity rather than the government. Briefly, after the private trade entity has received CCC approval, it makes a subauthorization to an importer who will purchase the commodities. The latter then deals with a U.S. exporter to arrange for delivery.

Simultaneously, the importer asks a foreign bank (approved applicant) to open a letter of credit in favor of the U.S. supplier, advised through the U.S. bank that holds the CCC commitment to reimburse. After shipment is made, the U.S. bank pays the exporter and applies to the Federal Reserve for reimbursement. Documents are shipped to the foreign importer so that possession of the commodities is facilitated upon arrival.

Barter Transactions

Under this program, the United States supplies agricultural commodities to developing countries. The latter, in turn, supply U.S. installations overseas (e.g., military bases) with required goods.

A foreign government wishing to take advantage of the barter program first makes an agreement with CCC concerning the types and quantities of goods to be exchanged. Then the foreign importer arranges for the opening of a performance letter of credit in favor of the CCC. This credit actually guarantees that the importing country will live up to its contract to supply U.S. overseas installations with specified goods.

U.S. agricultural commodities are shipped under a normal commercial letter of credit. The exporter, through the paying bank, receives reimbursement from the Federal Reserve in the usual manner. Similarly, as the importing country meets its obligation by supplying U.S. overseas bases, the Department of Agriculture is informed. The obligation of the foreign country under the barter contract and, therefore, the amount of the previously mentioned performance credit, is reduced correspondingly.

OVERSEAS PRIVATE INVESTMENT CORPORATION

The Overseas Private Investment Corporation (OPIC) was formed in 1971 to take over a number of programs previously offered through the Agency for International Development (AID).

Wholly owned by the U.S. Treasury, OPIC is functioning, in fact, as an agency of the government. Its objective is to stimulate and facilitate U.S. private equity and loan investments in friendly developing countries.

As a fundamental premise in all its activities, OPIC assists only with new investments that are financially sound, commercially viable, welcome by host countries, and generally responsive to the needs of host countries.

To the extent that OPIC's programs stimulate private investments in developing areas, they also promote world trade. Unlike Eximbank, however, OPIC does not require that goods bought under programs it sponsors be imported from the United States.

To achieve its basic purpose, OPIC offers the following programs:

Investment insurance

Guarantees

Direct loans

Preinvestment information, counseling, and cost sharing

Investment Insurance

To assist U.S. companies investing in developing countries, OPIC provides investment insurance for various types of risks. Three types of political risks may be covered.

Inconvertibility of profits or repatriation of the original investment.

Loss of investment due to expropriation or confiscation by the foreign government.

Damage to property resulting from war, revolution, or insurrection.

No protection is offered against normal business risks or against devaluation of a foreign currency.

Eligibility. Only new investments in certain developing countries are eligible for OPIC insurance. (A list is kept.) Insurance is, however, available for the expansion or modernization of existing enterprises. Application for insurance must be made with OPIC, and the investor must have received from OPIC a registration letter before an investment has been irrevocably committed.

Eligible investments must be made by a U.S. citizen or corporation, partnership, or association that is 50% or more U.S. owned.

Investments may be made with cash in convertible currencies, loans, machinery, services, processes, or technology. The investment must, however, be for a duration of at least three years.

Before OPIC issues an insurance contract, the investor has to get the foreign government's approval for the specific project. The U.S. government has entered into bilateral treaties with host governments under which the latter have the option of approving or not approving specific projects.

Insurance Amount. For each risk insured, two amounts are specified:

1. A "current insured amount": This places a limit on the amount of insurance compensation an investor can receive for any one year. For expropriation and war coverage, the current insured amount must equal at least the actual amount of capital at risk.
2. A "maximum insured amount": This may go up to 200% of the current insured amount on equity investments to cover eventual retained earnings. Additionally, principal and interest on any loan investments may also be covered.

Insurance Term. The maximum term for OPIC insurance is 20 years. More limited terms may, however, be imposed for certain very large investments in countries where OPIC's overall risk exposure is unusually high, or for investments in certain high-risk areas.

Investment Guarantees

An extended risk guarantee is made available by OPIC that provides coverage against all risks (including business risks) in certain economically viable projects. Guarantees are available for equity investments as well as for loans from U.S. financial institutions.

Equity Investments. Unlike the investment insurance discussed in the previous section, this program offers protection against losses incurred from an investment, even if the project fails for business reasons and is liquidated. Equity guarantees may be issued to investment companies, Edge Act subsidiaries of commercial banks, and industrial firms.

Compensation, in cases of business failure and liquidation, is limited to 50% of each equity holder's loss.

Loans. Loans made to private enterprises in developing countries is guaranteed 100% by OPIC. The proceeds of such loans may be used for buying raw materials, equipment, or services either from the United States or less developed countries.

The minimum amount of any guaranteed loan is $250,000. Loan amortization usually occurs over a period ranging between five and twenty years. Financial institutions are free to charge interest at prevailing market rates, but only subject to OPIC's approval. The OPIC minimum fee is 1¾ per annum on the outstanding guaranteed amount of the loan.

Normally, OPIC does not guarantee loans in excess of 50% of the project cost. Hence, other sources of financing are required to complete a particular venture.

Direct Loans

Where available, OPIC participates in project financing by making medium- and long-term loans in U.S. dollars or local currencies. The U.S. government usually obtains these currencies through other programs, such as CCC's sales of agricultural goods for local currencies discussed earlier. As with other OPIC programs, the consent of the host government is required before a loan may be granted.

Each loan request is evaluated by OPIC on its own merits, taking into consideration such factors as the viability of the project, its contribution to local economic and social development, the degree of U.S. private sector participation, project priority assigned by the host country, value of goods and services to be procured from the United States and developing countries, and so on.

Individual loan amounts generally range from $50,000 to $2 million although substantially larger loans may also be granted. Interest rates charged vary, depending on the risk involved and market conditions. Next to the usual interest charges, OPIC may also require a direct share in the financial success of a particular project. This "equity sweetener" may be in the form of convertible bonds, warrants to buy stocks, or some other arrangement.

Other Programs

Potential investors are offered general information on developing countries by OPIC. It may help U.S. firms in finding, planning, and developing potential investment projects. Also OPIC may actually investigate a potential project in the field and advise on a project's financial structure.

Preinvestment assistance may be given in the form of partial financial support for feasibility studies. If the study comes out favorably and investors decide to undertake the investment, they bear the entire cost. If the investors decide not to invest, they pay only one-half of the cost, with the remainder paid by OPIC. Also OPIC may be able to arrange the carrying of up to 80%

of costs for studies within the agribusiness field, such as food processing, marketing, storage, or distribution.

INTERNATIONAL INSTITUTIONS

There are a number of international organizations whose primary function is to assist the industrialization and general economic progress of developing countries. The International Bank for Reconstruction and Development, for instance, makes project loans for roads, power plants, steel mills, and so on, in developing countries. The Inter-American Development Bank has a similar purpose, but concentrates solely on Latin America. To the extent that these large projects require the importation of machinery, equipment, and know-how, loans that they grant directly assist in the financing of foreign trade. Similar organizations to the two already mentioned are the International Finance Corporation (IFC) and the International Development Association (IDA), both of which are affiliates of the World Bank. The IFC provides equity investment and/or partial financing of productive, private enterprises in developing countries. The IDA also serves this purpose, but while the IFC grants loans only up to about ten years, the IDA is willing to extend as long as fifty years.

What benefits do these international organizations provide U.S. exporters? First, to the extent that the machinery, equipment, and services needed for projects financed by these organizations originate in the United States, the suppliers get built-in export financing. They may, in fact, ship directly overseas but be reimbursed from the particular international organization itself. Second, if exporters through conversations with potential customers, hear of worthwhile projects that may qualify for financial assistance from one of the organizations, they may be instrumental in suggesting this to customers and may also assist in any negotiations necessary in Washington, D.C.—all in the hope of getting export orders if assistance is approved.

Third, a U.S. businessman may hear of a new project financed by one of these organizations on which he may wish to bid. Often borrowers advertise locally for bids and also inform the embassies of major countries. The Bureau of International Business Operations or other U.S. government agencies have information on projects for which bids may be offered.

CENTRAL BANK FINANCING IN ASIA

A number of countries in Asia have put in place export-import financing programs that are similar in some respects to programs of the U.S. Eximbank. Japanese and South Korean programs are described as examples although, of necessity, somewhat cursorily. For detailed information, the proper department within the respective central banks should be contacted.

Japan

Japan has achieved a position of world prominence in the export of capital goods, equipment, and technology—partly because of outstanding achievements in technology and partly because of the high degree of support from the Export-Import Bank of Japan (Japan Eximbank or OECD), which provides yen financing for exports, imports, and overseas investments.

Japan Eximbank. Japan's Eximbank is an independent governmental financial institution. Its programs rely heavily on participation by major commercial banks throughout the world. Exports are supported by parallel lending with these banks in the form of yen loans for major borrowings with medium- to long-term tenors (i.e., lengths of financing). The commercial part of the loan must be arranged by the participating commercial bank. Japan Eximbank adjusts the rate of its portion of the syndicated transaction so that the overall rate is within the consensus guidelines of the OECD.

Any qualified firm, foreign or domestic, may apply through Japan Eximbank for import (buyer) credit or export (supplier) credit. Eligibility is determined on the type of equipment, resources, raw material, or service that is involved. The Japanese content requirement is 50% of the contract value.

Financing Packages. Among the variety of credits and loans offered by the Japan Eximbank are the following:

Import Credit. Resources considered vital to the Japanese economy may qualify for import credits from Japan Eximbank. These include energy-related resources, raw materials, and manufactured goods. Japanese importers must apply directly to the Japan Eximbank.

Export Credit. Deferred payment credits for exports of major industrial equipment including ships is offered to domestic corporations. Japanese technical services abroad are also included in this category.

In this program, the foreign importer obtains the credit from the exporter who has requested that the Japan Eximbank make available supplier credits jointly to the exporter and a commercial bank. The credits are granted in yen but the foreign importers can usually obtain dollar-denominated credits from the exporter.

Overseas Investment Credits. The following qualify for overseas investment credits:

Equity participation in foreign corporations by Japanese corporations.

Long-term equity interest loans to foreign concerns, provided they also have equity participation from Japanese firms.

Equity participation in Japanese firms whose sole function is to make overseas investments.

Overseas projects directly operated by the borrower.

Direct investment loans are available to foreign governments for funds for equity participation in foreign corporations that have Japanese equity participation.

Overseas direct loans include tied loans for obtaining Japanese imports and untied loans for resources development projects and assistance to international development banks. Governmental loans are government-to-government agreements designed to assist economic development. Foreign governments or agencies may apply directly to the Japan Eximbank if they are directly responsible for economic development in their country and the project contains eligible export-import contracts.

Export Financing Terms. Credits are available only in yen, although importers can usually obtain dollar-denominated credit from Japanese exporters. Down payments required are 15% cash as stipulated by Japan Eximbank guidelines with the exception of ships, which require 20%.

The total Japanese suppliers' credits, including the commercial bank portion, cover 75 to 85% of the export contract. Currently, Japan Eximbank limits its participation to 60 to 70%, with the remainder loaned by commercial banks.

Repayment of principal plus interest is required in equal, semiannual installments beginning six months after shipment of the major portion of goods or completion of the project.

A requirement of export suppliers' credit is Ministry of International Trade and Industry insurance, obtained by the borrower, against both commercial and political risk. Unpaid balances of down payments and deferred payment portions require letters of credit, government guarantees, or letters of guarantee from major international banks, except in the case of government borrowers.

South Korea

With combined exports and imports up 65% in the past 10 years South Korea has become a major growth market. Its capital-intensive industries are active competitors in world markets and are subsidized through South Korea Export-Import Bank (South Korea Eximbank).

South Korea Eximbank. The most important activities of South Korea Eximbank are the direct loans to both foreign and domestic firms. Their purpose is to encourage the export of capital goods and services, overseas investment, and major resource development. The loans are low-cost with medium- to long-term financing arranged in conjunction with larger commercial banks throughout the world. As with all other programs of South Korea Eximbank, the domestic content requirement is 50% up to 75% depending on the particular product.

In all, the programs of the South Korea Eximbank include direct lending to both suppliers and buyers, relending facilities to foreign financial institutions, and the issuance of guarantees and export insurance.

Financing Packages. Among the variety of credits and loans offered by South Korea Eximbank are the following:

Export Credit. is extended by South Korea Eximbank for capital goods, which include industrial plants, steel structures, machinery, electrical equipment, ships, and vehicles (including parts). Installation and operation of plants abroad is also subsidized.

Overseas Project Credit. may be obtained for any facilities or equipment abroad in which most of the parts or materials required for installation, operation, or expansion are imported from South Korea. Similarly, *overseas investment credit* is available for foreign projects that make use of South Korean raw materials, exports, or simply promote economic cooperation with foreign countries.

Major Resources Development Credit. is designed to make funds available for foreign projects that will lead to a stabilization of the supply of natural resources or strengthen economic relationships with a country that supplies needed natural resources such as oil, coal, copper, lumber, and rubber. Even studies leading to the acquisition of mineral rights come under this program.

Direct Loans. are available to foreign importers for the purchase of South Korean capital goods and services. *Relending facilities* are also extended for projects with a minimum contract value of U.S. $1 million. Medium- and long-term direct loans must have an unconditional guarantee by the buyer's commercial bank, central bank, or government. For relending facilities, South Korea Eximbank, in effect, provides a U.S. dollar line of credit through a foreign financial institution.

Guarantees and Insurance. South Korea Eximbank provides financial guarantees for up to 100% of the principal plus interest to both foreign and South Korean financial institutions that cofinance international trade. These guarantees are available, however, only on loans whose repayment schedules extend for more than five years.

Foreign importers may also obtain 100% performance guarantees (for contract obligations) and advance payment guarantees. The latter provide for total cash refunds of down payments, in case the South Korean exporter fails to comply with the contract.

Export insurance coverage may be obtained through South Korea Eximbank to cover political, commercial, and even managerial risks. Exporters, manufacturers, and financial institutions involved in export transactions can obtain such policies for all export activity during a specified period of time or only for individual transactions. There are a total of nine insurance services that include export insurance, export finance insurance, export bill insurance, medium- and long-term credit insurance, buyer credit insurance, overseas construction work insurance, export bond insurance, and overseas investment insurance.

Financing Terms. All financing is available in U.S. dollars. For direct loans (contracts exceeding U.S. $1 million), 70% of the export contract value may be financed less the cash down payment. Relending facilities (contracts from U.S. $3 to $10 million) are available for 100% of the contract value less the cash down payment.

Predelivery export financing is available only for the local portion of the transaction at 70 to 90% of the import contract value less the cash down payment. Postdelivery export financing and other supplier credits cover 70% of the export contract value less the cash down payment. Cash down payments are required at a minimum of 15 to 20% of the total contract value.

Export credits extend from 181 days to 10 years while major resources development credits can extend to a maximum of 20 years. Direct loans are from three to ten years while relending facilities may be from two to five years.

Note that buyers must obtain guarantees covering 100% principal plus interest from a reputable commercial bank, central bank, or government, and that suppliers must obtain guarantees for 100% of credit transactions from a reputable commercial bank.

CHAPTER 5

Foreign Credit Insurance

Historically, international trade has been characterized by intense competition, and today is no exception. In addition to government supports and various export finance programs, there are currently more than 35 countries that have established their own Export Credit Agencies (ECAs) that offer direct assistance for the promotion of exports. Due to the substantial increase in trade and foreign investment that has taken place, the world has become too complex for us to take a one-country orientation. Multinational companies may be producing the same or similar products in several different countries. Often the attractiveness of the financing package will determine whether or not a sale is made. A multinational company may, therefore, wish to ship from one of its factories that is in the country that offers the best financing and insurance arrangements.

Similarly, when large industrial projects are sold, inputs may come from sources in several different countries. The selling company may have plants in a number of locations, with each producing one or more of the necessary components for the overall project. Alternatively, the main contracting company may have to buy all or part of the components from different firms in different countries. Again, the financing packages available in those countries may become crucial to the project.

As in the United States, most industrialized countries have set up financing and/or guarantee programs to assist their exporting companies, and even branches of foreign companies located in that country are frequently eligible for assistance. Often these programs are completely run by and dependent on the government; but, in some cases, private financing and/or guaranteeing institutions also play important roles.

A comprehensive review of the financing and insurance schemes of all major countries is clearly outside the scope of this book. It is, therefore, our purpose to give only selected examples of financial assistance available outside the United States. For this, we briefly examine the programs available in a few large, representative countries. Any reader wishing detailed information should refer to separate books on the subject, and since export promotion programs frequently undergo modifications, direct correspondence with the particular organization is advisable. A list of the government and private organizations in major countries that assist in export financing is given in Appendix 1.

UNITED KINGDOM

The United Kingdom has one of the oldest government-supported export credit programs in the world. Commercial credit and political risks connected with exports may be insured with the Export Credits Guarantee Department (ECGD), a separate department of the British government. There are also three private companies (Trade Indemnity Company, Credit Guarantee Insurance Company, and Credit Indemnity Company) that insure only against commercial credit (foreign exchange) risks of exporting, but not against political and transfer risks. Even though ECGD is an arm of the British government, it is commercially independent. Most insurance and guarantees granted are based on commercially sound considerations (referred to as Section 1 business). This means that, under normal circumstances, ECGD is expected to remain solvent without any government support. If unusual losses occur, however, ECGD is backed by the full credit of the British government.

Occasionally, business is undertaken that cannot be fully justified on commercial principles, but is considered to be in the national interest (referred to as Section 2 business).

The ECGD is one of the most successful national export credit insurers and many other programs have been patterned after it. Originally established in 1919, it has continually improved its coverage while, at the same time, reduced its premiums. Today, about one-third of all British exports are covered by ECGD.

Risks Covered

Generally, ECGD insures both commercial credit and political risk. Unlike the programs of Eximbank and FCIA, no separate political risk coverage is available. While coverage may vary slightly, depending on the type of policy, basically the risks insured are the following.

Commercial Credit Risks. There are three types of commercial credit risks.

1. Insolvency of the buyer.
2. Buyer's failure to pay within six months of due date for goods already accepted.
3. The buyer's failure to accept goods that have been shipped, provided

this nonacceptance was not caused by an action or noncompliance on the part of the exporter.

Under the first two commercial risks, ECGD covers 90% of the loss. Under the third risk, the exporter bears a first loss of 20% of the full purchase price. The ECGD covers 90% of the remaining amount. Under policies covering the export of specific pieces of capital equipment, no cover is given against the failure of private buyers to take up exported goods.

Political Risks. Several risks are insured:

1 Government action that blocks or delays payment of sterling to the exporter.
2 Cancellation of a valid import license or imposition of new import licensing restrictions in the buyer's country.
3 Cancellation or nonrenewal of a U.K. export license or imposition of new export licensing restrictions.
4 War between the buyer's country and the United Kingdom.
5 War, revolution, or similar disturbances in the buyer's country.
6 Additional handling, transportation, and/or insurance charges arising from an interruption or diversion of the voyage if these charges cannot be recovered from the buyer.
7 Any other cause of loss occurring outside the United Kingdom and not within the control of the exporter or the buyer.
8 Repudiation of the contract in cases where ECGD agrees that the buyer has government status.

Generally, ECGD covers 95% of any loss resulting from political risk. If the cause of the loss occurs before shipment, 90% is covered.

Suppliers' Credit—Types of Policies

Comprehensive Policies. Whenever sales are made on a repetitive basis, an exporter may wish to insure all his exports or at least those shipments going to certain clearly defined markets. To provide as broad a spread of risk as possible, ECGD prefers to cover all of an exporter's shipments. At somewhat higher premium rates, an exporter may, however, exclude certain markets from coverage. Sales under irrevocable letters of credit may also be excluded. In any case, the business that remains to be insured must still offer a reasonable spread of risk.

Exporters wishing comprehensive coverage have to agree to insure their entire turnover (sales) for either one or three years, or their turnover in certain markets for one year. A whole turnover policy for three years enjoys a more favorable premium rate.

An insured exporter makes a monthly declaration of the total amount of business transacted in each premium category, and is invoiced accordingly.

Credit Limits. Under the comprehensive policy, ECGD is not informed of most individual transactions. However, it does limit the amount of insurance that is available for shipments to buyers without adequate financial substance. If an exporter has no negative information on a new foreign buyer, he may deal with him up to £100. On repeat orders, the exporter may go up to a discretionary limit specified in the policy. Any sales in excess of the discretionary limit have to be approved by ECGD.

Types of Coverage. Comprehensive coverage is available in two types. Under the regular Comprehensive Guarantee, insurance starts with the date of contract. Under the Comprehensive Guarantee (Shipments), coverage starts only on the date of shipment. This latter policy, therefore, does not insure the risk of cancellation of a previously granted export license. Since the Comprehensive Guarantee (Shipments) covers fewer risks, it is also available at a lower premium.

Goods Covered. Sales that can generally be insured under a comprehensive policy include all types of consumer goods, as well as raw materials, semifinished products, and certain capital goods that show a recurrent pattern of similar business over an extended period of time. The terms under which goods are sold must follow those commonly accepted in the particular industry. For consumer goods, the maximum credit period is usually six months.

Extended Term Endorsement. For goods that require longer credits, the exporter can obtain extended term endorsements on comprehensive policies. A shipment made on extended terms has to be submitted to ECGD for prior approval. Credit terms of up to five years are allowed if required to be competitive in the industry. If warranted, ECGD may agree to longer terms.

Other Endorsements. The basic comprehensive policy may be amended to cover special features of an exporter's business. Some of the principal forms of endorsements are:

1 *Overseas Subsidiaries and Affiliates.* Companies shipping to controlled subsidiaries and affiliates outside the United Kingdom may wish to insure against political risks. (Commercial credit risks cannot be covered.) Resale of the goods by a foreign subsidiary to third parties can also be insured.

2 *Sales to Export Intermediaries.* Often export business is transacted through domestic intermediaries, such as export merchants or confirming houses. Since such intermediaries are sometimes poorly capitalized, a manufacturer may suffer losses due to insolvency of the intermediary, which may, in turn, be caused by failure to pay on the part of an overseas

buyer. To insure these risks, special coverage is available to U.K. manufacturers who sell through export intermediaries.

3 *Reexport on Non-U.K. Goods.* Since the United Kingdom is a trading nation, goods are often imported and, after packaging or light processing, reexported. The reexport of such non-U.K. goods can be insured through ECGD, provided they are not in direct competition with goods that are produced wholly or partly in the United Kingdom.

4 *Nonsterling Invoicing.* When payment for exports is due in a currency other than sterling, the ECGD policy can be amended to provide for payment of claims in the currency of invoicing.

5 *Overseas Inventory.* Sometimes, British firms maintain inventory in other countries, perhaps to allow them to make quick deliveries when required by local buyers. Due to political contingencies, such as war, revolution, expropriation, or revocation of reexport authority, control over goods abroad may be lost. To cover this risk, ECGD offers an "Overseas Stock Endorsement" to the basic comprehensive policy. The cost of this additional protection, which covers overseas inventory, is very modest.

   An exporter making use of the Overseas Stock Endorsement also has to offer for insurance coverage for the sales made from the inventory. These are covered by a "Sales-from-Overseas Stock Endorsements" which is also available to those exporters who do not require the Overseas Stock Endorsement.

Capital-Goods Policies. Many capital-goods exports are of a "once only" nature and it is, therefore, impossible to obtain a reasonable spread of risk. Coverage for each sale, therefore, has to be individually negotiated with ECGD.

Specific policy coverage is available either from date of contract or from date of shipment. Manufacturers and exporters of special-purpose equipment, who sell to government entities, are advised to get coverage commencing with the date of contract. No insurance is given against failure of private buyers to take delivery of exported capital goods.

Erection costs can also be covered by ECGD insurance, provided they are not included under a separate services policy.

Under specific policies, ECGD is prepared to insure for credit periods up to five years. Longer terms may also be available, if required to meet foreign competition.

At an early stage of negotiations between buyer and seller, ECGD is prepared to give an initial indication of availability and approximate cost of credit insurance. As negotiations enter a final stage, ECGD provides a binding offer of cover, which is usually held open for three months. There is no special charge for such an advance commitment.

Constructional Works and Services Policies. A constructional works contract is an agreement for the execution of a specific project. Included in one contract are provisions for the supply of goods as well as the performance of services. The entire amount due under such a project may be covered by an ECGD constructional works policy.

The United Kingdom, as an important trading country, exports not only goods but also a substantial quantity of services. Such services offered by U.K. individuals or companies to foreigners may include technical or professional assistance, overhaul or repairs carried out on ships or aircraft, supply of know-how, and so on. Where the services performed form a recurrent pattern of business and the period over which they are performed form is not in excess of 180 days, the ECGD coverage available is the same as the comprehensive policies earlier outlined.

For services where there is no continuing pattern of business, a Specific Services "Sums Due" policy is available. It insures all amounts due under the individual service contract.

Arbitration Cover. Many contracts with foreign state trading organizations, especially those of the communist countries, provide for arbitrations in a third country if a dispute arises under the contract. Insurance from ECGD is available for the eventuality that the exporter wins an arbitration dispute but the foreign buyer fails to implement the award. This type of arbitration coverage is given either by means of an endorsement to a comprehensive guarantee or as a provision within a specific policy.

100% Coverage Endorsement. Normal comprehensive and specific policies cover an exporter only up to 90 or 95%. This is an insurance practice that discourages selling to irresponsible buyers. As credit terms have lengthened substantially over past years, however, exporters of capital goods face the accumulation of uninsured portions of contract prices, resulting in frozen assent. To overcome this problem, ECGD is, under certain circumstances, prepared to increase its coverage to 100% one year after acceptance of the goods by the buyer. Total coverage is available on the following conditions:

The sales contract involves at least three years of credit to the buyer.

The sales contract provides for some payment in the first year.

During the first year, all obligations under the contract were met completely on time.

The 100% coverage facility is provided by an endorsement to a Specific Policy or, under a Comprehensive Policy, as an endorsement to an Extended Terms Approval issued for a particular contract. No levies are charged by ECGD for this facility.

Foreign Subcontractors. United Kingdom exporters of capital and engineering goods may subcontract part of the work to suppliers in other countries. Bilateral agreements have been concluded by ECGD with a number of countries, including Australia, Belgium, Denmark, France, Italy, the Netherlands, Norway, Sweden, Switzerland, and Germany. For subcontracts placed in these countries, ECGD is prepared to insure up to 30% of the value of the main contract. This provision may be particularly useful to multinational companies who supply all the components for a large project from plants located in a number of different countries.

In cases where the subcontracted portion exceeds 30%, or if the exporting country where the subcontractor is located has concluded no bilateral agreement with the United Kingdom, ECGD is prepared to discuss with the other credit insurer additional means of providing cover.

Short-Term Supplier Credit Financing

One of the chief advantages of ECGD insurance is that it makes it easier for the exporter to obtain financing for foreign receivables.

Assignment of Policy. When necessary, ECGD assists the exporter in permitting the assignment of rights under the policy to a bank or other financial institution. Depending on need, a whole policy, all transactions with a specified market, or all transactions with a specified buyer can be assigned.

A disadvantage of a straight policy assignment is that it does not cover the financing institution for all risks. First, there is the 5 to 10% risk retained by the exporter. Second, ECGD is not responsible if failure to pay by the overseas buyer is caused by a default on the part of the seller. Hence, a straight assignment will be satisfactory to a financing bank only if the exporter has sufficient substance to make such recourse worthwhile, if it should be necessary.

ECGD Guarantee. To make the financing bank's recourse to the exporter unnecessary, ECGD is prepared to issue a direct guarantee to the bank for a small additional premium. This means that ECGD unconditionally guarantees repayment of the bank loan. If recourse to the exporter is necessary, ECGD first pays the bank and then takes over the responsibility of collecting from the exporter. When ECGD issues its guarantee, the financing from the point of view of the bank is as good as making a loan to the British government. The rate charged by British banks for this type of loan is negotiable but generally low.

Eligibility. To make use of the ECGD guarantee to banks, exporters must have held comprehensive insurance coverage for at least 12 months. Then ECGD agrees to a limit for the financing it is prepared to guarantee, based on past experience and the specific exporter's general financial standing. Exporters also sign a recourse undertaking, giving ECGD the right to recover from them any amounts paid to a bank that are in excess of claims payable under the policy.

Medium-Term Supplier Credit Financing

Also, ECGD offers supplementary guarantees to financing banks when the terms of payment are two years or more, that is, when the export is covered by an Extended Terms Endorsement or by a specific policy. Banks who are the beneficiary of such a guarantee are willing to finance the transaction at a fixed, relatively low rate of interest. As under the short-term guarantee, the bank finances the exporter without recourse. However, ECGD retains recourse to the exporter for amounts not covered by the insurance.

Buyer Credit Financing

For large contracts requiring medium-term credits, it may be more desirable for a bank to finance the importer directly under an ECGD guarantee. This type of arrangement is particularly useful from the exporter's point of view for a number of reasons:

The exporter is paid in cash on delivery or as progress payments are made.

The exporter need not retain part of the risk.

For lightly capitalized exporters, potential difficulties are eliminated in getting additional ECGD guarantees for financing banks due to ECGD's right of recourse to the exporter.

Procedure. To qualify for an ECGD Buyer Credit Guarantee, the amount of a transaction must be in excess of £250,000. The importer is required to make a down payment amounting to at least 20% of the contract price against a bank guarantee for the same amount issued by the bank of the exporter. The bank guarantees to reimburse the importer in case the exporter fails to supply the merchandise as contracted. The remaining 80% is paid to the exporter directly (from the proceeds of a bank loan to the importer) or to a bank in the importer's locality. The bank loan is fully guaranteed by ECGD against nonpayment of principal and interest.

The exporter pays for ECGD's guarantee fee. This is appropriate since the exporter benefits from the guarantee by receiving immediate payment. Additional legal agreements that must be executed in connection with an ECGD buyer credit guarantee include

1. A supply contract between the British exporter and the overseas importer.
2. A loan agreement between a British bank and the overseas borrower. The latter may be the importer or a local bank acting on the importer's behalf. The guarantee of the importer's local bank may also be required.
3. A guarantee given by ECGD to the British lending bank to cover nonpayment of principal and interest by the borrower.

Terms. Generally, buyer credit guarantees are available for periods up to five years. Also, the ECGD is prepared to extend financial guarantees for longer periods if required for large projects, including the construction of oceangoing ships. In this case, the underlying contract must have a U.K. content of at least £2 million (£1 million for ships).

British banks have agreed to make loans under the Buyer Credit and Financial Guarantee facilities at a fixed, relatively low interest rate. Rates charged for new credits may change from time to time to reflect market conditions. Banks usually also charge a commitment fee on any unused portion of a credit facility.

Guarantees for Buying Programs. Sometimes, overseas buyers do not want to commit themselves to a specific British exporter. To meet this need, ECGD is willing, on a case-by-case basis, to guarantee a line of credit offered by a British bank or consortium of banks to the overseas buyer. The importer may then purchase required capital goods from one or more British suppliers. Under an ECGD guarantee the importer is assured that financing is available provided contracts are placed before the specified expiration date of the line of credit.

Refinancing

To provide the Clearing and Scottish banks with additional liquidity, eligible export paper can, under certain conditions, be refinanced by the Bank of England. To be eligible for refinancing, an export credit must have an original maturity of two years or more and must be covered by ECGD insurance. If these conditions apply, installments due within 18 months or 30% of all outstanding installments become "eligible" for potential refinancing. Any "eligible" amounts that are in excess of 5% of the particular bank's total deposits may finally be refinanced with the Bank of England.

FRANCE

The French foreign credit insurance program is administered by Compagnie Francaise d'Assurance pour le Commerce Exterieur (COFACE) and indirectly by the French government.

Similar to ECGD, COFACE provides only foreign credit insurance, but no financing. To help provide the needed funds for the financing of French exports, however, COFACE cooperates closely with private and nationalized banks, including Credit National, Banque Francaise de Commerce Exterieur (BFCE), and Banque de France.

Risks Covered

Under different circumstances and policies, COFACE insures the usual commercial and political risks, including inability to convert and transfer funds deposited by the buyer in his or her local currency. Also covered are losses due to natural catastrophes, such as floods, earthquakes, volcanic eruptions, and storms.

Types of Policies: Consumer Goods

Included under the definition of consumer goods are raw materials, semi-finished products, metals, foods, chemicals, pharmaceuticals, electrical appliances, and small tools. The credit period for such goods is usually limited to 180 days.

Two policies are available for the insurance of consumer goods exports:

GCP (General Comprehensive Policy). Insures against all risks, commercial as well as political.

PCT. Insures against political risks only.

Both the above, as is typical of short-term policies, require the exporter to insure his or her whole turnover, or at least enough to give the insurer a reasonable spread of risk, for commercial risks. COFACE allows the exclusion of all exports paid for by cash in advance or covered under irrevocable letters of credit confirmed by a French bank. Other requests for exclusions will be considered on a case-by-case basis. All insured exporters are required, however, to cover at least 50% of their export turnover.

The whole-turnover requirement applies only to commercial risks, not to political and preshipment risks. Exporters may choose the countries for which they wish to obtain political risks coverage.

Percentage Covered. Commercial credit risks in the United States and certain European countries are covered for 85%. The coverage for all other countries is generally 80%.

As far as political risks are concerned, the exporter may choose either 80 or 90% coverage. The higher percentage will, of course, be reflected in a higher premium.

Limits. On application by the exporter, COFACE establishes a limit up to which it is willing to insure sales to individual foreign buyers. As long as the exporter remains within these limits, there is no need to consult with the insurer before making a shipment.

For small sales to new customers, exporters may, in certain markets, proceed without prior COFACE approval. In these cases, however, commercial credit risk coverage is reduced to 50%.

Policy Riders. Two types of riders may be added to the General Comprehensive Policy.

Public Buyers. The straight GCP policy covers only sales to private buyers This special rider provides insurance on sales to public buyers. Such riders can be obtained to cover a single sale or all sales to government entities.

Preshipment Risks. A political risk or intervention by the French government may interrupt an exporter's marketing efforts prior to shipment. Riders to insure against these contingencies are available. However, COFACE offers no cover for cases when a private buyer cancels out of a contract or is unable to take delivery due to insolvency.

PCT: Political Risks Policy. The exporter may choose any countries for political risk coverage. Once having chosen, however, the exporter must insure all business with that particular country. As with the GCP policy, transactions paid by cash in advance or irrevocable confirmed letters of credit may be excluded. The exporter has a choice of 80 or 90% coverage. On application by the exporter, COFACE sets maximum limits up to which it is prepared to extend political risk insurance.

The basic PCT policy covers only private buyers. A rider is available that extends the insurance to public (government) buyers. Hence, a default in payment by the public buyer may also be covered since it constitutes, in fact, a political risk. Before contracting with a specific public buyer, the exporter wishing this coverage must obtain COFACE's permission.

Types of Policies: Light Machinery and Equipment

The range of policies under this heading are meant to ensure light machinery, capital goods, and similar products usually sold on credit terms of up to three years. The delivery period for goods covered may not be in excess of six months. Commercial credit risks and, optionally, political risks may be covered.

Two different types of policies are available for such items:

BE. Provides commercial credit risk insurance on a "whole-turnover" basis and political risk insurance on an optional basis. The wider spread of risk that the whole-turnover policy offers to the insurer permits a lower premium rate than specific (BI) policies.

BI. Provides insurance on a case-by-case basis for whichever specific sales the exporter wishes covered. Comprehensive or political-risk-only coverage is available at the exporter's option. Commercial credit risks alone cannot be covered under this policy.

Percentage Covered. On BE and BI policies, the percentages covered for political and commercial risks, respectively, are the same as those previously outlined.

COFACE Approval. On both whole-turnover (BE) and specific (BI) policies, the exporter must get COFACE's permission for each sales contract. Once COFACE has agreed, it issues a commitment to guarantee that is kept open for six months.

Riders. Normally, BE and BI policies cover only preshipment and commercial credit risks on sales to private buyers. Sales to public buyers can also be insured by means of special riders.

Types of Policies: Large Capital Goods and Projects

Issued by COFACE are insurance or guarantees to cover exports of heavy capital goods and large projects outside France undertaken by French companies.

Classification of Policies. Policies for suppliers' credits as well as for buyers' credits are available. Each of these two categories is further classified by COFACE into the following:

SP Policies. Insurance for sales to public buyers.
PR Policies. Insurance for sales to private buyers.

For suppliers' credit, each of these policy types may cover preshipment risks only, usual political and commercial credit risks, or both. For buyers' credits, there is, of course, no preshipment risk.

Percentage Covered. For suppliers' credits, political risk coverage is usually limited to 90% while commercial credit risk coverage does not exceed 85%. For buyers' credits there is an upper limit of 95% for both political and commercial credit risks.

Terms. Large projects and capital items usually require long credit terms. When required by competition and when customary in the particular market, COFACE is prepared to extend its insurance or financial guarantees up to ten years. For suppliers' credits in excess of five years, however, no action is taken until the agreement of a "committee for long-term exports" has been obtained. This committee meets periodically and is presided over by the director of foreign Economic Relations of the Ministry for the Economy and Finances.

Other Policies and Riders

Besides the short-, medium-, and long-term policies we have described, COFACE offers a number of useful additional coverages. These may be added as riders to existing policies or they may, in some cases, be obtainable as separate policies.

Guarantee of Security Deposits. Exporters and contractors are sometimes asked to put up security deposits to show "good faith" when bidding on projects abroad or to guarantee proper and timely performance of a contract.

Inherent in keeping deposits abroad are political, transfer, and foreign exchange risks. These risks may be insured by a rider to an existing policy or by a special policy. In either case, the insured may make claim to COFACE under the insurance independent of any preshipment or credit risk coverage that is also current.

Exchange risk coverage is generally extended directly to banks who place the security deposit for account of the exporter. Any adverse exchange fluctuations in excess of 0.1% is guaranteed to banks by COFACE. If, on the other hand, the exchange fluctuates more than 0.1% in favor of the bank, the resulting profit must be paid over to COFACE. Banks then, of course, are able to pass on the benefits of this exchange risk coverage to exporters and contractors for whose account the security deposits are maintained.

Overseas Inventory. A rider insuring against destruction or loss of inventory held outside France may be given in connection with a preshipment risk guarantee. The following risks are covered:

Reexport by the government of the country where the goods are located.

Capture, seizure, or detention by the same government.

War, revolution, or a natural disaster in the locality where the goods are located.

Exchange Risks. A COFACE guarantee of exchange risks is available only under very limited circumstances:

1 When invoicing in a foreign currency is an absolute condition of concluding the contract.
2 If the exporter has no other means of covering the risk.

In this case, COFACE guarantees any adverse exchange fluctuations in excess of 2%. Any fluctuation in excess of 2% that benefits the exporter must be turned over to COFACE.

Marketing Campaigns. A rather interesting feature of COFACE's many programs is its willingness to underwrite part of the inherent risk in marketing campaigns that French companies may undertake in foreign countries. An exporter conducting a foreign marketing campaign expects to incur such fixed expenses as establishment of an office, marketing studies, publicity, and so on. On the other hand, the exporter anticipates recovery of these expenses, over a period of years, by increased sales. If these sales do not materialize, all fixed expenses cannot be amortized as expected. In this case, COFACE is willing to cover part of the unamortized expenses. The proportion of fixed expenses that can be insured is between 50 and 70%, depending on the duration of the marketing program and other risk classifications.

Trade Fairs. Similar to the insurance of fixed expenses connected with marketing campaigns, COFACE is also willing to pay part of the expenses connected with participation in trade fairs abroad if expected sales do not materialize. Generally, 50% of nonamortized fixed expenses can be recovered.

Financing

As outlined in the previous sections, COFACE provides insurance to exporters and financial guarantees to banks that extend credit directly to foreign importers.

Assignments of Policies. Insurance policies may be assigned to banks and other financial institutions that extend export credits. Contrary to the program offered by ECGD, however, COFACE does not extend its complete, unconditional guarantee to financing institutions. Hence, for risks or portions of risks not covered by the insurance, banks have to rely on the credit standing of the exporter or foreign buyer who is being financed.

Financing Facilities. French commercial banks who finance exports can usually rediscount their paper with the BFCE or directly with the Banque de France. While credit insurance is not always a prerequisite for obtaining financing and subsequent rediscounting, the added security offered by COFACE insurance is certainly helpful in many cases.

In 1946 BFCE was organized to facilitate the financing of French exports. It discounts promissory notes executed by foreign importers and also accepts those executed by French exporters. These notes can, in turn, be rediscounted with the Banque de France.

Also, BFCE extends export credits to foreign buyers for maturities in excess of seven years. Similar to Eximbank's direct-loan program, the earlier maturities are financed by commercial banks. The rate of interest charged by BFCE is favorable when compared to normal commercial rates.

Other assistance in financing exports is also available from private sources, such as factoring, as well as some government-assisted programs.

GERMANY

In Germany, export credit insurance may be obtained from both public and private sources. The two private companies offering insurance are the Gerling-Konzern Speziale Kreditversicherungs-AG (GKS) and the Allgemeine Kreditversicherung-AG.

Under the Householdlaw of 1962, the West German government was authorized to offer credit and political risk insurance covering exports. To administer the program, the government commissioned two private concerns, Hermes Kreditversicherungs-AG and Deutsche Revisionsund Treuhand-AG. Applications by exporters are submitted to Hermes. The latter examines each application and submits it to an Interministerial Committee for Export Guarantees for approval or rejection. If approved, Hermes, acting as agent for the government, issues the actual guarantee. All Hermes export guarantees enjoy the full backing of the German government.

Similar to ACGD and COFACE, Hermes, as well as the private insurers, offers only credit guarantees but no financing. Financing may, however, be available from other governmental and private sources.

Risks Covered

Since export credit insurance in Germany is offered by both private insurers and the government, we must distinguish between the types of risks covered by each. Generally, however, the government insurance program enjoys much wider usage than export credit policies offered by private firms.

Private Insurers. Private insurers cover only commercial credit risks. It is understandable that private companies are only able to cover risks of nonpayment by individual foreign importers. Political and transfer risks, when they occur, usually affect many foreign importers simultaneously in the same country or region. It is, therefore, practically impossible for a private underwriter to get a sufficient diversification of any political and transfer risks. (Remember that under the FCIA policies, discussed in Chapter 3, private insurers underwrite only commercial credit risks while Eximbank underwrites political risk.)

All buyers in the remaining communist countries are, in essence, governmental or semi-governmental institutions. Hence, all risks of extending credit to these buyers are of a political nature.

Specific coverage offered by private firms includes nonpayment of foreign receivables resulting from commercial defaults by the foreign importer, such as bankruptcy or reorganization. Preshipment risks for specially manufactured capital goods may also be covered.

Hermes. German export insurance provides coverage against political, commercial credit, and preshipment risks. Exporters wishing coverage must insure both political and commercial credit risks; no separate political risk coverage is available. Preshipment risks may be insured separately or in conjunction with a regular policy coverage postshipment risks.

Political Risks. The government covers the usual political risks including

1 Nonpayment due to general moratoriums on repayment of debts and other governmental payment prohibitions.

2 Currency convertibility and transfer restrictions or the freezing of balances deposited in the local currency of the importer's country.
3 Losses from seizure, damage, or destruction of the goods that result from political causes and that cannot be covered by private insurance.

Commercial Credit Risks. As far as commercial credit risk coverage is concerned, the insurance differentiates between sales to private buyers and sales to governmental or semigovernmental entities. Export sales to private buyers may be insured against the commercial risk of insolvency or proven inability to pay on the part of the foreign debtor. Export sale to public buyers may be insured against nonpayment by the foreign debtor. Nonpayment occurs when a debt has not been paid within six months after its due date. In the case of shipments on a "documents-against-payment" basis, nonpayment is declared when documents have not been claimed within six months after arrival of the goods.

Preshipment Risks. Exporters of specially fabricated equipment may cover the risk that the equipment cannot be delivered due to a deteriorated financial position of the foreign buyer or due to bankruptcy or political occurrences in the foreign country. The amount of preshipment coverage includes all the out-of-pocket costs of the manufacturer (net of any recoveries) up to the point when it becomes obvious that delivery of the equipment to the importer cannot be effected.

Exporter Retention

Both the private insurers and Hermes require exporter retention of part of the risk. The percentage of retention varies, depending on the type of insurance. Gerling-Konzern, for instance, requires a 30% retention on the insurance of foreign commercial credit risks; on preshipment risk coverage, only a 15% retention is needed. Hermes requires retention by exporters according to the following schedule:

Percentage of Risk Required by Hermes to Be Retained by the Exporter	
Commercial credit risks (includes nonpayment by public buyers)	20%
Political risks	
Moratoriums, other payment prohibitions, convertibility, or transfer risks	15%
Other political risks	10%
Preshipment risks	15%

The portion of risk retained by the exporter may not be covered by other insurance. This assures that the exporter retains a stake in the transaction and, it is hoped, makes him careful in the selection of reputable and creditworthy foreign buyers.

Types of Policies

Private Insurers. Since private insurers need a good spread of risk, they favor comprehensive policies—primarily for the export of consumer goods. In this type of policy, the exporter is required to submit for insurance all sales made to importers in a previously specified list of countries. The underwriter, in turn, establishes limits for each foreign buyer. The exporter may make shipments up to these preestablished limits and be certain of insurance coverage. Any excesses beyond these limits must, of course, be first approved by the insurance company before being included under the coverage. Private insurers also issue specific policies covering the export of capital goods. In this case, the underwriter and the exporter come to a general agreement concerning the types of goods, countries, credit terms, and amounts for which insurance might be available. Each individual export, however, has to be reviewed and approved by the underwriters before commercial credit insurance becomes effective.

Preshipment risks for capital goods may be covered by special endorsements to specific policies.

Hermes. Separate policies with somewhat different provisions are available for sales to private and public (government) buyers. So-called *Ausfuhrgarantien* cover sales to private foreign firms; *Ausfuhrbuergschaften*, on the other hand, cover sales to foreign governments and other public bodies.

Insurance coverage against political and commercial risks is available in three different forms:

Comprehensive guarantee covering a number of different current export sales to several foreign buyers in various specified countries. This is similar to the other comprehensive policies discussed earlier. All sales to approved countries and buyers must be submitted for insurance and are covered up to preestablished limits.

Revolving guarantee covering repeat shipments to a single foreign buyer.

Specific guarantee covering a single foreign buyer. As with other specific policies, this one covers the export of capital goods.

The duration for which coverage is available depends on the nature of the goods and the terms customary in the particular line of trade. Usually the maximum period is five years, but exceptions are occasionally made. For capital goods exports, the foreign importer is required to make an appropriate down payment at the conclusion of the contract and/or at the time of delivery.

Policies covering the exportation of capital goods may include insurance for preshipment risks, provided the goods in question are specially manufactured or required a long production period.

In addition, policies may also be available to cover a number of special situations, such as the following:

1 Insurance against convertibility and transfer risks—this is, of course, less expensive than the "all risks" coverage discussed earlier. If exporters choose only convertibility (foreign exchange) and transfer risks insurance under the government program, they still have the option of insuring the commercial credit risk with a private underwriter.
2 Insurance covering inventory kept abroad on a consignment basis.
3 Guarantees for bank credits that are used to carry inventories of exported goods maintained abroad for eventual sales to local firms or individuals.
4 Foreign exchange risk coverage—since it is often hard to cover exchange risks that run in excess of two years, it is a stipulation of the policy that the export agreement be for a duration in excess of two years. The sales contract must be denominated in either U.S. dollars, pounds sterling, or Swiss francs. Only portions of the exchange risk that run more than two years may be insured with Hermes. On the exchange risk for the first two years, the exporter has the option of going uncovered or making arrangements in the private market. On the exchange risk beyond two years, the exporter has to bear any losses up to 3%. Any losses in excess of 3% will be compensated under the insurance. Conversely, any exchange gains in excess of 3% must be turned over to Hermes as agent for the government.

Cost

The cost of Hermes postshipment coverage differs, depending on whether the foreign buyer is a private firm or a governmental body. Sales to private firms (*Ausfuhrgarantien*) have generally been around 1.5% for the first six months and a small fraction for each additional month. If shipment is made on a documents-against-payment basis, the cost has been less than 1%. Sales to governmental buyers (*Ausfuhrbuergschaften*) have been between 0.5 and 1% as a base fee, depending on the amount of the transaction. There is also a small monthly maintenance fee for deferred payments.

Preshipment risks generally cost 1% of the insured amount. If, however, the same transaction is also covered under a regular postshipment policy (or if there is no postshipment risk at all, due to the way in which the transaction is structured) the cost is less.

Financing

The government and private insurance programs offer no direct financing of German exports.

Assignments. Insurance policies may, however, be assigned to commercial banks and other financing institutions, provided the assignor first obtains the written permission of the underwriter. Because a shipment is covered by assignable export credit insurance, financing from private or governmental sources is easier to obtain and less expensive.

AKA. A moderate percentage of German exports sold on medium-term credit may be discounted through Ausfuhrkredit G.m.b.H. (AKA). The latter is a syndicate of German banks that discounts medium-term export paper under one or more of three lines of credit.

Line "A." Under this line, billions of deutschemarks are available for financing commitments; somewhat less, however, may be outstanding for actual discounts. The difference in amounts that can be committed versus amounts actually financed is possible because not all commitments turn into actual discounts.

To obtain an export credit under line "A" an exporter, through a commercial bank, provides AKA with details of the transaction, as well as figures showing the importer's and his own creditworthiness. If AKA approves, the exporter issues promissory notes and presents them at AKA for discounting. In turn, AKA rediscounts 40% with the borrower's own bank and 60% with other banks that are owners of AKA, in proportion to their share ownership. If the credit term is two years or less, AKA rediscounts 25% with the borrower's own bank and 75% with other syndicate members. Only banks that are members of AKA may arrange line "A" credits for their customers.

Line "A" credits are available from one to eight years, depending on the nature of the transaction. Generally, only that portion which is guaranteed by Hermes may be discounted. The insurance policy, as well as foreign receivable, are assigned to AKA as security. Funding for the transaction, as well as any uninsured credit risk, however, is divided among the syndicate banks according to their degree of participation in AKA. Hence, AKA acts merely as a trustee and, therefore, requires no funds and assumes no risk.

Promissory notes arising from line "A" credits can be used as security for borrowings by commercial banks from the German central bank. This lends a certain amount of liquidity to line "A" export paper.

Line "B." This line represents a rediscount facility available to AKA at the German central bank. Similar to the "A" line, billions are available for commitments and slightly less for actual rediscounts. Unlike line "A" credits, banks making use of line "B" credits do not have to be members of AKA.

Under a line "B" credit, the commercial bank extends a credit to the exporter based on AKA's commitment to discount. In turn, AKA may rediscount the paper at the German central bank or it may sell the paper in the open market.

"B" line credits are available for terms of one to four years. Thirty percent must be self-financed by the exporter, compared to an average of twenty percent under line "A" credits, with the exact percentage varying, depending on the importer's country.

Line "C." In 1969 AKA introduced a third facility for the refinancing of buyer's credits. Generally, less has been allocated for this type of financing, and the "C" line has not enjoyed extensive usage.

Kreditanstalt fur Wideraufbau. The Kreditanstalt fur Wideraufbau (KfW) is a government credit institution originally formed to provide reconstruction loans. As one of its present activities, the KfW may provide medium-term export credits to developing countries. Specifically, it may supplement AKA's line "B" credits by financing the 30% exporter retention that is also guaranteed by Hermes. It may also provide financing for line "B" export credits with terms in excess of four years.

PART 2

Executing the Transactions

All export or import transactions involve several different parties to move goods from their place of origin to their destination. Foremost in this activity, of course, are the exporters and importers. Also important are the banks that provide financing, foreign exchange, money transfer, and other services; the shipping companies that contract to deliver the goods to their destination; and the insurance companies that protect the various interests in case of an unanticipated loss.

To spell out the rights and responsibilities of the various parties to a trade transaction requires numerous contracts and documents. A discussion of these vehicles of trade is the purpose of Part 2.

Underlying any trade transaction must be some form of contract between the buyer and seller. The nature of the contract may range from a mere verbal agreement between exporter and importer to a signed legal document with supporting schedules of hundreds of pages. Often, a failure to unambiguously specify the rights and duties of each party results in misunderstanding and conflict. Therefore, we shall discuss the general types of sales contracts and their major provisions in Chapter 6.

Immediately after signing a sales contract, either the exporter or importer (depending on the currency of payment) will find himself with a foreign exchange risk. Luckily this risk can be hedged, in most cases, primarily through the vehicle of a foreign exchange future contract. The general topic of foreign exchange is covered in Chapter 7.

The next step in a trade transaction is getting the export ready for shipment and obtaining payment. This requires a host of documents and contracts, such as bills of lading, drafts, invoices, inspection certificates, and so on. There are also some intermediaries, such as freight forwarders and customs brokers, who greatly help an exporter or importer in preparing the necessary documentation and passing goods through customs. The nature and purpose of these documents as well as the assistance that can be given by intermediaries is described in Chapter 8.

When shipping goods overseas, the risk of financial loss can be substantial, and few international traders can afford the loss of shipment due to perils of the sea. Moreover, any institution that finances a shipment would not be willing to assume the risk of loss due to such possibilities as water damage, fire, sinking of the ship, seizure in case of war, and so on. Luckily, the risks inherent in ocean shipments can be insured by means of a contract between the exporter or importer, on the one hand, and a marine underwriter, on the other. Ocean marine insurance is a rather complex area with many different risks and coverages. Chapter 9 discusses this topic.

CHAPTER 6

The Sales Contract

As a first step in exporting or importing, there must be some kind of contract between the buyer and seller, stipulating the rights and responsibilities of each party. If any conflict arises later between the two, reference is generally made to the sales contract, in an effort to resolve the misunderstanding. Therefore, it is important that the contract be negotiated with care, so that both buyer and seller are willing and able to function within its terms and know clearly and unambiguously what is expected of them.

Importers and exporters should be aware that many conflicts between buyers and sellers can be traced back to an incomplete or ambiguous contract. Arguments and litigation between customer and supplier seldom benefit either, and legal expenses incurred during a court case are often exorbitant. Moreover, the time and effort required by litigation is draining and diverts the merchant from his main business activities. Even if a court case is settled in favor of one party or the other, the ultimate result may be the loss of a customer or valuable source of supply. Not even the party in whose favor a court rules may benefit in the long run. The goal, therefore, should be to clearly establish the duties and rights of both parties from the beginning so that any chance of conflict is minimized.

In this chapter, we examine how a sales contract comes into being as well as consider the different kinds of contracts and main contract provisions, including terms of sales.

Occasionally, we will refer to Article 2 of the Uniform Commercial Code (UCC)—the codified law governing sales contracts in the United States (except Louisiana). It must be stressed that this is for illustrative purposes only. United States' laws apply only to sales contracts over which U.S. courts have jurisdiction. Many international sales contracts, however, provide for jurisdiction by the courts of some other country. In these cases, U.S. laws and legal practices do not apply.

Even in cases where the jurisdiction of U.S. courts is clearly established, the UCC may not be completely applicable. Statutes of the federal government may, for instance, take precedence over the UCC, which is state law.

Judges and juries may draw from common law rather than the UCC and, finally, provisions in the sales contract itself may take legal precedent over codified law. Once again, any reference to the UCC is merely illustrative.

CREATING THE SALES CONTRACT

Initiation

If a buyer and seller have not had previous dealings, an initial contact must be established between them. Perhaps a seller has heard from the trade development department of a bank that a particular buyer is interested in some of his products. The potential buyer may have written a letter of inquiry, possibly as a result of having seen the seller's advertisement or catalog. Alternatively, an agent or salesperson of the seller may have approached the buyer with an initial offer. Initiation toward the creation of a sales contract can occur in a number of ways:

A potential buyer sends a letter or telegram of inquiry to the supplier, asking for information on prices, qualities, and terms under which the latter is willing to ship. The supplier may then furnish the requested information and, at the same time, make a formal offer to sell a specified quantity and grade of goods at a fixed price and under other stipulated conditions.

A potential seller, knowing that another party is interested in his product, may submit an offer to sell at specified terms and conditions.

A buyer who is already familiar with the price and other terms under which a seller is willing to ship may submit a formal order for a specified quantity of goods at a stated price.

An offer to sell or an order requesting shipment is usually already legally binding for the party making the offer or placing the order. Therefore, it is important that an order or offer contain full details concerning the merchandise, including its grade and quality, quantity, price, terms of sale, delivery date, and other necessary specifications.

Response

Once a formal offer to buy or sell has been made, it is up to the other party to come up with an appropriate response. If all the terms outlined in the offer are satisfactory, the response might be a formal acceptance. Alternatively, some or all the conditions may not be acceptable, giving rise to further correspondence or face-to-face bargaining.

Sometimes, the respective conditions desired by the buyer and seller are similar, and only a slight compromise by either or both parties will finalize the arrangements. At other times, however, full agreement can be reached, if at all, only after prolonged bargaining and/or correspondence.

Acceptance

Once a seller's written offer has been formally accepted by the buyer, a sales contract is formed. One word of caution, however, is in order: The offer may have been made by a salesperson or agent who is unauthorized to make a binding commitment without prior approval of the head office. Therefore, the contract should contain a clause to the effect that the terms herein are irrevocable and that any changes must be accepted by all parties concerned.

A sales contract may also come into existence as the result of an order by a buyer. If the seller agrees with the specifications in the order and thinks he can comply with all the provisions, the seller may send a written and signed acknowledgment, thereby again completing a sales contract that is binding on both parties.

A seller may also accept an order by merely going ahead and shipping the merchandise desired in accordance with the buyer's specific shipping instructions. The UCC regulation applicable here (Article 2-206) states:

1 Unless otherwise unambiguously indicated by the language or circumstances (a) An offer to make a contract shall be construed as inviting acceptance in any manner and by any medium reasonable under the circumstances. (b) An offer to buy goods can be accepted merely by shipping the conforming goods.
2 Where the simple beginning of a requested performance is a reasonable mode of acceptance an offeror who is not notified of acceptance within a reasonable time may treat the offer as having elapsed before acceptance.

TYPES OF CONTRACTS

Sales contracts, in their simplest form, are merely accepted orders or offers that may arise through correspondence between buyer and seller. For large, complicated sales, however, a detailed contract must be carefully drawn. When there is a high degree of urgency, contracts may be arranged through cables, telexes, or over the telephone. We briefly examine the major types of contracts.

Verbal

The simplest type of contract is a verbal one. Typically, the buyer and seller meet face-to-face and discuss the basic conditions of sale. Having reached a mutually satisfactory agreement, they shake hands to indicate their agreement and willingness to live up to the terms negotiated. Often a face-to-face meeting is not even necessary; a buyer may simply telephone a supplier to place the order. The latter takes the buyer's verbal promise to accept delivery as sufficiently binding to make shipment.

For a verbal sales contract to be acceptable, there must be a great deal of trust and confidence between buyer and seller. Moreover, the transaction involved must be relatively simple in its terms and specifications. If there is any complexity at all, it may be difficult for the buyer and seller to remember the terms on which they agreed. Misunderstandings and differences in interpretation easily arise. One of the parties to the transaction may feel that the other has committed a breach and, as a result, does not feel obligated to his part of the contract. Since the original conditions were not put into writing, the actual agreement can never be accurately determined.

Despite the shortcomings, there are still many situations where verbal contracts are appropriate. When a buyer and seller have had many years of mutually satisfactory dealings of a fairly repetitive nature and there exists a great degree of trust and confidence, a verbal repeat order may be adequate. There are also certain specialized fields where almost all business is conducted via verbal agreements. Traders who buy and sell foreign currencies, for instance, do all their business over the telephone. A purchase and sale is finalized by a verbal agreement between two exchange traders who may never have met face-to-face. Confirmation of the deal is made in writing only after the fact.

As a general rule, when a verbal agreement has been made, it is a good idea to confirm it in writing. This way the underlying agreement is reaffirmed and any misunderstandings can usually be brought into the open before irreparable damage has been done.

Correspondence

Most typically, especially in international commerce, a sales contract comes into existence through a chain of correspondence between the exporter and importer. The importer may come in with an initial inquiry requesting a price quotation for a certain type and quantity of merchandise. The seller, in turn, responds with the desired information. Usually, this response can already be interpreted as an offer that is binding on the exporter, provided the importer accepts it within a reasonable period of time. Often, for the sake of simplicity, an order or an offer will have, at the end, some phrase like "Please acknowledge your acceptance of the provisions contained in this order (offer) by signing and returning the attached copy."

With respect to a "reasonable amount of time," Article 2-205 of the UCC states:

> An offer by a merchant to buy or sell goods in a signed writing which by its terms gives assurance that it will be held open is not revocable, for lack of consideration, during the time stated or if no time is stated for a reasonable time, but in no event may such period of irrevocability exceed three months; but any such term of assurance of a form supplied by the offeree must be separately signed by the offeror.

Sometimes, an offer (or order) will not be acceptable in its entirety to the potential buyer (or seller) and he will then come back with a counteroffer. In complicated deals, several letters and/or telegrams with offers and counteroffers may go back and forth before agreement is finally reached.

The point at which correspondence actually becomes a binding contract is sometimes difficult to determine. Courts have ruled, however, that a binding agreement can be represented by a file of correspondence (including telegraphic messages) between the two parties, even though a final agreement on all points between the buyer and seller may never have been explicitly spelled out.

We should note that in modern business an important role is still played by telegraphic and wire communication. Messages by cable or telex can be authenticated through testing arrangements between banks, as explained in Chapter 2. In cases where cable or wire service has been superseded by telexes or direct computer hookups, a good cable service should always be held in reserve as a backup system. It should be mentioned that the most recently developed media for communication, known as the Internet in the United States, is seldom used by banks because of a lack of security.

Printed Short Forms

Many firms have preprinted order and offer forms that when accepted, become contracts. This greatly simplifies buying and selling procedures in that details that are the same for most contracts of a particular firm need not be specifically typed each time. Major provisions are included in the printed part of the form. Variable provisions can be typed in as required.

One problem that occasionally arises with a form is that its fine print tends to favor the party who has issued it. Therefore, if the other party merely accepts the provisions, without attempting to negotiate more favorable terms, that party may be disadvantaged in case of a conflict. Therefore, forms preprinted by one of the parties are only acceptable when this is traditional in the industry, the amounts involved are small, there is a high degree of trust between the buyer and seller, or when enough previous business has gone on between the buyer and seller to make repeat orders fairly routine.

In those industries in which it has become traditional to have printed forms, the forms are usually drawn up by a trade association of firms in the specialized industry. Provisions in the contract form follow standard requirements of the industry, with blanks left to be filled in with appropriate details. A typical sales contract covering a specialized commodity is shown in Figure 6-1. Prepared by the Green Coffee Association of New York City, Inc., it is used for free on board (FOB) sales. A look at the main provisions is useful since they illustrate some of the items that should be included in a well-written international sales contract. Note, for instance, that details are given concerning the acceptable packaging of the green coffee. Other provisions include

F.O.B. CONTRACT
OF THE
GREEN COFFEE ASSOCIATION
OF
NEW YORK CITY, INC.
Effective June 6, 19__

Contract Seller's No. ______________

Buyer's No. ______________

Date ______________

SELLER: SOLD for account of ______________

BUYER: To ______________

QUANTITY: About ______________ (______) Bags/Tons of ______________ coffee
averaging ______________ per bag.

PACKAGING: Coffee must be packed in sound bags of uniform size made of sisal, henequen, jute, burlap, or similar woven material, without inner lining or outer covering of any other material, properly sewn by hand and/or machine.

DESCRIPTION: ______________
____
____

PRICE: At ______________ U.S. Currency, per ______________ net.
Free on board (F.O.B.) vessel at seaport(s) ______________

PAYMENT: ______________
____
____
____

SHIPMENT: During/Per ______________
from ______________ seaport(s) to ______________
by power-propelled vessel(s), by direct and/or recognized indirect route. Partial shipments permitted. Date of on-board Bill of Lading to be evidence of time of shipment, but is not conclusive proof.

ADVICE OF SHIPMENT: Telegraphic advice of shipment with name of vessel in which coffee is on-board, together with the quantity, description, and port of destination, must be transmitted direct, or through Seller's Agent/Broker, to the buyer as soon as known, but not later than on the day of arrival of vessel at destination stated on Contract. Where Sellers and Buyers in the Contracts involved are in the same area, such advice may be given by hand, or verbally, or by telephone, with written confirmation to be sent the same day.

WEIGHTS: (1) **DELIVERED WEIGHTS**: Coffee covered by this contract is to be weighed at port of discharge. Any variation from invoice weights to be adjusted at contract price.

(2) **SHIPPING WEIGHTS**: Coffee covered by this contract is sold on shipping weights. Any loss in weight exceeding ______ percent at port of discharge is for account of Seller at contract price.

(3) Coffee is to be weighed at the port of discharge within fifteen (15) calendar days after discharge from the vessel or fifteen (15) calendar days after all U.S.A. Government clearances have been received, whichever is later. Weighing expenses, if any, for account of Buyer.

INSURANCE: All Marine and War Risk insurance to be covered by the Buyer.

MARKINGS: Bags to be branded in English with the name of country of origin and otherwise to comply with laws and regulations of U.S. Government, in effect at time of shipment, governing marking of import merchandise. Any expense incurred by failure to comply with these regulations to be borne by Seller.

DUTIES AND TAXES: Any duty or tax whatsoever, imposed by the United States Government, or any authority in the United States, shall be borne by the Buyer.

RULINGS: The "Ruling on Coffee Contracts" of the Green Coffee Association of New York City, Inc., in effect on the date this contract is made, are incorporated for all purposes as a part of this agreement, and together herewith, constitute the entire contract. No variation or addition hereto shall be valid unless signed by the parties to the contract.

Seller guarantees that the terms printed on the reverse hereof, which by reference are made a part hereof, are identical with the terms as printed in By-Laws and Rules of the Green Coffee Association of New York City, Inc., heretofore adopted. If No Pass—No Sale terms are stipulated, then Guarantee Clause (a) shall not be applicable.

Exceptions to this guarantee are:

ACCEPTED:

Specimen

______________________ Seller

BY ______________________ Agent

______________________ Buyer

BY ______________________ Agent

______________________ Broker(s)

When this contract is executed by a person acting for another, such person hereby represents that he is fully authorized to commit his principal.

Figure 6-1. Short form sales contract (front and back), F.O.B.

TERMS AND CONDITIONS

ARBITRATION: All controversies relating to, in connection with, or arising out of this contract, its modification, making or the authority or obligations of the signatories hereto, and whether involving the principals, agents, brokers, or others who actually subscribe hereto, shall be settled by arbitration in accordinace with the "Rules of Arbitration" of the Green Coffee Association of New York City, Inc., as they exist at the time of the arbitration (including provisions as to payment of fees and expenses). Arbitration is the sole remedy hereunder, and it shall be held in accordance with the law of New York State, and judgment of any award may be entered in the courts of that State, or in any other court of competent jurisdiction. All notices or judicial service in reference to arbitration or enforcement shall be deemed given if transmitted as required by the aforesaid rules.

GUARANTEE: (a) If all or any of the coffee is refused admission into the United States by reason of any violation of the Federal Food, Drug and Cosmetic Act, which violation existed at the time the coffee arrived on board ship, seller is required, as to the amount not admitted and as soon as possible, to deliver replacement coffee in conformity to all the terms and conditions of this contract, excepting only the shipment terms. Any payment made for any coffee denied entry shall be refunded within ten (10) calendar days of denial of entry, and payment shall be made for the replacement delivery in accordance with the terms of this contract. Consequently, if Buyer removes the coffee from the dock, Seller's responsibility as to such portion hereunder ceases.

(b) Contracts containing the overstamp "No Pass—No Sale" on the face of the contract shall be interpreted to mean if any or all of the coffee is not admitted into the United States in its original condition by reason of failure to meet requirements of the Federal Food, Drug & Cosmetic Act, the contract shall be deemed to be null and void as to that portion of the coffee which is not admitted in its original condition. Any payment made for any coffee denied entry shall be refunded within ten (10) calendar days of denial of entry.

FORCE MAJEURE: (a) Seller and Buyer shall not be liable for delay in delivery, or delay in the performance of other acts required hereunder, when solely resulting from cause(s) wholly beyond his control, provided coffee is at specified seaport ready for shipment. Such causes shall include, but not be limited to, acts of God, acts of government, wars, revolutions, strikes, pestilence, floods, droughts, perils of the sea, or unavoidable interruption of transportation. Notice to this effect shall be given in writing at once on contracts specifying shipment from seaport. In no case shall the seller be excused by any such causes intervening before the arrival of the affected portion of the coffee in the foreign port of original shipment.

(b) Force Majeure shall not apply when Seller's inability to export is due to Seller's lack of export quota.

CLAIMS: Coffee shall be considered accepted as to quality unless within fifteen (15) calendar days after discharge of the coffee from the vessel or within fifteen (15) calendar days after all U.S.A. Government clearances have been received, whichever is later, either:

(a) Claims are settled by the parties hereto, or,

(b) Arbitration proceedings have been filed by one of the parties in accordance with the provisions hereof.

If neither has been done in the stated period, or if any chop or chops of the coffee has or have been removed from the dock before representative sealed samples have been drawn by the Green Coffee Association of New York City, Inc. in accordance with its rules, all claims as to quality regarding such chop or chops shall be unenforceable, for that portion so removed.

DELIVERY: (a) No more than five (5) chops may be tendered for each lot of 250 bags.

(b) Each chop of coffee tendered is to be uniform in grade and appearance. All expense necessary to make cofee uniform shall be for account of seller.

INSOLVENCY OR FINANCIAL FAILURE OF BUYER OR SELLER: If, at any time before the contract is fully executed, either party hereto shall meet with creditors because of inability generally to make payment of obligations when due, or shall suspend such payments, fail to meet his general trade obligations in the regular course of business, shall file a petition in bankruptcy or, for an arrangement, shall become insolvent, or commit an act of bankruptcy, then the other party may at his option, expresed in writing, declare the aforesaid to constitute a breach and default of this contract, and may, in addition to other remedies, decline to deliver further or make payment or may sell or purchase for the defaulter's account, and may collect damage for any injury or loss, or shall account for the profit, if any, occasioned by such sale or purchase.

BREACH OR DEFAULT OF CONTRACT: In the event either party hereto fails to perform, or breaches or repudiates this agreement, the other party shall be entitled to the remedies and relief provided for by the uniform Commercial Code of the State of New York. The computation and ascertainment of damages, or the determination of any other dispute as to relief, shall be made by the arbitrators in accordance with the Arbitration Clause herein.

Consequential damages shall not, however, be allowed.

CONTINGENCY: This contract is not contingent upon any other contract.

Figure 6-1. *(Continued)*

Detailed instructions on quantity, including a provision for weighing the goods at the port of discharge.

Description of the coffee by grade and type.

Price.

Exact method by which payment is to be effected.

Latest date on which advice of shipment must be made to the buyer.

Marine and war risk insurance to be arranged by the buyer.

Exactly how the bags of coffee must be marked, as well as a provision that any costs resulting from a failure to comply with marking regulations must be borne by the seller.

Any U.S. duties and taxes have to be borne by the buyer.

Other terms and conditions are printed on the reverse side of the contract form. Also, part of the contract are the "Rulings on Coffee Contracts" of the Green Coffee Association. These rulings consist of several pages of rules and trade practices that are common in the coffee trade, and their inclusion by reference allows for brevity on the actual sales contract form.

Detailed Contracts

With initial orders, or when large amounts of money are involved, the completion of a sales contract will be a bit more complicated than with the use of short forms as previously described. At best, there is a great deal of correspondence between buyer and seller before agreement can be reached on the final form. When major purchases, such as entire industrial plants are involved, correspondence will not do the job either. It is most likely that buyer and seller, as well as their respective lawyers and technical experts, must sit down together for several days or weeks of bargaining before all desired terms and conditions can be incorporated into a mutually agreed-on document. In such cases, all technical details must be outlined. Often the contract is accompanied by blueprints and detailed tolerance and performance specifications. If specifications concerning quality, tolerances, performance, or delivery are not met, the contract often provides for remedies or penalties to be paid by the seller. The net result of including all these specifications and details may well be a sales contract that, together with all appendixes and schedules, is as voluminous as an entire book.

CONTRACT PROVISIONS

Whether dealing through correspondence, a preprinted form, or a long form, there are certain key provisions that every contract should contain to avoid ambiguity and possible future conflicts. Other provisions, while desirable and even essential in some contracts, may be superfluous in others. Whether to include them depends on the type of goods involved, shipping and insurance complexities, and degree of trust and mutual confidence existing between buyer and seller. After a certain pattern has already been established, an initial contract will invariably take more time to work out than a repeat order.

Minimum Provisions

A complete sales contract should contain the following provisions as an absolute minimum:

Names and addresses of buyer and seller.

Description of goods, including price, weight, grade, and quantity specifications.

Shipping and delivery instructions and required documentation (including export licenses and permits).

Payment terms and instructions (including the payment of duties, taxes, and other fees).

Insurance coverage necessary while goods are in transit and designation of the party responsible for costs.

Additional Provisions

Other provisions, while they may not be necessary in all contracts, are still desirable and even essential in many cases. These include

Method of packaging and marking.

Inspections and tests allowed by the buyer before delivery is accepted.

Warranties of the seller concerning the quality and/or performance of the product.

Provision for bid and performance bonds or guarantees.

Remedies allowed by either party in case of default by the other.

Arbitration of disputes or claims that may arise.

Definition of jurisdiction under which any disputes shall be adjudicated.

Description of Goods

To avoid possible conflicts about quality, grade, quantity, or price, every effort should be made to describe the goods in the sales contract exactly as buyer and seller intend them to be.

Weight and Quantity. Confusion and misunderstanding on such things as weights and other quantity measures is not uncommon. A U.S. pound, for instance, is different from a European pound; similarly, a ton has a different real weight, depending on whether it is a short, metric, or long ton. Since these and other quantity terms may be ambiguous, careful definition in the sales contract is important.

Quality Description. Terms indicating grades or qualities are frequently harder to define than weights and quantities. A term for defining one particular degree of quality in one country may have a different meaning in another. Some abbreviations are in frequent enough use in one country or specific industry so that all those who are experienced readily understand them. Merchants sometimes forget, however, that in foreign countries and other industries, those abbreviations may not be known or may possess a different meaning.

It is useful to clarify the buyer's rights if the quality of the goods shipped is lower than intended in the sales contract—that is, can the shipment be rejected and sent back at the seller's expense, or does the buyer get a specified reduction in price?

Definitions. When writing a sales contract, international traders should take great care to clearly define their terms and avoid all ambiguous words or abbreviations. Detailed contracts often have, in one of the first articles, a definition of all terms. It may also be possible to clarify the description of goods by reference in the sales contract to catalog numbers, plans or drawings, engineering specifications, or even samples previously given to the buyer.

Prices. Price quotations can also be a source of misunderstanding. The basic price used as a reference may be a quotation in the seller's catalog, price list, or advertisement. This price, however, must be adjusted to correspond to the net amount quoted in the sales contract. Some typical adjustments might include

Quantity discounts.

Discounts for early payment.

The addition of finance charges in cases where deferred payment is allowed.

Addition of transportation and/or other charges.

Insurance fees.

Other discounts or surcharges that may apply to specific classes of buyers in particular countries or markets.

To help define exactly what is and is not included in the quoted price, reference in the sales contract may be made to the "Revised American Foreign Trade Definitions (1990)." However, this document gives only different terms of delivery and the seller's and buyer's responsibility. Other clarifying comments and definitions may have to be included in the sales contract to avoid ambiguity. Occasionally, the "International Rules for Interpretation of Trade Terms (1941)" are used. They are similar to the "Revised American Foreign Trade Definitions" but differ in a few details.

When deferred payment terms are offered, an exporter may wish to add a premium to the price to cover interest expenses until final payment is received and to compensate for the added risk inherent in the granting of terms. In some countries, importers are limited in the rate of interest they may legally pay on deferred payments. In such cases, any additional interest and risk expenses incurred by the exporter have to be built into the base price.

It is worth noting that when interest charges are included in the price quotation the importer ends up paying duty not only on the basic cost of the goods, but also on the interest. When deferred payment terms of several years are granted, interest charges may substantially increase the base price. If the merchandise in question carries a high import duty, a significant amount of unnecessary cost may be incurred by the importer. Therefore, it is to the importer's advantage to pay interest separately rather than having it built into the price.

Shipping and Delivery Instructions

Shipping Deadline. Usually, the buyer insists on a specified deadline or time interval within which shipment must be made. The meeting of these deadlines becomes especially important when dealing in seasonal goods, raw materials, or semiprocessed items required for further manufacture. If an importer of ornaments missed the Christmas season, due to late delivery, the losses could be substantial. Similarly, a manufacturer may need a certain raw material or subassembly in order to keep a plant in operation. If delivery is not received on time, the entire factory operation may come to a halt.

When timing is of the essence, importers will frequently not only specify a delivery deadline, but will also provide in the sales contract for remedies if these deadlines are not met. Sometimes, delays may be classified as those that are "excusable," that is, due to contingencies beyond the control of the exporter, and "inexcusable." Excusable delays may be caused by such things as war, government regulations, strikes, fire, or acts of God.

Interpretations of what constitutes an excusable delay may differ in various countries. In some, for instance, a strike is considered beyond the control of the seller, while in others it would represent an inexcusable delay. Once the buyer and seller have agreed on what constitutes a valid excuse for nonperformance, they must also specify what happens if nonperformance should occur under these circumstances. Common solutions are merely to postpone the delivery date, or to give either party the right to cancel the contract.

Typically, a contract might provide for no penalty in case of an excusable delay and a fixed or graduated fee for nonexcusable delays. An illustrative clause providing for delay penalties might read as follows:

> In the event that the availability for delivery of all or any portion of the contract equipment and materials are delayed for other than excusable causes beyond the delivery date, the seller shall pay to the purchaser actual damages at an equivalent rate of 0.15% of the total contract price per day beyond the delivery date stipulated plus 15 days grace period. In no case shall such payment exceed 5% of the contract price. It is understood, however, that no liquidated damages will be assessed for delays for minor items that will not affect the normal course of construction.

When a specific delivery deadline is stated, this generally means that the ocean bill of lading should be dated on or before the stipulated date. To make sure that the goods have actually been put on a vessel on time, the buyer should specifically request an "on board" bill of lading. Such ambiguous terms as "immediate" or "prompt" delivery should be avoided.

According to the UCC, if the parties to a sales contract have not agreed otherwise, delivery is due within a reasonable time (UCC 2-309). What constitutes a reasonable time depends on what is "acceptable commercial conduct" in view of the type of contract and the nature of the performance required under the circumstances (UCC 2-309 Official Comment). The UCC further states that if a time limit is given in the contract and if time is of the essence (e.g., seasonal goods), the buyer may refuse late delivery, recover damages resulting from the lateness, and be discharged from the obligation to pay for the merchandise (UCC 2-601).

As discussed in Chapter 13, a buyer can provide for the enforcement of a shipping deadline by an appropriate stipulation in a letter of credit. Alternatively, if an importer receives title documents against payment or acceptance of a draft drawn, it is necessary to make sure that the on-board bill of lading is dated on or before the shipping deadline before paying or accepting the draft.

Documents. An importer who wishes to claim a shipment at the dock to clear it through customs requires certain shipping documents. The most common of these are bills of lading, commercial invoices, consular invoices, and insurance policies or certificates. Other documents that may be required are detailed in Chapter 8. The important point to be stressed here is that an importer should specify in the sales contract exactly what documentation is required, the number of copies, and detailed information that is to be included on each piece of paper.

In many countries, goods may only be imported if the buyer has previously obtained a valid import license. Without a license, it may be impossible to pass goods through customs and they may be confiscated. The exporter should, therefore, make sure that the sales contract provides for the importer to obtain all necessary licenses. Importers also should make sure that exporters can obtain necessary licenses. Some countries have limited the quantities of certain goods that may be exported. Once this quantity restriction for any calendar period is reached, no further export licenses may be issued.

Delivery Terms. Another important item, which must be specified in the contract, is the delivery terms of sale. Terms such as "Ex Factory," "Free on Board" (FOB), "Free Along Side" (FAS), "Cost and Freight" (CFR), define the exact point at which delivery of goods to the seller takes place. All expenses and risks, up to that point, are usually included in the sales price. Similarly, any risks or losses, up to the point of delivery, are borne by the seller. Expenses, after the point of delivery, are for the account of the importer. If they are, nevertheless, paid by the exporter, they are specifically detailed on the invoice.

To avoid confusion and ambiguity in the use of delivery terms of trade, several attempts have been made in formulating uniform definitions. The industry standard is the "Revised American Foreign Trade Definitions (1990)." It clearly spells out the rights and obligations of both seller and buyer under different delivery terms. Since these definitions have no legal status, they must be included in the sales contract. Thus, it is advisable that each contract define the applicable delivery term by specific reference to the "Revised American Foreign Trade Definitions (1990)" or the "International Rules for the Interpretation of Trade Terms (1936)," which also finds some usage among international traders.

Some of the most commonly used delivery terms are summarized in the following paragraphs. For a more detailed description, the "Revised American Foreign Trade Definitions" is quoted in full in Appendix 2.

Ex Factory. Under this term, the seller is obligated to place the goods at the buyer's disposal at the point of origin, that is, the factory. The seller must, however, still assist the buyer in obtaining any documents the latter may need for exporting and/or importing the goods. The price quotation includes only the cost of making the goods available at the inland point of origin. All other costs, such as freight, insurance, export and import taxes, and so on, must be borne by the buyer. Since title passes at the factory or other stated origin, the buyer assumes all risks after the time when he or she is obligated to take delivery.

FOB (Free on Board). This delivery term may be subject to considerable ambiguity, unless it is specified on which conveyance the merchandise must be loaded. For instance, FOB may refer to loading on board of railway cars, trucks, lighters, barges, oceangoing vessels, aircraft, or other conveyances. It is, therefore, most important to specify exactly which conveyance is meant and the exact location, such as "FOB vessel New York City."

When FOB terms are quoted, the seller pays all charges until the goods are actually on board the named conveyance at the specified location. If terms are FOB vessel (named port of shipment), the buyer is obligated to furnish the seller a clean, on-board bill of lading. Again, the seller has to help the buyer with other documents needed for exportation and importation of the goods.

Since title passes when goods are loaded on board the conveyance, the seller assumes all risks up to that point, while the buyer is responsible for any damage or loss thereafter.

Once goods are loaded on board the named conveyance, subsequent transportation, insurance, and other charges must be paid by the buyer. If the actual cash outlay for any such charges is, in fact, made by the seller, it will be detailed and included in the invoice total.

FAS (Free Along Side). Under this delivery term, the seller is obligated to deliver the goods alongside the overseas vessel at the named port, within reach of the ship's loading tackle. The price quotation includes charges to that point, while subsequent levies (including storage, insurance, ocean transportation, and export taxes) must be borne by the importer.

CFR (Cost and Freight). This term differs from those previously mentioned in that the seller must provide and pay for transportation to the named point of destination. Any export taxes, plus other fees levied because of exportation, must also be paid by the seller.

In cases when an "on board" bill of lading is called for, title passes once goods have been loaded on board the vessel. When a received-for-shipment bill of lading is required, the title passes once the goods have been delivered to the ocean carrier's custody, which could be at the pier or warehouse of the carrier if the vessel is not yet ready for loading.

CIF (Cost, Insurance, and Freight). Basically, CIF terms are similar to CFR terms except that the seller is also obligated to provide and pay for ocean marine insurance. If war risk insurance is obtainable in the seller's market, he must also provide this type of coverage. The expense for war risk insurance, however, has to be borne by the buyer unless the seller has specifically agreed in the sales contract to provide such coverage at his expense.

As with CFR terms, title and, consequently, the assumption of risk, passes after goods are loaded on board the vessel ("on-board" bill of lading) or delivered to the custody of the ocean carrier ("received-for-shipment" bill of lading). Both CFR and CIF clearly indicate that the seller must provide and pay the unloading expenses at the port of destination of the goods.

The term "free out" is an added clause to the terms CFR or CIF, indicating the cost of unloading the goods is provided by the seller. Therefore, the invoices should clearly spell out "CFR free out" or "CIF free out," as the case may be. Also, the bill of lading should indicate "free out" next to the freight prepaid statement, because the clause is part of the sales contract and carries with it the contractual obligation of the seller.

DEQ. Under this term, the seller's price quotation includes all costs necessary to place the goods on the dock of the named port of importation. Specific costs borne by the seller include freight charges, export taxes and related fees, ocean marine and war risk insurance, fees for documents issued in the country of origin, costs of landing (wharfage, landing charges, and taxes), cost of customs entry in the country of importation, and customs duties and other taxes applicable to imports. To further clarify the DEQ delivery term, it is often referred to as "DEQ duty paid."

Since title passes only at the dock of the port of destination, the seller assumes all risks until the goods have been loaded onto the dock and the free time allowed on it has expired.

The DEQ term may be especially useful for importers who are buying for the first time from a given foreign supplier. When importers are quoted "DEQ-duty paid" terms, they know exactly what their landed cost will be. The foreign exporter has to worry about transportation charges, insurance and, most importantly, import duties and clearance through customs. Occasionally, imports may be subject to antidumping laws that may involve the importer in heavy fines. Only if DEQ or similar terms are used is the responsibility of violating antidumping laws placed on the foreign exporter where it really belongs.

Payment Instructions

To determine who is obligated to pay charges, such as freight, insurance, taxes, duties, and so on, reference should be made to the "Revised American Foreign Trade Definitions (1990)." Otherwise, details, as to who pays what, should be clearly and unambiguously specified in the sales contract.

Currency. The currency in which payment is due should be clearly specified in the contract. Quotations may be made in the currency of the exporter, importer, or third country. Often the exporters will prefer a quote in their own currency in order to reduce the foreign exchange risk and to enable them more easily to determine profit. Before accepting payment in the importer's or a third currency, exporters should make sure that payments can readily be converted into their own currency and that their exchange risk can be covered. Importers may prefer quotes in their own, the exporter's, or a third currency. Importers will prefer the latter two alternatives if the respective currencies are weak and they have a chance of profiting from a downward rate fluctuation or devaluation. Sometimes, exporters will wish to include, in their drafts on the importer, an exchange clause stipulating the rate at which a foreign currency payment will be converted. From the importer's point of view, such a clause is tantamount to being invoiced in a foreign currency and he runs roughly the same risks. If an exchange clause is to be used, it is important that this be first so specified in the sales contract; if, however, it is included without prior authorization, the importer would be justified in dishonoring the draft and refusing the shipment. Indeed, the existence of an exchange clause may make it more difficult for importers to cover their exchange risk.

A special exchange risk arises when long-term contracts are denominated in a currency foreign to the exporter. The latter may receive payment over a number of years in a foreign currency. For such long periods of time, it may be difficult or impossible to get forward exchange cover. The exporter may, therefore, wish to include an escalation clause providing for compensatory payments in case of adverse exchange fluctuations.

Generally, exporters are advised not to quote prices in a foreign currency, unless it enjoys a fair degree of stability or a forward market exists for covering the exchange risk. Exporters may quote in a foreign currency today only to find that the next day, or a few days later, the currency has devalued. Since a price quotation is a binding commitment, substantial losses may result. However, in an effort to reach an agreement, it is often the case that payment will be in a foreign currency and at a future date. To enable the parties to agree on an acceptable unit price and minimize exposure to exchange fluctuations, money market rates for the two currencies can be used. Since the forward market usually reflects the net accessible interest differential between the two currencies, an acceptable unit price may be established by utilizing these rates. (See Chapter 7.)

Payment Terms. The sales contract should specify the exact payment terms. The terms that are negotiated in any particular contract depend on competitive practices, the custom in the industry, the financial strength and reputation of the buyer, and the buyer's and seller's relative bargaining strength. Terms that may potentially be used include the following:

Cash in Advance. Since the seller receives payment before shipping the goods, this is clearly the most desirable method from the exporter's point of view. Competitive practices usually make this payment term impractical to obtain, except for small shipments or the sale of goods that have to be especially manufactured for a highly specialized end use.

Irrevocable Letter of Credit. When the credit is issued by a prime bank of excellent standing or confirmed by a reputable bank in the exporter's locality, this term is almost as safe from the exporter's point of view as cash in advance. As long as exporters comply with the documentation specified in the credit within the stipulated time period, they can be assured of payment. When negotiating the sales contract, exporters should make sure that only those documents are required which they can readily obtain. Similarly, when stipulating the documents required under a letter of credit, the importer should be guided solely by the previously negotiated contract.

Revocable Letter of Credit. Since this instrument may be revoked at any time by the importer or the importer's bank, it is clearly less safe than an irrevocable credit. Nevertheless, it may be used when a high degree of trust exists between buyer and seller, between affiliated companies, or when the underlying commodity is readily salable at a good price in the open market. Note, however, that some banks refuse to issue or advise a revocable letter of credit.

Documents Against Payment. Under this payment term, shipping documents are turned over to the importer against payment of a sight draft for the amount due drawn on him by the exporter. While the exporter or his bank retains control over the shipment until payment is received, there is, nevertheless, a considerable amount of risk for the exporter: The importer may, for instance, simply refuse to accept the shipment. By that time, the goods are usually on the high seas or at a foreign port and can probably not be disposed of except at a reduced price.

Documents Against Acceptance. In this case documents are turned over to the importer on acceptance of a time draft drawn on him. The tenure of the draft is for a stipulated period of time such as 30, 60, 90, or 180 days. In addition to all the risks mentioned under "Documents Against Payment," the exporter runs the additional danger that the accepted draft may not be paid at maturity.

Consignments. Sometimes, the exporter may wish to retain title to the goods while at the same time physically turning them over to the importer to allow the arrangement of sales and deliveries to final customers. This can be achieved by consignment terms. The goods are actually sent to the importer to allow the latter to display and/or warehouse them. Title, however, remains with the exporter. Once the importer has made a final sale, there is the obligation to pay the consignor (exporter) promptly for the merchandise involved. Clearly, by giving up physical possession of the goods, the exporter runs a substantial risk unless the consignee is of undoubted integrity.

Open Account. In U.S. domestic commerce the term most commonly used is the open account. This is certainly the least cumbersome method. The seller merely ships the goods to the buyer and separately mails the buyer the title documents and invoice calling for payment within a stipulated period of time. Before a seller agrees to ship on open-account terms, it is necessary to ascertain the honesty and financial strength of the buyer. Usually, in domestic transactions, this represents no problem. To get a complete credit history on any particular buyer, the seller merely contacts his local bank. The latter, through its banking relationships gets into contact with a bank, some other financial institution, or a credit agency that has intimate knowledge of the buyer's business, financial strength, reputation, and payment habits. Since information generally is freely exchanged in this country, credit reports by banks and others are quite reliable.

In international commerce, open account terms are usually used only between large companies of undoubted repute and firms having a long history of satisfactory dealings during which a high degree of mutual confidence has been developed.

It is most important that the exact payment terms be specified in the sales contract. In the United States, the UCC provides that whenever exact payment terms are not specified, payment must be made at the time and place at which the buyer is to receive the goods. (This is stipulated in UCC 2-310[a].) When international shipments are involved, such a broad statement of law leaves a great deal to interpretation with possible conflicts and ambiguities.

Some of the terms that have been outlined, such as documents against acceptance, provide for deferred payment. In such cases, and in situations where there is an unauthorized delay in payment by the buyer, it will be to the seller's advantage to have a clause in the contract providing for the payment of interest at a specified rate for the deferred period.

Packaging and Marking

Proper packaging can be extremely important, depending on the type of product and its destination. Ocean voyages may be most damaging to goods that are not properly packaged. Goods subject to breakage have to be crated, and those subject to moisture must be wrapped in plastic. Others may require some special treatment or coating before shipment, while others have to be refrigerated during transit.

Customs Regulations. The markings of outer and inner boxes are often subject to strict control at the country of destination. Each country has its own regulations—for example, the system of weights and measures to be used to show quantity of content, language to be used on the boxes, and so on.

Improper packaging and markings may prevent the goods from getting safely to their destination or may cause local customs authorities either to reject the shipment or levy a heavy fine against the consignee. Thus, it is in the best interest of the importer to specify clearly in the sales contract the packaging and marking required. If an exporter does not comply with packing and marking instruction, the importer is justified in refusing to accept the shipment.

Typical Clause. A typical contract clause covering packing and marking instruction may read as follows:

> The seller shall prepare all equipment for export shipment in accordance with the best commercial practices and standard marine insurance requirements. The seller shall assume full responsibility for any damage sustained due to faulty or inadequate preparation. The seller shall indicate shipping marks on all containers and same on all packing lists, invoices and other shipping documents, the contract number, gross and net weights, dimensions of container and other identification marks or reference numbers as may be required. The seller shall certify on each invoice rendered the value of the export packing and inland freight as an aid to the purchaser in establishing the net value of the equipment for import duty purposes.

Warranties of the Seller, Guarantees, and Inspections

Warranties. It is, of course, to the advantage of the buyer to have warranties of the seller included in the contract. If the seller guarantees not only against product defects, but also for proper performance, he may be liable not only for replacing a defective product but also for consequential damages. A clear definition in the contract of exactly what is and is not warranted is, therefore, advisable. A typical warranty clause might read as follows:

> The seller shall warrant that the design, material, and workmanship will be of the highest grade and consistent with the established and generally accepted standards for equipment of this type; and that it will be in full conformity with the specification and seller's offer.
>
> The seller agrees that this warranty will survive acceptance of and payment for the equipment, whether any defect shall be patent or latent, for one year after satisfactory full load operation, but not to exceed 30 months after the date of delivery to the port of exit of final shipment under the contract.
>
> The seller agrees that this warranty will survive acceptance of and payment for the equipment whether any defect shall be patent or latent for one year after satisfactory full-load operation but not to exceed 30 months after the date of delivery to the port of exit of final shipment under the contract.
>
> The seller's entire obligation under this warranty shall be to repair or, at his option, replace any part of the equipment which, under the specified use and proper maintenance, proves defective within one year from the date of satisfactory full-load operation of the unit concerned.

Performance Guarantee. Sometimes, exporters are expected to back up their warranties with bank performance credit (in the form of a standby credit), guarantees, or performance bonds. If delivery or performance does not comply with previously agreed-on specifications, the importer has the right to draw under the guarantee or bond.

Inspection. Sometimes, a buyer may wish to have the right to inspect the merchandise or equipment while it is being manufactured. In this case, an inspection clause should be included in the contract. A typical inspection clause might read as follows:

> The seller shall allow and shall require any subcontractor to allow the buyer, or his authorized representative access to their premises, at all reasonable times, to inspect the conditions and progress of manufacture, production, or testing of the equipment, prior to the delivery thereof.
>
> After any inspection or test, the buyer may reject the equipment or any component thereof, for any defect or nonconformance to the contract specification. Notice of rejection will be conveyed in writing and will state the respects in which the equipment is defective or not, in conformance with the contract specification. The seller shall promptly make good the defect or ensure that the equipment complies with the contract specifications.

When shipments are made on a documentary-collection basis, the buyer may wish to have the right to inspect the merchandise before accepting or paying the draft. If this will be the case, it must be clearly stipulated in the contract. Moreover, if the goods are defective, the contract should specify whether the buyer may buy them at a reduced price, or if they should be returned to the seller at the latter's expense.

The UCC provides that, unless otherwise agreed, the buyer of goods has the right to inspect them before acceptance and payment. The buyer is not, however, entitled to inspect the merchandise, if the contract provides for cash on delivery or payment against title documents unless, again, the contrary is specifically agreed on in the contract (UCC 2-513[1]). Some contracts may provide that while payment is to be made against title documents, it is not actually due until the goods are available for inspection. If the title document arrives before the goods (as it often does), the buyer is then not obligated to pay until the goods also arrive and are available for inspection (UCC 2-513, Comment 5).

In practice, it is often difficult or impossible for an importer receiving goods on a documents-against-payment basis to inspect them prior to payment. To claim goods from the carrier requires a negotiable bill of lading. To obtain the negotiable bill of lading, however, the importer must first pay the sight draft.

Arbitration and Jurisdiction of Disputes

If disputes arise between buyer and seller, they can be amicably settled between the parties, taken to court, or settled by arbitration. Unless disputes can be settled directly between the parties, the next best alternative is arbitration. Court procedures tend to be time consuming, costly, and sometimes judges may not be familiar with the specific practices of the industry and laws that apply to a particular case.

Advantages of Arbitration. Arbitration, on the other hand, is often faster and less costly than the courts, and the decision is made by people who are well informed about the practices and problems in the particular industry. The parties can, of course, always agree to arbitration after a dispute arises. It is safer, however, to include an arbitration clause in the sales agreement.

Arbitration Clause. The arbitration clause should specify an arbitration tribunal to which a dispute will be referred. There are many reputable arbitration associations, such as the International Chamber of Commerce, American Arbitration Association, Inter American Commercial Arbitration Commission, and many others. Some trade associations have their own arbitration tribunals. In addition to the number of arbitrators and their selection, the contract should specify the place where the arbitration is to be held, how the cost of the arbitration is to be divided, and the scope of the arbitration. Regarding this last point, the parties may wish to limit the scope to only certain parts of the contract or a specific aspect of a particular dispute.

Alternatively, it may be specified that arbitration applies to any possible conflict arising out of the sales contract. A sample arbitration clause follows:

> Any controversy between the parties arising out of or relating to this contract, or the breach thereof, shall be settled by arbitration according to the rules then prevailing of the American Arbitration Association or such other rules as it may designate. The American Arbitration Association is hereby authorized to make arrangements for any such arbitration to be held under such rules in New York, unless the parties hereto agree upon some other location. This contract shall be enforceable and judgment on any award rendered by all or a majority of the arbitrators may be entered in any court of any country having jurisdiction and, for this purpose, the parties hereby consent and agree that the courts of the State of New York have jurisdiction.
>
> To the extent that any controversy or claim arising out of the contract cannot be settled by arbitration as herein provided, the parties consent to the jurisdiction of the courts of the State of New York for the resolution of such controversy and/or adjudication of such claim.

Adjudication of Disputes. Note from the previous clause that any dispute that cannot be settled by arbitration shall be adjudicated by the courts of the State of New York. It is important, in any contract, that the parties define exactly under the laws of what country or state any dispute is to be adjudicated.

Patent Protection

The seller's products may be subject to patent protection and, as a result, he may wish to prevent the purchaser from duplicating the product or allowing it to be duplicated. Conversely, the buyer may wish to be protected against any patent infringement suit brought as a result of an infringement by the seller. In the latter case, a clause such as the following, might be included in the sales contract:

> The seller shall defend any suit or proceeding brought against the purchaser so far as based on a claim that the equipment or any part thereof constitutes an infringement of any patent. The seller shall pay all damages and costs awarded therein against the purchaser. In case said equipment or any part thereof is in such suit held to constitute infringement and the use of said equipment or part is enjoined, the seller shall at his own expense either procure for the purchaser the right to continue using said equipment or part, or modify it so it becomes noninfringing without affecting the quality or performance or any guarantees on the original article.

Trademarks

A "trademark" as defined in Section 45 of the 1945 Act, includes any word, name, symbol, device, or any combination of these, adopted and used by manufacturers or merchants to identify their goods and distinguish them from those manufactured or sold by others. In short, it is a brand name used on goods moving in channels of trade.

The primary function of a trademark is to distinguish one person's goods from those of another; but the trademark also serves to indicate to purchasers that the quality of the goods bearing the mark remains constant, and it serves as the focal point of advertising to create and maintain a demand for the product.

How Trademark Rights Are Established and Protected. Rights in a trademark are established by adoption and actual use of the mark on goods moving in trade. Use ordinarily must continue, if the rights are to be maintained. No rights exist until there has been actual use; and a trademark may not be registered until the goods bearing the mark have been sold or shipped in interstate, foreign, or territorial commerce.

A trademark may be owned by an individual, firm, partnership, corporation, association, or other collective group. The first U.S. trademark-registration act was passed in 1881. The present registration act was passed on July 5, 1946, effective July 5, 1947 (popularly known as the Lanham Act).

Trademark rights are protected under common law, but registration results in material advantages to the trademark owner. It constitutes notice of the registrant's claim of ownership, and it creates certain presumptions of ownership, validity, and exclusive right to use the mark on the goods listed in the registration. In Figure 6-2 applications are for trademark shown. The first is a corporate application, and the second is a partnership application.

Termination of Contract

Circumstances beyond the control of either the buyer or the seller may require a termination of the contract. If an excusable delay, for instance, becomes a permanent condition, it makes little sense to continue the contract. Similarly, if for any reason it becomes obvious that the seller cannot perform under the contract (even though the cause is nonexcusable), or if the buyer has become insolvent, there should be some kind of a provision for terminating the contract. A sample termination clause may read as follows:

> If any delay in delivery or failure in contractual performance, other than an excusable delay, shall continue for a consecutive period of 60 calendar days, the purchaser may, after giving the seller 30 days' notice in writing, at his option, terminate this contract as to any equipment not then completed. The purchaser may recover any amounts having been paid on account to the seller for equipment not completed and may at this option purchase other equipment or material of similar characteristics, charging the seller with any excess cost incurred by reason of such purchase.

(Instructions on reverse side)

SERVICE MARK APPLICATION, PRINCIPAL REGISTER, WITH DECLARATION (Corporation)	MARK *(identify the mark)* CLASS NO. *(if known)*

TO THE COMMISSIONER OF PATENTS AND TRADEMARKS:

NAME OF CORPORATION [1]

STATE OR COUNTRY OF INCORPORATION

BUSINESS ADDRESS OF CORPORATION

The above identified applicant has adopted and is using the service mark shown in the accompanying drawing[2] for the following services: ____

____,

and requests that said mark be registered in the United States Patent and Trademark Office on the Principal Register established by the Act of July 5, 1946.

The service mark was first used in connection with the services[3] on ______________ *(date)* ; was first used in connection with the services[3] rendered in ______________ *(type of commerce)* commerce[4] on ______________ *(date)* ; and is now in use in such commerce.

5

The mark is used by[6] ____

____

and five specimens showing the mark as actually used are presented herewith.

7

____,
(name of officer of corporation)

being hereby warned that willful false statements and the like so made are punishable by fine or imprisonment, or both, under Section 1001 of Title 18 of the United States Code and that such willful false statements may jeopardize the validity of the application or any registration resulting therefrom, declares that he/she is

____
(official title)

of applicant corporation and is authorized to execute this instrument on behalf of said corporation; he/she believes said corporation to be the owner of the service mark sought to be registered; to the best of his/her knowledge and belief no other person, firm, corporation, or association has the right to use said mark in commerce, either in the identical form or in such near resemblance thereto as may be likely, when applied to the services of such other person, to cause confusion, or to cause mistake, or to deceive; the facts set forth in this application are true; and all statements made of his/her own knowledge are true and all statements made on information and belief are believed to be true.

____
(name of corporation)

By ______________________________
(signature of officer of corporation, and official title of officer)

____
(date)

PTO Form 4.7a (Service Mark) (Corporation) — Patent and Trademark Office - U.S. DEPT. of COMMERCE

(over)

Figure 6-2. Application for trademark.

REPRESENTATION

If the applicant is not domiciled in the United States, a domestic representative must be designated. See Form 4.4.

If applicant wishes to furnish a power of attorney, see Form 4.2. An attorney at law is not required to furnish a power.

FOOTNOTES

1 If applicant is an association or other similar type of juristic entity, change "corporation" throughout to an appropriate designation.

2 If registration is sought for a word or numeral mark not depicted in any special form, the drawing may be the mark typed in capital letters on letter-size bond paper; otherwise, the drawing should be made with india ink on a good grade of bond paper or on bristol board. If the mark is of a nature that a drawing is not practicable, insert a description of the mark instead of reference to the drawing.

3 If more than one item of services in a class is set forth and the dates given for that class apply to only one of the items listed, insert the name of the item to which the dates apply.

4 Type of commerce should be specified as "interstate," "territorial," "foreign," or other type of commerce which may lawfully be regulated by Congress. Foreign applicants relying upon use must specify commerce which Congress may regulate, using wording such as commerce with the United States or commerce between the United States and a foreign country.

5 If the mark is other than a coined, arbitrary or fanciful mark, and the mark is believed to have acquired a secondary meaning, insert whichever of the following paragraphs is applicable:

a) The mark has become distinctive of applicant's services as a result of substantially exclusive and continuous use in ______________________ *(type of commerce)* commerce for the five years next preceding the date of filing of this application.

b) The mark has become distinctive of applicant's services as evidenced by the showing submitted separately.

6 State the manner or method of using the mark in the sale or advertising of the services.

7 The required fee of $35.00 for each class must be submitted. (An application to register the same mark for goods and/or services in more than one class may be filed; however, goods and/or services, and dates of use, by class, must be set out separately, and specimens and a fee for each class are required.)

Patent and Trademark Office - U.S. DEPT. of COMMERCE

Figure 6-2. *(Continued)*

(Instructions on reverse side)

SERVICE MARK APPLICATION, PRINCIPAL REGISTER, WITH DECLARATION (Partnership)	MARK *(identify the mark)*
	CLASS NO. *(if known)*

TO THE COMMISSIONER OF PATENTS AND TRADEMARKS:

NAME OF PARTNERSHIP

NAMES OF PARTNERS

BUSINESS ADDRESS OF PARTNERSHIP

CITIZENSHIP OF PARTNERS

The above identified applicant has adopted and is using the service mark shown in the accompanying drawing[1] for the following services: ______________________________

______________________________,

and requests that said mark be registered in the United States Patent and Trademark Office on the Principal Register established by the Act of July 5, 1946.

The service mark was first used in connection with the services[2] on ______________ *(date)*; was first used in connection with the services[2] rendered in ______________ *(type of commerce)* commerce[3] on ______________ *(date)*; and is now in use in such commerce.

4

The mark is used by[5] ______________________________

____

and five specimens showing the mark as actually used are presented herewith.

6

______________________________ *(name of partner)*,

being hereby warned that willful false statements and the like so made are punishable by fine or imprisonment, or both, under Section 1001 of Title 18 of the United States Code and that such willful false statements may jeopardize the validity of the application or any registration resulting therefrom, declares that he/she is a partner of applicant partnership; he/she believes said partnership to be the owner of the service mark sought to be registered; to the best of his/her knowledge and belief no other person, firm, corporation, or association has the right to use said mark in commerce, either in the identical form or in such near resemblance thereto as may be likely, when applied to the services of such other person, to cause confusion, or to cause mistake, or to deceive; the facts set forth in this application are true; and all statements made of his/her own knowledge are true and all statements made on information and belief are believed to be true.

______________________________ *(signature of partner)*

______________________________ *(date)*

PTO Form 4.7a (Service Mark) (Partnership) — Patent and Trademark Office - U.S. DEPT. of COMMERCE

(over)

Figure 6-2. *(Continued)*

PTO Form 4.7a (Service Mark) (Partnership)

REPRESENTATION

If the applicant is not domiciled in the United States, a domestic representative must be designated. See Form 4.4.

If applicant wishes to furnish a power of attorney, see Form 4.2. An attorney at law is not required to furnish a power.

FOOTNOTES

1 If registration is sought for a word or numeral mark not depicted in any special form, the drawing may be the mark typed in capital letters on letter-size bond paper; otherwise, the drawing should be made with india ink on a good grade of bond paper or on bristol board. If the mark is of a nature that a drawing is not practicable, insert a description of the mark instead of reference to the drawing.

2 If more than one item of services in a class is set forth and the dates given for that class apply to only one of the items listed, insert the name of the item to which the dates apply.

3 Type of commerce should be specified as "interstate," "territorial," "foreign," or other type of commerce which may lawfully be regulated by Congress. Foreign applicants relying upon use must specify commerce which Congress may regulate, using wording such as commerce with the United States or commerce between the United States and a foreign country.

4 If the mark is other than a coined, arbitrary or fanciful mark, and the mark is believed to have acquired a secondary meaning, insert whichever of the following paragraphs is applicable:

a) The mark has become distinctive of applicant's services as a result of substantially exclusive and continuous use in ______________________ *(type of commerce)* commerce for the five years next preceding the date of filing of this application.

b) The mark has become distinctive of applicant's services as evidenced by the showing submitted separately.

5 State the manner or method of using the mark in the sale or advertising of the services.

6 The required fee of $35.00 for each class must be submitted. (An application to register the same mark for goods and/or services in more than one class may be filed; however, goods and/or services, and dates of use, by class, must be set out separately, and specimens and a fee for each class are required.)

Patent and Trademark Office - U.S. DEPT. of COMMERCE

Figure 6-2. *(Continued)*

CHAPTER 7

Foreign Exchange Operations

Foreign exchange in the United States is very different today from what it was 25 years ago. In the early 1970s the bulk of foreign exchange trading involved either sight payments for import-export transactions or forward contracts to hedge time drafts denominated in foreign currencies. At that time, the bulk of trade for the United States was in U.S. dollars, and foreign currency fiduciary transactions were sporadic. Today there are many more types of operations that require foreign exchange, including new instruments for spot and future transactions used in both hedging and speculation. Edouard Balladur convinced the authorities in Brussels and other European central bankers to expand the band to 15% on either side of parity for European currencies. These changes, in fact, amounted to a depreciation of many currencies.

It is relevant to mention that foreign exchange is no longer the exclusive domain of large commercial banks but is being transacted with increasing frequency in small- and medium-sized banks. Multinational corporations and joint ventures are also trading with increasing frequency through their various subsidiaries in major money centers of the world (i.e., without going through local banks) in order to settle transactions or renew fiduciary investments.

EXCHANGE FLUCTUATIONS

For those who engage in international commerce, there are a variety of risks. One arises from the fact that each country has its own currency. When payments for goods, services, and investments have to be made across international boundaries, one currency must be exchanged for another.

The need to exchange currencies would cause no problem if the money of a particular country could always be bought and sold at a fixed and invariable price with the monies of all other countries. Unfortunately, the real world is more complicated. The price of one currency in terms of others usually undergoes continuous fluctuations simply because the currencies of the world, like other commodities, follow laws of supply and demand. On one particular day, for instance, there may be a strong demand for German marks, causing their price to rise against other currencies. This means that more dollars or other currencies may be required to buy a specific quantity of marks. On another day, the demand for marks may be weak, causing their price in terms of dollars and other currencies to decline.

The relationship that different currencies have to each other, that is, the ratio or rate at which one currency can be sold for another, undergoes constant fluctuation. Rates may change many times a day to reflect up-to-date supply and demand conditions of those who are in the market to buy or sell currencies. The specific rates at any one time represent a distillation of economic pressures (such as interest rates or the actions of a central bank), world news (weather, revolutions, etc.), and the basic interaction of all the financial markets.

Predictions of economists with respect to exchange rates are often at significant variance with what the market eventually determines those rates to be. Even granting that the tools with which economists work have been refined to a state of near adequacy, it must still be remembered that most economic predictions, including those of exchange rates, are based on probabilities, and that news, one of the biggest components of those probabilities, cannot by its very nature be known in advance. Political events in particular, such as decisions of parliaments, outcome of elections, or even mundane announcements of economic data, can obviously have an effect on the value of a nation's currency.

International Monetary Fund

In an effort to stabilize exchange rates, that is, to eliminate the sometimes wide and erratic fluctuations in the open market price for a particular currency, most of the countries of the world have joined in forming the IMF. Until the late 1960s, the IMF had substantial influence over the rates at which currencies could be exchanged.

Shortly after it was established in 1944, the IMF set parities or fixed prices for most currencies in terms of U.S. dollars. In turn, the U.S. dollar was tied to gold at $35 per ounce as far as international settlements between central banks were concerned. Then the Fund ruled that none of the currencies could deviate more than 1% on either side of the fixed price. To prevent its currency from fluctuating beyond the permitted parity band, each government was obligated to intervene in the free exchange markets.

In December 1961, at the so-called Smithsonian Agreement between key member nations of the IMF, the permitted band of fluctuation was widened to 2¼% on either side of parity. This change was the culmination of several years of turmoil in foreign exchange markets due to weakness of the U.S. dollar and relative strength of the West German mark, Japanese yen, and other currencies. While the 2¼% parity bands were in effect, governments were obligated to intervene to prevent exchange rates from moving outside those band limits. For instance, after the Smithsonian Agreement the British pound was set at a parity or central rate of $2.60547 per pound. This means that during the short period the agreement was in effect, the pound was not allowed to fluctuate outside the limits of $2.5471 and $2.6643. If demand for the pound was strong, its price against the dollar would rise. This meant that many people would want to buy pounds and get rid of their excess dollars. However, when the price approached the upper limit of $2.6643, the Bank of England would be obligated to intervene. It would do so by buying the excess dollars that people wanted to sell. Alternatively, when the demand for the pound was weak, people would try to buy dollars with their excess pounds. The price of pounds would drop until it approached the lower intervention point and the Bank of England would have to sell dollars and other convertible currencies that it had in reserve, thereby buying up the excess pounds that people wanted to sell.

Parity Changes

Until the late 1960s, the system established by the IMF worked successfully. Occasionally, however, there was so much buying or selling pressure on a currency that the respective central bank could or would no longer intervene. The result was a general downward or upward valuation of that currency against the dollar and, therefore, against all other currencies. Since the formation of the IMF, a few currencies were devalued against the dollar. Some experienced several devaluations over a number of years. A few strong currencies, during this period, were revalued one or more times, that is, their price in terms of the dollar and other currencies was increased.

Reliance on the U.S. Dollar

By now it should be clear that the monetary system set up by the IMF put great reliance on the U.S. dollar as the key currency. As long as the dollar remained strong, stable, and, for central banks, convertible into gold, it could be used as the standard for all other currencies. For a number of reasons, however—the large dollar investments abroad by U.S. companies, the recovery of Western Europe after World War II, and a deteriorating U.S. balance of trade—the dollar itself came under heavy selling pressure. Many people wanted to sell dollars and instead hold currencies that were strong at the time, such as the Japanese yen, West German mark, Dutch guilder, and so on. As these currencies reached their upper intervention levels, the respective central banks were forced to buy the excess dollars. In theory, the central banks could always trade in these dollars they bought for U.S. gold; in practice, however, the dollars held abroad totaled many times the U.S. gold resources at Fort Knox. It was obvious that if all the central banks attempted to exchange their excess dollars for gold, the United States would be forced to suspend gold payments.

This is exactly what happened in August 1971. In an effort to force other countries to revalue their currencies at more realistic exchange rates against the dollar, the United States suspended the redemption of dollars for gold. This left other countries the choice to do one of two things: (1) either to revalue their currencies upward to a point where dollars would stop flowing in or (2) to buy an unlimited supply of dollars to support their currencies at a cheaper parity.

Most major industrial countries adopted a combination of the two choices. They let their currency values float upward against the dollar; at the same time, to prevent too high a revaluation which would hurt their ability to export, and maintain more or less orderly conditions in the foreign exchange markets, central banks, from time to time, intervened on either the buying or selling side, as conditions warranted. The result of this development was the Smithsonian Agreement of 1971. In addition to widening the permitted band of currency fluctuations to 2 ¼% on either side of parity, the Smithsonian Agreement formalized a change in the basic parity of the U.S. dollar vis-à-vis some strong convertible currencies. During the fall of 1993, when the French franc was under constant pressure, the French government headed by Prime Minister Edouard Balladur convinced the authorities in Brussels and other European central bankers to expand the band to 15% on either side of parity for European currencies. These changes amounted to a *de facto* depreciation of many currencies.

Suspensions of IMF Parity Bands

Contrary to expectations, the Smithsonian Agreement did not resolve the international monetary problems that led up to its establishment. Corporations, banks, and individuals, usually for legitimate business purposes, continued to sell large quantities of dollars against such stronger currencies as Japanese yen, West German marks, and Swiss francs. The central banks of strong-currency countries were forced to buy enormous quantities of dollars to keep their currencies from moving outside the widened IMF parity bands.

Even a further devaluation of the U.S. dollar in early 1973 did not stop the heavy demand for stronger currencies. The result was that a number of countries decided to stop supporting the IMF parity bands and let their currencies float against the dollar. Specifically, several European countries decided to permit their currencies to float jointly against the dollar while maintaining a 2 ¼% maximum fluctuation against each other. These included West Germany, Belgium, the Netherlands, Luxembourg, Denmark, Norway, and Austria. Other countries decided individually to allow their currencies to float against the U.S. dollar.

The effect of these developments was, in fact, a suspension of previous IMF parity bands. Most major currencies were allowed to float freely against the dollar as dictated by fundamental forces of supply and demand. Governments were no longer prepared to buy or sell dollars or other currencies to keep their own currencies within relatively narrow parity bands. Governments would, however, intervene in the exchange markets at their own option to prevent erratic fluctuations and help provide orderly market conditions.

It is likely that the present system of freely floating rates, guided only by supply and demand forces, will remain a viable long-term solution. This seems borne out by higher levels of speculation, which can have a stabilizing effect on exchange rates, a growing number of financial instruments that involve various currencies, and even the speed with which large transactions can be effected, all of which directly affect short-term supply and demand.

One thing that can be predicted with certainty is that exchange rates will continue to fluctuate, with specific currencies experiencing alternating phases of relative strength and weakness. Different rates of inflation in various countries, as well as different interest rate structures, will maintain their influence on imports and exports of goods and capital. In the short term, exchange rates must fluctuate to compensate for day-to-day changes in supply and demand. In the long term, exchange rates usually have to adjust to reflect fundamental changes in the balance of payments positions of various countries.

Later in this chapter, we examine how exporters, importers, and foreign investors may protect themselves against exchange fluctuations. The more we may expect exchange rates to fluctuate, the more important such protection becomes for the orderly and prosperous conduct of international commerce.

EXCHANGE CONTROLS

For a number of reasons, including the stabilization of their currencies, many governments have, at some time, resorted to exchange controls. This often means that the central bank assumes the task of restricting the free movement of currencies by becoming either buyer or seller for all foreign exchange transactions. Most other foreign exchange trading firms and traders are eliminated. Thus, for example, when importers must settle the cost of imports, their banks must obtain the required foreign exchange directly from the central bank where it may or may not be available. Such an encumbrance of foreign exchange usually isolates that nation's currency and brings about its depreciation on world foreign exchange markets.

Purpose

The purpose of exchange controls may be varied, depending on the needs of the particular country imposing them. Controls have been imposed by different countries for the following reasons:

To regulate the import and export of certain types of goods (e.g., prevent importation of luxuries and make sure sufficient exchange is available for such essentials as foods, raw materials, and industrial machinery).

To provide a means of allocating scarce foreign exchange resources.

To prevent the flight of capital from a specific country/currency.

To prevent an excessive inflow of foreign currencies.

It is interesting to note that, historically, most exchange controls have been imposed by countries with limited foreign exchange resources who had to regulate the outflow of exchange. More recently, a number of industrially advanced countries, such as Switzerland, have imposed restrictions to prevent the speculative inflow of foreign currencies. The sudden inflow of large amounts of foreign currency not only increases the exchange rate of a nation's currency, which affects its exports, but it also opens up greater downside risk for the currency when the exchange rates begin to move in the other direction.

The underlying reason why exchange controls are deemed necessary is the unwillingness of governments to allow free play to the market forces of supply and demand. Without exchange controls, currencies would appreciate or depreciate to their "natural" levels in relation to other currencies. Such a situation would, of course, frustrate many a domestic economic, anti-inflationary, or development policy.

Many more types of exchange controls than those cited below are possible. Indeed, governments have been most ingenious in thinking up new methods of preventing undesirable inflows or outflows of currencies. Their ingenuity is surpassed only by that of speculators, merchants, and investors who manage to find loopholes through which they can legally circumvent the restrictions. Of course, every time a loophole is found, the respective government has the option of imposing a new round of restrictions in an endeavor to close the opening.

Types of Controls

Since exchange controls may have a substantial impact on the activities of foreign merchants and investors, a brief look at some of the most commonly used is useful.

Import Licensing. To prevent undesirable imports, particularly luxuries or products that would compete with infant local industries, some countries require importers to obtain a government license approving a specific import. Only desirable imports are licensed in unlimited amounts. Less desirable goods may be limited by quantity restrictions or excluded altogether.

To discourage the importation of certain types of goods, some governments require that importers place a local currency cash deposit with a commercial or central bank for a fixed period of time before a valid import license will be issued. Specific requirements vary, of course, depending on the country that has established such a regulation. Different deposit percentages may be required for various classes of goods. Moreover, the specific requirements may vary, depending on the country of origin of goods imported. Some governments have imposed deposit requirements as high as 10,000% of the value of the imported merchandise.

Tariffs and Quota Restrictions. The importation of luxuries, as well as goods that would compete unduly with local industries, may be limited by a high tariff. Absolute quantity restrictions concerning the amount of goods that may be imported over a given period, say one year, may also be imposed. Low tariffs may be charged on goods considered to be desirable imports contributing to a country's economic development.

Multiple Exchange Rates. A large number of countries have resorted to a system of multiple exchange rates as a control mechanism. This system may be used to encourage exports and tourism, on one hand, and to control the outflow of currencies for undesirable foreign expenditures, on the other. Multiple exchange rates may also be used by countries with strong currencies to limit the inflow of money for speculative or investment purposes.

Countries employing a system of multiple exchange rates to preserve and allocate scarce foreign exchange typically set a more favorable rate for desirable imports, such as essential food items, commodities, and industrial equipment. These types of products can, therefore, be imported relatively cheaply, since the foreign exchange required for their purchase can be obtained through the local central bank at a relatively favorable rate of exchange. Foreign exchange for imported goods that are considered less desirable is sold by the central bank only at a relatively high price. Since more of the importer's domestic currency units are required to buy such goods, their importation is discouraged. Several different exchange rates may exist in some countries for imports of different product categories.

During the currency turbulences discussed earlier, a number of industrially developed countries adopted multiple exchange rates to discourage the inflow of foreign currencies for investment and speculative purposes. Several governments established a separate exchange rate to be used only for trade transactions. This rate remains fairly stable and is allowed to fluctuate only within relatively narrow bands. If a rate threatens to move outside the band, the government intervenes on either the selling or buying side as necessary. The rate applicable for exchange transactions into and out of the currency for purposes of investment and speculation, in contrast, is allowed to float freely according to market supply and demand.

When a currency is relatively strong, exporters may benefit from a dual-rate structure, since foreign importers can obtain the required currency at a supported price that may be lower than the freely floating rate. Moreover, since rates established for trade transactions are only allowed to fluctuate within narrow limits, the chance of losses due to violent fluctuations is minimized. Those who demand a particular currency for investment or speculative purposes, on the other hand, are asked to pay a dearer rate of exchange. Moreover, since the rate for nontrade transactions is allowed to fluctuate freely according to market forces, the danger of losses resulting from sudden, unanticipated fluctuations is increased. The dearer price for the currency and greater uncertainty surrounding it has tended to limit speculative inflows.

Capital Controls. Countries wishing to stem speculative inflows of currencies have also imposed capital restrictions. Germany, for instance, required its residents who borrowed money abroad for purposes other than financing of trade transactions to place a substantial portion of the borrowed money with the central bank in a noninterest-bearing deposit. The ability of local banks to pay interest on deposits from nonresidents has also been curtailed in a number of countries. Some countries have even imposed a negative interest rate for certain deposits by nonresidents. Nonresidents may also be prohibited from buying certain local currency-denominated bonds and real estate.

Waiting Lists. Those countries with scarce foreign exchange resources have resorted to the simple device of a waiting list to allocate the limited exchange available. Local importers who wish to pay for purchased goods or for goods they plan to buy from abroad have to apply at the local central bank or finance ministry for the needed exchange. They are then put on a waiting list. Once exchange becomes available, the necessary conversion may be made and the foreign exporter will receive payment. Before that time, however, the payment in local currency remains in a blocked account in a local bank.

IMPLICATIONS FOR TRADERS

What do various exchange controls and recent monetary developments mean to those firms engaged in international trade and investment?

Wider Fluctuations

Before the floating of major currencies, the international merchant and investor could find some comfort in the narrow range of fluctuations allowed by the IMF. This is no longer true, since fluctuations are, at present, governed primarily by free market forces of supply and demand. Day-to-day as well as long-term fluctuations in the prices of various currencies are bound to be substantially wider than they were before. Therefore, the risk for the merchant and investor of not covering foreign exchange exposure has become greater.

Price of Imports and Exports

Goods that are imported from countries whose currencies have been valued upward are likely to be more expensive; consequently, goods exported to these countries will be cheaper for the foreign importers. The relative competitive position of importers and exporters in world markets, therefore, changes accordingly.

Covering and Hedging

Due to possibly wider exchange fluctuations, greater uncertainties in the exchange markets, and exchange controls, it may be more difficult for merchants and investors to cover or hedge their currency risks. Banks and other institutions that are willing to cover exchange risks for commercial firms may require a wider profit margin to compensate for additional risks. Forward contracts for certain currencies or maturities may not be readily available. Exchange controls in some countries may even make it impossible or very expensive to cover or hedge by buying a foreign currency at spot and then depositing the proceeds at a local bank until needed.

Direct Investment

The desire of some countries to limit the inflow of foreign funds may make it more difficult for companies who wish to set up or expand foreign subsidiaries and affiliates. Restrictions by some countries inhibiting the outflow of capital have made it harder for investors to send money abroad. Multiple exchange rates may make currencies bought for purposes of investment more expensive than currencies bought in payment for imports.

Scarcity of Exchange

Exporters who sell to countries with limited foreign exchange resources may find it difficult to get payment in hard currency. Local currency may be in a blocked account. The waiting line for local currency to be converted may be several months, or even years.

Continuing Uncertainty

Whatever new monetary systems evolve over the years, it is obvious that currency values will continue to fluctuate relative to one another, reflecting supply and demand conditions. Countries seem more willing to allow their currencies to float for prolonged periods of time to help them overcome fundamental payment disequilibria. Besides, intervention from central banks, even on a massive scale, has not always been successful. Major moves in foreign exchange are often only temporarily slowed by such action. The international merchant and investor will, therefore, have to pay careful attention to foreign exchange risks and opportunities.

THE MARKET FOR FOREIGN EXCHANGE

Recent developments have shown that, in the long run, no governmental action or international agreement can overrule the basic laws of supply and demand. It will, therefore, be useful to examine those factors that constitute the supply and demand for foreign exchange.

Supply

On the supply side, there is first the export of goods and services. If goods are sold abroad, the importing company will first pay for them with its local currency. But the importing company has to eventually buy dollars with its own currency or the U.S. exporter who receives foreign currency as payment has to sell against dollars. In either case, the amount of foreign currencies offered in the market will increase.

The same effect will result if foreigners purchase anything else from the United States, such as real estate, stocks, or bonds. Again, dollars must be purchased with local currencies, thus putting more of these currencies on the market.

Interest and dividends earned on U.S. capital lent or invested abroad will also increase the supply of foreign exchange. The same is true for the repayment of dollar loans made abroad and repatriations of previously invested capital. In all these cases, foreign currency has to be sold for dollars, thus augmenting the supply of foreign currencies in the exchange market.

There are other sources of foreign exchange supply, such as foreign tourist spending in the United States, gold exports, and so on. The idea is the same, however. Foreigners wish to buy or repay something for which they need dollars. To do this, they must offer their local currencies in the market, thereby increasing the supply of foreign exchange.

Demand

On the demand side, there is the import of goods and services from abroad. Either the U.S. importer has to make payment in a foreign currency or the foreign exporter must convert dollars into local currency. In either case, there will be a market demand for foreign exchange.

A large source of demand for foreign exchange has been for U.S. investments abroad. United States companies can normally generate only dollars. But factories using local labor and materials must pay in local currency. Consequently, U.S. companies investing overseas wish to buy foreign exchange for dollars, thus generating heavy demand.

The demand for foreign exchange is really the mirror image of the demand for supply, such as the spending of U.S. tourists abroad, interest and dividends on foreign capital invested in the United States, repayment by U.S. residents of loans contracted in other currencies, and gold imports.

The Marketplace

A marketplace for foreign exchange is, in essence, any place where foreign exchange is bought and sold in large amounts. The major markets today are in large cities, such as London, New York, Frankfort, Amsterdam, Milan, and others. The marketplaces, as well as individual banks and dealers, are linked with a modern communication network consisting of telephones, telexes, and computers. Buy and sell transactions can be negotiated and executed in a matter of seconds.

Role of Banks

Banks play the most important role in foreign exchange markets. When a company wishes to buy or sell foreign exchange, it will most probably contact its bank. Each bank that is active in the exchange market has several *nostro* accounts (foreign currency accounts) with banks abroad in each major country. Balances maintained in these *nostro* accounts may be considered an inventory of foreign exchange that can be drawn on to fill customers' demands. Alternatively, these accounts are replenished with foreign exchange bought from customers. Banks usually have credit lines from their correspondents abroad. If a heavy demand for a particular currency exhausts a bank's *nostro* accounts, it can often borrow or go into overdraft for a short period of time.

Foreign Exchange Traders

Each bank that is active in exchange trading has traders that buy and sell foreign currencies. These traders are very attuned to the market, since they are in contact not only with their customers, but also with other domestic banks, brokers, and foreign banks. If a customer wishes to buy or sell foreign exchange, a bank trader quotes a price and agrees to the transaction immediately. As soon thereafter as practicable, however, some traders try to find a counterpart for that purchase or sale. Thus, if a customer bought, say, $1 million worth of German marks, the bank's trader might try to buy from another bank, broker, or customer the same amount of marks sold, so that the bank's position remains even. For its services as a middleman the bank earns the spread between the bid and asked price.

Occasionally, when a trader is very confident in an expected price movement, a trader may also take a long or short position in one or more currencies. If he gambles on a long position, he buys more of a particular currency than he sells. Conversely, if he expects a downward movement in the price of a currency he may go short, selling more of the currency than he buys. If the trader's bullish or bearish expectations come true, a profit is earned. On the other hand, if there is a price movement opposite from the one expected, losses may be substantial.

INSTRUMENTS OF FOREIGN EXCHANGE

Working closely with the exchange traders usually involves a bank's remittance department, which sends and receives from abroad remittances on behalf of customers.

Remittances Abroad

For outgoing remittances, the customer or remitting party, which may be a domestic correspondent bank acting on behalf of its customer, pays in domestic currency, either by issuing a check to the remitting bank or authorizing the bank to debit his account. The bank then makes the remittance abroad via a foreign correspondent bank.

U.S. Dollar Remittances. One alternative is to credit the foreign correspondent's U.S. dollar account with the amount of the remittance and, at the same time, send it an advice by air mail, giving the name and address of the beneficiary and asking the foreign correspondent to make payment in its local currency at the prevailing rate of exchange. In this case, the foreign correspondent bank makes the conversion into foreign currency.

Foreign Currency Remittances. Another alternative is for the domestic remitting bank itself to make the conversion to foreign currency. In this case, the remittance department may issue and sell for dollars a foreign currency draft drawn on its overseas correspondent with which it has a local currency (*nostro*) account. Alternatively, it may telex the correspondent, asking it to pay the beneficiary in local currency and debit of its *nostro* account. In either case, the actual conversion to foreign currency is performed by computer, telegraphic transfer, mail remittance, or a foreign currency draft. The basic principle, in all cases, is the same: The remitting bank sells the needed foreign exchange for dollars. It uses for the sale the inventory of *nostro* balances that it maintains with banks in countries whose currency is sold. The communication merely instructs the foreign correspondent to debit the *nostro* account of the remitting bank and pay the amount to the beneficiary.

Service for Domestic Correspondents. Large, international U.S. banks offer a foreign currency draft service to domestic correspondents. Small- and medium-sized banks find it too costly to maintain an inventory of foreign exchange in the form of *nostro* accounts abroad. Drafts may, therefore, be drawn in a domestic correspondent's own name on *nostro* accounts maintained by a large bank with its overseas correspondents. The domestic correspondent is thereby able to sell foreign currency drafts to customers who require them. After selling a draft to a customer, the domestic correspondent notifies the large bank so that the latter knows a drawing has been made on one of its *nostro* accounts. The large bank, in turn, notifies its overseas correspondent to authorize the drawing. At the same time, it debits the dollar equivalent to the account that the domestic correspondent maintains on its books. The latter will, of course, in turn, charge the dollar account of its customer who bought the foreign currency draft.

Under this service, the foreign correspondent must be specifically authorized to honor the drawing. Occasionally, it may occur that the draft arrives at the overseas bank before the authorization. This may happen when the person requesting the draft flies directly overseas and promptly presents the draft at the drawee bank. Whenever a potential danger exists that the draft may arrive before the authorization, it is wise to request that the overseas bank be advised by telex rather than mail.

For the convenience of domestic correspondents, large banks periodically issue rate sheets giving fixed buying and selling rates for exchange of major currencies. These publications may be used for exchange transactions involving small amounts up to $5,000 or $10,000, depending on the currency. The prices on the rate sheet will, of course, be at least a day old, but the differences will usually be nominal. For larger transactions, domestic correspondents should contact the foreign exchange traders of the large bank by telephone or telex to get an up-to-date quotation.

Incoming Remittances

Incoming remittances for domestic customers may be received either in dollars or foreign currency.

Dollar Remittances. If received in dollars, the beneficiary can be promptly paid, either by crediting his account or issuing a check. In this case, the conversion has already been made by the foreign remitting bank that maintains a dollar account in the United States.

Foreign Currency Remittances. Foreign-currency payments may be received by mail, cable, telex, computer, or draft. The basic procedure of making the conversion into U.S. dollars is the same in all cases.

Mail and Cable Remittances. If the remittance is transacted in a foreign currency, the remittance department receives advice by mail or telex that its *nostro* account with a foreign correspondent has been credited. The remittance department, again in consultation with the foreign exchange traders, makes the conversion to domestic currency and pays the beneficiary, either by issuing a check or crediting his account. Sometimes, a merchant may not wish to convert foreign currency receipts into dollars. A merchant may, for instance, have a payment to make in the same currency and, therefore, wishes to avoid two conversions. For this reason, banks will usually consult with recipients of foreign currency before converting the funds to dollars. In some countries with exchange controls, however, nonresidents may not maintain local currency deposits; in these cases, a conversion into dollars may become mandatory.

Instructions to the Bank. Exporters who invoice in foreign currencies will frequently be beneficiaries of foreign currency remittances. If exporters do not maintain an account abroad, they should instruct the importer from whom payment is due to place the currency with a specified local bank for the account of their U.S. bank. The latter will, in turn, pay the exporter an equivalent amount of dollars at the current rate of exchange. If at all possible, the U.S. bank should be advised of the date on which its *nostro* account will be credited. In this manner it can plan its foreign exchange position and pay out dollars to the beneficiary on the same day.

When customers cannot advise the exact date when funds will be received, their U.S. banks will generally not be able to credit their accounts with dollars until one or more days later. Thus, the beneficiary incurs the opportunity loss of not having the immediate use of the funds.

Sometimes, a beneficiary who knows exactly when he will receive foreign exchange will shop with a number of banks to obtain the best conversion rate. The bank giving the highest bid will get the business. The buying bank then tells the beneficiary the name of the overseas correspondent with which the money should be deposited to the credit of its *nostro* account. The beneficiary should then telex the overseas remitter to give instructions as to when and where the money should be deposited.

Sight Drafts. Beneficiaries may also receive payment by means of a foreign currency draft. This is, in fact, a check drawn on a local bank of the country in whose currency it is denominated. These drafts can be sold for domestic currency to a U.S. bank. The latter then sends the draft to the foreign bank for collection, that is, for having the proceeds credited to one of its *nostro* accounts or converted into dollars and debited to a dollar account that a foreign bank keeps on the books for the U.S. bank. In either case, it usually takes several days before the domestic bank will have available the proceeds for the foreign currency draft. To reflect this time delay in obtaining the money, foreign currency drafts may be bought at a slightly less favorable rate of exchange than immediately available money, such as telex or computer transfers.

Time Drafts. Time drafts denominated in foreign currencies may be discounted by the U.S. bank. This way, the U.S. exporter can immediately obtain the face value of the draft minus discount charges. Many merchants prefer to discount their drafts to obtain immediate cash. When a U.S. bank discounts a time draft (as well as when it buys a sight draft), it usually retains full recourse to the beneficiary in case of eventual nonpayment by the drawee.

Generalized Procedure. Whether beneficiaries are advised by telex or mail that foreign currency has been credited to accounts at their disposal at foreign banks, or whether they receive a foreign currency draft, the principle of making the conversion is the same: A domestic bank buys the foreign currency represented by the telegraphic or mail transfer or foreign currency draft. The foreign bank is instructed to debit the account of the seller or to exchange and credit the amount to the *nostro* account of the buying bank. The latter's inventory of foreign exchange is thus increased.

Other instruments of foreign exchange often sold to domestic banks include foreign travelers' checks and dividend and interest coupons denominated in foreign currency.

Alternative Instruments

As explained in the previous section, money can be remitted from one country to another by cable transfer, telex, computer, mail, or draft. The fastest method, telex or computer, is the most advisable when relatively large amounts are involved. The time and interest saved can be substantial.

The basic rate at which banks buy and sell foreign exchange is the telegraphic transfer (TT) rate. Buying rates for mail transfers, foreign currency drafts, travelers' checks, and similar instruments are all based on the TT rate, but may be slightly less favorable to reflect the greater time required for collection. Foreign currency usance drafts are also bought based on the TT rate, but interest to maturity is deducted for the time that still has to elapse until maturity.

TYPES OF TRANSACTIONS

Spot Exchange

When foreign exchange is bought and sold for immediate delivery (in one or two business days), the transaction takes place in the so-called spot market. If a merchant buys French francs for spot delivery, for instance, the selling bank instructs its Paris branch or French correspondent bank to hold the francs at the merchant's disposal. The merchant may then give further instructions, such as for the money to be used to invest in French securities or to pay a named French exporter who has recently shipped merchandise. There are two basic methods of quoting exchange rates:

1 Quotes of the number of units of domestic currency that are required to buy one unit of foreign currency: For instance, if the U.S. dollar is the domestic currency, it may take $1.9210 to buy one pound sterling, $0.6470 to buy one German mark, $0.1931 to buy one French franc, and so on.
2 Quotes of the number of units of foreign currency that may be purchased with one unit of domestic currency: Hence, one U.S. dollar may buy 0.5205 pound sterling, 1.5455 German marks, or 5.1795 French francs.

In the United States, it is common practice to use the first method. This means that foreign exchange is quoted in the cents or in the dollars and cents required to buy one unit of foreign currency.

Spot exchange is sold at the spot rate. Actually, each bank or dealer, at any one time, is prepared to quote two spot rates for each currency: one at which the bank or dealer is willing to buy and the other at which the bank or dealer is willing to sell. Spot sterling may, for example, be quoted as $1.9210–12. Thus, a bank buying sterling may bid $1.9210 for each pound. When selling sterling, however, the bank will demand a larger amount of dollars, that is, $1.9212 for each pound it sells. The buying rate is also called the bid rate, while the selling rate may be referred to as the offered rate. The small spread between the bid and offered rate is determined by the market and represents the collective judgment of exchange dealers as to what their profit margin should be, given the degree of risk they see in the transaction.

Future Exchange

Many times, merchants have a need to buy or sell exchange at an approximate or exact date in the future. They may, for instance, have entered into a sales contract whereby they are obligated to deliver goods in three months, with payment to be received in a foreign currency on the date of delivery. If exporters know that in three months they will receive a certain sum of foreign exchange, they will probably want to sell against their own currency. Alternatively, importers may contract to receive merchandise in one month, with payment in a foreign currency due 30 days after delivery. Hence, they know that in two months a certain amount of foreign exchange will be needed.

When foreign traders know that they will have to either buy or sell foreign exchange at a certain time in the future, they can simply wait until that future time arrives and make their purchase or sale in the prevailing spot market. Alternatively, they can buy or sell the exchange immediately, but for delivery at a certain point in the future. The latter type of purchase or sale takes place in the future market. Thus, exporters who know they will receive foreign exchange in three months are able to sell future receipts that day, but for delivery in three months. Importers who are aware that they will need exchange in two months can buy it now, but for delivery in two months, that is, when it is actually needed.

When dealing in future or forward exchange, delivery of the currency and the counterpart funds is not made until the specified future date. The price to be paid for the currency, however, is fixed immediately at the time of sale.

The future exchange market is a separate market involving the sale or purchase of foreign currencies for delivery at a stipulated time in the future. Typical future dates for which exchange may be bought and sold are one, two, three, and six months. This means that actual delivery of the currency bought or sold, as well as of the counterpart funds, takes place exactly in the stated number of months from the contract date of the future contract.

Odd Dates. In most important currencies, future transactions can also be arranged for so-called odd dates. Thus, if I know that in exactly 43 days I will need a certain amount of Swiss francs, my bank may be able to sell them to me today for future delivery in exactly 43 days.

Option Dates. Often a merchant knows only approximately when a certain amount of exchange will be needed. To satisfy those needs, banks are often willing to execute future exchange option contracts. A typical option period is one month. Other option dates may, however, also be available to satisfy specific needs.

Through an option contract, a bank's customer is given the option of delivering or receiving the currency in question (depending on whether the contract is to sell or buy) at any time during a specifically defined period. While customers have some choice as to *when* they may receive or deliver the exchange, they *are* obligated to receive or deliver at some time during the period stipulated. Thus, the option is only for the delivery date and does not give the customer the right to cancel out of the contract altogether.

Due to exchange restrictions, banks may be unwilling to write option contracts in certain currencies. It may be especially difficult to write options in currencies of countries that prohibit or limit deposits in local currencies by foreign institutions.

Close-Outs. Occasionally, a bank's client may not want to take delivery of future exchange for which he has contracted. Alternatively, a client who has sold exchange for future delivery may not be in a position to deliver the amount contracted. When this occurs, the bank closes out the contract at spot rates prevailing when the decision not to make delivery was made. For instance, if all or part of a merchant's forward purchase of exchange is not taken up, the bank buys it back at its prevailing spot rate. Any difference between the original forward selling rate and the current spot buying rate is debited or credited to the customer's account.

Future Rates. Just as banks quote spot rates for each major currency, they also quote separate rates for future transactions. Not only must buy and sell rates be quoted for each currency, but the rates also differ, depending on how far into the future the delivery is to take place. The buy and sell rates for delivery of sterling in three months are usually different from the respective rates for delivery in one month.

Depending on market conditions, expectations of traders and speculators, and differences in interest rates between countries, future rates may be higher or lower than the respective spot rate for each currency. If future rates are higher, the currency is said to be selling at a premium in the future market. Such a premium may reflect a strong currency and expectations by traders and investors that spot rates may be moving upward in the near future. If future rates are quoted below the respective spot rate, the currency in the future market is said to be selling at a discount. This may reflect a weak currency and expectations that spot rates may be moving lower.

Occasionally, future rates may also be the same as spot rates. The spread between buying and selling rates, however, is always wider in the future market. Therefore, the future rate can only be equal to the spot rate on either the selling or buying side. A typical future quote may thus read "par—five points discount." This means that the selling side is at par, that is, the same as the spot rate; the buying side is at five points discount from the respective spot rate.

While the relative strength or weakness of a currency can sometimes be gauged by whether its future rates are at a premium or discount, this is not *always* the case. As discussed later, premiums or discounts are also related to market interest rate differentials in the two countries involved. Currencies of countries with relatively high interest rates tend to sell at a future discount, while currencies of countries with relatively low interest rates tend to sell at a forward premium.

Price Quotations. A future rate may be quoted either as an outright price or as a discount or premium over spot. An outright quote is merely a direct statement of the number of dollars and cents required to buy one unit of the exchange for future delivery at a specified date or during a specified option period. The outright quote is usually used in transactions between banks and their customers.

Quotations in terms of discount or premium over spot are usually made in the interbank market and between banks and brokers. Since spot rates are often quoted to four decimal points, the premium or discount is quoted in number of points over or under spot. One point is equivalent to $0.0001. Hence, if the bank's bid (buying) rate for spot sterling is 1.9689, while the three months future bid rate is 1.9639, the future sterling is said to be selling at a discount of 50 points. If three months sterling is quoted at 30 points premium on the bid side, based on the same spot rate, the forward rate would be 1.9719.

Premiums and discounts over spot may also be applied to the offered (selling) side of spot rates. Hence, a quote for spot sterling, as well as for selected future dates, may read as follows:

	Buying	Selling
Spot (Dec. 1)	$1.9689	$1.9692
One month	65	60 discount
Two months	100	93 discount
Three months	190	182 discount
Six months	380	370 discount

To get the outright forward rate, the points, expressed as a decimal, are added to the spot rate when forward exchange is selling at a premium.

Conversely, when forward exchange is selling at a discount, the points, expressed as a decimal, are subtracted from the spot rate.

Since predictions of changes in exchange rates are increasingly uncertain as they project further into the future, the spread between a bank's sell and buy rates tends to become wider for delivery dates that extend further into the future than normal (routine) forward exchange transactions. From the customer's point of view, the "cheapest" way of buying and selling future exchange is for one of the standard periods, that is, one, two, three, or six months. Odd dates and option contracts, however, give the customer added flexibility but may be more difficult and risky for the bank. Consequently, odd dates and option contracts may prove to be more expensive than standard dates.

Quotes on Options. When giving option rates to customers, the bank always quotes the rate most favorable to itself during the option period. This is natural, since the customer can exercise the option at any time during the specified period. The bank must therefore assume that the customer will exercise the option at a time most unfavorable to the bank. If, for instance, a bank's spot selling rate for sterling is $1.9692 and the *discount* for one, two, and three months is 60, 93, and 182 points, respectively, customers wishing an option to buy sterling at any time during the three-month period would be charged $1.9692 for each pound. The customers would not therefore get the benefit of the discount existing on the future sterling. If they wish an option to buy sterling at any time during the third month, the rate would be $1.9599, that is, the bank's spot selling rate minus the 93 points discount prevailing at the end of the second month.

To take another illustration, assume the spot selling rate for sterling is $1.9692 and future sterling is selling at a *premium* of 6, 11, and 15 points for one, two, and three months, respectively. An option contract allowing the customer to take delivery of the sterling at any time during the three months would cost $1.9707 per pound (the $1.9692 spot rate plus 15 points of premium for three months sterling). This means that customers would have to pay the full premium prevailing on three months sterling. Again, the bank assumes that the option will be exercised at the most unfavorable time for itself, that is, at the end of the three-month period. Similarly, if the customer wishes an option to buy sterling any time during the second month, the price would be $1.9703 (the spot rate plus 11 points premium).

Similar rate calculations for option contracts can be made for customers wishing to sell sterling. Assume, for instance, the bank's buying rate for forward sterling is at a discount of 65, 100, and 190 basis points for one, two, and three months respectively, and the bank's spot buying rate is $1.9689. A customer wishing an opportunity to sell the bank sterling at any time during the three months would be quoted a rate of $1.9499 for each pound (the bank's spot buying rate of $1.9689 minus the discount of 190 basis points for three months sterling). The bank assumes that the option will be exercised at the time most disadvantageous to itself, that is, at the end of the option period.

Cost of Future Contracts. A person buying or selling exchange for future delivery generally has the option of alternatively consummating the transaction in the spot market. A merchant who needs a foreign currency in three months, for instance, may buy it immediately in the spot market and deposit the proceeds with a foreign bank until needed. (Exchange controls designed to keep foreign currencies out may make this option impossible in some countries.) The interest differential of keeping the exchange on deposit in foreign currency rather than in dollars may, therefore, be compared to the alternative cost of buying the exchange for future delivery. Similarly, a merchant expecting to receive payment in a foreign currency in three months may be able to borrow an equal amount of foreign currency and immediately convert it into dollars at the spot rate. When the actual foreign currency receivable comes in three months, it can be used to liquidate the loan. Again, it will be of interest to compare the cost of borrowing minus the interest that may be obtained by depositing dollars for three months, with the alternative cost of selling the exchange in the forward market for three months delivery.

For reasons previously outlined, it is desirable to express the premium or discount of forward exchange as a percent per annum. This can be done by using a simple formula:

$$\frac{\text{Discount or Premium} \times 1200}{\text{Spot rate} \times \text{number of months of future contract}} = \%\text{ per annum}$$

For instance, if three months forward sterling is selling at a discount of 182 points at 2.331 (the spot rate is 2.3513), the calculations would be as follows:

$$\frac{0.0182 \times 1200}{2.3513 \times 3} = \frac{7.2800}{} = 3.10\%\text{ per annum discount}$$

Alternatively, if one month sterling is selling at a premium of 40 points at \$2.3553 (the spot rate is \$2.3513), the calculation would be as follows:

$$\frac{0.0040 \times 1200}{2.3513 \times 1} = \frac{4.8000}{2.3513} = 2.04\%\text{ per annum premium}$$

Swap Transactions

A swap involves simultaneous transactions in both the spot and future markets in opposite directions. It may, alternatively, involve two simultaneous transactions in the future market in opposite directions.

Types of Swaps. A swap involving a simultaneous spot and future transaction takes on one of two generalized forms:

A purchase of spot exchange with a simultaneous sale of future exchange in the same currency and amount. Hence, for whatever reason, a businessman or banker may wish to purchase one million German marks in the spot market but simultaneously sell them back for delivery in, say, three months.

A sale of spot exchange with a simultaneous purchase of the same amount and currency for future delivery. A businessman or banker may thus wish to sell one million marks at spot and simultaneously buy them back for future delivery at a fixed date.

Swap Rates. A "swap rate" may be defined as the margin between the spot and forward rates of exchange of a particular swap transaction. It is expressed in terms of a premium or a discount as compared to the spot rate or may be converted to a per annum percentage. The latter is calculated with the same formula used when expressing a forward premium or discount as a percent per annum.

A swap transaction yields a premium

1 If the spot exchange is bought while simultaneously the future exchange is sold at a premium over spot.
2 If the spot exchange is sold while, at the same time, the future exchange is bought at a discount.

A swap transaction yields a discount

1 If the spot exchange is bought while the future exchange is simultaneously sold at a discount.
2 If the spot exchange is sold while, at the same time, the future exchange is bought at a premium.

As an example, assume that quotes for German marks for selected dates are as follows:

	Buying	Selling
Spot	0.3117	0.3119
One Month	8	10 premium
Three Months	20	25 premium
Six Months	35	43 premium

Given this rate structure, if a merchant or banker buys spot marks at market rates he has to pay $0.3119 for each mark. If he simultaneously sells marks for delivery in six months, he will receive $0.3154 for each mark (the spot rate plus 35 points premium). The swap premium, expressed as a percentage per annum, comes to:

$$\frac{0.0035 \times 1200}{0.3119 \times 6} = \frac{0.7000}{0.3119} = 2.24\% \text{ per annum}$$

Hence, if a merchant or banker bought spot marks for dollars and simultaneously sold the marks forward for delivery in six months, he would have made 2.24% per annum on the transaction. Whether this type of transaction is profitable or not depends entirely on the interest rate structure of the two countries. If, for instance, to do the swap the banker or merchant has to borrow dollars at 8% per annum, while the six-months investment in marks yields only 5% per annum, the transaction is clearly unprofitable. The 2.24% per annum does not fully compensate for the 3% per annum interest rate differential. If the interest rate differential had been less than 2.24% per annum, the transaction would have been profitable.

As the previous example indicates, swap rates are closely related to differences in interest rate levels in the two countries whose currencies are involved. Under normal conditions, swap rates (and, therefore, forward rates) tend to move to equal out differences in interest rates between the two countries. If one of the countries has a higher interest rate structure than another, for instance, its forward currency will probably be selling at a discount. An investor buying that country's currency at spot to make an investment and selling it forward to cover the exposure, will probably lose part of the interest rate advantage in the swap, due to the forward discount. Similarly, a lender who takes up money in a relatively high interest rate currency and swaps it into a low interest rate currency, may earn a premium on the swap that partly or totally offsets the interest rate differential.

Uses of Swaps. Merchants and investors may wish to use swaps for taking advantage of interest rate differentials in foreign markets. If a better rate can be obtained on U.K. treasury bills than for similar U.S. instruments, a U.S. businessman with temporary excess liquidity may wish to buy spot sterling and invest it in the United Kingdom. To protect himself against a possible sterling devaluation, he will wish to simultaneously sell sterling for delivery at a fixed future date when his treasury bills mature. Of course, the per annum percentage of discount or premium on forward sterling has to be respectively subtracted from or added to the interest rate differential in the two markets to calculate the net benefit of engaging in the swap transaction.

Bankers use swaps to make foreign currency loans and investments. Again, the swap transaction itself may yield a discount or premium that must be considered as part of the overall interest cost. Swaps from one currency into another are an integral part of the Eurocurrency market, which is discussed in Chapter 11. Eurodollars may, for instance, be swapped into marks or some other currency and invested in fixed deposits or money market instruments in that currency for the duration of the swap. This type of swap transaction may be attractive if it gives a fractional yield advantage, taking into consideration the interest rate differential in the two currency markets, as well as the swap premium or discount.

EXCHANGE RISKS AND OPPORTUNITIES

The fact that currency values constantly fluctuate imposes a degree of risk on the international merchant or investor who is to receive or pay a currency other than his own. The risk is further aggravated by the possibility of a major devaluation or revaluation of a currency in which a merchant or investor may have a net liability, net asset, or receivable.

When looking at foreign exchange, it is not enough, however, to look only at the risk side. Wherever there are risks, there are usually also some opportunities. The businessman who has a long position in a currency that is about to revalue stands to make a handsome profit. We, therefore, look at both risks and opportunities that may be present from the exporter's, importer's, and investor's points of view. Simultaneously, we examine ways through which a businessman with an open exchange position may be able to cover or hedge risk. Before proceeding, however, a general definition of covering and hedging may be useful.

"Covering" may be defined as safeguarding against an exchange risk that results from an actual foreign currency liability (payable) or asset (receivable) that a businessman may have and that matures on a definite or approximate date in the future.

"Hedging," on the other hand, is the act of safeguarding against an exchange-related risk with no fixed maturity date. When a businessman hedges an exchange-related risk, he may actually create an open foreign exchange position with the purpose of offsetting another open position (such as an inventory position) he is running in the opposite direction.

The theory behind both covering and hedging is that a foreign merchant, investor, or manufacturer should concentrate on and take risks only in the line of business he or she knows best. Producers of machinery may be able to manufacture and sell abroad quality products at a profit. They probably know little about the intricacies of foreign exchange and expected currency movements. It would, therefore, be wise to let other professionals—bankers—assume any foreign exchange risks that may be present.

The Exporter

If an exporter concludes the sales contract in his own currency, he does not run an exchange risk. It is up to the importer to make a fixed amount of the exporter's currency available at a stipulated date. There is no need for the exporter to convert foreign currency into his own, and consequently he faces no risk.

Invoicing in Foreign Currencies. Exchange risks and opportunities will be present when an exporter concludes a sales contract with a buyer in a foreign currency. This may be the currency of the importer's own country or a third currency in which it may be convenient to denominate an international trade transaction. In either case, the exporter will receive, at a stipulated date, a certain amount of money in a currency that is foreign to him. He will thus have to convert it, that is, sell it for his own country's currency.

The exporter already knows, at the time he signs the contract, the amount of foreign exchange to be received, as well as the exact, or at least approximate, date of payment. The exporter does not, however, know the spot rate of exchange that will prevail at the time the money is actually received. Thus, if spot rates move up in the interim between signing of the contract and receipt of the foreign money, the exporter will receive more of his own currency than he might have originally anticipated. On the other hand, if spot rates move down (caused either by a devaluation of the foreign currency or revaluation of the domestic one), the exporter will receive less and may, as a result, incur a loss on the transactions.

In view of the previously discussed type of transaction, it should be of some interest to the exporter whether he receives payment in a relatively strong or weak currency. If the currency is weak, there exists a good possibility of a downward movement in the exchange or even a devaluation that may result in substantial losses to the merchant. (The same results would come, of course, from a revaluation of the exporter's own currency.) If the currency is strong, the possibility of an upward movement in rates or a revaluation may result in a nice profit.

Covering—General. If an exporter, at the signing of a sales contract, knows he will receive a certain amount of foreign currency at some time in the future, he can cover the exchange risk by selling the expected receipts in the future market. An exporter will thereby be able to fix, at the signing of the contract, the rate at which the foreign currency will be converted into his own. Delivery of the actual exchange to the bank that enters into the future contract does not, of course, take place until the planned date or receipt from the foreign importer.

If the expected date of receipt of the foreign currency falls on a date that is exactly one, two, three, or some other monthly period from the date on which the exporter makes the forward contract, one of the standard date contracts can be used. If the exporter knows the exact date when the foreign money will come in, but it doesn't happen to fall on one of the standard dates, the exporter can ask his bank to execute a future option contract. If, for instance, the exporter knows in advance that the foreign currency receipt for a sale will be arriving in the month of July, he can ask his bank for the option to deliver the exchange any time during that month. The rate of exchange is, of course, fixed at the time the contract is written, so that the exporter knows exactly the amount of his own currency that will be received.

Covering a Revaluation-Prone Currency. If the foreign currency of payment is strong or revaluation prone, future rates are probably at a premium over spot. In this case, the amount of home currency the exporter will receive will be more than what is indicated by spot rates at the time the forward contract is written. Thus, if the sales contract was based on prevailing spot rates, the execution of a future contract will result in a windfall exchange profit for the exporter. An exporter will, therefore, find it desirable to invoice in a revaluation-prone currency.

When selling to a country whose currency is strong, an exporter may well argue that there is no need to cover the exchange risk. In this case, he foregoes the premium on the forward exchange but stands to benefit from any upward movement in exchange rates or actual revaluation of the currency. It must be remembered, however, that the exporter would probably be wise to engage only in the line of business he knows best and not participate in foreign exchange speculation of any kind. If this line of reasoning is accepted, the exporter should take the sure (but smaller) gain of a forward exchange premium over the more ephemeral windfall profit that could be earned if he did not cover and if spot exchange rates were to move up by the time payment was received.

Covering in Devaluation-Prone Currency. If the currency of payment is weak or devaluation prone, forward exchange will most likely be selling at a discount. In covering exchange risk, the exporter will thus incur a cost due to his need to sell the forward exchange at a lower price than the spot rate prevailing at the time of signing the contract. To make up for this cost, the exporter may wish to adjust the prices for goods upward before signing the sales contract.

Alternative Means of Covering. As an alternative to entering into a future contract with his bank, the exporter may also be able to cover exchange risk by borrowing, at the time he signs the sales contract, an amount of foreign currency that is equal to the expected future proceeds. The exporter can then immediately convert the borrowed money into his own currency at the prevailing spot rate, thereby fixing the amount of his own currency received from the sale. When payment from the overseas importer is finally received, the exporter can use it to repay the loan he previously took on the same currency. Of course, the exporter has to pay interest for the duration of the foreign currency loan. This interest minus interest received or saved by having the dollars available earlier may be considered to be the cost of the covering operation. Sometimes, when future exchange rates are at a large discount or when it is difficult to find a bank willing to enter into a future contract for a certain currency or time period, this last covering alternative may be cheaper or more readily available. The vehicle is, of course, open only to an exporter who has the capacity to borrow in the particular foreign market or the Eurocurrency market.

Leads and Lags. Businessmen may deliberately speed up or slow down the settlement of international debts to take advantage of possible revaluations or devaluations. If payment of an obligation is accelerated, this is called a "lead"; if payment is slowed down, it is called a "lag."

Exporters who invoice in a revaluation-prone currency may wish to lag payments they expect to receive for their products. The longer they wait, the more chance there is for an upward movement in the exchange rate and, therefore, a higher value of their account receivable once received and converted into domestic currency.

Exporters who invoice in a devaluation-prone currency, on the other hand, tend to lead by pushing for payment as early as possible. The sooner they get paid, the less risk there will be of experiencing a loss at conversion due to a possible devaluation of the currency in which the receivable is denominated.

The Importer

Invoicing in Foreign Currencies. The importer who contracts for payment in the exporter's currency, or a third currency, does not know the spot rate that will prevail when the actual payment has to be made. If the currency of payment is weak or devaluation prone, the spot rates might be lower at the time payment has to be made. In this case, the importer can buy the required foreign currency at a cheaper price and thus stands to earn an extra exchange profit. On the other hand, if the foreign currency is strong or revaluation prone, the importer may have to pay more of his own currency to obtain the fixed amount of foreign exchange required. In this case, he will have to pay more than might have originally been calculated and thus may incur substantial losses.

Invoicing in Own Currency. On the surface, it would appear that the importer who is invoiced in his own currency does not run an exchange risk, since he can fix exactly the amount he has to pay, leaving the responsibility of conversion to the exporter's local currency up to the latter. Closer examination reveals, however, that in certain situations the importer may still run an exchange-related risk. Assume, for instance, that the importer has already bought for inventory and has made the required payment. While the goods are still in inventory, the currency of the exporter's country is devalued. This means that competitors can now buy the goods more cheaply than the carrying value of the importer's inventory; and it may result in a general decline in market prices for the goods in question. The importer will, therefore, be able to sell his inventory only at lower prices than he originally anticipated.

Covering a Revaluation-Prone Currency. The importer who buys abroad in foreign currency knows at least approximately when payment must be made. If the importer is invoiced in a revaluation-prone currency, he runs the risk of having to pay a higher price for the specific currency needed if exchange rates move up or if there is a revaluation after the sales contract is signed but before payment is made. The same risk is also incurred if the exporter's own currency should devalue between the time he signs the sales contract and the time payment is made.

The conventional way of covering exchange risk is for the importer immediately to buy the foreign exchange for future delivery at the date when actually needed. Again, odd dates or option dates can probably be arranged as required.

If the foreign currency in question is strong or revaluation prone, its forward rate will probably be at a premium. In this case, the importer has to put up more of his own currency to buy the needed forward exchange. He therefore incurs a cost for covering this open currency position.

One alternative way of covering the risk is to buy the foreign currency required immediately on signing of the contract at the prevailing spot rate. The money can then be invested in the exporter's country or the Eurocurrency market until the actual payment falls due. If this avenue is followed, the importer must put up his own currency immediately at the signing of the contract; measured against this is the interest the importer earns by investing the money until actually needed.

Covering a Devaluation-Prone Currency. If the foreign currency in which payment has to be made is weak or devaluation prone, the importer may decide that covering is not necessary. If rates do indeed weaken or the currency devalues, he will be able to buy the needed exchange at a lower price, thus making a profit. The importer might, on the other hand, decide not to gamble on a possible devaluation, but reap the smaller but certain profit that he can get by covering immediately.

Hedging the Inventory Risk. Let us assume that an importer buys from a devaluation-prone country and has already paid for the merchandise. To protect against a possible decline in the value of his inventory resulting from a devaluation in the exporter's currency, the importer may wish to hedge. He can do this by selling the exporter's currency in the forward market for an amount equal to the approximate value of his inventory. If a devaluation occurs, he will be able to cover the forward sale at a lower price, and thereby earn a profit on the exchange transaction. This profit will, it is hoped, offset any loss he may incur on the value of the inventory. The importer should, of course, reduce the amount of his hedge as he sells off his inventory.

It is important to note that before actual payment is made, no hedge is necessary if the transaction is invoiced in the weaker currency; if a devaluation occurs, the importer will be able to buy the foreign currency he needs at a lower price, thus offsetting any inventory losses.

Decision on Hedging. The decision whether or not to hedge must be carefully weighed. When hedging, the merchant does not merely cover an existing risk, but takes a new *additional* risk in the opposite direction. If an expected devaluation of the exporter's currency does not take place, for instance, but there is instead an opposite upward move in spot exchange rates, the hedge can only be undone at a cost to the importer. Hedging is, therefore, useful only if the additional risk and expense is not too great. If, for instance, the forward exchange an importer would have to sell to carry out the hedging operation is already at a large discount, hedging will not be worth the additional expense. Generally, hedging is only useful if there is a real danger of a significant revaluation or devaluation and if the cost is reasonable—a situation that, in practice, rarely occurs.

Leads and Lags. Importers who are invoiced in a revaluation-prone currency will wish to lead as much as possible. The sooner they pay their strong currency obligations, the less chance there is of paying a higher price for the currency if an upward movement in the exchange rate actually occurs.

Importers who are invoiced in a devaluation prone currency will wish to benefit as much as possible from an actual devaluation. If the devaluation occurs before payment for the obligation has been made, it will take fewer units of the importer's currency to buy the same number of units of the weak currency in which the account payable is denominated. Importers, in this situation, wish to lag, that is, they wish to postpone payment as long as possible.

The Investor

New Investments. The foreign investor who knows he has to make a payment abroad at some time in the future runs the same risks and may enjoy the same opportunities as the importer who is invoiced in a foreign currency. If the currency of the country in which the investment is to be made devalues in the interim, the investor will require fewer of his domestic currency units to buy foreign currency. On the other hand, if the foreign currency revalues before the investment is made, more will have to be paid for the required foreign currency.

Similar to the importer, when an investor knows he has to make a foreign currency payment at a roughly determinable future date, he can do one of two things to cover his risk:

1 Buy the needed exchange in the future market for delivery on the date it is needed.
2 Buy the exchange immediately at the prevailing spot rate and invest the proceeds until they are needed.

The relative cost of the two alternatives may be compared based on current interest rate differentials and forward exchange premiums or discounts.

Existing Investments—Stocks and Bonds. If investments in stocks or bonds are made in a devaluation-prone foreign currency, they will be worth fewer units of domestic currency if a devaluation of the foreign currency or revaluation of the domestic currency actually occurs. To cover this risk, the investor may wish to sell forward the weaker currency. The delivery date of the forward sale should coincide with the time at which the investor expects to liquidate the investment and convert the proceeds back to his own currency.

If the weak currency is selling at a large discount in the forward market, the investor may find it too expensive to cover his exchange risk. An alternative worth considering in this case is the maintenance of an open long position in the foreign currency, in the hope that no devaluation—or only a modest one—will occur. Consequently, it is suggested that there is no absolute rule telling an investor when to and when not to cover his risk. Each case must be considered on its own merits, taking into consideration the cost of covering versus the potential losses of maintaining an open position.

If the local currency in which an investment has been made revalues, an investor will reap a nice windfall profit. Not only will stocks and bonds be worth more in the investor's home currency, but any dividends and interest he receives will be converted at a higher and thus more favorable, rate of exchange.

An investor who expects to receive interest or dividends from abroad may wish to postpone the actual remittance if he expects an upward valuation of the foreign currency. He thereby hopes to get a better price for the exchange he sells after the revaluation has occurred.

If, on the other hand, the foreign currency is devaluation prone, the investor will wish to remit his dividends and interest immediately when received. He may even be able to anticipate the receipt of dividends and interest by borrowing in the local market and exchanging the proceeds for his own currency at the prevailing spot rate. The foreign currency loan can then be repaid as local currency dividends are declared or interest is received. Cover by means of a forward sale of the currency could also be arranged as an alternative.

Existing Investments—Fixed Assets. The situation becomes more cloudy when we assume that a depreciation or appreciation of the foreign currency occurs after an investment in fixed assets has been made.

If the investor buys such fixed assets as real estate, machinery, equipment, the short-run effect on a devaluation will reduce the book-carrying value of his investment in terms of his home currency. The longer-run effect of a devaluation, however, may well be a general increase in prices of the country that has devalued. Fixed assets and inventory may thus be worth more in terms of the local currency than they were before. This price increase may, in the long run, wholly or partially offset the book loss that is incurred as a result of the devaluation.

Any profits remitted from abroad will buy fewer units of the investor's home currency after the foreign currency is devalued. Whether the devaluation might eventually increase the profits made by the overseas branch or subsidiary (e.g., because of higher prices) cannot be determined a priori.

A net investor in fixed assets or inventory in a foreign country that subsequently revalues its currency makes a book profit. Moreover, dividends remitted back to the home country will buy more of the investor's own currency resulting in higher profits. Whether a revaluation will set into motion deflationary forces that would tend to reduce local prices and profits is a question that cannot be answered deductively. Recent experience, as well as the commitment by practically all governments to maintain high degrees of employment and purchasing power, would indicate that such deflationary periods are unlikely.

A businessman who has invested in real estate, other fixed assets, or in a foreign subsidiary or affiliate may wish to guard against a possible devaluation of the foreign currency or revaluation of his own currency. If a parity change appears imminent, there are a number of ways through which an investor can be protected. If an investor has a controlling interest in a producing company abroad, it would certainly be desirable to remit profits as soon as possible. If he also exports to the subsidiary, payment for such merchandise should be remitted without delay. More generally, all obligations in stronger currencies should be paid as soon as possible. If an undesirable parity change seems imminent, it may be a good idea to accumulate inventory of imported materials, using borrowings in local currency to finance such an accumulation. Generally, it is desirable for an investor to borrow as much as possible in the weaker currency. If the subsidiary has assets, such as cash and accounts receivable that are denominated in a stronger currency, it is desirable to delay their conversion into the local, weaker currency.

If the forward discount is not too great, an investor may also be able to hedge by selling the weaker currency in the forward market. He then hopes to buy the currency in question at a cheaper price after the parity change has occurred, thus offsetting any book loss on the investment.

CHAPTER 8

Shipping and Collection

When buyers and sellers know one another and enjoy trust in their business relationships, shipping and collection documents are reduced to a bare minimum. Commercial invoices and house-to-house transport documents are usually all that are necessary to effect transactions efficiently. However, in the absence of established business relationships, particularly if there is any reason for distrust, or if government exchange controls are, in effect, in the buyer's or seller's country, special handling formalities will be necessary.

Shipping merchandise to a foreign country and collecting payment requires a great deal of paperwork. Documents are needed to spell out contractual rights and duties of the parties concerned; some are needed to collect and remit payments; and others are required merely for information and to satisfy governmental stipulations concerning the exporting and importing countries.

The documents covered in this chapter can be classified into three basic types:

Negotiable money paper, which evidences an obligation payable in money.

Commodity paper, which evidences an obligation to deliver goods.

Other documents, which are required for information or to satisfy governmental requirements.

Organizations that give assistance in preparing documents and expediting shipments are also discussed.

NEGOTIABLE MONEY PAPER

A negotiable money instrument is a written promise or order to pay that may be easily transferred (negotiated) from one person to another. Indeed, it is this ready transferability that makes a negotiable money instrument very popular in modern business, particularly in the conduct of international trade.

It is really a short-form type of contract that acknowledges a financial obligation from one person to another.

Examples of negotiable money paper used in international trade are *drafts* and *promissory notes*. A draft that is accepted by the buyer or a promissory note signed by the obligor often evidence a financial obligation arising out of international trade. The rights to this obligation may be transferred from one owner to another merely by selling or discounting the instrument. An exporter may, for instance, sell to his bank a time draft that has been accepted by the importer. A negotiable money instrument may thereby become a useful medium for the transfer of rights to receive payment in money.

When negotiable money paper is denominated in a foreign currency, it may be used as a means of holding foreign exchange by a merchant who requires it for business reasons. An importer, for instance, who must pay sterling in 90 days could buy a sterling draft maturing in 90 days. This represents an alternative way of arranging forward exchange cover.

Legal Basis

The U.S. law governing negotiable instruments is the Uniform Commercial Code (UCC) in 49 states (Louisiana being the exception). Article 3 of the UCC outlines the law of commercial paper. In cases where the UCC is silent or unclear, further interpretations can be found in numerous court decisions passed down on the subject over the years. Basically, the UCC codifies established business and banking practices and previous court decisions.

The United Kingdom's negotiable instruments law was codified in the Bills of Exchange Act of 1882. It is similar to the UCC in its major provisions and applications. Indeed, laws and practices governing negotiable instruments are similar in most countries. This universal recognition of negotiable money instruments may be counted as an important advantage that makes them particularly adaptable for facilitating international payments.

However, the laws governing negotiable instruments in various countries may vary in their details. A brief review of U.S. law is given. If questions arise regarding detailed or specific issues (concerning either U.S. laws or the laws of a specific foreign country) merchants are advised to seek legal counsel.

Conditions for Negotiability

To be a truly negotiable instrument under U.S. law, a number of specific requirements must be met.

In Writing. Any typed or handwritten form is acceptable. Pencil is not recommended because this makes it easy to enter subsequent, unauthorized alterations.

Signed. The instrument must be signed by the maker or drawer. Any authorized signature is satisfactory, as long as the person signing is legally competent to do so. Instruments signed by infants, alcoholics, drug addicts, or persons declared legally insane are not valid and, therefore, not negotiable under the law.

Unconditional Promise or Order to Pay. To be unconditional, the promise or order must stand on its own feet without reference to any outside contingency. To be considered a promise or order, it must be stated positively without any contingencies attached. Thus, such a phrase as "to be paid at the buyer's convenience," would never be accepted as an unconditional order, while merely the word "pay" would, indeed, so qualify.

A Sum Certain in Money. The instrument must be certain concerning the amount of money to be paid. In cases where the exact amount is not stated but is readily determinable, the writing is acceptable. For instance, if it is a promise to pay a certain sum of money plus interest at a stated rate for a fixed period of time, the total is readily determinable and the negotiability of the instrument is not impaired.

The instrument must be payable in money. The denomination of the currency has no effect on negotiability; an instrument calling for payment in a foreign currency is still considered negotiable. It may be satisfied by payment of that number of dollars that the stated foreign currency will purchase at the buying rate for that currency on the day on which the instrument is payable.

Payable on Demand or at a Definite Time. If payable on demand, that is, on presentment, the instrument is negotiable. If it is payable at a future time that is definite and determinable, it is also negotiable. For instance, if a draft is payable 90 days from the date of sight, the future date of payment can readily be determined once the date of sight is known. The instrument is, therefore, negotiable. On the other hand, if the draft reads, "Payable 90 days after the arrival of the (named) vessel," the future date is not determinable as long as the vessel has not arrived, since there is always a chance that it may never arrive. This instrument is not negotiable under the law.

Payable to Order or Bearer. If the instrument is payable to the order of a named person, that person must endorse it before it can be transferred to someone else. If the instrument is made out to bearer, anyone holding it has title to it. In this case, it can be transferred from one person to another by mere delivery.

With all the previously mentioned requirements, it would appear that a negotiable instrument must be complicated. Actually, the reverse is true: the simpler the instrument, the better chance it has of meeting all the requirements. A mere dated statement, such as:

June 20, 19––
I promise to pay John Doe $1,000 in 90 days.
Joe Smith

is fully negotiable under Article 3 of the UCC.

Types of Negotiable Money Paper

Although there are a number of different kinds of negotiable money paper, they all share the essential characteristics previously outlined. They are generally concisely worded documents in which each word, due to repeated usage in commerce and interpretation by the courts, has a specific meaning.

Promissory Note. The simplest kind of negotiable money paper is the promissory note. It is an unconditional promise in writing made by one person to another and signed by the maker, engaging to pay on demand or at a fixed or determinable time a sum certain in money to order or to bearer. A promissory note is, therefore, two-party paper where the issuer (maker) promises to pay a second person.

Draft. Another negotiable money instrument is the draft or bill of exchange. It is an unconditional order in writing addressed by one person to another and signed by the person giving it, requiring the person to whom it is addressed to pay on demand or at a fixed or determinable future time a sum certain in money to order or to bearer.

There are usually three parties to a draft: First, the drawer who issues, signs, and sends the draft to the second party, the drawee. The draft is addressed to the drawee, asking him either to pay or accept and pay when due the amount indicated on the draft. The drawee, if he accepts the draft, is the primary obligor. Last, there is the payee who is to receive payment made by the drawee. The payee and drawer may be the same person. The payee may also be a third party or, most typically, the bank at which the drawer has his account. A draft is referred to as three-party paper. A typical draft is illustrated in Figure 8-1.

Acceptance. A draft is typically accepted by the drawee when he writes anywhere on it, but most typically across the face of it, the word "accepted," the date, and his signature. Other words with a similar meaning, such as "good" or "OK" can be used, and just the drawee's signature and the date are sufficient to indicate acceptance under UCC 3-410(1). Usually, the acceptor also writes on the draft the location or bank at which it is payable. A drawee is not liable for payment of a draft unless and until he accepts it. An acceptance is illustrated in Figure 8-2.

Acceptances must be payable at some fixed or determinable future time. When payable after a stated number of days, the computation of the final maturity differs depending on the wording of the draft. If it is payable "at so many (e.g., 90) days *sight*," it matures that many days after the date of acceptance. If it is payable "so many (e.g., 90) days after *date*, it matures that many days after the original date on the draft.

Acceptance by the drawee may be general or qualified. If it is general, the acceptor gives his complete assent to the order contained in the draft, thus creating an unquestioned liability to pay according to the stated terms.

DRAFT

$ 6,000.00 ----- AT SIGHT ----- Oct. 31 19 --

Pay to the order of John Doe & Company

------ Six Thousand Dollars ------ Dollars

Value received and charge the same to account of

John Doe & Company

To Richard Roe & Company
No. 170 Park Avenue
76 125 New York, NY 10003

John Doe

Figure 8-1. Filled-in draft form. (Note that tenor specification "at sight" is equivalent to "on demand.")

If acceptance is qualified, the acceptor limits his liability in some manner. He does this by writing the qualification directly on the draft above his signature. An importer, for instance, may wish to make his financial obligation contingent on proper arrival of the merchandise.

When an acceptance is qualified, the draft is no longer a truly negotiable instrument. A holder of a draft may refuse a qualified acceptance and treat the instrument as dishonored. Where a holder agrees to a qualified acceptance, however, the drawer and each endorser who does not affirmatively assent to the qualification is discharged of any further liability if the primary obligor refuses to honor the instrument. Qualified acceptances are relatively rare.

Check. A check is a special type of draft. The drawer is the person signing the check, the drawee is the bank where he has an account, and the payee is the beneficiary, that is, the person in whose favor the check is made out. Thus, a check is an unconditional order by the drawer or maker, asking his bank to pay a certain amount of money to a third party, the payee.

Banker's Draft. A slightly different type of draft is a banker's draft. It is an order from one bank (the drawer) to another (the drawee) with whom it normally maintains a correspondent relationship, to pay to a named person (the payee) a specified sum of money on demand. Banker's drafts are sometimes used to make payments for imports from abroad. A customer may, for instance, ask his bank to issue a draft for a specified amount in a specified currency payable to a named person. Of course, the customer is charged with the dollar countervalue of the draft plus bank handling charges.

Bank Money Order. A bank money order is similar to a banker's draft. It is a draft in which a bank orders money to be paid to a named person or

DRAFT

$ 6,000.00 ---- AT TWENTY DAYS SIGHT ---- Oct. 31 19--

Pay to the order of John Doe & Company

------ Six Thousand Dollars ------ Dollars

Value received and charge the same to account of

To Richard Roe & Company
170 Park Avenue
No.
76 125 New York, NY 10003

Accepted Payable on Nov. 20, 19-- at 170 Park Ave. New York, NY by Richard Roe, President

John Doe & Company
John Doe

Figure 8-2. Filled-in acceptance.

to bearer. There is no separate drawee and the order is drawn on the issuing bank itself.

Other kinds of negotiable money instruments include certificates of deposit, which really are promissory notes issued by banks in consideration of time deposits maintained with them.

Transfers and Endorsements

The ownership of a negotiable money instrument may easily be transferred from one person to another. Generally, the transferee acquires all the transferor's rights to the instrument as well as any security interest that may be attached to it.

Transfer and Negotiation. A negotiable instrument may be transferred from one person to another either in exchange for value or merely as a gift. When an instrument that is payable to the order of a named person is transferred for value, the transferee (i.e., the person receiving the instrument) receives the enforceable right to have the unqualified endorsement of the transferor.

Negotiation takes effect only when the endorsement is made and only then is the transferee considered the new owner (see UCC 3-201(3)). However, this applies only to the transfer for value of an instrument payable to order or specially endorsed. It does not apply to instruments payable or endorsed to bearer or endorsed in blank. It also does not apply to a gift (see UCC 3-201, official comment).

Negotiation of an instrument is its transfer in such a form that the transferee becomes the holder. Hence, negotiation of an instrument payable to the order of a named person is completed once it has been properly endorsed and delivered to the new holder. Paper that is payable to bearer is negotiated by mere delivery. In this case, no endorsement is necessary (see UCC 3-202(1)).

Endorsements. An endorsement consists of a signature and related comments by or on behalf of the owner of a negotiable instrument. The endorsement serves to transfer the title of an order instrument to the transferee, that is, to the person to whom it is negotiated. An effective endorsement must be on the instrument itself or on a paper so firmly affixed as to become a part thereof (UCC3-202(2)).

An endorser, by writing his name on the instrument, makes the following implied warranties:

The instrument is genuine in all respects in what it purports to be.

He has a good title to the instrument.

All prior parties to the instrument had the capacity to contract.

The paper, at the time of endorsement, is a valid, enforceable obligation.

If the instrument is dishonored and all necessary procedures are taken, the endorser will pay the holder the amount due.

There are four basic types of endorsements:

1 *Blank.* This is the most common type of endorsement. It specifies no endorsee and consists only of the endorser's signature. The instrument, therefore, becomes payable to bearer and any further negotiations can be effected by mere delivery. The endorser in blank becomes liable to all subsequent holders, should the instrument be dishonored by the person primarily obligated to pay at maturity. An endorser of a draft, before acceptance, warrants that it will be accepted and eventually paid.

2 *Special.* This type of endorsement specifies the name to whom or to whose order the instrument is to be paid. Before further negotiation can take place, the instrument has to be endorsed, in turn, by the special endorsee.

   A holder of a blank endorsed instrument can make it payable to a specific person only (possibly himself). He merely fills in, above the signature of the endorser, a phrase, such as "pay to the order of," followed by the name of the endorsee desired. This changes a blank to a special endorsement.

3 *Restrictive or Conditional.* By adding certain phrases before his signature, an endorser may put some kind of restriction to its further negotiation. For instance, the endorsement may read "Pay to Mr. X only" or "For deposit to my account only." This has the effect of limiting any further negotiation of the instrument, except for the purpose or under the condition specified. The endorsee may be appointed the agent of the endorser with such a restriction as "for collection," or "as agent." The endorsement may also be made conditional by stipulating that the instrument can only be transferred on some stated condition. Other types of restrictive or conditional endorsements are also possible.

4 *Qualified.* If an endorser wants to limit his liability he may precede his signature with a phrase, such as "without recourse." A qualified endorsement makes the endorser a mere assignor of the title of the instrument. The qualification does not, however, affect the passage of title nor does it limit the instrument's negotiability.

Most frequently, negotiable instruments are endorsed "with recourse," which means that the holder of the instrument may look to any of the prior endorsers for payment if the ultimate obligor refuses to pay or accept and pay the instrument. If an endorser qualifies his signature with the words "without recourse," he eliminates himself (and himself only) from the chain of people who can be made liable for payment in case the ultimate obligor fails to honor the instrument.

Holder in Due Course

One of the important advantages of negotiable money paper that makes its use in commerce so desirable is that a holder in due course enjoys certain rights in connection with the instrument that are totally separate from the underlying transaction that originally gave rise to the instrument. To be considered a holder in due course, a third party (i.e., one who was not party to the underlying trade or other transaction that gave rise to the instrument) must take the instrument

1 For value.
2 In good faith.
3 Without notice that it is overdue or has been dishonored or of any defense against or claim to it on the part of any person (see UCC 3-302).

Advantages. A holder in due course of an instrument enjoys the advantages of being entitled to payment regardless of any personal defenses that may be put up by the ultimate obligor. To elaborate further on this, we must first realize that usually some kind of transaction between the drawer or maker and the drawee gives rise to a negotiable instrument. For instance, the drawer of a draft might be an exporter shipping goods to the drawee, that is, the importer. The latter does not wish to pay for the goods immediately because he has to sell them and wait for payment until he has the necessary funds. The exporter, who strongly wishes to make the sale, agrees to draw a draft on the importer payable 90 days after the date of the draft. The importer agrees to accept the draft.

Let us assume that the importer has received the merchandise in question and has found it to be defective. The importer therefore, feels that he has no obligation to honor the acceptance when it matures. The exporter, as holder of the trade acceptance, can now go to court to make a counterclaim of defective merchandise. Since both parties to the suit and countersuit were parties to the underlying transaction, the claims of each can be examined together by one court of law. The outcome is uncertain and depends on the merits of each party's claim, particularly whether the merchandise was really defective and, therefore, not in accordance with the underlying sales contract.

Now let us change the situation slightly and say that the exporter, needing money immediately, discounted the accepted draft with a third party, probably his bank. The bank, having, in fact, bought the negotiable money instrument for value, becomes a holder in due course and will present the acceptance to the importer for payment on the due date. In this case, the importer has to pay the acceptance regardless of whether or not the underlying merchandise was defective. If the bank goes to court to demand payment, the importer/acceptor will be compelled to pay based only on the fact that he accepted the draft without any reference to the underlying sales contract. If the goods are indeed defective, the importer can, of course, bring an entirely separate court action against the exporter. In this suit, however, the court will be concerned only with whether or not the exporter complied with the contract and not at all with payment or nonpayment of the acceptance to a third party holder in due course.

There is active consideration of limiting the rights of a holder in due course in cases where the underlying merchandise delivered is found to be defective. Some groups interested in the rights of consumers have succeeded in limiting a consumer's liability of payment for defective merchandise, even in cases where his installment paper has been negotiated by the seller of the defective merchandise to a holder in due course, such as a consumer finance company or bank.

The previously discussed situation illustrates valuable characteristic of negotiable money instruments. A holder in due course is entitled to payment, regardless of certain defenses that may be put up by the maker of a note or the drawee of a draft. Specifically, even if there is lack of consideration or if some provision of the underlying contract remains unfilled, a holder in due course of a negotiable money instrument is still entitled to payment.

Additionally, a holder in due course takes the instrument free from all claims to it by any person. Hence, even if the instrument was originally stolen, an innocent purchaser in due course who knows nothing of the theft has the right to collect payment when due.

Permissible Defenses. There are a number of defenses by other parties that are capable of preventing even a holder in due course from collecting payment. These include

1. Infancy on the part of the maker or obligor.
2. Other incapacity, duress, or illegality of the transaction, which would render the obligation of the party a nullity.
3. Such misrepresentation as has induced the party to sign the instrument with neither knowledge nor reasonable opportunity to obtain knowledge of its character or essential terms.
4. Forgery, that is, if the person never really signed the instrument.

Primary and Secondary Liability

We have already noted that on each negotiable instrument there is a primary obligor who is liable for payment of the amount on the instrument. Only if the primary obligor does not pay do endorsers and the original drawer of a draft become liable.

We, therefore, can make a dichotomy between a primary and a secondary obligor. The primary obligor is the one liable for payment as a result of the underlying transaction that gave rise to the negotiable instrument in the first place. Usually, the drawer of a draft has performed some kind of service or has sold goods to the obligor (drawee) for which the latter, instead of paying cash, accepted the instrument, thereby obligating himself to pay at a fixed future time. Thus, the primary obligor on a draft is the drawee. The primary obligor on a promissory note or certificate of deposit is the maker.

The drawer of an accepted draft has the option of holding it until maturity, at which time, on presenting it to the primary obligor, he hopes to get payment. Alternatively, if the drawer needs cash immediately, he may sell the instrument to a third party for cash or some other consideration. Since the third party can collect cash only at some future date, such a sale is usually made at a discount. Of course, to effect the sale, the drawer endorses and delivers the instrument to the third party, who thereby becomes a holder in due course. The third party again may sell and endorse the instrument over to a fourth party, and so on. Whoever the holder is when the instrument matures will present it to the primary obligor (the drawee) for payment. If the primary obligor refuses to pay, the last holder has recourse to all prior endorsers (except those who qualified their endorsement as being without recourse), as well as to the drawer. Thus, those secondarily liable are the endorsers of a negotiable instrument or drawer of a draft. Each endorser has recourse to prior endorsers until the chain ends where it started, namely, with the drawer. The drawer, when he originally negotiated the instrument for a consideration, undertook that it would be honored by the primary obligor. If not so honored, the drawer becomes liable as secondary obligor.

Use of Negotiable Money Instruments in Foreign Trade

All types of negotiable instruments enjoy usage throughout the world. The one that is used most frequently in foreign trade, however, is the draft and its variations, such as the acceptance, banker's draft, check, and international money order.

A draft accepted by a buyer of merchandise is called a trade acceptance. A typical trade acceptance is illustrated in Figure 8-3. A draft accepted by a bank is called a banker's acceptance. When a draft is accepted by a prime bank, it becomes the obligation of a financially strong and reputable organization. There is no doubt that the bank will meet its obligation at maturity. Bankers' acceptances enjoy a wide market and are important tools in the financing of international trade.

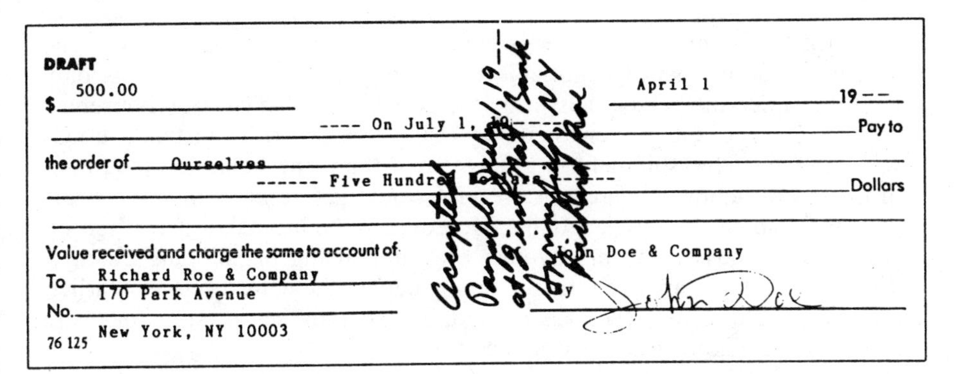

DRAFT

$ 500.00 April 1 19--

---- On July 1, 19---- Pay to

the order of Ourselves

------ Five Hundred Dollars ------ Dollars

Value received and charge the same to account of John Doe & Company

To Richard Roe & Company
170 Park Avenue
No.
New York, NY 10003
76 125

By John Doe

Accepted

Figure 8-3. Filled-in trade acceptance.

When drawing a draft on someone in a foreign country, the question sometimes arises whether it should comply with the negotiable instruments law of the drawer's or the drawee's country. The general rule is that the instrument should comply with the laws of the country where it is issued, that is, the country of a drawer of a draft or the maker of a promissory note. This is especially important when recourse against the beneficiary, that is, the drawer, is an integral part of and precondition to the financial transaction.

COMMODITY PAPER

Commodity paper symbolically represents some merchandise that may be either in transit or in storage. The most important kinds of commodity paper are bills of lading and warehouse receipts. Also considered to be commodity paper are dock receipts, dock warrants, and any other documents that in the regular course of business or financing evidence that the person in possession of them is entitled to receive, hold, and dispose of the goods they cover (UCC 1-201 (15)). The law governing these documents of title is outlined in Article 7 of the UCC. However, there are also a number of federal laws, such as the Federal Bill of Lading Act, that apply to interstate and international shipments.

Commodity paper may be negotiable or nonnegotiable. When nonnegotiable, it is basically a receipt for the goods issued by a warehouse or carrier. Its only significance is that it evidences either a storage or shipping contract. Even as such, however, it can be an important vehicle for financing, such as nonnegotiable warehouse receipts issued in the name of a bank.

When commodity paper is negotiable, it not only represents a shipping or storage contract, but the paper itself carries title to the goods. If the paper is issued to bearer or has been endorsed in blank, title to it can be transferred by mere delivery. If a specific person is named in the instrument, he must endorse it first, before title can be transferred by delivery (UCC 7-501 (3)).

Negotiable commodity paper is similar to negotiable money paper. The holder in due course of negotiable commodity paper, however, gets only the title, which the person delivering the goods to the bailee (warehouseman or carrier) has or has power to convey (UCC 7-503). If, for instance, goods were delivered for shipment or storage by a thief, the bona fide purchaser of the bill of lading or warehouse receipt would get no more than the rights the thief had in the stolen goods. Moreover, a bailee has a prior lien on goods in his possession in payment of warehousing or shipping charges. This is different from a negotiable money paper where, as discussed earlier, a holder in due course receives a valid, and in some cases, superior claim against the obligor on the instrument.

Bills of Lading

The bill of lading is the most important of all shipping documents. It must be issued by the navigation company that owns the vessel or its agent. The full name and address of both the navigation company and agent, if applicable, must appear. The following format is typical:

XYZ Corporation
1 World Trade Center
New York, NY 10038

as agents for:

Eastern Navigation Company,
incorporated in New York at
11 Broadway, New York, NY 10274

In those cases where the primary business address is different from the incorporation address, either may be used. If the shipper presents a printed bill of lading that does not show full names and addresses of the owners of the shipping line on the heading, then it can be given at the bottom of the document. This requirement applies to all types of bills of lading, including:

1 *Liner Bill of Lading.* A transport document issued for shipment on scheduled port calls through scheduled trade routes.
2 *Combined/Multimodal Transport Bill of Lading.* A transport document providing for more than one mode of transport for the goods from a scheduled point of departure to a scheduled place of delivery.
3 *Tanker Bill of Lading.* A transport document often used for the transportation of liquid industrial elements or crude oil, usually governed by a charter party agreement. (A charter party agreement is between the owner of the goods and the party paying for the freight, usually the seller, but sometimes the buyer.)

4 *NVOCC (nonvessel operating common carrier) Bill of Lading.* A transport document that utilizes the ships of vessel operators and provides ocean shipping services, although the "shippers" do not operate the ships themselves.

In its usual form, the bill of lading serves three functions:

It is a contract between the steamship company (carrier) and exporter (shipper) in which the former agrees to carry the goods from the port of shipment to the port of destination.

It is a receipt for the goods.

A negotiable bill of lading is a document establishing title rights to the goods.

The bill of lading, as a title document, is most important when financing is involved. Usually, the ocean bill of lading is made out in the name of the exporter who endorses it over to the bank that finances the shipment while in transit. The bank retains title to the goods while they are being financed. If the loan financing the shipment is not repaid, the bank can use the bill of lading to claim the merchandise from the shipping company. The bank can, therefore, sell the goods, liquidating the loan with the proceeds. In practice, this is, of course, rarely done, since the loan is practically always repaid in the normal course of trade.

The carrier, as well as the bank, has no responsibility for the authenticity of the description of the goods in the bill of lading. The bill of lading is taken by the bank entirely at its face value. Both the importer and banker who has a financial interest in the goods must rely on the honesty of the exporter.

The most common bill of lading used in international trade is the ocean bill of lading. It comes in many varieties, and a brief description is useful.

Straight (Nonnegotiable) versus Order Bill of Lading. Under a straight bill of lading, the shipment is consigned to a specific party, normally the importer. The shipping company, in this case, delivers the cargo at the port of destination to anyone who can prove that he is the party named in the bill of lading.

The actual bill is not needed to receive delivery of the goods. In this case, both the shipper and the bank lose control over the goods, and title cannot be transferred to any third parties by mere endorsement and delivery of the bill of lading. (Prior to delivery to the ultimate consignee, however, the shipper may direct the carrier to deliver the goods to another, different consignee (see UCC 7-303).) The nonnegotiable bill of lading is, therefore, not good collateral. It is rarely used in ocean transport where the exporter or the bank generally wish to retain title to the goods until they have been paid or the importer has acknowledged a financial obligation by accepting a draft drawn on him. The straight bill might be used for cash in advance, open account, or consignment shipments when no financing is involved and the exporter is willing to lose control over the goods, either because he has been paid already or because he trusts the importer completely.

A negotiable or order bill of lading contains a phrase, such as "Consigned to the order of (a named party)." The consignee or holder can transfer title to the negotiable commodity paper by endorsement and delivery. Since ocean shipments are generally financed, most ocean bills are in negotiable form. They may be made out either to the order of the bank or order of the exporter who endorses it in blank. The latter is the preferred practice because it is the way banks get bearer documents that they do not have to endorse themselves to pass title over to another party.

Since order bills of lading represent goods in transit that are probably readily marketable and fully insured, these documents are considered good collateral by banks. Generally, however, a bank would not find the collateral of an order bill of lading satisfactory by itself. It usually looks to the party being financed as the primary source of repayment.

Although anyone presenting an order bill of lading to the shipping company can get possession of the goods, the bill also contains the name and address of the ultimate consignee—that is, the importer—together with a request that he be notified when the shipment reaches its final destination. Probably, by the time the goods have arrived, the consignee has also already received the bill of lading (which is usually sent by airmail), so that he can get possession of the merchandise immediately.

"On-Board" versus "Received-for-Shipment" Bill of Lading. An on-board bill of lading certifies, by signature of the captain of the vessel or his representative, that the goods have actually been loaded on board the ship that will carry them to their destination. The only way an importer can make sure that the goods are shipped on or before the date stipulated in the sales contract is to insist on an on-board bill of lading dated no later than the latest permitted date of shipment. This will also tell the importer approximately when his shipment is scheduled to arrive. Most sales contracts (and letters of credit) do, indeed, stipulate on-board bills of lading. On-board bills of lading are also important because war risk insurance generally becomes effective only after the goods have been loaded on board the vessel.

A received-for-shipment bill of lading merely acknowledges that the steamship company has received the goods for shipment. It does not state that the vessel carrying them is in port or shipping space is available. Hence, goods may be at the dock for weeks and even months before actual shipment takes place. Therefore, any bill of lading, in order for it to serve as a guarantee of receipt of merchandise on board the vessel, must clearly contain one of the following types of statements on the face of the document:

1 Shipped On Board s/s *Esperanza*, dated ______.
2 Laden On Board s/s *Esperanza*, dated ______.
3 On Board s/s *Esperanza*, dated ______.

The printed or cut-off date perforated on the bill of lading does not warrant the taking on board of the merchandise. The date should appear, whether handwritten or stamped, next to the previously outlined three alternatives.

When goods are perishable or seasonal, a received-for-shipment bill of lading should never be satisfactory to an importer.

A received-for-shipment bill of lading can be converted into an on-board bill, merely by stamping it "on-board," and including the name of the vessel, date, and signature of the captain or someone authorized by him.

If an exporter, for some reason, does not get an on-board bill of lading, he should follow through with the steamship company to make sure that the goods are loaded as soon as possible.

Clean versus Foul Bill of Lading. When the shipping company receives boxes that are damaged or in poor condition so that they might not survive the ocean voyage, it is so noted on the bill of lading, which then becomes a foul bill. The reason for the notation is to limit the liability of the carrier from subsequent damage claims on packages already in poor condition when they were received. It is important for exporters to get a clean bill of lading, that is, one that has no such notation as to damaged packages. Foul bills of lading are generally not acceptable under letters of credit.

The exporter can get a clean bill substituted for a foul one by replacing the damaged boxes. Alternatively, if the damage is slight and the boxes cannot be replaced, the exporter might be able to give a letter of indemnity to the shipping company, holding it harmless of any damages that may result during the voyage and thus inducing it to issue a clean bill of lading. The latter solution is not entirely satisfactory, since the exporter waives his rights to claim damages from the carrier. In certain instances, however, this may be the only available alternative.

The following are some of the statements used to qualify a bill of lading as a foul bill of lading:

1 Bags torn and contents leaking.
2 Barrels damaged.
3 Equipment showing "rust."
4 Cartons wet.
5 Crates broken.

In other words, the bill of lading must show the defective nature of the merchandise or packaging. Note, however, that the following stamps:

1 Shipper's load and count: ______.
2 Contents said to be: ______.

are not considered to declare a defect of either the goods or the packaging.

Forwarder's Bill of Lading. A freight forwarder may consolidate the shipments of several exporters in order to get a lower bulk rate from the carrier. To evidence receipt of the goods, the forwarder issues his own bill of lading. This is a nonnegotiable instrument that serves merely as the forwarder's receipt and contract with the exporter to arrange for ocean shipment. Such a bill of lading in no way obligates the steamship company and is no assurance that the goods have been loaded on board a vessel. A forwarder's bill of lading is not acceptable under a letter of credit, unless specifically permitted. The freight forwarder, of course, gets an ocean bill of lading from the steamship company for the consolidated shipment.

Unless otherwise stated in the underlying letter of credit, the acceptance of such a bill of lading under a letter of credit must be expressly authorized by the issuer of the credit or strictly comply with Pub. 500. Furthermore, it must show the full name and address of the navigation line as well as the agent for that line. Pub. 500, established by the International Chamber of Commerce in Paris, presents guidelines on documentary letters of credit and other instruments used in financing global trade.

Through Bill of Lading. This is not really an ocean bill but is actually a bill of lading issued by a railroad company or trucker. It contains all the information that is usually in an ocean bill of lading. The through bill of lading, in fact, represents the railroad's or trucker's obligation to see to it that the goods get shipped from the inland point of origin to the inland point of destination. Generally, all rail, truck, and ocean freight is prepaid, and the railroad or trucker arranges for payment to the steamship company at the port of departure.

The through bill of lading can be useful to an exporter who does not have a forwarding agent at the port to take delivery of the goods from the railroad or truck and put the goods on board the vessel. It may also be advantageous for the exporter to know in advance the total cost of freight. On the other hand, since no ocean bill of lading is available, it may be difficult to arrange for financing of the shipment. Moreover, some follow-up by the exporter may be required to make sure that the rail shipment arrives at the seaport and the vessel gets loaded before the deadline called for in the sale contract. Due to the inherent uncertainty of shipment, some letters of credit prohibit the use of a through bill.

The previous discussion outlines some of the main kinds of bills of lading. The one most commonly used and the most desirable, from the financing bank's point of view, is the clean, on-board, order bill of lading; fortunately, most bills of lading are of this type.

B/L Copies. Ocean bills of lading are usually issued in several copies, the number depending on the needs of the importer. The importer generally requires at least two signed copies, one to get possession of the goods from the steamship company and one to clear them through customs. Additionally, the exporter may wish to send an unsigned copy directly to the importer for his information.

Any one of the signed copies of a negotiable bill of lading is enough to get possession of the goods from the carrier. Hence, a bank that has a financial interest in the shipment requires that it have possession of all signed, original copies in order to be sure no one is able to claim the goods without its permission.

Standardized Forms. Most clauses on modern bills of lading are standardized, as provided by the rules of the Carriage of Goods by Sea Act passed in Congress in 1936. Several other countries have enacted laws with similar provisions.

Freight Collect. Occasionally, goods are sent out "freight collect." Steamship companies generally don't like to accept freight collect shipments unless the consignee is well known and of undoubted business integrity. In most cases today, freight is prepaid by the exporter, who adds it to his invoice total. When freight is not prepaid, the carrier has a first lien on the merchandise, subject to payment of freight.

Airbill. A bill of lading issued by an air carrier is usually in nonnegotiable form. This means that most air shipments are consigned directly to the importer. A negotiable bill of lading would be of limited use in the case of air shipments, since the merchandise will probably, in most cases, arrive before the title document. Since banks and the exporter generally lose control over the merchandise when airbills are used, financing of an air shipment becomes more difficult when the underlying goods must be used as collateral.

Dock Receipt

This is a nonnegotiable receipt issued by a steamship company indicating that the goods have been delivered to the dock. Generally, the receipt is given to the railroad or trucker who delivers the goods and, in turn, gives the dock receipt to the exporter.

A dock receipt contains full details on the shipment, including the name of the shipper, vessel, port of destination, any numbers and marks on the packages, a general description of the goods, and gross weight and cubic measurement of each package. If some packages are damaged or in poor condition, this is also noted on the dock receipt and it becomes a foul receipt.

The dock receipt is used to make up the bill of lading, and the date of the receipt becomes the date of the received-for-shipment bill of lading. If there are notations on the dock receipt concerning damaged packages, this is transferred to the bill of lading, which then becomes a foul instrument.

Warehouse Receipt

A warehouse receipt is a document of title issued by a warehouseman covering the storage of goods in a terminal or field warehouse. The holder of a negotiable or nonnegotiable warehouse receipt generally has title to the goods in storage.

OTHER EXPORT DOCUMENTS

Commercial Invoice

The main purpose of the commercial invoice is to serve as an authoritative description of the goods shipped. It contains full details on grades, quality, price per unit, and total price of the shipment, as well as the nature of the price quotation, such as FOB vessel, CIF port of destination, and so on.

Other important information on the invoice includes:

Names and addresses of both exporter and importer.

Number of packages, their weight, and any marks on them.

Payment terms (i.e., letter of credit, documentary draft, cash in advance, etc.) including the currency, place, and time of payment.

A detailed statement of other expenses, such as transportation, insurance, and fees that are collectible from the importer and, therefore, part of the invoice total.

Name of vessel, ports of departure and destination.

Any export and/or import permit numbers that may be applicable.

While the commercial invoice concerns primarily the seller and the buyer, there may be other interested parties, such as banks and governments. Some foreign governments, for instance, have special regulations for commercial invoices, such as requiring them to be translated into the local language or requiring the use of metric weights and other measurements. Several customs authorities and other regulatory agencies also insist on complete consistency between the different documents. Thus, the numbers and marks on the commercial and consular invoices, the insurance certificate, and the bill of lading must agree exactly.

Failure to comply with government and customs regulations may result in heavy fines for the importer or even failure by the authorities to allow importation of the goods. It is, therefore, extremely important for the exporter to learn what the local requirements are and to comply with them exactly.

Packing List

This is an addendum to the commercial invoice and identifies the exact content of individual packages. Occasionally, a detailed packing list helps identification of specific items by the importer and facilitates clearance through customs. As with the commercial invoice, the customs authorities of the importing country may levy heavy fines if there are any inaccuracies or misrepresentations.

Consular Invoice

Many countries require that shipments be accompanied by consular invoices whose main purpose is to provide information to local customs officials on the goods being imported. Generally, special blank forms are available at foreign consular offices. Exporters must use meticulous care in filling out the forms, since even minor inaccuracies may delay customs clearance in the importing country and, in addition, could involve the importer in heavy fines.

After the exporter or his forwarding agent has filled out the consular invoice form, it must generally be presented and sworn to at the foreign consulate at the U.S. port of shipment.

Insurance Policy or Certificate

Practically all foreign shipments are to be insured, and an appropriate policy or certificate must accompany the other shipping documents. Chapter 9 discusses ocean marine insurance coverage.

Shipper's Export Declaration

In an effort to compile export statistics, the U.S. government requires the completion of an export declaration on a Department of Commerce form. The completed form must be filed with U.S. customs authorities. Information given on the form must accurately describe the shipment and it must also agree with the validation export license, when required, for the particular goods.

Export License

Most goods shipped from the United States can be exported under a general license, and thus no special license is required. A few strategic items, however, demand a special validation license, which may be obtained, on application, from the U.S. Department of Commerce. Detailed regulations on export licenses are given in the "Comprehensive Export Schedule" published by the Department of Commerce.

Inspection Certificate

The importer has to take, at face value, the description of the merchandise as stated on the commercial invoice, bill of lading, and other documents. Usually, the importer will have made payment before he has a chance to personally inspect the merchandise. Thus, a great degree of confidence in the honesty and ability to perform, as promised by the exporter, is required.

One way the importer can attempt to protect himself is to require, as part of the export documentation, a certificate of inspection by a reputable, independent inspection company located at the port of origin. This company, which may be the importer's own agent, will inspect the quality and quantity of goods shipped to make sure they are in agreement with the commercial invoice and underlying sales contract. The inspection certificate summarizes the results found by the inspecting company. If the shipment is deemed not to be up to previously agreed-on standards, the importer and intermediary banks will know this through qualifications on the inspection certificate. In that case, not all the documents are in order and no payment has to be made.

Certificate of Origin

In some instances, the United States may have a tariff treaty with another country, giving a more favorable rate if the item is of U.S. manufacture. In other instances, it may be easier to get financing for the export of goods of primarily U.S. origin. As we have seen in Chapters 3 and 4, FCIA insurance, Eximbank guarantees, and Eximbank financing are available only for exports of goods that are essentially of U.S. origin. In such instances, a certificate of U.S. origin may be required.

Banks should exercise a great deal of caution in examining this document when it is under an export letter of credit. If the issuing bank requires the certificate of origin to be issued by a chamber of commerce, it must invariably be issued on the letterhead of that *particular* chamber of commerce. For instance, if the Greater Chamber of Commerce of Paradise City is required to issue the certificate of origin, then a mere certification on a preprinted certificate of origin that is only attested by the Chamber of Commerce of Paradise City will not suffice (i.e., it must be issued by the *Greater* Chamber of Commerce of Paradise City). The negotiating/paying bank may, unfortunately, find that documents are held at the exporter's disposal for this irregularity. Figures 8-4 and 8-5 show certificates of origin issued by a chamber of commerce and attested by a chamber of commerce, respectively.

ASSISTANCE WITH EXPORT DOCUMENTS—FOREIGN FREIGHT FORWARDER

Getting together the proper export documentation for a shipment can be difficult and time consuming, especially in view of the high degree of government regulations. It may be advisable for an exporter to use the services of a freight forwarder whose job is to take care of all the required details.

All freight forwarders must be licensed and bonded under the rules of the Federal Maritime Commission. Some of the services performed by freight forwarders include the following:

Paradiseo Chamber of Commerce

1 Main Street
Paradiseo City

June 4, 19__

CERTIFICATE OF ORIGIN

Messrs. HACI Industrial Pumps,
7215 Mempho Lane,
Nellore, India.

Gentlemen,

The Paradiseo Chamber of Commerce, certifies to the best of its knowledge and belief, that 9 crates SIMA ISC Pumps, under Letter of Credit No.E-123456 advised by ABC American Bank, and under import licence No. GA 14541217; are manufactured by Industrial Supplies Company in the United States of America, with the prevailing laws and regulations.

Industrial Supplies Company has its principal offices at 23, Yirvon Street, Kings County.

PARADISEO CHAMBER OF COMMERCE

Signature
By ______________________

(Name and title)

Figure 8-4. Certificate of origin issued by a chamber of commerce.

Engagement of Ocean Cargo or Air Space Needed for the Shipment. Due to his thorough knowledge of the industry it is sometimes easier for the freight forwarder to get space on a vessel. Moreover, because of his familiarity with the shipping market, he may even be able to get lower freight rates than a small manufacturer with no such experience.

Arrangement for Ocean Marine Insurance. Many freight forwarders are also insurance brokers, which enables them to know exactly what

CERTIFICATE OF ORIGIN

SHIPPER/EXPORTER	DOCUMENT NO.
Industrial Supplies Company 23 Yirvon street Kings County, NY	E-123456
	EXPORT REFERENCES Ahanda Forwarding
CONSIGNEE HACI Industrial Pumps 7215 Mempho Lane Nellore, India.	FORWARDING AGENT - REFERENCES Ahanda Forwarding 1729 Main Lane Brooklyn, NY
	POINT AND COUNTRY OF ORIGIN USA
NOTIFY PARTY as above	DOMESTIC ROUTING/EXPORT INSTRUCTIONS Inland Routing to Pier No.7
PIER OR AIRPORT Brooklyn Pier No.7	
VESSEL (Flag) s/s Pipeda — PORT OF LOADING New York	ONWARD INLAND ROUTING as above
AIR/SEA PORT OF DISCHARGE Nellore — FOR TRANSSHIPMENT TO --------	

PARTICULARS FURNISHED BY SHIPPER

MARKS AND NUMBERS	NO. OF PKGS.	DESCRIPTION OF PACKAGES AND GOODS	GROSS WEIGHT	MEASUREMENT
SIMA ISC PUMPS 1 to 9	9 crates	SIMA ISC Pumps	3,267 Lbs.	9m3

The undersigned John Symski (Owner or Agent), does hereby declare for the above named shipper, the goods as described above were shipped on the above date and consigned as indicated and are products of the United States of America.

Dated at Paradiseo City on the 4th day of June 19--

Sworn to before me this 4th day of June 19--

Notary Public SEAL John Symski
SIGNATURE OF OWNER OR AGENT

The Paradiseo Chamber of Commerce, Paradiseo City, a recognized Chamber of Commerce under the laws of the State of Paradiseo, has examined the manufacturer's invoice or shipper's affidavit concerning the origin of the merchandise, and, according to the best of its knowledge and belief, finds that the products named originated in the United States of North America.

Secretary

PRINTED IN U S A

Figure 8-5. Certificate attesting to origin but not issued by a chamber of commerce.

insurance is needed and where to obtain the best rates for the particular coverage desired. Some freight forwarders carry their own insurance policies under which they can cover the occasional exporter whose limited volume may not warrant a policy of his own. A freight forwarder can also be of assistance in collecting insurance claims.

Delivery of the Freight to the Vessel by Rail, Truck, or Lighter (a Barge) as May Be Required. Sometimes the goods have to be picked up at the railroad siding and delivered to the dock. The freight forwarder may additionally follow up on a shipment from the factory to the ultimate destination to ensure a continuous smooth, and rapid flow of the goods.

Preparing the Necessary Export Documentation, Knowledge of What Is Required by All Parties, Including the Specific Import Regulation of the Various Foreign Countries. The freight forwarder also makes sure the requirements of the U.S. government, as well as those of the financing bank, are properly met. Occasionally, to save time, an exporter sends a commercial invoice, draft, and other shipping documents to the freight forwarder. The latter combines these with the ocean bill of lading which he has, in the meantime, obtained from the steamship company, and sends the whole package to the bank so that it can check the documents and make prompt payment under a letter of credit or send the item out for collection.

Consolidation of Smaller Shipments to Get More Favorable Cargo Rates. We have already noted that, in this connection, the freight forwarder issues his own bill of lading. Shipments thus consolidated are usually consigned to a foreign affiliate or correspondent of the freight forwarder. The affiliate or correspondent receives the goods, passes them through customs, and finally delivers them to the ultimate consignees in accordance with instructions received from the U.S. forwarder.

In some instances, the forwarder may be able to supply the exporter with information on business conditions, sales outlets, potential agents or representatives, credit condition, and so on, of certain foreign countries.

As seen from this list, the services of a freight forwarder are manifold and can be most valuable, especially to the small- or medium-sized exporter with only limited experience.

IMPORT DOCUMENTS

Generally, import documents required are the same as those used for exports.

Consular Invoice

Like other countries, the United States requires a consular invoice for most of its imports. The main purpose of the U.S. consular invoice is to give customs sufficient data to assess the import duty, as well as provide statistical records.

The consular invoice must contain a detailed description of the merchandise, including its grade, quality, quantity, and purchase price, as well as any marks, numbers, or symbols. Also given must be ports of departure and entry, names of buyer and seller, currency of purchase, and amount of any special charges, such as for insurance, freight, and commission.

Indemnities

Occasionally, a shipment of goods will arrive before the respective documents. To allow the importer to get the goods without the documents, his bank may be willing to issue an indemnity or guarantee to the steamship company. In it, the bank agrees to hold the carrier harmless for any consequences of releasing the goods without a bill of lading. The bank also agrees to submit the bill of lading to the carrier as soon as it is received. Based on this bank indemnity, the steamship company issues a carrier's certificate that serves in lieu of a bill of lading in allowing the importer to pick up the goods at the dock.

The importer who requests the letter of guarantee or the letter of indemnity to be issued on his behalf without an original bill of lading is required to certify in writing that he will reimburse the bank for all payments made by that bank, plus costs, interest, and legal expenses or fees, whether or not his bank is held liable for any damages resulting from issuing such an undertaking in favor of the steamship company.

A noncustomer of a bank, under a documentary collection, may also request the domiciled bank to issue a letter of guarantee/indemnity in favor of a steamship company, provided he supplies a counterindemnity from his bank, satisfying the credit risk requirements of the domiciled bank. It is worth noting here that all steamship guarantees/indemnities must be recorded by the bank as contingent liabilities and be booked against the credit facilities of the party requesting such a guarantee/indemnity.

Similarly, an airway release will enable the importer to take possession of his goods before transport documents are received by his bank or the domiciled bank, provided the goods are consigned in the name of the bank issuing such a release. Again, an airway release must be recorded by the bank and booked against the credit facilities of the party requesting such a release.

Import Duties

To assure that import duties will be paid, importers, both in the United States and abroad, often have to file a bond or bank guarantee with the collector of customs. In many foreign countries, banks issue guarantees for the payment of import duties as part of the regular credit facilities available to worthy customers. Such guarantees must be recorded in the books of the bank.

Services of Customhouse Broker

To help with the complex procedure of getting goods through customs, an importer may wish to use the services of a customhouse broker who knows and keeps up to date on important laws and administrative regulations. The services of a customhouse broker include watching for the arrival of the vessel, preparing and filing entry at the customhouse, paying on behalf of the importer the estimated duty, preparing and notarizing all necessary affidavits after the customs examination, delivering the goods according to the importer's instructions, and watching for the final liquidation of the customs entry. Considering the valuable services performed, the fees of a customhouse broker are usually modest.

In the United States, a customhouse broker may also operate at the same time as a freight forwarder.

CHAPTER 9

Ocean Marine and Air Cargo Insurance

Shipping, banking, financing, and insurance are the four essential ingredients of foreign trade. Among them, they have generated millions of jobs for U.S. manufacturers, farmers, exporters, importers, customhouse brokers, freight forwarders, and so on, and billions in revenues. This chapter focuses on insurance, specifically marine and air cargo insurance since the majority of shipments to and from the United States travel by seagoing vessels and cargo aircraft.

THE NEED FOR INSURANCE

The reason that practically all marine and air shipments are insured is the fact that such shipments are exposed to a number of hazards. The safety of shipping has, of course, improved greatly since early sailing days, but damage or loss of cargo (sea or air) is still a real possibility from such diverse causes as fire, stranding, collision, rolling of the ship/aircraft, hijacking by terrorists, theft, and so on.

Limited Liability of Carriers

Due to greater dangers inherent in marine and air shipments, the liability for damages is much more limited than for land carriers. Historically, sea voyages were considered joint ventures between ship owners and cargo owners, and thus the risks were shared. They still are today, and the concept is extended to air cargo shipments. As discussed under "Types of Losses," if any part of a total venture has to be sacrificed for the safety of the rest, all those who benefit from the sacrifice must pay a pro rata share to the party who suffered the loss.

Despite their limited liability, ocean carriers and air cargo operators are responsible for losses that may result from failure to exercise due diligence before the beginning of the voyage or flight. If the vessel or the aircraft is overloaded or is not properly insulated, manned, or equipped the carrier can be held responsible for any resulting damage to the cargo. The burden of proving the exercise of due diligence rests on the carrier. This can, however, be proven by merely showing that the vessel or plane was properly loaded, staffed and equipped before it started. If these few prerequisites are met, the carrier may be excused from the payment of damages to cargo even though, strictly speaking, the carrier may be wholly or partly at fault.

The duties, rights, and liabilities of ocean carriers are detailed in the 1936 Carriage of Goods by the Sea Act, which provides that the liability of carriers for damages is limited to $500 per package. The air carriers' liability is detailed in the amendment of the Hague Convention of September 28, 1955, stating that the liability shall not exceed $20 per kilogram of goods lost. This and further acts restricting the liability of carriers make proper insurance most important.

Financing

Most marine and air shipments are insured because they are financed by banking institutions. Usually, sellers want to get their cash immediately, and thus may request an irrevocable letter of credit. Buyers, on the other hand, do not generally want to pay until they take delivery of the goods. Banks and other financial institutions are asked to extend credit during the interim, with the goods serving as collateral. They, therefore, naturally insist on complete insurance coverage. Banks and other financial institutions may be named in insurance policies as interested parties. This appears in the policy as a banker's or factor's endorsement and covers banks or other financial institutions for their interest in the venture. A typical statement in an insurance policy nominates a bank as the "Assured Party" thus making said bank the beneficiary of the policy.

ARRANGING FOR INSURANCE

Whether the exporter or importer is responsible for arranging marine/air insurance depends on the shipment terms of sale. If reference is made to the Revised American Foreign Trade Definitions (1990), the terms of sale specified in the contract determine who is responsible for arranging insurance. If CIF terms are quoted, the exporter arranges the insurance and its cost is included in the price quotation. If FOB, C&F, FAS, or similar terms are used, the importer is responsible for arranging the insurance. In this case, the buyer's insurance may cover the goods for the entire voyage, from the warehouse of the supplier to the warehouse of the buyer, or it may only cover the period after title to the goods (therefore, responsibility) passes to the buyer. Alternatively, the sales contract may still stipulate that insurance is to be arranged by the exporter for account of the importer. The exporter then arranges for the insurance, but specifically itemizes its cost on the invoice. The exporter's basic price quotation does not include the cost of insurance. It is, however, included in the total as a specifically enumerated cost that the exporter incurred acting at the request of the importer.

Arranged by Exporter

Whether the delivery terms are FOB, CIF, FAS, or some others, the exporter enjoys certain advantages if he is the one who arranges marine/air insurance.

Coverage of Entire Voyage. If the importer arranges insurance, coverage may commence only when responsibility for the goods passes over to him. If the delivery terms specify FOB or FAS, for instance, the portion of the voyage before title passes may not be covered by the importer. Separate arrangements covering part of the voyage would, therefore, have to be made by the exporter.

The need for separate insurance is avoided if the exporter makes all the arrangements. He will then probably wish to obtain warehouse-to-warehouse coverage for the entire voyage. After the importer pays for the shipment, insurance documents can easily be turned over to him, together with the negotiable bill of lading giving him title (i.e., an insurable interest) to the goods as well as other shipping documents. The importer may, therefore, also be confident that the portion of the voyage for which he is responsible is adequately covered. He may, for instance, specify the desired insurance coverage in the sales contract and letter of credit. Unless the exporter submits documentation evidencing the type of insurance specified, he or she will not be paid.

Assurance of Adequate Coverage. If the importer arranges the insurance, the exporter may never know whether or not the coverage is adequate. It may be argued that after the point where responsibility transfers to the importer, the exporter doesn't care whether adequate insurance is maintained or not. As a practical matter, however, there are many situations where the exporter does care. Even though the responsibility for the goods is theoretically his, the importer may not be willing or able to accept and pay for them. Perhaps, the goods were damaged while in transit, resulting in the importer's refusal. An exporter may, therefore, have to make a claim, even after he is theoretically no longer responsible. In this case, he certainly is interested in the adequacy of insurance coverage. When shipping on an open account or collection basis, it is especially important for the exporter to maintain adequate coverage before he receives payment for the goods.

Assurance of Payment of Claims. If an exporter experiences a loss, he certainly wants to make sure a valid insurance claim will be paid promptly and in a currency he can use. If the importer arranges insurance, the exporter may not even have access to the policy. His ability to demonstrate an insurable interest and collect payment from an underwriter he does not know is severely limited. Since the policy is made out in the name of the importer, it may be impossible for the exporter to collect.

Sometimes the exact point when a loss occurred during a voyage cannot readily be determined. If two underwriters are involved, there may be lengthy disputes as to which of them is responsible, while the claim remains unpaid. Such conflict can be avoided if one and the same underwriter insures the entire voyage.

Easier Financing. A bank that finances an international trade transaction will probably wish to obtain negotiable insurance documents to make sure the shipment is properly insured and to be able to collect directly from the underwriter in case of difficulty. As a practical matter, this insurance documentation is most readily available to the bank if the exporter makes the arrangements. Moreover, insurance documents can readily be transferred from one financial institution to another that may have an insurable interest in a particular shipment.

Arrangement by Importer

There may be instances when ocean cargo insurance arranged by an importer is mandatory. A number of countries that are short on hard exchange insist that their importers insure locally. Moreover, several countries require locally arranged coverage as a means of building up their insurance industries. The exporter who wishes to sell to this type of market has no alternative but to go along with the restriction. He may, however, still take out some supplemental insurance in his own country to go into effect if the claim cannot be collected through insurance arranged by the importer. Such supplemental insurance is readily offered by many insurance companies and is commonly known as contingency insurance.

Insurance arranged by the importer may also be satisfactory if the latter's underwriter is known to be a company of undoubted reputation and the exporter can find a way of making sure adequate coverage in a negotiable form is arranged. The exporter may, for instance, require a copy of the policy or certificate to be sent to him directly by the underwriter or by the customer. This enables the exporter to examine the insurance document to make sure adequate protection is maintained.

Types of Policies

In a broad sense, ocean cargo policies can be divided into two basic types. Occasionally, merchants find it useful to take out a separate policy for each shipment. Firms having a more substantial trade volume, on the other hand, may find it useful to take out an open policy covering all their shipments for a defined period of time, to specific markets, and over defined routes. We may, therefore, distinguish between specific and open policies.

Specific Policies. Specific or special policies are written for each individual shipment. This policy is useful for the incidental exporter or importer who wishes to get separate coverage for each shipment he makes or receives. Since only a few shipments are made each year, the policy can be tailored to each movement of goods without putting an undue burden on the exporter or the underwriter.

Open Policies. Open policies, on the other hand, are recommended for exporters and importers who do a larger volume of business. An open policy provides coverage for all goods shipped by the insured while the policy is in effect. The policy may be good for a previously agreed on time interval, such as one year, or it may run indefinitely. In the latter case, it is usually subject to cancellation by either party upon 30 days' written or telegraphic notice. Cancellation does not, of course, apply to any shipment that is dispatched before the cancellation's effective date, as long as the shipment is promptly reported to the insurance company in the usual manner.

Reporting Each Shipment. Under an open policy, the shipper must inform the underwriter, as soon as practical, about each shipment that is insured. Particulars to be communicated to the underwriter include the value and description of the goods, name of the carrying vessel/aircraft, date and place of sailing/departure and destination. If the insured is an exporter, he usually informs the underwriter by sending him a copy of the cargo declaration made out by the shipper on forms supplied by the underwriter. If the insured is an importer, however, he may not be in a position to report details until the goods have actually arrived at their destination.

Premiums are billed at the end of each month, based on shipments reported during that period. If the insured deliberately fails to report a shipment, the insurance company has the option of canceling that policy. Unintentional errors, omissions, or delays in reporting, on the other hand, are usually excused. The insurance company retains the right to inspect the insured's records to make sure all insured shipments are reported and appropriate premiums paid.

Insurance Certificate. When an open policy is used, the instrument evidencing insurance on a specific shipment is not the policy itself (as would be the case with a specific policy). Rather, an insurance certificate is employed. This is prepared by the exporter on a form supplied by the insurance company. The original of this form becomes the certificate that serves as the shipping document evidencing insurance coverage. It takes the place of the insurance policy and can be used to convey all the rights of the original policy to anyone having an ownership interest in the shipment. The certificate generally contains a phrase, such as "Losses are payable to the order of (named person) on surrender of this certificate." Since the named person can endorse the certificate over to someone else who may have an interest in the shipment, the certificate becomes a quasinegotiable instrument.

The certificate does not contain all the detailed terms of the master policy. Indeed, the information contained in it is limited, so that the bank and the importer sometimes cannot determine whether insurance coverage is adequate. For this reason, banks are generally careful in accepting certificates under a letter of credit, unless specifically permitted or unless the certificate contains enough detail to allow a judgment that adequate insurance has been obtained in accordance with the provisions of the credit. To meet requirements set by banks and others as to knowing full details on extent of coverage, underwriters sometimes issue specific policies in lieu of certificates under an open policy.

Obtaining the Proper Insurance

Practically all ocean marine insurance underwritten in the United States is placed through brokers. A broker acts as agent for the insured, and for his services receives a commission from the underwriter with whom the insurance is placed.

Services of Brokers. The broker has the advantage of being familiar not only with the technicalities of marine/air insurance, but also has an unbiased overview of the coverage and premium rates offered by all insurance companies. He is in a good position to obtain for his client the coverage that best fits his needs at the lowest possible cost.

A marine/air insurance broker may also be able to offer other valuable services. He can assist in getting payment of claims for losses sustained by the insured, especially with the more complicated particular and general average losses. If an underwriter is unreasonable in delaying payment on a justified claim, the broker may often advantageously intercede on behalf of the customer.

Since a broker gets paid for his services, shippers are well advised to put their brokers to work in helping them obtain proper insurance, settling claims on marine/air shipments, and so on.

Broker's Own Policy. Occasionally, a broker takes out his own open policy and issues so-called cover notes against it on behalf of clients who do not have the volume of business to warrant having their own open policy. It is important to note that such brokers' cover notes are not acceptable in lieu of insurance policies or certificates without specific agreement between the buyer and seller. If a letter of credit is involved, banks will generally not accept cover notes without being specially permitted to do so in the credit.

A shipper or importer who accepts a cover note should be aware that he will not know for sure whether the broker's open policy with the underwriter contains the specific coverage needed. While the broker may, in some instances, be held responsible for any misrepresentations that might be made, brokers generally do not have sufficient financial resources to pay legal claims made against them.

Amount of Insurance

The need for maintaining adequate insurance has already been stressed. Generally, the recommended minimum amount is the CIF value of the merchandise plus 10% for other fees (such as bank charges, export and import duties, etc.), and normal margin of profit. Insurance for customs duties is usually separately computed from other marine and war risk insurance, primarily since rates for customs duty insurance are substantially lower.

Probably, the best way of determining needed insurance is to estimate the market value of the merchandise at the port of destination and obtain coverage for that amount. Policies are also available that provide for reimbursement at the highest market value for the goods during a defined period while in transit. This type of valuation clause is often used in connection with shipments of commodities, such as coffee, cocoa, and rubber, whose prices tend to undergo wide fluctuations. Other methods of arriving at a valuation of goods may also be agreed on by the insurer and the insured to meet individual needs.

Cost

The rates charged by insurance companies depend on many different factors. Important determinants include the type of coverage desired, shipping routes, types of conveyances, duration of voyage, and nature of goods shipped. Each individual shipper's past loss experience is also important. After a period of favorable experience, rates may be lowered. Conversely, a shipper with a bad loss record may find his insurance premiums increased.

When negotiating an open policy, the insured tells the underwriter the goods he expects to ship, where he expects to ship them, and the extent of coverage desired. Taking all factors into consideration, the underwriter then gives the shipper a complete rate schedule. The shipper, therefore, knows how much his exact shipping costs will be. This helps exporters to arrive at exact price quotations in cases when the cost of insurance is included in the cost quoted to the foreign importer.

Loss Prevention Service

Many brokers and underwriters have a loss prevention service; it is usually offered free of charge, since it benefits not only the insured, but also the underwriters. Sometimes, a shipper may get repeated claims from an overseas importer. Through the loss prevention service, an underwriter or broker can turn such problems over to a specialized staff. Perhaps, unnecessary losses are being incurred because of faulty packaging or some other cause that can be remedied. A packaging expert may, for instance, be able to isolate the problem and recommend corrective action. The shipper benefits from such a loss prevention service because it assists in keeping down premium rates.

It may be advisable for shippers to choose underwriters or brokers who have a loss prevention service. A company without such a service merely increases its premiums when a shipper's loss experience goes up. A more constructive approach, in contrast, is offered by a company that puts up a team of experts to help solve the underlying problems causing the losses.

GENERAL POLICY PROVISION

Each ocean cargo policy has a number of clauses that specify the parameters within which the insurance will be operative. Items, such as the name of parties to the insurance contract, types of goods, valuation of goods, types of conveyances, voyages covered, and limitation of the underwriter's liability, must be specified. A description of some of the most important general policy provisions is helpful for an understanding of ocean marine insurance.

The Insured Party

Anyone having an insurable interest in a shipment may take out ocean cargo insurance. This may be the exporter, importer, or a financial institution. If the insured cannot demonstrate that he has an insurable interest in the goods, the policy is not valid. Hence, on FOB, FAS, cost and freight, and similar shipments, the exporter does not, strictly speaking, have an insurable interest beyond the point of title transfer. He may, nevertheless, be acting as agent for the importer in obtaining cargo insurance. Insurance obtained as agent for someone else who has an insurable interest is considered to be valid.

Insurance policies often contain a phrase, such as "loss, if any, payable to insured or order." This, in fact, makes the policy seminegotiable. Losses may be payable to anyone to whom insurance and title documents have been negotiated and who has an insurable interest. Losses may also be made payable to an interested third party, such as a financial institution, by inserting the name of the third party in the special space provided on the policy.

Insured Goods

Insurance coverage is limited to "lawful goods and merchandise." Hence, any illicit or contraband shipment cannot be covered. The basic types of goods that are expected to be shipped under the policy are usually listed. Coverage is not, however, limited only to those goods listed. If other lawful goods are shipped, these may also be insured, provided the underwriter is informed of their nature and, if necessary, an additional premium is paid.

Valuation

Before marine insurance goes into effect, the underwriter and the insured agree on the value of the goods to be covered. Premiums are then paid, based on this value. If a total or partial loss occurs, the underwriter makes reimbursement determined by the previously agreed-on value. The importance of maintaining adequate insurance, based on landed value plus profit, has been outlined earlier in "Amount of Insurance."

Types of Conveyances

Ocean Vessels. Coverage is usually granted for all mechanically propelled iron or steel vessels and connecting conveyances. Barges and sailing vessels are specifically excluded when used as connecting conveyances.

Air Shipments. Shipments made by aircraft and connecting conveyances are also covered. Policies generally contain a special clause that specifies the types of risks insured if shipment is by aircraft or connecting conveyances. The policy may also contain a clause reading, "Wherever the words 'ship,' 'vessel,' 'seaworthiness,' 'ship or vessel owner' appear in this policy, they are deemed to include also the words 'aircraft,' 'airworthiness,' or 'aircraft owner.'"

Coverage on air shipments is usually for all risks of external loss or damage. This does not, however, include war risks. Losses due to strikes, riots, and civil commotion are usually covered but may also be excluded if the premium for such insurance would be too high. Also excluded may be damages due to changes in atmospheric pressure, heat, or cold.

Premium rates on air cargo shipments may be lower than those for ocean shipments because of the shorter time required and, therefore, reduced chances for pilferage.

Mail or Parcel Post. Cargo insurance may also be valid for first class or registered mail, registered, government insured, or ordinary parcel post, by air or otherwise.

If insurance for shipments by either air, mail, or parcel post is not desired, these respective clauses may be crossed out and marked "void."

Voyages Covered

The geographic limits where insured voyages may take place are usually specified. At one extreme, the voyage clause may be limited to operations between only two designated ports, as between New York and London. At the other extreme, a liberal voyage clause may read, "At and from ports and/or places in the world to ports and/or places in the world."

Limit of Liability

To limit his overall risk, the underwriter generally specifies clear money limits to the liability he is willing to assume. Upper liability limits are usually attached to the following:

Maximum amount that may be shipped on any one vessel, aircraft, or connection conveyance.

Maximum amount that may be shipped on deck of any one vessel.

Maximum amount in any one package shipped by mail or parcel post.

Sometimes, the maximum amount permitted on any one vessel or aircraft has to be exceeded. If the shipper informs the underwriter of the excess before loading, coverage can usually be arranged by special agreement.

TYPES OF LOSSES

Most of today's marine insurance practices can be traced back many years. In fact, even a modern policy contains some of the same wording as Lloyd's Policy of 1779 and earlier policies. To the uninitiated, the practices and language of marine insurance often seem unclear. Some attempts have been made to modernize the language but a number of traditional expressions and phrases still exist because their meaning has become clearly defined through centuries of trade practices and court decisions. Hence, even if the phrasing may be somewhat difficult for those not familiar with ocean marine insurance, to those who are initiated, the rights and duties of both underwriter and insured are clear and unambiguous.

Marine insurance recognizes four different types of losses. The type of coverage that underwriters give differs, depending on the nature of the loss suffered. An understanding of the different losses is, therefore, essential as a prerequisite for understanding ocean marine insurance.

Total Loss

The occurrence of one of the perils of the sea, fire, or some other cause may result in a total loss of the entire shipment. A "constructive total loss" might also occur when the cost of salvaging the shipment would be more than the salvaged value of the merchandise. A shipment might be abandoned by the insured or the underwriter if any further efforts at salvage would be fruitless.

Most policies provide for the payment of a total loss resulting from an insured peril up to the insured amount.

Total Loss of Part of Shipment

When a shipment consists of separate parts, units, or packages, insurance can generally be obtained that considers the loss of any one or more units as a total loss. This may be desirable from the point of view of the insured, since total losses are the easiest to adjust.

Particular Average

The word "average," as used in the insurance industry, often causes confusion to the layman. Actually, it has nothing to do with the normally accepted meaning for average. Rather, it means a partial loss. A particular average loss, therefore, is a partial loss that is suffered by the one whose goods are partly lost or damaged. When there is a particular average loss, other interests in the voyage (such as the carrier and other cargo owners whose goods were not damaged) do *not* contribute to the partial recovery of the one suffering the loss.

An example of a particular average (partial loss) occurs when a storm or fire damages part of the shipper's cargo and no one else's cargo has to be sacrificed to save the voyage. The cargo owner whose goods were damaged looks to his insurance company for payment, provided, of course, his policy covers the specific type of loss suffered.

Since most losses experienced by shippers are partial, that is, of the particular average nature, it is important to know exactly what provisions for such a partial loss are in the insurance policy. Underwriters sometimes limit their liability for particular averages.

General Average

Sometimes, when threatened by a peril of the sea or some other hazard, part of the cargo or vessel must be sacrificed to save the whole venture. For instance, during a storm, a portion of the cargo may have to be jettisoned to save the vessel and remaining cargo. Today, the most typical cause for general average losses is fire where, in the process of its being put out, some goods are damaged by water. In such cases, it is established, under maritime law, that those interests whose property was saved must contribute proportionally to cover the losses of the one whose property was voluntarily sacrificed. Thus, a shipper, even if his goods remain undamaged, may have a general average claim levied against him.

SCOPE OF INSURANCE COVERAGE

So far, we have considered only the types of losses that may occur, with these losses defined in accordance with long-standing ocean marine insurance practices as total, part of a total shipment, particular, or general. Another question is under what circumstances the underwriter will pay when one of these losses occurs. Given the occurrence of a loss, whether or not the underwriter will reimburse under the policy, as well as the amount of any payment, may depend on whether the loss is defined as total, particular, or general.

Perils Clause

While ocean marine coverage can be written to fit individual needs, all policies contain the so-called perils clause:

> Touching the adventure and perils which the Company (Underwriter) is contented to bear, and take upon itself, they are of the seas, fires, assailing thieves, jettison, barratry of the Master or Mariners, and all other like perils, losses or misfortunes that have or shall come to the hurt, detriment or damage of said goods and merchandise, or any part thereof except as may be otherwise provided for herein or endorsed hereon.

This clause is a somewhat updated version of the one that appeared in Lloyd's Policy of 1779. The perils clause outlines the basic risks that the underwriters are prepared to assume:

Perils of the seas, such as damage resulting from heavy winds and waves.

Fires, including consequential damages resulting from a fire or efforts to extinguish it.

The taking of cargo by force by assailing thieves.

Coverage under the basic perils clause does not include clandestine theft or pilferage, nor does it include piracy.

Jettison or the voluntary throwing overboard of part of the cargo to lighten the vessel and save the remainder of the venture.

Barratry or deliberate negligence, theft, fraud, or other misconduct on the part of the ship's officers or crew.

Like perils of the same specific nature as already listed.

It is important to note that the extent of coverage against hazards enumerated in the perils clause may be curtailed in other clauses of the same policy. To highlight this, the sample perils clause previously discussed ends with the phrase "except as may be otherwise provided for herein or endorsed hereon."

Additional coverage against risks not listed in the perils clause may also be provided in other sections of the policy or in a separate policy in the case of war risks coverage.

Qualifications on Particular Average

If a total or a general average loss results from the occurrence of an insured peril, most policies provide for full reimbursement to the insured who suffered the loss. Interestingly enough, the same is not generally true for particular average. Ocean cargo policies may contain clauses that in some way narrow the underwriter's liability in case of a partial loss. Since most claims under ocean marine policies arise from partial losses, it is important for the insured to understand the coverage he has available and, alternatively, the risks he is taking on himself. We shall, therefore, examine the typical particular average qualifications that may be found in a marine policy.

Free of Particular Average (FPA). The words "free of" followed by other words or phrases mean that the underwriter assumes no responsibility for whatever is enumerated. Hence, if a policy reads "free of particular average," the underwriter will not pay any particular average claims. Since the insured must, therefore, assume the risk for any and all partial losses, this is the most restrictive qualification on an insurance policy.

A clause with a similar meaning might read "free of average unless general." This means that general average claims are covered, while particular average claims are not.

FPA—American Conditions (FPA—AC). "Free of particular average unless *caused* by the vessel being stranded, sunk, burnt, on fire, or in collision." This clause is substantially more liberal to the insured than the straight FPA clause. It means that the underwriter assumes the risk for a partial loss or damage if it was directly caused by a stranding, sinking, collision, or fire. In all other cases, the underwriter assumes no responsibility for partial losses.

FPA—English Conditions (FPA—EC). "Warranted free from particular average unless the vessel or craft be stranded, sunk, or burnt, on fire, or in collision." This clause is slightly more liberal than FPA—AC. Under the U.S. conditions, a reimbursable partial loss must be directly caused by a stranding, sinking, burning, or collision, while the English conditions provide for insurance payments if the vessel was stranded, sunk, or burnt at some time during the voyage. There is no need to show that the stranding, sinking, or burning was the direct cause of the particular loss.

To avoid possible confusion, it must be pointed out that the terms "American conditions" or "English conditions" refer merely to the historical origin of these clauses. In modern ocean marine insurance practices, there is no necessary correlation between the names of these clauses and insurance practices in the United States and the United Kingdom, respectively. FPA—AC and FPA—EC are specialized insurance terms used in many different countries.

Franchise Clause

> Free of particular average under 3% unless general or vessel/aircraft is stranded, sunk, crashed, burnt, on fire, or in collision with any substance other than water, each case or shipping package separately insured.

Payment by underwriters for particular average is often qualified by a franchise clause, such as the one previously quoted. The purpose of this clause is to avoid the payment of many small claims that involve costly processing relative to the amount involved. The franchise clause states that the underwriter pays only if the amount of the claim is in excess of a previously agreed-on franchise limit. This limit varies, depending on the nature of the merchandise and type of coverage desired. It is usually expressed as a percentage of particular damage as compared to the total amount of insurance.

It is interesting to note that, in contrast to the deductible clause commonly found in automobile and other "land-type" insurance, the franchise clause of ocean marine policies provides for payment of the *entire* partial loss as long as the franchise percentage is exceeded.

In the previously mentioned sample clause, if the vessel has been stranded, sunk, burnt, on fire, or in collision, the franchise percentage is waived and losses from the specifically enumerated sea perils are recoverable, regardless of the percentage. General average claims are also reimbursed without regard to the franchise percentage. For other perils enumerated in the perils clause, the franchise percentage would apply.

The franchise clause provides substantially broader coverage than the other particular average clauses. The scope of the previously quoted simple clause is further expanded by the provision that each case or shipping package is separately insured. Hence, the loss of one package is considered a total loss of part of a shipment.

On-Deck Shipments

Insurance coverage for on-deck shipments may be somewhat different from the more usual under-deck shipments. Cargo that is stored on deck, rather than in the hold of the vessel, may be subject to additional hazards. Consequently, insurance policies frequently have some special clauses for on-deck cargo. On such clause, for instance, is that the underwriter will not pay particular average for on-deck cargo unless the loss is caused by stranding, sinking, burning, or collision of the vessel, or if the cargo has to be jettisoned or is washed overboard.

An on-deck shipment is defined as one involving an on-deck bill of lading. If the bill of lading provides for storage in the ship's hold and the carrier stores it on deck without permission of the insured, for purposes of the insurance, the shipment is considered to be below deck. This arrangement provides maximum protection to the insured if the carrier performs an unauthorized act. Of course, even though the insurance company may pay the claim of the insured, it may be able, in turn, to hold the carrier responsible for the damage.

The establishment of containerization has brought some changes to insurance coverage for on-deck shipments. On modern container ships, up to one-third of all containers may be stored on deck. Moreover, the insured does not know whether the container holding his cargo will be stored on or below deck. Hence, the practice has evolved for insurance of containerized shipments to be treated the same, as far as extent of coverage and cost is concerned, regardless of whether the container is stored on or below deck. Nevertheless, containers stored on deck may be slightly more vulnerable to damage by water and atmospheric changes, particularly if the container is not watertight. The roof of such containers is often constructed of thin metal, and damage that allows water to enter is possible.

Additional Coverage

The basic perils clause lists only a limited number of perils that are covered in case of a total, particular, or general loss. Exporters and importers who wish coverage against other hazards can usually obtain the desired insurance.

The different possible types of insurance coverage are limited only by the nature of the merchandise, the underwriter's willingness to assume a particular risk, and the insured's willingness to pay an appropriate premium. Marine insurance policies are often written for the specific need of the shipper and requirements of the particular merchandise. A number of the clauses providing more extended coverage have been standardized by the American Institute of Marine Underwriters.

Explosion Clause. Since explosion is not covered in the basic perils clause, it must be included by a special provision if such coverage is desired by the insured. Damage or loss resulting from war, strikes, riots, or civil commotions, however, are excluded from coverage under the explosion clause.

Warehouse, Forwarding, and Lost Packages Clause

> These assurers agree to pay any landing, warehousing, forwarding and special charges for which this policy in the absence of any average warranty contained herein would be liable. Also to pay the insured value of any package or packages which may be totally lost in loading, transhipment or discharge.

Normal warehousing, forwarding, and similar charges are not, of course, borne by the underwriter. Such charges may, however, have to be incurred to minimize a loss. If any such charges incurred in preventing a loss would be recoverable under a "with average" policy (i.e., one that reimburses total as well as partial losses for all insured perils), they are also recoverable even if the policy contains a free of particular average clause. It is to the underwriter's advantage to reimburse expenses incurred in salvaging goods because such action could prevent the occurrence of an insured loss.

Regarding lost packages, under the previously quoted clause, it need not be shown that any packages were lost as a result of one of the insured perils.

As long as a package is totally lost in loading, transhipment, or discharge, it is covered by the insurance.

Inchmaree Clause. Any loss resulting from the bursting of boilers, breakage of shafts, a latent defect in the machinery, hull, or appurtenances or from errors in navigation or management of the vessel may be covered by the so-called Inchmaree clause. This clause came into fashion after a British court ruled, in the case of the SS *Inchmaree*, that the enumerated hazards are not perils of the sea and, therefore, not insured unless a special clause is added to the policy.

While the hazards enumerated in the Inchmaree clause can cause most serious damage to the hull and machinery of the vessel, a consequential loss to cargo may also be possible. The Inchmaree clause was originally included only in hull insurance policies. It was later also adapted to cargo policies and is now one of the standardized American Institute Cargo Clauses.

Other Hazards. Some of the additional risks for which coverage may be desired include the following:

- Theft and pilferage
- Fresh water damage
- Damage due to sweat or moisture inside the ship's hold
- Rust
- Damage caused by contact with other cargo or fuel oil
- Breakage or leakage of containers through carelessness in handling or improper storage

Additional risks that can or should be covered depend on a number of factors, such as the goods involved, quality of packaging, past experience of the insured, and most importantly, the amount of premium the insured is willing to pay. Insurance for some hazards may only be obtained at an exorbitant premium, which may make it more economical for the trader to carry the risks.

Depending on the nature of the goods, certain types of coverage may not be necessary. For instance, it makes little sense to insure against pilferage or rust if one is shipping bulk commodities, such as coal or grains.

"All Risks" Coverage

> To pay for physical loss or damage from any external cause, irrespective of percentage, excluding such risks as are excepted by the FC&S Warranty and the SR&CC Warranty in this policy, also excluding claims for delay, loss of market and inherent risk.

The previously quoted clause provides substantially more protection than the basic perils clause. Any physical loss due to an external cause is covered by "all risks" insurance. Specifically *excluded* from coverage, however, are the following:

1 Claims for delays in the delivering the goods to the final destination; deterioration, such as spoilage due to inherent nature of the goods; and loss of market (perhaps due to late delivery).
2 Risks resulting from war, whether declared or not, or from weapons of war. The exclusion from coverage for these risks is usually specified in a "free of capture and seizure" (FC&S) clause. Insurance against war risks may be available under a separate war risks policy.
3 Losses (including theft, pilferage, breakage, or destruction of property) resulting from strikes, locked-out workers, riots, and civil commotions. Exclusion from coverage of these risks is usually specified in a so-called SR&CC (strikes, riots, and civil commotions) clause. Insurance against SR&CC risks may, however, be obtainable by a separate endorsement to the ocean cargo policy or through separate war risks insurance. If a separate endorsement or policy covers these risks, such insurance extends only to direct damage to the merchandise, but does not cover resulting damages, such as time delays, loss of market, or added expenses that may occur due to the need to transship the goods as a result of the disturbance. In some circumstances, with the underwriter willing, such consequential losses can also be covered. In this case, however, consequential damages can only be collected when there is a direct and unbroken link between the peril covered and specific loss suffered.

If there is a prolonged disturbance such as a major dock strike, SR&CC coverage may involve underwriters in substantial losses. For this reason, insurers reserve the right to cancel this type of coverage with only 48 hours' notice (similar to the cancellation provision for war risk policies).

Since "all risks" coverage is very broad, it has become popular in today's insurance market. Traders must, however, not be misled by the terminology of "all risks." As previously indicated, some important hazards are not covered even under a so-called all risks policy. Moreover, other risks of damage may be specifically excluded from coverage. The risk of leaking shipping containers, for instance, may be excluded. Similarly, when insuring uncrated automobiles, it is customary to exclude risks of marring, denting, scratching, or chipping, unless caused by the vessel's being stranded, sunk, burned, on fire, or in collision. Other exclusions depend on the susceptibility of certain types of goods to damage, as well as the premium that the insured is willing to pay.

Finally, all risks coverage is more expensive than a more limited policy. Depending on the nature of the goods, the route of shipment, and other factors, all-inclusive all risks insurance may not be necessary. It makes little sense to pay high premiums for extended insurance coverage that is not really needed.

DURATION OF COVERAGE

So far, we have considered the different hazards to which ocean shipments may be susceptible and the types of insurance coverage available. A different, and, for exporters and importers, a most important question is the points in time when coverage commences and when it terminates. Unless some specific extension to the policy is made, insurance is only effective while goods are on the high seas. For foreign merchants and financing institutions, this leaves gaps in time during which they may still be susceptible to substantial losses. In an effort to meet demand for more comprehensive coverage, underwriters have come up with a number of riders that extend the time when insurance is available.

Warehouse-to-Warehouse Clause

This clause provides coverage not only while the vessel is at sea, but from inland point of origin to inland point of destination. Demand for this type of comprehensive coverage has been so strong that most cargo insurance policies presently contain some kind of version of the warehouse-to-warehouse clause. Aside from its broad coverage in terms of time, the warehouse-to-warehouse clause offers the advantage of providing insurance by the same underwriter for the entire voyage. If, as an alternative, different underwriters insure the land and sea portions of the voyage, disputes may easily arise as to where, during transit, a particular shipment of merchandise was damaged. The actual point at which damage occurred may be difficult or impossible to determine. If one underwriter insures the entire voyage, such disputes are easily avoided.

Under the warehouse-to-warehouse clause, goods are covered from the time they leave the warehouse or store of the shipper, during ordinary transit and transshipment, and until they reach their final destination. After the goods are unloaded from the overseas vessel, however, a time limit is imposed, during which coverage is still effective. If the final destination is within the limits of the port of discharge, the time limit is 15 days. If it is outside such limits, 30 days are allowed. Should the permitted time be exceeded or should there be a transshipment due to circumstances beyond the control of the insured, coverage continues in return for payment of an additional premium. In this case, the insured must give prompt notice of the uncontrollable delay to the underwriter.

Craft etc. Clause

This clause provides coverage whenever a lighter (barge) or other such craft is used to load or unload an overseas vessel. If a lighter or other such craft is sunk, stranded, or burned, and all the goods on it are lost, this is considered a total loss, and recovery may be made accordingly. If part of the goods are salvaged, the free-of-particular-average clause would govern.

Deviation Clause

> This insurance shall not be vitiated by any unintentional error in description of vessel, voyage or interest, or by deviation, over-carriage, change of voyage, transhipment or any other interruption of the ordinary course of transit, from causes beyond the control of the Insured. It is agreed, however, that any such error, deviation or other occurrence mentioned above shall be reported to the Company as soon as known to the Insured, and additional premium paid if required.

This clause is self-explanatory. It is again important to note that the insured is covered only if the deviation is caused by circumstances beyond his control. The insured is obligated to promptly report any error in description or occurrence of a deviation to the insurance company. An additional premium may be payable for continuation of coverage.

Shore Clause

> Where this insurance by its terms covers while on docks, wharves or elsewhere on shore, and/or during land transportation, it shall include the risks of collision, derailment, overturning or other accident to the conveyance, fire, lightning, sprinkler leakage, cyclones, hurricanes, earthquakes, floods (meaning the rising of navigable waters), and/or collapse or subsidence of docks or wharves, even though the insurance be otherwise FPA.

When warehouse-to-warehouse coverage is in effect, insurance is required for risks that are common during the land part of a voyage. The perils covered while goods are on land are outlined in the previously quoted clause. All insured losses that occur while goods are on land are paid in their entirety, even though coverage during the sea portion of a voyage may be limited by an FPA or franchise clause.

Marine Extension Clauses

Marine extension clauses (MECs) were initiated during World War II to give the insured continuous protection in case of deviations, delays, or other variations of the voyage. These clauses remained in force even after the war. They provide for automatic continuation of coverage at no additional premium when the course of transit is interrupted or suspended due to circumstances beyond the control of the insured. There are presently seven MECs, whose major provisions may be summarized as follows:

1 The first MEC provides for insurance coverage from the time goods leave the warehouse, at the place named in the policy, until they arrive at the final destination named in the policy—despite any deviation or delays that may occur. It, in fact, broadens the basic warehouse-to-warehouse clause by omitting the phrase "during the ordinary course of transit."
2 Specific coverage is given during any deviation, delay, forced discharge, transshipment, or "any other variation of the adventure arising from the exercise of a liberty granted to the shipowner or charterer under the contract of affreightment."
3 It may occur that, under a bill of lading or other contract, a shipowner or charterer may terminate a shipment at a port other than the original destination. If this happens, the third MEC provides for continuation of the insurance until goods are either forwarded to the original destination, another final destination, or sold.
4 The fourth MEC provides for termination of insurance coverage 15 days after goods arrive at their final port, if the goods are resold. If resold goods are forwarded to another destination not covered by the insurance, coverage terminates when the goods are again put into transit or at the expiration of 15 days, whichever occurs first.
5 The fifth MEC provides for continuation of insurance coverage, provided the insured pays an additional premium under two circumstances:
   a. If there is a change in voyage at the discretion of the insured
   b. If there has been an omission or error in the description of the interest, vessel, or voyage
6 Any loss, damage, or expense resulting from a delay or inherent vice, or nature of the goods is specifically excluded from insurance coverage. Hence, it is emphasized that MECs cover only the time period during any delay but do not cover losses caused by the delay. Only losses caused by hazards specifically insured against elsewhere in the policy are covered.
7 The last MEC emphasizes that no extension of coverage is granted unless the course of transit is suspended or interrupted due to circumstances beyond the control of the insured. In case of a voluntary change of voyage insurance, coverage may be extended through payment of an additional premium as provided in MEC 5.

LIMITATIONS TO CARGO INSURANCE

A number of hazards are usually *not* covered by marine/air insurance policies. The most typical of these are losses resulting from:

The inherent nature or vice of the merchandise itself (e.g., the deterioration of perishable goods, improper packaging, ordinary wear and tear).

Loss of market due to delays.

If a shipment itself is illegal or the shipper knowingly fails to give some important information to the underwriter, the insurance policy may be voided.

A venture is legal if it complies with the laws of the country under whose flag it operates as well as with any international agreements to which that country may be a party.

Memorandum Clause

Sometimes, an insurance policy will contain a so-called memorandum clause that lists special articles for which the underwriter will not pay particular average. For other specifically listed commodities, particular average may be paid only if it exceeds a certain franchise percentage. Clauses of this nature are included for goods that may be particularly susceptible for certain types of losses. In such cases, the cost of complete insurance coverage would require a prohibitively high premium.

Labels and Machinery Clauses

At times, two additional special clauses are included. These clauses concern the underwriter's liability in case of damaged labels or parts of machinery. The labels clause provides that if labels on packages are damaged due to an insured peril, the underwriter is responsible only for obtaining and affixing new labels.

The machinery clause similarly states that if a part of a machine is damaged, the insurance company is not liable for the cost of the whole machine, but only for getting and installing a new part.

OBLIGATIONS AND WARRANTIES

Sue, Labor, and Travel Clauses

Property may sometimes be imperiled, but it can be salvaged if a timely effort is made. To be certain that a maximum effort is made, most policies contain a "sue, labor, and travel" clause. This obligates the insured to take any possible action that will save the merchandise from loss or further loss if some damage has already occurred. The underwriter, in turn, agrees to reimburse the insured for expenditures incurred up to the proportion that the insured amount bears to the total value of the property at risk.

Information

When shipping under an open policy, the insured has to declare all shipments promptly to the insurer, giving details concerning the type of goods shipped, terms of sale, value of shipment, port of origin and destination, and so on. The insured may not knowingly withhold any information that might alter the underwriter's evaluation of the risk inherent in the voyage. If such information is deliberately withheld, the usual penalty is voiding of the insurance policy.

Seaworthiness of Vessel and Airworthiness of Aircraft

It has already been pointed out that the carrier has certain responsibilities, such as providing for the seaworthiness of the vessel or the airworthiness of the aircraft and maintaining either on their previously arranged courses and itineraries. Although the shipper should actually look to the carrier for damages resulting from such things as an unseaworthy vessel and unairworthy aircraft, this principle is usually waived by the underwriter in favor of the insured. The appropriate clause may read as follows:

> The seaworthiness of the vessel and the airworthiness of the aircraft as between the insured and the insurers is hereby admitted and the wrongful act or misconduct of the shipowner or his servants causing a loss is not to defeat the recovery by an innocent insured if the loss in the absence of such wrongful act or misconduct would have been a loss recoverable on the policy.

Thus, if damage results through a fault of the carrier, the insurance company will pay the shipper, but will itself take recourse for damages to the carrier. This is commonly referred to as the right of subrogation—that is, when the insurer pays a loss, it acquires any right of recovery the insured may have against a third party responsible for the loss, such as, in the above case, the carrier.

WAR RISK INSURANCE

War risk coverage is not part of the usual ocean cargo policy. A separate war risk policy is available, however. If such insurance is obtained, it is advisable to get it from the same insurer that also underwrites the regular ocean marine policy for the same cargo. Sometimes, when a loss occurs, it is hard to determine whether it was caused by a war risk or some other peril. Hence, having the same underwriter for both policies avoids potential disputes.

Risks Covered

Similar to the marine policy, war risk insurance contains a basic perils clause outlining the risk covered. The following war hazards may be insured:

Capture, seizure, destruction, or damage by men-of-war.

Piracy, takings at sea, arrests, restraints, detainments, and other warlike operations; acts of kings, princes, and peoples in prosecution of hostilities or in the application of sanctions under international agreements.

Aerial bombardment.

Floating or stationary mines and stray or derelict torpedoes.

Weapons of war employing atomic or nuclear fission and/or fusion or other like reaction or radioactive force or matter.

As with ocean marine risk coverage, war risk insurance covers only actual physical loss or damage to goods insured. Losses due to delays, deterioration, and loss of market are specifically excluded.

Period of Validity

War risk coverage is effective after the goods are loaded on an overseas vessel. When loaded on a lighter craft or similar vessel, coverage is also provided against mines and stray or derelict torpedoes. When the ship arrives at the overseas destination and goods remain on the vessel, the insurance is good only for 15 days after arrival. Coverage is no longer provided once goods have been discharged at the overseas port.

If goods are moved from one vessel to another, they are covered while being transferred and when on the new carrying vessel. Again, however, after any vessel with the goods on it has been in a port for more than 15 days, the coverage ceases.

If there is a deviation, overcarriage, change in voyage, error, or unintentional omission in the description of interest, vessel, or voyage, the war risk coverage remains effective provided the insured promptly informs the underwriter and pays any additional premium which may be required. This provision is similar to the deviation clause of an ocean marine policy. The latter, however, provides for continuation of coverage without payment of an additional premium.

For aircraft shipments or connecting conveyances the same principles apply. Once goods have been discharged at an overseas airport, coverage is no longer provided. Goods transported from one aircraft to another aircraft in another airport, for example, KLM Aircargo arriving at Kennedy Airport but continuing to Pittsburgh via LaGuardia, should have insurance coverage up to the airport of the final destination.

Limitations

War risk policies are generally "free from any claim based upon loss of or frustration of the insured voyage caused by arrests, restraints, or detainments." Thus, if the voyage is frustrated without any actual harm being done to the cargo, no insurance cover is provided.

The insurance also does not cover any loss or damage caused by the following:

Commandeering, preemption, requisition, or nationalization by the government of the country to or from which the goods are insured (this type of risk may be coverable under export credit insurance against political risks).

Seizure or destruction under quarantine or customs regulations.

Delay, deterioration, and/or loss of market.

Air and Mail Shipments

While shipments by oceangoing vessel are insured against war risks only from the time they are loaded onto the vessel until the time of discharge, shipments by mail are insured continuously from the time they leave the sender's premises until they are delivered to the consignee. Shipments by air are generally insured under the same conditions as shipments by overseas vessel. Of course, no coverage is provided against mines and torpedoes.

Cancellation

It is easy for underwriters to provide war risk coverage in times of general peace. If war breaks out, however, heavy damages may result in only a few days. For this reason, underwriters reserve the right to cancel war risk policies with 48 hours' notice. Such cancellation does not, of course, affect shipments already at sea.

INSURANCE CLAIMS

Insurable Interest

Whenever an actual loss occurs, it is important that the one having an interest in the merchandise can get fair, efficient, and rapid adjustment of his claims. While insurance is often arranged by the exporter, a loss is generally discovered by the importer after he has already paid for the merchandise and is, therefore, the rightful owner. Consequently, claims are usually made by the importer. We have already noted that insurance policies and certificates are quasi-negotiable, and thus may be endorsed over to the person having an ownership interest in the merchandise, for example, the importer.

A basic prerequisite for having a claim recognized by the underwriter is that the one making the claim has an insurable interest in the goods. This does not necessarily require full ownership. Susceptibility to financial loss by the claimee if the shipment is lost or damaged is sufficient to demonstrate an insurable interest. Claims can be made by the shipper, importer, financial institution, or even a carrier that has a first lien on goods for unpaid freight charges.

Survey of Claim

A claim is usually registered by the importer with a local correspondent or agent of the underwriter. For convenience, names and addresses of local agents and correspondents may be listed on the back of policies and certificates. An expert then conducts a survey to determine:

A loss has indeed occurred.
Cause of the loss.
Amount of the loss.
Whether the policyholder has a financial interest.
Whether the particular peril that caused the loss is covered by the policy.
Whether there are any limiting clauses in the policy that may affect the underwriter's obligation to pay.

Settlement of Claim

The survey report, together with a copy of the bill of lading, the commercial invoice, the insurance certificate, a covering letter requesting payment, and other documents that may be required in specific instances are sent to the insurance company for processing. Occasionally, in clearcut cases, the local agent may be authorized to make payment himself.

Total Loss

A total loss is the easiest one to adjust. All that is needed is to send the survey and other documents to the underwriter or his agent who will, it is hoped, make prompt payment.

Partial Loss

The same general documents are needed for a particular average claim. In this case, however, the surveyor has to determine what the property is worth in damaged condition, as well as what it would be worth in undamaged condition—thus computing a percentage of damage. This percentage is then applied to the value for which the merchandise is insured to come up with the required payment.

General Average Loss

General average claims are the most difficult to adjust. Before a general average claim from the insured is accepted, there has to be some risk that threatens all interests of the venture, both the vessel and the cargo, followed by a voluntary sacrifice for avoiding or reducing the loss for the common good of all interests. Finally, there must be some practical effect of the sacrifice, with at least some part of the value saved.

To make an assessment of all the interests involved and to justify all claims may take months of work by the surveyor and hundreds of pages of testimony, assessment, and conclusions. In the interim, all the parties that might be assessed, before being able to claim their merchandise, have to provide some kind of security for the payment they may eventually have to make. Where the party contributing to the general average loss is not covered by insurance, either a cash deposit or a general average bond by a bonding company will be required. Generally, the underwriter pays general average contributions only in the proportion that the insured value of the merchandise bears to the total value.

To help unravel general average claims, reference is often made to the York Antwerp Rules, which govern the adjustments of general and other losses.

REINSURANCE

The sinking of a giant supertanker or the crash of a Boeing 747 cargo aircraft may cause the loss of human lives and surely will involve the loss of millions of dollars of cargo, not to mention the ship or the aircraft. Such losses are great enough to strain the resources of the largest insurance company, and even if no loss of life is involved, require enormous compensation and indemnity to the owners of the tankers, aircrafts, and cargoes. Most underwriters safeguard against such excessive and extraordinary risk through reinsurance.

The Act of Reinsurance

Whenever the cargo of a vessel is valued at multimillions of dollars, the insurance will be placed with more than one insurance company. The necessity for this precaution becomes obvious when one considers that huge compensations and indemnifications must be paid out of revenues earned from selling insurance. If insurance companies provide remedy for the loss of multimillion dollar cargoes in a single voyage, and if one or more such casualties should occur, gigantic losses must be met, honored, and processed without danger to the financial structure of the insurance company and risk to the stockholders' equity.

Reinsurance is the procedure and modus operandi through which an underwriter passes on to another the whole or certain percentages of the risks that he, the designated underwriter, has insured for the owners of the tanker or the cargo.

Direct insurance and reinsurance are distinguished from one another as follows:

1 Direct insurance is the original insurance given to the owner of the ship or the merchant owning the cargo.
2 Reinsurance is the act of insuring a cargo by the first underwriter with subsequent underwriters.

Ever increasing dependency on energy and energy-related products brought about the creation of supertankers and hypertankers in the 1970s. Their purpose was to move the maximum amount of crude oil possible, with the greatest economy. Each time one of these multimillion dollar vessels is sunk, repercussions are felt throughout the board rooms of many insurers. And yet, reinsurance makes the risk manageable, and compensation is possible for all parties incurring financial loss.

Reinsurance is not a process with which the insured parties need be concerned, as it does not affect the negotiations of individual policies. Nevertheless, it is a practice to be aware of in that it makes possible coverage of enormous amounts through the mutual sharing of risk by the underwriters involved.

PART 3

Financing Techniques and Vehicles

Every shipment from an exporter to an importer requires some kind of financing while in transit. In addition, the exporter usually needs funds to manufacture or buy the item to be exported. Similarly, the importer also has to carry the goods in inventory until he is able to sell them to the ultimate buyer. Finally, the accounts receivable created by the sale require financing until payment is received. Hence, each export may represent a series of financing transactions, starting with manufacture or purchase, going through shipment, and ending up with sale to the ultimate consumer and receipt of proceeds by the importer.

The trade cycle can be financed in many different ways. The exact method or combination of methods used for any one transaction depends on such factors as the relative financial strength of the exporter and importer, their degree of mutual trust, the currency of invoice, availability of bank lines to the exporter or importer, and availability and cost of credit in the different countries. A financially strong exporter may be able to finance the entire cycle out of his own funds and, thus, not demand payment from the importer until the latter has sold the goods and has received payment. Alternatively, a strong importer may be able and willing to give the exporter an advance to buy or manufacture the goods exported. In between these two extremes are countless ways of financing the trade cycle through a combination of exporter, importer, and intermediary financial institutions.

When a bank or some other financial institution helps to finance a shipment, it may be done on an unsecured or secured basis. If the company requiring financing enjoys a strong financial position and its principles are known to be of undoubted integrity, unsecured financing is usually available. Very often, however, export/import companies, by the very nature of their business, operate on limited capital. A need may, therefore, exist to use the actual merchandise being shipped as collateral. Some specific techniques and vehicles of unsecured and secured lending are discussed in Chapter 10.

Since the Eurocurrency market has become a very specialized means for financing international trade and investment, Chapter 11 is devoted entirely to this topic.

When an exporter has a considerable degree of trust in the financial strength and integrity of an importer, he may be willing to allow release of title documents for shipped goods on payment by the importer of a sight draft drawn on him. Since the draft, which is sent by airmail, usually arrives and must be paid well before arrival of the goods, which are sent by seamail, this method shifts the main financing burden on the importer. To allow somewhat longer terms, an exporter may be willing to draw a time draft of a specified number of days on the importer. In this case, the importer gets the title documents on acceptance of the draft, with payment not due until the time stipulated on the trade acceptance has expired. This shifts more or all of the financing burden to the exporter who may, as a result, need some assistance from his bank. Allowing the release of title documents against payment of a sight draft or acceptance of a time draft by the importer is often referred to as shipping on a foreign-collection basis. This topic is discussed in Chapter 12.

When an importer is less well known to the exporter or certain exchange restrictions prevail in the importer's country, the exporter may wish to have the importer's promise of payment backed by a prime foreign or domestic bank. The importer, in turn, may not wish payment to be released to the exporter before he is reasonably assured that the goods in question have been shipped. A banking vehicle that meets these objectives has luckily been developed in the form of the letter of credit. Chapter 13 discusses general letter of credit procedures and Chapter 14 examines different types of letters of credit and how some of these may be used as financing tools.

CHAPTER 10

Financing Techniques

In any business transaction, it is the provider's main concern to receive payment for the goods or services supplied and avoid delays or losses of payment due to financial problems on the part of the buyer. On the other hand, the buyer of these goods or receiver of these services is concerned about the quality of the goods or services received and whether they are financed at the most advantageous terms possible. Both parties are thus concerned about financing. We first consider unsecured and then secured lines of credit.

UNSECURED CREDIT

A large part of international trade is financed through unsecured credit lines that companies have available at their banks. For customers with undoubted credit standing, banks are usually willing to make credit available without specific collateral. An authorized official of the company merely signs a promissory note that is delivered to the bank as evidence of the debt. When the note is due, it may be repaid, or the loan may be rolled over. In the latter case, the customer delivers a new note to the bank for the extended period.

Often the purpose of short-term unsecured borrowings is not specifically stated. The company may require the money for "general corporate purposes" or "for working capital." In this case, the money is usually used to buy raw material, carry on the manufacturing process, and/or to finance inventory and accounts receivable. If the credit is taken down for the medium term (one to five years), it may be utilized for buying machinery, building a new plant, or carrying long-term receivables. For such medium-term credits, there is usually a formal, written term loan agreement, which spells out the purpose of the borrowing, maximum amount, rate, repayment schedule and covenants that the borrower is expected to observe while the loan is outstanding.

How can unsecured short- or medium-term credit be used for financing exports and imports? If the borrowing company buys all or part of its raw materials and/or finished goods from abroad, part of the credit will probably be used for financing these imports and carrying in inventory the imported items before they are processed and sold. Conversely, a borrower who exports may use all or part of his unsecured credit line to buy goods for export, carry inventory that will eventually be exported, and/or carry foreign receivables. If the exports or imports are such capital items as machinery, industrial plants, computers, or airplanes, the credit required for the transaction may be for periods in excess of one year. In this case, an unsecured medium-term loan may be used to finance international trade.

The portion of an unsecured credit that is used for financing foreign trade may never be specifically spelled out or known to the company or bank. It is, nevertheless, most important for prime companies who rely heavily on foreign sources of supply or export a significant portion of their products.

SECURED FINANCING

Many situations arise when a borrower's financial position is not strong enough to induce a financial institution to give him unsecured credit. This means that in order to get the needed money, he has to put up some kind of collateral. Usually, firms engaged in trading act primarily as middlemen and, therefore, operate on a relatively low markup. Often, they have to carry (finance) the goods while in transit and inventory. Moreover, once sold, the trading company may also have to carry the accounts receivable until final payment. Turning a respectable profit on such an operation means operating on limited net worth relative to the overall funds required to carry inventory and receivables. To induce a bank or other financial institution to put up the money may require some sort of collateral.

To provide collateral in its simplest form, a company may be able to deposit some readily salable Treasury bills, bonds, or other securities. Precious metals (e.g., silver) can also be used as collateral, since they can easily be stored in the bank's vault. If the person seeking a loan owns some real estate, this can be mortgaged as security. Basically, anything readily salable that has sufficient value and can be assigned to the financial institution can serve as good collateral for a loan.

Firms engaged in trading often do not have stocks, bonds, and similar collateral, since they require every penny they can get to carry their inventory and receivables. They, therefore, must find other methods of furnishing their bankers with required security. Fortunately, legal methods have been devised whereby the company's own stock in trade can be used as collateral for a loan. Through various means, inventory owned by the borrower can be assigned to or brought under the control of the financing institution. Similarly, accounts receivable can be assigned to a bank or finance company or sold outright to a factor to provide required financing. Hence, when we talk about secured financing of international trade, we mean having explored various ways by which the actual goods being traded can be used as collateral for a loan. In this chapter, we examine three possible vehicles, namely, the negotiable bill of lading, the warehouse receipt, and the trust receipt. In the last section, another vehicle for financing trade, the banker's acceptance, is discussed.

It must be stressed that in this chapter we are primarily considering methods of secured financing of international trade as are practiced in the United States. The commercial codes of other countries may differ substantially from that of the United States. Moreover, some instruments of secured financing may be different abroad, in form as well as usage. Hence, before permitting merchandise to be released abroad against a trust receipt or accepting a foreign warehouse receipt as security, a businessperson or banker is well advised to first get some competent legal counsel from the country in question.

Many U.S. export and import transactions do, however, fall under U.S. law for all or part of the trade cycle. Moreover, sales contracts, as well as credit agreements with bankers, may specifically stipulate that U.S. laws should apply in cases of conflict. A review of the prevalent U.S. commercial code and practices is, therefore, useful.

It is also advisable for exporters, importers, and commercial bankers to check backgrounds on all foreign and domestic entities with whom they may transact business. Resources in the United States include lists published by the U.S. Treasury Department, Washington, D.C. of Foreign Assets Control Regulations. Also see the list of Denial Orders published by the Department of Commerce in Washington, D.C.

SECURED FINANCING UNDER THE UCC

The purpose of developing the UCC was to simplify, modernize, and clarify commercial law. Its objective has been to reduce legal uncertainties and make commercial law uniform throughout the United States.

Purpose of Article 9

Article 9 of the UCC specifically deals with secured transactions. The previous body of law differentiated among various types of secured transactions and often made it legally difficult and administratively cumbersome for creditors to extend secured financing. Article 9, in contrast, recognizes that all secured transactions have much in common and that earlier distinctions among types are largely unnecessary. It completely sidesteps, for instance, the question of whether title to goods serving as collateral rests with the lender or the borrower. The real key and central thread running through all secured transactions is that goods are used to collateralize a loan. If the bank is not paid according to agreed terms, the lender may take over the goods and dispose of them in whole or partial settlement of the debt.

To give recognition to this unifying theme, Article 9 defines a "security interest" as existing whenever goods serve as collateral for payment or performance of an obligation. It thereby effectively avoids the question of which party actually has title to the goods as not being germane to the secured transaction per se.

The UCC governs only commercial transactions that are subject to state law. Hence, Article 9 does not cover a security interest that is subject to any federal law, such as the Civil Aeronautics Act, Ship Mortgage Act, or Federal Bill of Lading Act.

Security Agreement

A security interest in specific personal property may be established through a simple written contract between the parties, that is, the lender and the borrower. As long as no other law is violated, the parties may make whatever stipulations they wish in the security agreement.

A security agreement must be signed by the debtor and describe the property that is to serve as collateral. Other provisions usually present in a security agreement include the following:

Amount and terms of indebtedness.

Maintenance of proper insurance on the property by the debtor.

Prohibition of any other liens on the same property.

In addition to the previously listed provisions, many security agreements also contain a so-called after-acquired property clause or floating lien, especially when current assets that turn over in the normal course of business are being financed. Other clauses of the security agreement may provide for a plaster lien on all assets, the disposition of proceeds from sale of collateral, and dominion over the collateral.

Floating Lien. The after-acquired property clause provides a lien not only on specified goods presently owned by the debtor but on all similar property that the debtor may acquire in the future. This is a so-called floating lien, since it "floats" forward in time to include all similar assets as they turn over in the normal course of business. A floating lien is especially useful when financing inventory or accounts receivable.

Plaster Lien. A security agreement may cover specified assets only or it may refer to all the assets of an individual or firm. If all assets, both those presently owned and any that may be acquired in the future, serve as collateral, the security interest is called a "plaster lien."

Proceeds. When financing involves assets that are ultimately sold, it is useful to provide for a security interest in the proceeds of such a sale. In describing the collateral in the security agreement, use of the word "proceeds" is sufficient to obtain a security interest in proceeds of any type (for instance, cash or accounts receivable).

Dominion over Collateral. A security agreement may allow a debtor to use, commingle, and sell any part of the collateral. Hence, the debtor may have actual dominion over the collateral that he has pledged to the financing institution. If proceeds are also included in the security agreement, these must be turned over promptly to the financing institution.

Creation of Security Interest

A valid security interest in personal property is created when the following conditions are met:

There is a properly signed security agreement between the creditor and the debtor.

The creditor has given a loan or other value to the debtor.

The debtor has ownership or assignable rights to the collateral.

Perfection of Security Interest

A security interest by itself is of limited value if it is not enforceable against third parties, such as other secured creditors, other unsecured creditors, or a trustee in bankruptcy. To be valid against such third parties, a security interest must be perfected. This can be done in one of two ways.

Possessory Collateral. If the secured party has physical possession of the collateral, no further action is required to perfect the security interest. For instance, if a financing bank has possession of a negotiable bill of lading or warehouse receipt, or if a similar nonnegotiable instrument is consigned to the bank, its security interest is perfected against third parties. No further action to achieve perfection is required.

Nonpossessory Collateral. To perfect a security interest in collateral that is not in possession of the secured party requires filing with the appropriate state authority, usually the secretary of state. If two different creditors file for the same collateral, the one who has filed first receives a preferential right to the collateral in case of a conflict.

By filing, the fact that a security interest attaches to certain goods becomes public knowledge. Any potential lenders or other interested parties can check public records to see whether a prior lien exists on goods that they are about to finance or acquire. The act of filing, therefore, protects innocent parties who may otherwise get stuck financing or buying property in which someone else already has a security interest.

In view of the first to file rule, it is clear that a secured party should file as soon as possible. It is permissible to file as soon as a security agreement exists. No actual loan has to be made (hence, no actual security interest has to exist) prior to filing.

When filing is necessary, the secured party must send to the appropriate state authority a financing statement that contains the following information:

Addresses of the debtor and of the secured party.

Statement indicating the nature of the collateral (a general description of the goods is adequate).

Signatures of the secured party and the debtor.

In New York, the borrower does not have to sign the financing statement provided he has signed the security agreement and thereby has given the financing institution the right to file.

A financing statement with a maturity date is valid until 60 days after its expiration. Usually, however, no maturity date is given and the filing is good for five years, at which time it may be renewed. The form of a typical financing statement is shown in Figure 10-1.

Specific Collateral

Depending on the nature and use of the specific property, UCC rules that are applicable to any specific secured transaction may vary. The UCC differentiates broadly among three classifications of collateral:

Tangibles (consumer goods, equipment, farm products, and inventory).

Intangibles (accounts receivable, contract rights, and general intangibles).

Semi-intangibles (chattel paper and documents).

Tangibles. When tangible goods are being financed, these often have to be in the physical possession of the borrower. In the case of machinery and equipment, for instance, the items being financed are of no use, unless they are located at the debtor's place of business and are used to manufacture a salable product.

A similar situation often exists with inventory. It too must usually be under the control of the borrower, since it consists either of raw material awaiting production, goods in process, or finished goods awaiting sale. In some instances, however, it may be possible to store inventory in an independent warehouse thereby bringing it under the direct, possessory control of the financing institution.

Whenever tangible goods are under the dominion of the borrower, it represents nonpossessory collateral. A security interest must, therefore, be perfected by filing a financial statement with the appropriate state authority.

This FINANCING STATEMENT is presented to a Filing Officer for filing pursuant to the Uniform Commercial Code.

No. of Additional Sheets Presented:

3. Maturity Date (optional):

1. Debtor(s) (Last Name First) and Address(es)

2. Secured Party(ies): Name(s) and Address(es):

4. For Filing Officer: Date, Time, No. Filing Office

5. This Financing Statement covers the following types (or items) of property:

6. Assignee(s) of Secured Party and Address(es)

☐ Proceeds are also covered. ☐ Products of the Collateral are also covered.

7. ☐ The described crops are growing or to be grown on: *
☐ The described goods are or are to be affixed to: *
* (Describe Real Estate Below):

8. Describe Real Estate Here:

9. Name(s) of Record Owner(s):

No. & Street | Town or City | County | Section | Block | Lot

10. This statement is filed without the debtor's signature to perfect a security interest in collateral (check appropriate box)

☐ under a security agreement signed by debtor authorizing secured party to file this statement.
☐ already subject to a security interest in another jurisdiction when it was brought into this state.
☐ which is proceeds of the original collateral described above in which a security interest was perfected:

SPECIMEN

By ______________________ (Signature(s) of Debtor(s)

By ______________________ Signature(s) of Secured Party(ies)

(1) Filing Officer Copy — Numerical

(9/65) NY STANDARD FORM - FORM UCC-1 —

Figure 10-1. Financing statement.

The financing of inventory as nonpossessory collateral presents some special legal problems:

Some parts of inventory that serve as collateral for a loan may easily become commingled with other parts, thereby making them difficult to identify.

Inventory is eventually sold to buyers who purchase it in the normal course of business and want a good title without having to search for liens.

The sale of inventory creates proceeds in the form of cash or accounts receivable.

By including in the security agreement an after-acquired property clause (floating lien), a lender may make new advances as the borrower acquires new inventory. There is no need to enter into a separate security agreement each time, and the burden of policing an inventory financing transaction is thereby greatly reduced. Moreover, by proper filing, a creditor may also acquire a perfected security interest in any products or proceeds, such as finished goods, accounts receivable, and cash. A creditor who takes inventory as collateral should, therefore, always file for products and proceeds by checking the appropriate box on the financing statement.

A creditor has no rights against someone who purchases the inventory in the normal course of business. The latter takes title to the purchased goods, free of any security interest that may exist in favor of a creditor. The creditor does, of course, have a legal right to the proceeds of the sale, as previously outlined. He should, therefore, make sure that all proceeds are promptly turned over to him. The rights of an innocent purchaser in due course of the inventory are, however, completely protected.

Intangibles. Accounts receivable, contract rights, and other intangibles are, by definition, flimsy documents of which it is impossible to have real physical possession. Since the security interest in this type of collateral cannot be perfected by possession, proper filing under the UCC is necessary.

Semi-Intangibles. Instruments such as chattel paper, negotiable title documents, promissory notes, stocks, and bonds are considered to be semi-intangibles. A secured lender is usually able to take possession of this type of collateral. A security interest may, therefore, be perfected through possession.

If a creditor releases a title document against a trust receipt, a security interest is perfected automatically for an additional 21 days. To perfect a security interest beyond 21 days requires filing of a financing statement.

Regardless of whether or not a creditor has filed a financing statement, the debtor who has physical possession of title documents may negotiate them to a holder in due course. The latter receives title to the documents free of any liens that the creditor may have. Hence, the good title of an innocent purchaser in due course is protected.

Unlike the situation with a negotiable instrument, title to goods covered by a nonnegotiable document is not locked in the instrument itself. A holder of a nonnegotiable document, therefore, has to perfect his security interest in the goods directly. This can be done by one of the following methods:

Having the nonnegotiable document issued in the name of the secured party.

Giving the party who has possession of the goods, such as a warehouseman, notification of the secured party's interest.

Filing a financing statement as to the goods.

Priority

Article 9 of the UCC outlines specific rules governing priorities in cases where two or more creditors have a security interest in the same collateral. If each security interest is perfected by filing, the creditor who filed first has a priority. Hence, when the first financing statement filed covers all assets of a borrower with a plaster lien, the effect is to cut off other lenders to the same borrower from a priority interest in all assets.

A priority lien based on the "first to file" rule may be defeated in two instances.

Bankruptcy. If the security interest was given within four months prior to bankruptcy, this might be termed a preferential transfer under the Federal Bankruptcy Act. In this case, a referee in bankruptcy might set aside the prior claim of a secured party in favor of other, unsecured creditors. The Federal Bankruptcy Act may thus supersede the UCC, which is state law.

Purchase Money Security Interest. A seller of goods who, in lieu of immediate payment, takes a security interest in the goods sold is said to have a purchase money security interest. The same also applies to a lender who makes funds available to enable the purchase of some personal property and who takes a security interest in that property.

Filing and notification requirements to perfect a purchase money security interest differ, depending on the nature of the collateral. If proper notification and/or filing is made, however, the holder of a purchase money security interest may have preference in the special collateral, even if another creditor has filed a floating or plaster lien on all the debtor's assets.

BILL OF LADING AS TITLE DOCUMENT

It is explained in Chapter 8 that a negotiable bill of lading, properly endorsed, gives title to the holder. Most typically, an exporter might have the bill of lading made out to his order. The exporter then adds his unqualified endorsement by signing his name in the same manner that he would endorse any other negotiable instrument. The bill of lading is then turned over to the exporter's bank, which acquires a possessory interest in it. The bank might have paid the exporter under a letter of credit and now holds the negotiable bill of lading as collateral. This title document is required to enable the importer to pick up the shipped goods from the steamship company. The bank may insist on either full payment from the importer or, at least, the importer's acceptance of a usance draft drawn on him or his bank for the value of the import before releasing the negotiable bill of lading to him.

Possible Sale of Collateral

If the importer does not pay or accept the draft, the financing institution keeps the negotiable title document and, therefore, a possessory interest in the merchandise. The bank can use the bill of lading to pick up goods from the pier, sell them in the open market, and with the proceeds liquidate the advance it has given to the exporter.

Recourse to Exporter or Importer

If the proceeds of the sale are not enough to repay the full amount of the advance, the bank may or may not have recourse to the exporter and importer, depending on the underlying agreement between the parties. If the exporter was paid under an irrevocable letter of credit, the financing bank does not have recourse to him. Since, in this case, financing is for the account of the importer, however, the latter's bank has full recourse to him if he refuses payment and if the proceeds from sale of the goods are inadequate to liquidate the advance. If, on the other hand, the export is made on a documents-against-payment or acceptance (collection) basis, financing is for account of the exporter and the bank usually retains full recourse to him. Chapters 12 through 14 discuss financing tied to outward collections and letters of credit. The point stressed here is that a negotiable bill of lading is a useful tool that serves as possessory collateral for an advance made to finance a trade transaction.

WAREHOUSE RECEIPT FINANCING

While goods are in transit and under the control of a steamship company, title is often represented by a negotiable bill of lading, which, in turn, may be used to collateralize a loan. It may, however, also be necessary to finance the goods prior to shipment as well as after arrival at their destination.

Uses

Exporters, for instance, may have to store goods prior to shipment, perhaps awaiting the arrival of a vessel. They may also be buying shipments in piecemeal lots over a period of time, and, therefore, must store and finance the goods until a complete shipment has been assembled. In either case, they may wish to use goods they hold in inventory as collateral for a loan.

Importers who receive shipments may not be in a position to pay for them right away. If they have no immediate buyer, they may have to store the goods until they are able to sell them. Only after receipt of the proceeds from the ultimate buyers can they pay the exporters or intermediary financing banks. Again, the goods may be required by the financing institution as collateral for an advance.

A ready vehicle for providing loan collateral exists in the warehouse receipt. We shall, therefore, examine the qualifications for an eligible field warehouse and warehouseman, the kinds of warehouse receipts, and the general procedure for warehouse receipt financing.

A warehouse receipt, besides being employed on either end of an international trade transaction, may also be used domestically. A manufacturer, for instance, may use a warehouse receipt as a vehicle to bring adequate inventory close to the ultimate point of sale without turning it over to a middleman, such as a distributor, dealer, or wholesaler. The usual procedure is to set up a field warehouse at the middleman's location. If and when the middleman needs some of the goods, he can pay for them and at the same time obtain an authorization to withdraw a fixed quantity from the warehouse. Once the goods are safely in a field warehouse, it may also be possible to arrange financing for them with or without recourse to the manufacturer. While this procedure is used primarily for domestic shipments, it may also become helpful in facilitating foreign trade transactions.

The Warehouse and Warehouseman

Types of Warehouses. There are basically two types of warehouses: terminal (also called metropolitan) and field.

A terminal (metropolitan) warehouse is a large storage area serving a number of different businesses. It is a separate location owned and operated by an independent warehouse company. Since a terminal warehouse is geographically removed from the depositor's place of business, it is often not very convenient for him to deposit and withdraw inventory as needed. A terminal warehouse is utilized by businesses that require additional storage capacity; it is not primarily used as a financing tool.

To overcome the locational inconvenience of a terminal warehouse, the field warehouse has come into common use. It is established right at the depositor's place of business and is usually a segregated part of his own warehouse or storage area. A field warehouse arrangement is established primarily as a tool to facilitate secured financing and not to provide additional storage facilities.

Independent Warehouse Company. A field warehouse, even though it exists at the depositor's place of business, must be run by an independent company engaged in the business of storing goods. The fact that the warehouse company is an independent third party is very important to the lender. A financing institution, before approving the use of a specific warehouse company, usually conducts a thorough investigation of it to determine the quality of its management, its reputation, methods of operation, and financial strength.

The premises of the field warehouse itself must be leased or subleased from the depositor by the warehouse company. The warehouse must be segregated from the premises of the depositor by some kind of barrier and under the constant control—that is, lock and key—of the warehouseman, an employee of the warehouse company. It is permissible, however, for the warehouseman or his deputy to have been an ex-employee of the depositor. While acting for the warehouse company, however, he is in its employ and it also pays his salary. Only the warehouseman or his authorized and bonded deputy may have access to the premises.

To indicate to all parties concerned that the segregated part of the depositor's premises is a field warehouse under the control of the warehouse company, adequate public notice must be posted.

The warehouse company and warehouseman must establish general operating procedures, including proper inventory control and records.

Insurance. The carrying of adequate insurance by the warehouse company is particularly important, both to the depositor and the financing bank. If any loss should occur due to the fault of the warehouse company or its warehouseman, the former is usually not strong enough financially to make up for the loss. The depositor to a field warehouse, on the other hand, is usually a merchant who cannot afford any loss, regardless of whose fault it is. Insurance against different risks should, therefore, be arranged by both the warehouse company and the depositor.

The warehouse company may be held liable for losses resulting from negligence to the warehouseman or any of its other employees including

Theft of goods by an employee of the warehouse company or by others.

Damage to goods caused by improper handling or lack or reasonable care.

Issuance of fraudulent warehouse receipts by authorized employees.

Misdescription of goods.

Delivery of goods to the wrong person, that is, one who does not present a validly endorsed negotiable receipt or a valid and properly signed delivery order.

The previously outlined risks can usually be covered through insurance against theft and other crime, legal liability for damage to or loss of stored goods, and bonds assuring the fidelity of employees, as well as performance bonds that assure delivery of goods in storage to the proper warehouse receipt holder. Sometimes, special insurance coverage against such hazards as leakage for liquid goods stored in tanks may also be advisable.

The depositor of the goods should carry insurance against all loss or damage to goods that cannot be ascribed to negligence of the warehouse company or its employees. So-called "all risks policies" are available to cover all or most contingencies.

Since the financing institution has a direct stake in the goods stored, it should make sure that proper coverage is maintained and that any insurance proceeds are turned over directly to itself. Financing institutions usually require certified copies of insurance policies maintained by depositors. In some cases, they may require a copy of the policy maintained by the warehouse company. Lenders should also demand a loss-payable endorsement, which provides that any insurance benefit payments are made by the underwriter directly to the financing institution.

If there is a loss or damage of stored property, and if insurance coverage is inadequate, a financing institution, of course, always retains recourse to the borrower for the full amount of the loan plus interest. Since borrowers requiring warehouse receipt financing are probably weak, in terms of their own capital resources, not much reliance should be put on this recourse provision. Complete insurance coverage against all conceivable losses is, therefore, all the more important, not only to the lender, but also to the borrower.

Cost. The cost of field warehousing usually varies from 1 to 2% per annum on the gross value of the goods stored. The depositor also pays all out-of-pocket costs of the warehouseman, including the salary of his bonded representative. Additionally, the work required by banks or other financing institutions in policing and servicing warehouse receipt loans is considerably higher than for most other types of lending. Bank interest charges for warehouse receipt financing are thus generally higher than for conventional types of credit.

Warehouse Receipts

A warehouse receipt symbolically represents the goods stored in a warehouse. There are two different types of warehouse receipts, negotiable and nonnegotiable.

A negotiable receipt is made out to the order of a named person or to bearer and is, therefore, negotiable commodity paper that may serve as possessory collateral. Delivery of goods stored against a negotiable receipt is made to the bearer of a properly endorsed receipt on surrender of it to the warehouseman.

A nonnegotiable warehouse receipt is made out to a specific party. Only the named person or institution may authorize release of goods from the warehouse. The nonnegotiable receipt may be transferred or assigned to another party. The warehouse company, however, must be so notified by the transferer before the transfer or assignment becomes effective. A nonnegotiable receipt in itself, therefore, does not convey title and cannot be used as possessory collateral.

Prudent bankers and risk managers must inspect goods stored in warehouses before contemplating the financing of warehouse receipts because such goods might have deteriorated or spoiled during the storage period or might have been damaged during transport from the unloading point of the vessel/aircraft to the actual warehouse.

Bitter disputes and lengthy litigation can be avoided if risk managers insist on physical inspection. It is true that bankers are not experts in general merchandise or the morphology of chemical compounds, yet they can enlist inspectorate or surveillance agencies in the fulfillment of this delicate and essential task.

Advantage of Nonnegotiable Receipt. Surrender of a nonnegotiable receipt to the warehouseman is *not* necessary to get release of all or part of the stored merchandise. All that is needed is a delivery order signed by the party in whose name the receipt is issued (usually the financing institution) instructing the warehouseman exactly what types and quantities of goods are to be released to the person named in the order.

The fact that the receipt itself is not needed to obtain release of goods from a warehouse makes nonnegotiable warehouse receipts more suitable than negotiable receipts for some types of bank financing. If the bank holds a negotiable receipt and wishes to authorize release of only part of the stored merchandise, it must nevertheless surrender the warehouse receipt. A bank representative must go to the field warehouse to get the merchandise released and obtain a new receipt for what remains in the storage area. Alternatively, the bank could endorse the receipt over to its customer, thereby allowing him to make the withdrawal himself. Then the bank has to trust the customer to take the correct, authorized amount out of the warehouse, and to turn the newly issued receipt promptly over to the bank. This cumbersome and sometimes risky procedure can be greatly simplified by using a nonnegotiable receipt. In this case, the financing institution wishing to authorize a release of only part of the goods can simply issue a delivery order for the exact amount or number of units it wishes released. The delivery order can be turned over to the customer, who picks up the needed merchandise himself at the field warehouse, that is, his own place of business.

Because of the advantages previously outlined, most warehouse receipts issued to financing institutions are nonnegotiable. The only significant exceptions are negotiable receipts covering grains and other commodities that are actually traded on the exchanges.

Form of Warehouse Receipt. A warehouse receipt does not have to be in any specific form. The UCC states, however, that unless the warehouse receipt contains certain information and terms, the warehouseman is liable for damages caused to persons as a result of such omission. Hence, as a practical matter, a domestically issued warehouse receipt must contain at least the following information (UCC 7-202):

Location of the warehouse where the goods are stored.

Date of issue of the receipt.

The consecutive number of the receipt. (As a control procedure, all receipts issued by a warehouse company should be consecutively numbered.)

A statement whether the goods in storage will be delivered to bearer, to the order of a specified person, or only to a specified person. This merely means the receipt has to indicate whether it is negotiable or nonnegotiable.

The rate of storage and handling charges. (When goods are stored under a field warehousing arrangement, a statement of that fact is sufficient on a negotiable receipt.)

A description of the goods or of the packages containing them. The warehouse company is responsible for delivering goods of the nature and type described in the receipt. Often warehouse companies are not in a position to inspect merchandise deposited with them. They therefore add a disclaimer on the receipt such as "boxes said to contain" merchandise of a certain description.

Signature of the warehouseman or his authorized agent.

If the receipt is issued for goods that the warehouseman owns, either jointly or in common with others, the fact of such ownership must be stated.

A statement of the amount of any advances made and of any liabilities incurred for which the warehouseman claims a lien or security interest on the goods. (If the exact amount is unknown, a statement of the fact that advances have been made or liabilities incurred and their purpose is sufficient.)

Financing Procedure

Agreement with Warehouse Company. As a first step in setting up a field warehouse financing arrangement, the depositor and the warehouse company sign a contract outlining the particulars of the arrangement, such as the location of the warehouse, fees, duration of the contract, and so on. A valid field warehouse is then established at the merchant's place of business. Merchandise is stored in the warehouse, and receipts are issued to the bank or other lending institutions.

Margin. The percentage of total value that a bank or other financing institution is willing to advance against warehouse receipts depends on the financial strength of the borrower, as well as the particular merchandise being stored. If it is a readily salable commodity that can, perhaps, even be traded on one of the exchanges, the lender will be willing to advance a relatively high percentage of the value of the goods stored. If, at the other extreme, the goods are perishable, seasonal, or style oriented, only a very low percentage will be advanced. Indeed, in the latter cases, no warehouse receipt financing may be possible at all.

When determining a proper margin, a lender has to take into consideration not only a possible decline in market price of the collateral, but also the cost of actually liquidating the merchandise, if it becomes necessary to do so. A warehouse company has a prior lien on all stored merchandise subject to payment of storage charges. Moreover, it is usually in times when a borrower is in financial difficulties that storage charges go into arrears. Additionally, there are selling expenses, brokerage fees, loading and transportation charges and so on, which have to be paid out of the gross sales proceeds. It should also be remembered that financial trouble of a borrower may well coincide with a substantial decline in the market value of his stored inventory. Lenders are, therefore, well advised to calculate conservatively the percentage of margin that they are willing to advance.

Releasing Privileges. To be useful to the borrower, a warehouse receipt financing arrangement must allow the borrower to withdraw goods from the warehouse when needed. Therefore, the lender and merchant usually work out an arrangement, specifying the circumstances under which releases from the warehouse may be authorized. The financing institution has several alternatives with regard to releasing privileges. At one extreme, the creditor may allow delivery of goods only against cash payment or substitution of similar collateral. On the more liberal side, some goods may be released without payment. In this case, a stipulated quantity of goods may be released against trust receipt. The debtor is thus given the opportunity to sell the goods and collect payment before reimbursement by the financing institution. Once payment for the amount released has been made, the releasing privilege is reinstated.

A financing institution may also authorize a warehouseman to release a stipulated quantity of goods to the depositor without a specific delivery order. Again, the borrower is then obligated to replace the collateral or repay part of the loan before any more releases may be made.

Usually, when releasing privileges are granted, the percentage of the value of goods stored against which the bank is willing to make a loan (i.e., the margin) is computed, based on the gross value minus the value of the releasing privileges.

Protection of Lender

Extending credit against warehouse receipts usually requires a considerable amount of checking and policing by the lending institution. It must make certain that the grade, quality, and quantity of merchandise agreed on is indeed what is deposited in the warehouse. The warehouseman is responsible only for the goods as they are described in the warehouse receipt. Unless the receipt specifically stipulates the quality or grade, the warehouseman is not responsible. If the goods are packaged, there is no guarantee, short of actual spot-checking, that the packages contain the purported goods. In this case, the receipt states that the packages are "said to contain" the described goods. In this manner, the warehouseman is relieved of responsibility. This recalls a certain instance, a number of years ago, when warehouse receipts were issued against salad oil allegedly stored in tanks. The tanks were actually full of water, causing substantial loss to financial institutions that had extended loans against receipts—apparently without ever bothering to open one or a few of the tanks to check their contents.

Other dangers of which a lender should be aware include improper release of goods without knowledge and permission of the receipt holder. Sometimes, a conflict of interest may arise because the clerk who has control over the keys of the field warehouse is a former employee of the borrower.

The warehouseman is not responsible for any decline in value of the goods due to normal deterioration or any other cause. Hence, the lender has to make sure that he is advancing a conservative percentage against the current value of the merchandise.

The rights of a holder in due course of commodity paper may be defeated in certain instances. A negotiable or nonnegotiable warehouse receipt is no guarantee of title if the depositor had no valid title to the goods in the first place. If some kind of fraud exists, for instance, whereby the borrower does not have full title to the goods, or if there are other liens on the same commodities, the bank may find itself without any real security.

The need for the lender to accept receipts of only the most reputable warehouses should be obvious. Additionally, the bank should conduct periodic inspections to review the warehouseman's operating procedures and spot-check the inventory. To determine periodically the condition, quality, and grade of the merchandise, the services of an independent appraiser may be needed.

Lastly, the financing institution should not rely entirely on the value of the collateral. As with any other loan, the financing institution should conduct a complete investigation and credit analysis on the borrower, including his general financial strength as well as reputation and honesty.

In summary, when extending a loan secured by a warehouse receipt, a financing institution may be subject to substantial risks. To control the degree of risk, it should consider the integrity of the warehouseman, adequacy of the warehouse facilities, nature of the commodity, financial strength and reputation of the borrower, and sufficiency of the insurance.

TRUST RECEIPT FINANCING

There may be situations where storage of collateral in an independently controlled field warehouse is impractical. An importer may require the goods for further processing or displaying in order to make the final sale. In such cases, a financing institution that has a great degree of trust in the importer may be willing to release the negotiable bill of lading, and thereby also the goods, to the importer against the signing of a trust receipt. After the importer has made his final sale and received the proceeds, he can pay the financing institution that granted the advance.

Other purposes for wishing release of documents from the financing institution without prior payment, include clearance of the goods through customs, inspection of the goods, or obtainment of clearance by the Pure Food and Drug Administration and other U.S. government agencies.

Credit Agreement

In some cases, the release of title documents against a trust receipt might be done at the request and risk of the exporter. Most typically, however, it is accomplished under a separate credit arrangement between the U.S. bank and the importer. The U.S. bank pays the sight draft drawn by the exporter on the importer, thereby actually giving the latter a loan to pay for his imports and allowing him to further process and sell the merchandise. The risk, in this case, is assumed by the U.S. bank, which bases its decision on a prior credit evaluation and open credit line it may have for the importer.

Agreement by the Trustee

The trust receipt signed by the customer is usually on the bank's own form. By signing the trust receipt the customer agrees to and states the terms given in Figure 10-2.

Prudent banking principles require the customer's signature to be verified and compared favorably with a specimen held on the bank's premises. Favorable comparison, however, is not enough; the signer must be fully authorized and empowered by his corporation to sign trust receipts, and his signature must bind irrevocably the borrowing entity.

Acknowledgment of Security Interest. The trustee acknowledges receipt and possession of the relevant documents in trust for the entruster, that is, the financing institution. At the same time, the trustee grants a security interest in the documents and underlying goods to the financing institution. The latter also retains a security interest in any accounts receivable, other contract rights, as well as cash proceeds that arise from any sale of the collateral.

Statement of Purpose. The reason why the trustee wishes the documents released is stated. The most typical purposes include:

To take possession and sell the goods and to pay the proceeds over to the financing institution.

TRUST RECEIPT

New York, NY, ..., 19...

The undersigned (hereinafter called the "Trustee") acknowledges receipt from the ABC AMERICAN BANK, N.A., AS AGENT (hereinafter called "ABC American Bank") for... (hereinafter called the "Entruster") of the following described documents (which, together with the goods represented by such documents and all additions and/or accessions to or products of such goods, are herein called the "Collateral") and further acknowledges the existence of, or hereby grants, a security interest in favor of the Entruster in the Collateral and any accounts and contract rights relating thereto and in the proceeds thereof:

DOCUMENTS (give full description, including marks and numbers):

The security interest acknowledged or granted hereby secures payment of any and all Liabilities of the Trustee to the Entruster. The term "Liabilities" shall include any and all indebtedness, obligations and liabilities of any kind of the Trustee to the Entruster and also to others to the extent of their participations granted to or interests therein created or acquired for them by the Entruster, now or hereafter existing, arising directly between the Trustee and the Entruster or acquired outright, conditionally or as collateral security from another by the Entruster, absolute or contingent, joint and/or several, secured or unsecured, due or not due, contractual or tortious, liquidated or unliquidated, arising by operation of law or otherwise, direct or indirect, including, but without limiting the generality of the foregoing, indebtedness, obligations or liabilities to the Entruster of the Trustee as a member of any partnership, syndicate, association or other group, and whether incurred by the Trustee as principal, surety, indorser, guarantor, accommodation party or otherwise.

PURPOSE: In consideration of the delivery of such Collateral, the Trustee agrees to hold the Collateral in trust for the Entruster, without liberty to pledge or otherwise encumber the same, solely for the purpose designated: (<u>One of the following must be designated by an X in the box provided</u>.)

[] (1) To sell or procure, the sale of the goods and to pay and deliver to ABC American Bank the proceeds of all sales as and when received by the Trustee.

[] (2) To exchange or procure the exchange of such document (after arranging for entry of the goods through customs, if required) for a negotiable warehouse receipt covering such goods, issud to the order of ABC American Bank by a warehouse acceptable to ABC American Bank, and to deliver such warehouse receipt to ABC American Bank.

[] (3) To arrange entry of the goods through customs (if required) and/or examine them, in a manner preliminary or necessary to their manufacture, processing and/or sale; and, immediately after examination, either to (<u>strike out whichever [*] is inapplicable</u>.):

Figure 10-2. Trust receipt.

* honor a draft drawn on the Trustee at ______________________
for ______________________ by ______________________

* pay ______________________________ to ABC American Bank

or, if the Trustee shall not accept the goods, to deliver to ABC American Bank title documents satisfactory to ABC American Bank covering the goods.

[] (4) To arrange entry of the goods through customs and examination of them by (strike out whichever [*] is inapplicable):

* U.S. Department of Agriculture

* U.S. Department of Health, Education and Welfare, Food and Drug Administration

in a manner preliminary or necessary to their manufacture, processing and/or sale; and, immmediately after the governmnet agency has approved the goods, to notify ABC American Bank thereof and to (strike out whichever is inapplicable):

* honor a draft drawn on the Trustee at ______________________
for ______________________ by ______________________

* pay ______________________________ to ABC American Bank

or, if the goods are not approved by the government agency, to deliver to ABC American Bank title documents satisfactory to ABC American Bank, and the Gevernmental detention notice, covering the goods.

[] (5)

For the same consideration as expressed above, the Trustee further agrees with the Entruster as follows:

1. The Trustee will pay all expenses and charges (including shipping and storage charges and taxes) in connection with the Collateral and any proceeds thereof, and will at all times while the same are in its hands hold the Collateral and proceeds separate and distinct from any property of the Trustee and capable of identification and will show such separation in all its records and entries.

2. The delivery of the documents and goods is temporarily made to the Trustee for convenience only, without novation and without giving the Trustee any title thereto, except as trustee for the Entruster for the purpose herein designated.

3. The Trustee will account to the Entruster for the Collateral by delivering to the Entruster or to ABC American Bank, immediately upon receipt thereof by the Trustee, all proceeds of every disposition of the Collateral, in whatever form received, to be applied by the Entruster to the paymnet of any Liabilities. If such proceeds be instruments or chattel paper they shall not be so applied until paid,

Figure 10-2. *(Continued)*

the Entruster, however, to have the option at any time to sell or discount any such instrument or chattel paper and so apply the net proceeds hereof, conditionally upon final payment of such instrument or chattel paper. Neither the Entruster nor ABC American Bank shall be required to take any steps necessary to preserve any rights against prior parties to any of the Collateral.

4. At any time and from time to time, upon demand of the Entruster or ABC American Bank, the Trustee will: (a) keep and stamp or otherwise mark any and all documents and chattel paper and its individual books and records relating to inventory, accounts and contracts rights in such manner as the Entruster or ABC American Bank may require; (b) permit representatives of the Entruster or ABC American Bank at any time to inspect its inventory and to inspect and make abstracts from the Trustee's books and records pertaining to inventory, accounts, contract rights, chattel paper, instruments and documents; (c) deliver to the Entruster or ABC American Bank on demand accurate records and copies of all accounts with respect to the Collateral or proceeds thereof; and (d) give, execute, deliver, file and/or record any notice, statement, instrument, document, agreement or other papers that may be necessary or desirable, or that the Entruster or ABC American Bank may request, in order to create, preserve, perfect or validate any security interest granted herein or pursuant hereto or to enable the Entruster to exercise and enforce its rights hereunder or with respect to such security interest. The Trustee covenants that there will be no offsets or credits against any claims or accounts constituting proceeds of the Colateral and guarantees payment of said claims and accounts in full.

5. The Entruster may at any time it deems itself insecure, without notice or demand, declare all Liabilities immediately due and payable and this agreement in default, and thereafter the Entruster shall have the remedies of a secured party under the Uniform Commercial Code of New York subject to other applicable law, including, without limitation, the right to take possession of the Collateral and any proceeds thereof, and for that purpose the Entruster or ABC American Bank may, so far as the Trustee can give authority therefor, enter upon any premises on which the Collateral or any proceeds thereof may be situated and remove the same therefrom. The Trustee will make the Collateral available to the Entruster or ABC American Bank at a place to be designated by the Entruster or ABC American Bank which is reasonably convenient to both parties. If notice is required by law, five day's prior written notice of the time and place of any public sale thereof or of the time after which any private sale or any other intended disposition thereof is to be made shall be reasonable notice to the Trustee. Expenses of retaking, holding, preparing for sale, selling or the like shall include the Entruster's reasonable attorneys' fees and legal expenses.

6. Neither the Entruster nor ABC American Bank shall be responsible for the correctness, validity or genuineness of any documents referred to herein or for the existence, character, quantity, quality, condition, value or delivery of any goods purported to be represented thereby.

7. The Trustee will, at the expense of the Trustee, keep the goods fully insured in favor of, and to the satisfaction of, the Entruster against all insurable risks to which the goods may be subject, the insurance policies to be satisfactory to the Entruster and payable to the Entruster and the Trustee as their interests may appear, and the Trustee will deposit the insurance policies with the Entruster or ABC American Bank on demand. All proceeds of such insurance shall be subject to the trust hereunder, and the Trustee will forthwith pay over to the Entruster or ABC American Bank all such proceeds received by the Trustee.

Figure 10-2. *(Continued)*

8. No right or power of the Entruster shall be deemed to be waived by any conduct or inaction or knowledge of the Entruster, and no waiver of any right or power and no consent of the Entruster shall be valid or effective unless in writing signed by it or by ABC National Bank. The rights and powers herein given the Entruster are in addition to all others however arising.

9. The Trustee will furnish promptly such documents as the Entruster or ABC American Bank may reasonably request in order to protect or enforce the Entruster's rights hereunder and, in connection with any goods in bond, such duly executed customs forms as may be required to obtain possession of the goods.

10. At the expense of the Trustee, the Entruster or ABC American Bank is hereby irrevocably authorized to file one or more financing statements under the Uniform Commercial Code naming the Trustee as debtor and the Entruster as secured party and indicating the types, or describing the items, of Collateral herein specified. Without the prior written consent of the Entruster, the Trustee will not file or authorize or permit to be filed in any jurisdiction any such financing or like statement covering the Collateral herein specified.

11. If this Trust Receipt is signed by two or more parties, it shall be the joint and several obligation of such parties. This Trust Receipt shall be construed according to the laws of the State of New York. Unless the context otherwise requires, all terms used herein which are defined in the Uniform Commercial Code shall have the meanings therein stated.

Name................................
(corporation or firm)

Authorized
Signature...........................

Name................................
(individual)

Figure 10-2. *(Continued)*

To deposit the goods in a warehouse and arrange for the issuance of a negotiable or nonnegotiable warehouse receipt in favor of the financing institution. The warehouse receipt must be delivered promptly to the entruster.

To pass the goods through customs and/or to inspect them either himself or, if required, have them inspected by the Department of Agriculture, the Department of Health, Education, and Welfare, or the Pure Food and Drug Administration. If the goods are acceptable, the trustee promises to pay for them promptly or to honor a sight or time draft drawn on him.

If the goods are rejected, the title documents must be returned to the entruster.

Segregation of Collateral. The trustee is usually required to hold the collateral and any proceeds separate from his own property and to keep them specifically identifiable. This also means that the trustee's records have to reflect the collateral nature of the goods in question. Practically speaking, segregation of the collateral property may not always be feasible. Component parts that are acquired under a trust receipt may lose their individual identity as they are processed into finished goods. Since the UCC allows a security interest to be maintained not only in the original collateral, but also in products and proceeds, trust receipt financing of goods that lose all or part of their identity is greatly facilitated.

Turnover of Proceeds. All proceeds from sale of the collateral have to be turned over to the entruster. Proceeds are usually in the form of accounts receivable or cash. The financing institution may use any proceeds received to liquidate its advances to the trustee.

Insurance. The trustee agrees to, at his own expense, keep the goods fully insured against all insurable risks. Payments from the insurance company have to be made directly to the entruster.

Financing Statement. The trustee authorizes the financing institution to file a financing statement and other documents that may be required under the UCC.

Risks Assumed by the Entruster

The person authorizing the release of title documents on trust receipt—be it the foreign exporter or the U.S. bank—must realize that certain risks are being taken that have to be evaluated. After all, physical possession of the goods is being turned over to the trustee in the hope that he will turn over the proceeds of any sale to the entruster. Consequently, trust receipt financing, as the term implies, requires a great agree of trust in the integrity of the customer acting as trustee.

Financial Strength of Trustee. In evaluating a potential trustee, the entruster will first wish to look at his general financial strength. When the bank extends financing against trust receipts, does it depend entirely on the proper sale of the goods so financed? Does the importer have a net worth cushion that can be relied upon for repayment if something goes wrong? It is not advisable to extend trust receipt financing unless a substantial cushion exists, not only in terms of net worth, but also in terms of profitable operation of the business over a reasonable past period of years.

Integrity of Trustee. Most important also are the reputation, honesty, and integrity of the trustee. He or she must be expected to live up to the letter of the agreement entered into when signing the trust receipt. The documents and goods may be used only for the purpose specifically stipulated. As soon as the importer receives proceeds from the sale of the goods, they must be turned over to the bank. This last point is of special significance in trust receipt financing. The banker should be careful to estimate as closely as possible the time it will take the trustee to process and/or sell the goods. Trust receipt privileges should never be longer than the duration of time needed to complete the transaction. It has happened that an importer requested trust receipt privileges for 60 days when only 30 days were required to complete the transaction. Therefore, the trustee had the use of bank borrowings for an additional 30 days and used these funds to speculate in commodities; he promptly lost them, and had to declare bankruptcy. The bank, as a result, lost most of the money it had lent to him. This illustrates the importance of careful policing by the entruster of the time for which trust receipts are outstanding.

Nature of Goods. The nature of the goods financed should also be an important consideration. Ideally, the goods should be readily salable commodities and specifically separated and identifiable on the trustee's premises. When the goods are mixed or mingled with others by further processing or manufacturing, specific identification of them by the entruster becomes difficult or impossible. In this case, if the bank wishes to reclaim the goods because of financial difficulty of the trustee, it would be impossible to do so. Moreover, when the goods are intermingled, the bank may run into disputes with other entrusters and creditors to determine what belongs to whom.

Other Creditors. This leads to another consideration, namely, whether the trustee is getting trust receipt accommodations from other financial institutions. If he is, policing of the individual transaction becomes more difficult and the chances of conflict with another entruster when repossessing the merchandise or claiming proceeds becomes more likely.

Ultimate Buyers. Finally, the customers to whom the trustee ultimately sells the goods must be considered. They should be of sufficient financial strength that they can be relied upon to make payment when due. Special caution should be exercised when the trustee not only sells to a customer, but also buys from him. In this case, the possibility exists that rather than paying the trustee for the merchandise, the customer will attempt to set off claims that he might have against the trustee.

Trust Receipts and the UCC

Article 9 of the UCC outlines the law governing trust receipts and similar devices, such as conditional sales, chattel mortgages, and factor's liens. To simplify the law and minimize conflict, all these devices, including the trust receipt, are replaced by a single lien called a "security interest."

To establish and perfect a security interest in title documents, such as bills of lading and warehouse receipts, mere possession of the respective negotiable instrument is adequate. When a secured party does not have possession of the documents (e.g., when he releases them against a trust receipt), filing with an appropriate state authority is necessary to perfect the security interest. This filing becomes a public document available to anyone interested. It assures that trust receipts and similar security interests cannot be used to establish secret liens. The danger of a trustee's obtaining financing twice based on the same collateral is thereby greatly reduced.

Up to 21 days from the date of the signing of a trust receipt, a temporary perfection of the security interest is in effect without the entruster's filing, provided the security interest arises out of new value given by the entruster. To perfect the security interest beyond 21 days, however, the entruster must file a financing statement before expiration of the 21 days or he must take repossession of the title documents or goods themselves. An entruster should, therefore, file the required statement as soon as the security interest is established.

It is important for an entruster to note that a security interest under a trust receipt arrangement is subordinated to the rights of a bona fide purchaser, pledgee, or mortgagee of the negotiable title document or of the goods. This is true whether the security interest is perfected by the entruster's filing or not. If a trustee in the normal course of business sells the goods represented by a bill of lading or warehouse receipt, the bona fide buyer acquires title irrespective of any security interest that the entruster may have. The entruster could never successfully move against a bona fide buyer for recovery of the merchandise. A bank releasing documents under a trust receipt must, therefore, make sure that the proceeds of any sale are promptly turned over to it to liquidate the advance.

Use of Trust Receipts Abroad

Outside the United States, the trust receipt serving the purposes, as previously outlined, is commonly used only in the United Kingdom. In Europe and other parts of the world, the trust receipt is rarely used. Consequently, it is advisable for U.S. exporters to first investigate the laws of the relevant country before allowing the release of documents to a foreign importer. Additionally, even when such a release of documents takes place in a country, such as the United Kingdom where local laws are favorable, all the elements of trust in the importer previously discussed must be present.

It is probably a good practice for a U.S. exporter not to allow release of documents against a trust receipt, unless he has so much confidence in the foreign importer that he would ship to him on open-account terms. If that is not the case, it is much better to leave it to the importer's local bank as to whether or not it wishes to release the documents against trust receipt or some similar instrument at its own risk and based on its own business relations with the importer. The foreign bank not only knows the financial strength and honesty of the importer, but it is also more familiar with local laws governing trust receipts than the faraway exporter can ever hope to be.

BANKERS' ACCEPTANCES

A time draft drawn on and accepted by a bank is called a "banker's acceptance." It usually arises from international trade transactions where there is an underlying obligation of a buyer of goods to make payment to a seller at some future time. Many bankers' acceptances are created when payment is made by means of letters of credit. Bankers' acceptances may also be created when payment for international trade transactions takes place on a collection- or open-account basis. In all these instances, the drawee bank, by accepting a draft, assumes the obligation of making payment at maturity on behalf of the buyer or his bank.

There are also other situations that may lend themselves to the creation of a banker's acceptance—the domestic shipment of merchandise, the storage of readily marketable commodities, and the creation of foreign exchange. Theoretically, acceptances can be created in any currency. In practice, however, those that are most actively traded are in sterling and U.S. dollars. Our discussion concerns itself only with U.S. dollar acceptances.

Acceptance Agreement

An importer wishing acceptance financing is usually requested to execute an acceptance agreement in favor of the bank. The party being financed agrees with the bank that funds will be provided to pay the acceptance no later than one day prior to the maturity of the instrument. The agreement also gives the bank a purchase money security interest in the goods involved. Hence, if title documents are released on trust receipt, the financing bank is put in a preferred position vis-à-vis other creditors as far as the specific goods are concerned.

A typical acceptance agreement is shown in Figure 10-3.

Eligibility

One of the key advantages of U.S. dollar bankers' acceptances is that they can be readily sold in the open market. Bankers' acceptances thus serve as a vehicle for channeling nonbank funds into the financing of trade. Commercial banks may also discount bankers' acceptances with the Federal Reserve. To be eligible for such discounting, the acceptances must strictly comply with the rules laid down in Regulation C of the Federal Reserve Board. They must be for:

Importation and exportation of goods—this includes not only the shipment of goods between the United States and foreign countries, but also shipments between two foreign countries.

Storage of readily marketable staples, either domestically or in any foreign country.

Domestic trade transactions involving the movement or storage of readily marketable staples.

Creation of dollar exchange.

By far, the largest proportion of acceptances are created as the result of international trade transactions. Many foreign traders in the United States

A C C E P T A N C E   A G R E E M E N T

Date...........

To: ABC American Bank, N.A.
1 York Street
New York, NY 10003

Please accept the draft(s) drawn on you (the "Bank") by ....
(Insert "the under-

.... for a total sum of .... Dollars ($):
signed" or name of other drawer)

Number	Date	Tenor	Amount

The description of particular drafts need not be inserted above when inappropriate. This Acceptance Agreement is a continuing agreement, and this Agreement and the below-mentioned Underlying Agreement(s) shall apply to any draft or drafts which may hereafter be accepted by the Bank at the request of the undersigned (whether or not described above), including all drafts issued in extension or renewal of any thereof.

Acceptance of each such draft will be under and in accordance with facilities previously arranged by the undersigned with the Bank. The undersigned represents to the Bank that the tenor of each draft presented for acceptance hereunder will not be in excess of the estimated time required to complete the relative underlying transaction.

In consideration of the acceptance by the Bank of any draft hereunder, the undersigned agrees that all of the terms and conditions of each Application and Agreement for Commercial Credit relating to said draft(s), General Loan and Collateral Agreement and/or other Security or Letter of Credit Agreement executed by the undersigned and heretofore or herewith delivered to the Bank or by which the undersigned may be otherwise bound (the "Underlying Agreement(s)") shall be applicable to said draft(s) and the Bnak's acceptance thereof and any and all obligations and liabilities of the undersigned with respect thereto, and the Underlying Agreement(s) is (are) by this reference made a part of this Acceptance Agreement.

If and to the extent not already provided in the Underlying Agreement(s), the undersigned further agrees (a) to pay to the Bank at its Main Office, in United States currency, the amount of each such acceptance (together with all unpaid charges of, and expenses paid or incurred by, the Bank in connection therewith, and

Figure 10-3. Acceptance agreement.

interest where chargeable), on demand but in any event not later than one business day prior to maturity; (b) that, in addition to any and all other security, any and all bills of lading, warehouse receipts and other documents of title attached to any such draft, and the goods covered thereby, shall be security for all obligations and liabilities of the undersigned to the Bank mentioned herein or in the Underlying Agreement(s), and the undersigned hereby grants or confirms unto the bank a security interest in any and all thereof and the proceeds and products thereof; (c) if the Bank delivers to or upon the order of the undersigned any of such documents and/or goods prior to the Bank's having received payment of any such draft, to sign and deliver to the Bank a trust receipt or other security agreement therefor complying with the requirements of the Uniform Commercial Code, or other applicable statute, and a financing or other statement in the form specified in the relataive statute, and to pay all filing fees in connection therewith; and (d) to keep such goods adequately covered by insurance in amounts, against risks, in companies and as may be otherwise satisfactory to the Bank, and to assign the policies or certificates of insurance to the Bank, or to make any loss or adjustment payable to the Bank, at its option, and to furnish the Bank, if demanded, with evidence of acceptance by the insurers of such assignments, and should the insurance for any reason be unsatisfactory to the Bank, the Bank may, at the expense of the undersigned, obtain insurance satisfactory to the Bank.

The right is expressly granted to the Bank, at its discretion, to file one or more financing statements under the Uniform Commercial Code naming the undersigned as debtor and the Bank as secured party and indicating therein the types or describing the items of collateral herein or in any of the Underlying Agreements specified.

....
(Name)

....
(Address)

....

....
(Title)

PLEASE SIGN OFFICIALLY

Figure 10-3. *(Continued)*

and abroad have found acceptance financing a convenient and relatively inexpensive vehicle. It must be stressed that acceptances can be created for trade not only between the United States and other countries, but also between third countries. This highlights the importance of the U.S. dollar for the financing of world trade.

Federal Reserve eligibility requirements also require a banker's acceptance not to exceed 180 days, and to be created within less than 45 days from the on-board bill of lading date. The nature of the merchandise should be specified and vague terms such as "general merchandise" should be avoided.

Domestic Transactions. Domestic trade is only rarely financed by way of bankers' acceptances. Regulation C states that a member bank may accept a draft for financing a domestic movement of goods only if shipping documents conveying title to the goods are in the possession of the accepting bank at the time of acceptance. Since most domestic shipments are made on open-account terms, involving no negotiable bill of lading, the creation of bankers' acceptances is often impractical.

International Transactions. The requirements for documentation on the part of the bank is much less stringent when foreign trade is financed through bankers' acceptances. It would, of course, be desirable for the bank to have title documents in its possession when creating the acceptance. In international trade, especially when shipments between third countries are being financed, this is, however, often impractical or impossible. The Federal Reserve is, therefore, generally satisfied if the accepting bank has on file the following information:

1. Value of the merchandise being shipped and financed.
2. General description of the merchandise.
3. Ports of origin and destination of the shipment.
4. Date of shipment.
5. Certification by the company or bank being financed that the merchandise is not being financed by any other bankers' acceptances.

This information may be supplied in different ways. A copy of shipping documents would be best. It is, however, sufficient to have the information in the form of an official letter or tested cable from the borrower. The important thing is that the accepting bank obtains and has on file satisfactory evidence (documentary or otherwise) showing the nature of the commercial transaction on which the extension of bank credit is based (Federal Reserve Regulation C, Section 203.1(a)(1), footnote).

Generally, a separate acceptance is executed for each shipment. Sometimes, when many small shipments occur, it may be desirable to combine them into one draft. In this case, for an acceptance to be eligible, it must show on its reverse side, or on an attachment, the previously listed details for each specific transaction included.

Acceptance financing is primarily used for trade in commodities, raw materials, food items, textiles, and other consumer goods, such as cars, appliances, and so on. These types of goods are generally sold to the final consumer or user within a few months. Acceptance financing is thus always short-term financing. Indeed, one of the Federal Reserve stipulations is that only acceptances with original tenures of six months or less are eligible for rediscounting.

Storage. The storage of readily marketable staples in the United States or any foreign country may be financed by means of bankers' acceptances. To qualify as a readily marketable staple, a product or commodity must be:

> The subject of constant dealings in ready markets with such frequent quotations of price as to make (a) the price easily and definitely ascertainable, and (b) the staple itself easy to realize upon by sale at any time. (Federal Reserve Regulation C, Section 203.1 (a) (3), footnote.)

A bank may only create eligible acceptances to finance storage if the transaction is secured throughout. This means that the financing institution must have in its possession a warehouse receipt or some other document giving it title to the commodities for the entire financing period.

A merchant who wishes to finance the storage of goods by way of acceptances submits to his bank a warehouse receipt conveying title to the goods, together with a draft. The bank accepts and discounts the draft, crediting the merchant with the net proceeds.

Acceptance financing of stored goods should only be used if the commodities are expected to enter into the channels of trade in a relatively short period of time. This means that the goods should be promptly sold, exported, or entered into the manufacturing process.

At present, acceptance financing is only rarely used for goods stored either domestically or abroad. In domestic trade, borrowers have preferred to finance stored goods via loans rather than acceptances. When goods are stored abroad, it may sometimes be difficult to obtain title documents that could qualify the transactions for acceptance financing.

Dollar Exchange. A number of foreign countries rely on one or a limited number of crops for their foreign exchange earnings. Since the export season for these crops is of limited duration, a shortage of foreign exchange may develop just before the start of the season. To overcome this temporary shortage, banks in the exporting country may draw dollar drafts on U.S. banks. The U.S. banks accept the drafts, discount them, and credit the net proceeds to foreign banks. No more than three months later, the agricultural country should receive foreign exchange as its annual crop is exported. The dollar acceptances can, therefore, be liquidated (paid) with the proceeds.

Dollar exchange bills do not arise from specific trade transactions. They anticipate proceeds from exports that will be forthcoming within a three-month period. Regulation C of the Federal Reserve limits the maximum tenure of dollar exchange bills to three months.

Presently, only a small proportion of total bankers' acceptances outstanding are used to create dollar exchange. The probable reason for this is that as former agricultural countries have expanded and diversified their industries, the seasonal nature of exports has been alleviated.

The Acceptance Market

Acceptances are generally created only by well-known banks of undoubted credit standing. A banker's acceptance, therefore, becomes a very safe and liquid investment for those wishing to put their money to use for short periods of time.

A bank, after having created and discounted an eligible acceptance, may hold it in its own portfolio until maturity, sell the acceptance to one of its customers or to an acceptance dealer, or rediscount it at the Federal Reserve.

Easy Credit Period. In periods of adequate liquidity, when banks have enough lendable funds, they often hold their acceptances in their own portfolios until maturity. They thereby earn the corresponding discount charges for their own account. In such periods of liquidity, banks are indifferent as to whether they finance a transaction by means of an advance or an acceptance. Acceptance financing has no decisive advantage over loan financing from the bank's point of view.

Tight Credit Periods. In periods of tight credit, the situation changes drastically. When the bank makes a loan, it has to use its own funds. When it creates an acceptance, it can sell the instrument in the open market. Thus, while it lends its good name to the transaction, the bank does not have to use any of its own funds when it provides financing on an acceptance basis.

Investors in Acceptances. Banks sell acceptances that they do not wish to keep in their own portfolios, either through acceptance dealers or directly to bank customers. Foreign governments and central banks have often found acceptances to be useful investments for their excess dollar liquidity. Acceptances by prime U.S. banks are very safe and generally give a somewhat higher yield than U.S. Treasury bills. Foreign and domestic commercial banks and companies may also wish to invest their excess liquidity in bankers' acceptances. Occasionally, an individual may find it useful to put temporary cash holdings into acceptances. It must must be remembered, however, that the acceptance market deals only in large amounts. The purchase of acceptances in amounts totaling below, say $25,000, is generally not welcome by bankers and acceptance dealers.

Cost

The cost of acceptance financing may be broken down into three parts: the bank's acceptance fee, the discount charges, and any supporting balance requirements that the bank may impose.

Acceptance Fee. The prime bankers' acceptance commission is 1.5% per annum (although, in some cases, a higher fee is negotiated). It is the fee charged by banks for lending their names to a transaction when they accept a draft drawn on them. The 1.5% acceptance fee has traditionally been applied to customers with the best credit standing. Competitive pressures in the acceptance financing market have, however, forced banks to apply the same 1.5% per annum rate to customers who, while their credit is still considered good, would not be classified in the "prime" category. However, customers with a credit rating below the "good" category may have to pay an acceptance fee in excess of 1.5% per annum.

There has been some pressure on the 1.5% per annum commission rate. Sometimes, when banks are considering all the costs of acceptance financing, cheaper funds have been available through the Eurodollar market. To meet these competitive pressures, there have been instances when banks charged somewhat less than the standard 1.5% per annum fee.

While, by and large, the 1.5% per annum still stands as the minimum commission charge, it is likely to continue to come under increasing pressure because of competitive means of trade financing.

Discount Charges. The second cost element consists of the normal discount charges. This is basically a market rate that reflects the prevailing cost of money. It is the rate at which short-term investors are willing to buy bankers' acceptances. The discount rate generally stands in some kind of close relationship with other, similar instruments used for short-term investments, such as Treasury bills, commercial paper, and certificates of deposit.

Supporting Balances. Finally, some banks may be willing to do acceptance financing only for customers who keep supporting demand deposits in their current accounts. The informal balance requirement with regard to acceptance financing is generally far less stringent than for loans, and in many cases, competitive pressures have entirely done away with supporting balance requirements. The approximate amount of balances demanded by the bank varies with market conditions, the credit standing of the customer, and the bank's own desire to engage in acceptance rather than loan financing.

Prepayment

Since acceptances are tied to a specific trade transaction, the underlying transaction may be completed before maturity of the acceptance. An importer, for instance, may be able to sell the goods and receive proceeds well before the maturity of the banker's acceptance that was used for financing. In such cases, most banks prefer their customer to prepay the acceptances. Since banks generally are willing to refund a portion of the discount charges in case of prepayments, the importer saves some expenses. Moreover, the bank makes sure that the proceeds of any specific transaction it is financing are not diverted into speculative or unauthorized activities.

Even though a bank's customer may be required to prepay an acceptance, a bank will never prepay its own acceptance liability prior to maturity.

Advantages of Acceptance Financing

Acceptance financing is especially attractive during periods of tight liquidity. At such times, commercial banks may simply not have enough liquid funds to meet all the loan demands of their customers. The acceptance market then becomes a most useful means of channeling short-term liquid funds of companies; foreign, central, and commercial banks; and other investors into the financing of foreign trade. When money is tight, acceptance financing is not necessarily cheaper than loans. It may, however, be the only practical way to obtain financing.

Sometimes, there may also be a cost advantage in acceptance financing. This primarily revolves around the prevailing market rates for acceptance discounting as compared to loans and the need to maintain lower compensating demand balances with banks. The determination as to which vehicle is less expensive depends very much on market conditions prevailing at any time, as well as on each company's individual liquidity position. For instance, often a company must maintain certain balances with its bank to meet current working needs, regardless of the type of financing it uses. In this case, the normally required level of working balances cannot be counted as a cost of loan versus acceptance financing.

Bankers, as a matter of policy, often prefer to finance only specific trade transactions of a self-liquidating nature. Acceptances lend themselves well to this type of requirement, since the customer is forced to identify the underlying transaction. Thus, aside from factors of liquidity, acceptance financing may be more palatable to some bankers than loan financing because the purpose of the transaction and source of payback is clearly specified.

Acceptances and Smaller Banks

The names of most small- and medium-sized banks are not sufficiently well known for their acceptances to enjoy wide marketability. How can such banks nevertheless make use of the acceptance vehicle for financing their clients' exports and imports? The answer, as expected, is through a correspondent relationship with a large, city bank whose name is well recognized in the market. The small bank may finance a customer's exports and imports by extending an unsecured loan, discounting a foreign trade acceptance, advancing against outward collections, or other means. At the same time, in order to also take advantage of the acceptance correspondent, the latter accepts the draft, discounts it, and credits the small bank with the net proceeds. The latter can then use the cash that has been raised for financing legitimate trade transactions. Of course, the underlying transaction must have all the elements needed to make it eligible for acceptance financing.

Once the underlying trade transaction has been completed—that is, payment from the ultimate buyer has been received—the proceeds are used to liquidate the advance extended by the small bank. The latter, in turn, uses the proceeds to repay the acceptance to the city correspondent at or before maturity.

Ineligible Acceptances

Traditionally, bankers have been very careful to create only acceptances that strictly comply with all the eligibility requirements of the Federal Reserve.

In recent years, however, the eligibility regulations have been interpreted as governing only the ability of bankers to rediscount the accepted draft with the Federal Reserve. If there is no need or intention to rediscount, then generally it appears, at present, perfectly legal for banks to create acceptances that do not conform to the regulations in one or more respects.

A number of banks have found it useful to create acceptances that are not eligible for rediscount at the Federal Reserve. The instruments may still be financing a trade transaction, but some of the information required for eligibility may be missing. Banks creating ineligible acceptances either hold them in their own portfolio or sell them to investors interested in this kind of an instrument, either directly or through an acceptance dealer.

To the extent that a private market exists for these ineligible acceptances, they can be considered a useful financing tool. The use of ineligible acceptances grew to more than $500 million during the tight money period in 1970. As money became more readily available, the use of ineligible acceptances also diminished.

Risks in Financing

Following are the major risks of the financing operations discussed.

Refusal of the Merchandise. If the buyer refuses to receive the merchandise, he must support his position with documentary evidence that the seller has not fulfilled his obligations under the terms of the agreement. It is true that banks deal in documents and not in goods, yet if the bank has accepted the goods as part of the collateral in the extension of credit to its customer, the bank may also suffer if, for instance, the buyer of the underlying goods refuses the merchandise because of a subsequent softening of the price of these goods in world markets.

Delayed Payment. The buyer may slow payment for the goods and the bank will suffer the consequent delay in recovering the funds. A careful examination of the credit histories of potential clients is the best protection against this kind of risk.

Political Disturbance. The buyer's country may suffer from political unrest; consequently, the U.S. bank and its customer (the exporter) may decide that the risks are too high and withdraw the shipment. They could then look for another buyer in a different market or attempt to sell the merchandise locally. However, under these circumstances, the sale of the goods may not always cover the financing.

Banks with several well-placed networks overseas are in a better position to find buyers in those markets. In such instances, however, risk management must continue to be directly involved in order to evaluate further risks and assist in enlisting inspectorate companies to minimize the possibility of losses.

CHAPTER 11

Eurocurrency

THE MARKET

The most misunderstood of all foreign market operations is the Eurocurrency market. As an initial approach to the subject, it might be helpful to think of the Eurocurrency market as a market in external currencies, since accounts denominated in these currencies constitute an asset or liability in a bank outside their country of origin. For example, French francs deposited in London are external francs and, as such, are called Eurocurrencies or offshore currencies. Of all the currencies that make up this market, the most important is the Eurodollar.

Eurodollars

Perhaps, the best way of defining Eurocurrencies is to describe the way one such currency—the Eurodollar—is said to have come into general usage. During the early 1950s, the communist countries of Eastern Europe had sizable U.S. dollar balances that they held in New York. This was unsatisfactory to them for several reasons: First, if they kept the money in demand deposits, no interest could be earned because of U.S. banking law prohibiting payment of any interest on demand balances. Second, even if the money was put into time deposits, the rate of interest that could be paid would be very low due to interest ceilings then imposed by Regulation Q of the Federal Reserve. Lastly, the Eastern European countries did not want to disclose their identities as owners of these funds because they were afraid the balances might be blocked by the U.S. government in case of a political or military conflict.

The solution to the problem seems simple, at least in retrospect. Instead of depositing the dollars with a bank in the United States, why not deposit them with a bank in England. To do this, the foreign trade bank of any particular Eastern European country would merely have to ask its bank in New York to charge its account with the amount in question and credit it to the account of a London-based bank. The London bank that would receive the deposit could be a European bank or London-based branch of a U.S. bank. It could even be a branch of the same U.S. bank that had originally held the direct deposit of the Eastern European country. In this way, a new asset and liability would be created on the books of the London bank. On the liability side, it would now have a deposit from an Eastern European foreign trade bank. On the asset side, it would have a corresponding increase in the dollar balance it maintained with either one of its correspondent banks in New York or, in the case of a branch, its head office. It is important to note that the actual dollars would never leave the United States. They would only be transferred from one account to another or, perhaps, from one U.S. bank to another.

Part of the reason the communist foreign trade bank would deposit the dollars in London, rather than in New York, would be to get a better interest rate. To be able to pay this rate, the London bank would have to rapidly find a use for its newly acquired dollar deposit. Completing this illustration, then let us assume that the London bank could place the Eurodollar deposit with an Italian bank at a rate that was fractionally higher than its own interest obligation. To effect the actual transfer of the dollars, the London bank would merely instruct its New York correspondent to debit (charge) the amount in question to its dollar account and pass a corresponding credit to a dollar account maintained by the Italian bank at the same or some other U.S. bank. Again, the dollars would merely be transferred from one account to another and would not leave the country. A new deposit liability and corresponding asset would, however, be created on the books of the Italian bank. The deposit liability would be to the London bank that placed the Eurodollars with the Italian bank. The asset would be represented by an increase in the Italian bank's dollar deposits in the United States.

Let us assume that the Italian bank had a commercial customer who imported from the United States and, therefore, had a maturing dollar obligation. To allow this customer to finance his dollar-denominated imports, the Italian bank might wish to lend him its newly acquired Eurodollars. Thus, in this example, the funds would ultimately be used to pay a U.S. exporter. The transaction would be executed by means of a request from the Italian bank to its U.S. correspondent to debit its dollar account and to pay the money to the U.S. exporter in settlement of the account receivable he would have coming to him from the Italian importer. The asset on the Italian bank's balance sheet would now become a Eurodollar loan to the Italian importer.

Of course, at the maturity of his Eurodollar loan, the Italian importer would have to find dollars from somewhere (perhaps, by buying them against lire) to repay the loan. The Italian bank, in turn, would have to repay the London bank at the expiration of the time originally set for the deposit. The London bank would then in turn, repay (or renew) the deposit of the East Europeans.

To summarize, a Eurodollar is a U.S. dollar deposit that is being redeposited with banks or lent to companies, individuals, or governments outside the United States. Note that the actual dollars never leave the United States. It is, however, the dollar deposit at a U.S. bank that is being traded in Europe.

Market Growth

While the Eastern Europeans are often credited with starting the Eurodollar market, other capitalists soon caught on to this most useful tool of finance. Companies, banks, and individuals from all over the world started to deposit their dollars with banks in London. The reasons for this were similar to the ones already outlined—primarily the desire to earn a higher interest rate than was permitted in the United States. London, because of its expertise and long-established role as a world financial center, became the chief marketplace for Eurodollar deposits and lending. Eurodollars are also traded in other major cities, such as Paris and Milan. An active Eurodollar market has also developed in Nassau; while the dollars are deposited with banks or branches of U.S. banks there, the actual trading is done out of New York and Toronto.

It is estimated that the size of this market is about $1,750 billion and still growing. It has been stimulated particularly by the financing of large crude oil shipments for which the contract agreements are mostly drawn in U.S. dollars.

Asian Dollars

There has also been the growth of an Asian dollar market, based primarily in Singapore, Tokyo, and some other cities of noncommunist Asia. These dollars are no different from the ones we already discussed, except that instead of being deposited with a London or other European bank, they are deposited with an Asian bank. A Eurodollar may become an Asian dollar deposit when a London-based bank asks its New York correspondent to debit its own account and credit the amount in question to the dollar account maintained in New York by a Singapore- or other Asian-based bank. More broadly, Asian dollars are created whenever dollars are placed on deposit with an Asian bank by another bank, corporation, or individual. Again, the actual dollars never leave the United States but are merely transferred from one account or bank to another in the United States. An Asian depository bank will probably wish to lend the dollars to a local customer—perhaps, an Asian firm that imports from the United States—who happens to be in need of dollars.

Other Eurocurrencies

Sometimes, banks and other holders of Eurodollars may find it profitable to convert them into other currencies, such as German marks, Swiss francs, or Dutch guilders. Usually, the conversion of Eurodollars into other currencies is done by means of a swap transaction, that is, a spot purchase of the currency against dollars and a simultaneous forward sale of the currency for dollars. The motivation for swapping Eurodollars into other currencies is usually the ability to take advantage of interest rate differentials between dollars and the other currency in question.

When the other currency into which dollars are swapped is deposited outside its own home country, it is called a "Eurocurrency." Thus, we have what is commonly called the Eurocurrencies market. A Eurocurrency is basically a deposit denominated in one of the key convertible currencies being traded (i.e., redeposited and/or lent) in countries other than the currency's home country. Again, the actual pounds, francs, marks, and so on, never leave their respective home countries; only the deposits in a local bank are being traded externally. To emphasize the fact that Eurocurrencies are deposits traded outside their home countries, they are also often referred to as offshore currencies.

Today, the great bulk of the offshore currencies market consists of Eurodollars. Other European and Asian currencies do, however, play increasingly important roles.

Sources of Eurocurrencies

The sources of Eurocurrency deposits are varied, and since some of them move over numbered accounts, are not known exactly. Part of the supply comes from wealthy individuals in such places as South America, the Middle East, and Canada who choose not to keep all their money invested in their home country. Another important source is large, multinational corporations that have excess liquidity that they choose to invest in the relatively high-yielding market for Eurodollars or other offshore currencies. As part of their international cash management, for instance, it may be possible for companies periodically to transfer receipts in different currencies to a central consolidation account in London. There, the money can earn a good interest rate until it is needed for further investments, profit remittance to the company's home country, or some other purpose.

Another source of Eurocurrencies may be swaps out of a local currency. This is usually done to take advantage of interest rate differentials. Assume, for instance, that mark deposits for three months can be obtained in Germany for 5% per annum, while Eurodollars yield 7% per annum. On the surface, it would appear that it will benefit banks in Germany to gather up marks and convert them into dollars. At the end of three months, however, the bank engaging in this operation has to change the dollars back into marks to repay its mark obligation. The original exchange rate, of course, will reflect the interest rate differential, and if the mark has, in the meantime, become more expensive, losses may result that are well in excess of the interest rate differential gained. To cover against such potential exchange losses, the German bank could generally buy three months' forward marks at the same time it sells the marks for dollars. Thus, it could engage in a swap transaction like the ones described in Chapter 7. If the three months' forward premium on the mark is only, say, 1% per annum, the swap transaction still would yield a net interest rate differential of 1% per annum. Indeed, under the given interest rate, it could be assumed that it would be advantageous to swap marks into Eurodollars, as long as the forward premium of marks bought for delivery three months hence was less than at the rate of 2% per annum.

The last important source of deposits comes from governments and central banks. As a result of heavy overseas investment by U.S. companies, cumulative U.S. balance of payments deficits, accumulation of exchange by oil-rich Arab countries, speculative currency flows, and international interest rate differentials, foreign governments and central banks have been accumulating enormous quantities of dollars. Traditionally, these dollars were invested in U.S. Treasury bills, certificates of deposit, bankers' acceptances, and other money market instruments. With the growth of the Eurodollar market, however, central banks also started to place their dollars in London, primarily to obtain a better yield.

Uses of Eurocurrencies

The large pool of Eurocurrencies from the previously mentioned sources is utilized in many different ways. Certainly, a good part of the money is used to finance international trade, although it is difficult to determine how large a portion flows into this area. Eurodollars and other offshore currencies may be converted (swapped) into local currencies of specific countries. These local currencies can then be used to finance working capital, plant expansion, trade, and other commercial and governmental activities. Governments, both national and local, may wish to borrow in the offshore markets to finance balance of payment deficits, expansion of nationalized industries, education, and so on. Eurocurrencies may also be repatriated to their home country to provide needed financing in periods of liquidity shortage. Finally, Eurocurrencies may be used to help companies and banks in their covering and hedging operations. Each of these uses is discussed in more detail later in the chapter.

Eurocurrency Flows

To further illustrate the possible sources and uses of offshore currencies, it will be interesting to follow a hypothetical Eurodollar deposit from its creation through the various hands it may move until it finally either ceases to be a Eurodollar or multiplies through a process of credit expansion.

Assume that a large Italian car manufacturer receives $10 million for his sales in the United States. For his own reasons he does not immediately want to convert the proceeds into Italian lire, but prefers to keep the money in dollars. If the money stays in a demand deposit at a U.S. bank, no interest is earned. Also, a time deposit may not offer as good a yield as can be obtained in the Eurodollar market. Assume that the $10 million is at first on deposit in a demand account at the Chase Manhattan Bank. To transfer the money to London, the Italian car manufacturer asks the Chase Manhattan Bank to debit its account and transfer (credit) the $10 million to its London branch for the purpose of establishing a six-months' Eurodollar deposit at the prevailing rate of interest, say, 6% per annum. The Chase Manhattan branch in London now has a $10 million credit in the account it maintains with its head office in New York. Offsetting this asset, it also has a deposit liability to the Italian company for an equal amount.

Now, assume that Chase London does not have an immediate commercial borrower for the money. A German bank, however, is willing to take the money at six months' deposit for 6.5% per annum. Since Chase London earns ⅛ of 1% per annum on the transaction, it redeposits the money with the German bank. Assume the latter's New York correspondent is the Citibank N.A. The German bank requests that its account at Citibank be credited with the $10 million. Chase New York does this by debiting the account of its London office and transferring the money to Citibank via the New York clearing.

The German bank now has $10 million in its favor at Citibank, offset by a deposit liability to Chase Manhattan's branch in London. The German bank may now do several things with this newly acquired dollar deposit:

1. Redeposit it with another bank.
2. Lend it to a German importer who needs dollars to pay an obligation. In this case, the money is credited to the account of the U.S. exporter and, in fact, leaves the Eurodollar market. (The deposit liabilities on the books of the London and German banks, as well as the offsetting assets, remain, of course, until the maturity of the deposit at the end of the six-month period when the German importer has to obtain dollars to repay the bank loan.)
3. Sell the dollars to a German importer against marks for a similar purpose as previously outlined. To cover its future dollar liability, the bank would probably simultaneously buy an equivalent amount of dollars for delivery in six months.
4. Swap the money into German marks and lend the proceeds to a local company for working capital.
5. If no commercial demand for dollars exists, the German central bank may finally buy them to maintain what it considers a satisfactory exchange rate of its local currency against the dollar. This means the account of the German commercial bank at Citibank is debited and the account of the central bank credited. The central bank may dó several things with these newly acquired dollars:
   - **a.** Leave them in a demand deposit in New York. Since such demand deposits earn no interest, this alternative is an unlikely choice.
   - **b.** Invest the money in Treasury bills, certificates of deposit, bankers' acceptances, or some other money market instruments available in the United States.

c. Deposit the money in the Eurodollar market. This alternative is the most interesting, since it actually creates additional Eurodollars. The German central bank may instruct Citibank to credit the money to the account maintained in New York by Citibank's London branch for the purpose of setting up a six-month Eurodollar deposit at 6%. The cycle has gone one full turn, and another $10 million Eurodollar deposit has been created.

A similar deposit-creating transaction, such as the one outlined in 5c., occurs if any direct or indirect recipient of a Eurocurrency loan deposits some or all of the proceeds with a Eurobank. For instance, assume that a British firm borrows Eurodollars to pay for an import of Polish linens; it pays these dollars to the Polish exporter. The latter may use the newly acquired dollars to pay for imports from the United States. In this case, again, the money leaves the Eurodollar market. If, on the other hand the Polish firm (or central bank) has no immediate need for the dollars, it may choose to deposit all or part of them in the Eurodollar market as a short-term investment. Again, additional Eurocurrency deposits are created.

Interbank Trading

The previously outlined possible uses for Eurocurrencies represent "end uses," in that a loan is made to a commercial concern or government that needs the money to finance a specific activity or meet a financial obligation. In addition, an active trading in Eurocurrency deposits between financial institutions has developed. A bank may not find sufficient commercial and governmental outlets for its offshore currency deposits. It will, in this case, try to place the excess with another bank, hopefully earning ⅛ or 1/16% of a percent per annum spread in the process. Often banks will take short-term deposits and place them at a longer term, hoping to profit from the usually prevailing liquidity preference that makes the interest rate on short-term deposits lower than that on longer-term deposits. In this way, an active interbank market in offshore currencies has developed.

Rates at which interbank deposits can be placed, constantly vary, depending on supply and demand conditions, as well as rates at which a particular currency can be swapped (i.e., bought or sold with forward cover) into and out of other currencies. The so-called interbank rate has become an important cornerstone on which interest rates for practically all Eurocurrency loans are based. The interbank-offered rates for each day are quoted on the financial pages of most major newspapers.

Deposits

Eurocurrency deposits are most typically made at call or for 1-, 2-, 3-, 6-, or 12-months' maturities. Generally, fixed deposits for other maturities (including two or more years') can also be arranged in specific instances. The rate paid for such deposits is based on current market conditions at the time the deposit is made, and is fixed for the term of the deposit. The rates that are bid for deposits fluctuate constantly to reflect general market conditions, a particular bank's need for funds, and its evaluation of future interest rate and foreign exchange developments. When negotiating to take on a large deposit for longer maturities (i.e., one or more years), a bank may try to find an exact counterpart in the form of a user of a Eurocurrency for the same amount and term. Of course, the rate paid by the final use plus any gain or loss in any swap that may be involved will be in excess of the rate paid for the deposit, thus allowing the bank to earn money for its services.

One of the principal challenges for Eurobankers has been the marshaling of new resources required for financing an increasing volume of trade and investment. One innovation that has helped in opening new sources of funds is the negotiable certificate of deposit issued in Eurodollars and other Eurocurrencies. Investors are often willing to place their money in this type of vehicle because of its greater liquidity. There is an active secondary market in Eurodollar certificates of deposit. Consequently, an investor who needs ready cash before the maturity of the investment can usually find a willing buyer.

COMMERCIAL USES OF OFFSHORE CURRENCIES

In contrast to interbank trading, we may differentiate among a number of possible commercial uses of Eurocurrencies. We emphasize their usefulness in financing of foreign trade. Other uses, such as swaps into local currencies, financing balance of payments deficits, financing of investments, and so on, may, however, be equally or even more important in terms of volume of Eurocurrency funds employed.

Financing of International Trade

One of the chief advantages of the offshore currencies market is that its growth has added another dimension to international liquidity and the financing of trade. Traditionally, much international trade has been financed in pounds sterling and U.S. dollars. Balance of payments restrictions, as well as general tightness of credit in the United States and the United Kingdom, however, have limited the use of the respective currencies. A good part of the financing gap thus created was filled by the growth of the Eurocurrencies market.

U.S. Imports. Imports to the United States may be financed in Eurocurrencies. Take, for instance, the financing of diamond imports that originate in South Africa and are cut in Antwerp or Tel Aviv. The South African exporter will probably wish to receive rand at the time he submits his airway bill of lading under a letter of credit. The proceeds in dollars, however, will not be forthcoming until several months later when the diamonds are sold to the ultimate consumer in the United States, the world's largest diamond importing country. Belgian and Israeli diamond cutters can finance their processing operation by borrowing Eurodollars. Proceeds of the dollar loan are converted to South African rand and paid to the exporter. After the diamonds have been cut and sold to a U.S. diamond merchant, the proceeds of the dollar-denominated sale can be used to repay the loan in the same currency.

This type of transaction does not necessarily have to be financed in Eurodollars. If, for instance, the South African exporter would be willing to ship under a time letter of credit, he would, in fact, be financing the transaction. Alternatively, the transaction could also be financed on a loan or acceptance basis in domestic U.S. dollars, sterling, or some other currency. The choice of one vehicle in preference to another depends largely on cost and money availability. United States loans or acceptance financing may be more expensive than Eurodollars. It may also be that financing in the U.S. market is simply not available, due to tightness of internal money market conditions caused by a domestic economic boom and Federal Reserve efforts to limit the growth of the domestic money supply.

In this example, financing of the trade transaction in dollars is especially useful, since the proceeds from the ultimate sale are also in dollars. Hence, these proceeds can be used directly to repay the Eurodollar loan without conversion or currency risk. Had financing been arranged in some other currency, say sterling, the borrower would first have to convert the dollar sales proceeds into sterling to repay the loan. An exchange loss might be incurred if sterling should appreciate against the dollar before the loan was repaid. This exchange risk could, of course, be covered through a forward purchase of sterling.

It is interesting to note that if any of the diamonds were ultimately sold to the United Kingdom, financing in domestic or Eurosterling might be a useful alternative. In this case, since the final proceeds would be in the same currency as the financing, no exchange risk would be incurred.

U.S. Exports. Exports from the United States may also be financed in Eurocurrencies. One instance might be the export of a Boeing 747 airplane for $35 million to KLM of Holland. Due to the large amount of money involved, the purchasing airline will generally wish to arrange for medium- to long-term credit to finance the purchase. Assume, for our example, that seven years' credit is desired, with repayment over 14 equal semiannual installments.

Boeing will, of course, wish to receive the proceeds of its sale immediately on delivery of the aircraft. Now, assume that the Eximbank is willing to finance one-half of the transaction, that is, the last 3½ years' maturities. Commercial bank financing must, therefore, be arranged for those installments maturing in the first 3½ years. This can be done in U.S. or Eurodollar markets, depending on where the money can be obtained most easily and cheaply. If financing is arranged in Eurodollars, KLM would typically get a 3½ year loan for $17.5 million from a London-based bank or branch, with repayment in seven equal semiannual installments. Most probably, the interest rate would be on a fluctuating basis, set each three or six months and tied to the interbank (offered) rate prevailing on the date of each rollover.

The proceeds of the Eurodollar loan (as well as the other half, financed by Eximbank) would, of course, be turned over directly to Boeing in payment for the aircraft. As the 747 operates over the years, it will generate income, perhaps, even in dollars, to repay the loans by Eximbank and the commercial bank. Again, if the loan is in dollars, the borrower has no exchange risk, there is a steady and dependable source of dollars to eventually repay the loan.

In the case of KLM, for instance, a certain portion of its airline tickets would be sold in the United States. This might, over a number of years, supply enough funds to repay the dollar loans taken out to purchase the aircraft.

Similar financing arrangements can often be made for U.S. exporters of other capital goods or turnkey industrial plants. Ideally, the machinery or plant will eventually turn out a product that can be sold in dollar markets. Proceeds from ultimate sale of the product can, therefore, be used to repay the loan over a number of years. A potential exchange risk of having income generated in one currency yet loan payments due in another is thereby avoided. If the final product is expected to be sold for currencies other than dollars, it may be advisable to obtain financing in these same currencies.

Intercompany Debt. Many U.S. headquartered multinational companies sell goods on a regular basis to their foreign subsidiaries and affiliates. This gives rise to intercompany payables that show up as "accounts receivable from foreign affiliates" on the books of the parent company. The carrying of these intercompany accounts for a certain period of time before payment, actually represents a method of financing exports by the parent company. Most typically, the U.S. company uses its regular lines of credit available at U.S. banks for providing working capital.

A monkey wrench was thrown into this type of intercompany financing through the U.S. government's limitations on foreign direct investment by U.S. companies. Under the previously existing Office of Foreign Direct Investment (ODFI) regulations, an increase of export credit beyond the terms that are customary in the industry represented an outflow of capital. To remain within their ceiling of permitted overseas investment, a number of companies had to sell their accounts receivables to a foreign bank or overseas branch of a U.S. bank. As long as this overseas banking institution financed the purchase with offshore currencies, such a sale was considered an inflow of capital, thereby again bringing the U.S. company within its OFDI ceiling.

As mentioned previously, OFDI restrictions were suspended in early 1974. As long as they existed, however, the Eurocurrencies market represented a useful vehicle for financing increased U.S. exports to affiliated foreign companies.

Third-World Trade. Trade between third-world countries can also be financed in Eurocurrencies. Assume, for instance, that a company in Japan sells some industrial equipment to a company in Romania. Since the U.S. dollar is a key trading currency, the Romanian importer might have arranged for the opening of a dollar sight letter of credit in favor of the Japanese exporter. After the expiration of, say, six months, the Romanian importer, through his bank, will repay the Eurodollar loan, perhaps from the proceeds of some exports to the United States or simply by buying the needed dollars from his central bank.

There is no reason why the previously outlined transaction could not be financed in U.S. domestic dollars, perhaps, using a straight advance or a banker's acceptance as the vehicle. Whether to arrange financing in domestic currency, Eurodollars, or some other currency, depends primarily on money availability, relative cost, and regulatory requirements. If, for instance, a country's exchange restrictions put a limit on the amount of that nation's currency that could be used for financing trade not originating in that country, then financing in the offshore market would represent one viable alternative. Similarly, under previously existing Federal Reserve guidelines limiting U.S. bank loans to foreign obligors, the offshore market supplied an important dimension of liquidity to finance third-world-country trade.

While the previous examples are hypothetical, they should illustrate the varied uses to which Eurocurrencies can be put to finance international trade. The Eurodollar is an extremely flexible vehicle for financing exports and imports. The only limits are considerations of cost and the imagination of merchants, manufacturers, and their bankers.

Swaps into Local Currencies. A local company in Italy may be in need of some funds for the financing of plant expansion or inventory. It can, of course, always go to its local bankers to borrow the required lire. However, it may be more advantageous for it to borrow the needed funds in the offshore market. The company could, for instance, borrow Eurodollars and sell them for lire that it can use as needed. Since repayment of the loan ultimately has to be made in dollars, it may—at the time of the spot sale of dollars—wish to purchase dollars forward for delivery at the time when the Eurodollar loan matures. If Eurodollars can be borrowed for, say, 9% per annum and the forward purchase of dollars cost an additional 2% (on the assumption that the forward dollar is selling at a premium against the lire), the net cost to the Italian company will be 11%. This may or may not be cheaper than direct lire borrowing, depending on money market conditions at the time of takedown. Alternatively, the Italian borrower may have a steady income in dollars (perhaps from dollar-denominated exports) that can be used to repay loan installments and, therefore, make covering unnecessary.

The borrowing of Eurocurrencies and swapping of same into local money will be advantageous when the cost—after due consideration for gain or loss on the swap—is lower than direct borrowings in local currencies. It may also be that, due to credit restraint, local currency borrowings are not available. In such cases, the Eurocurrencies market represents an important source of added liquidity.

When Eurodollars are swapped into local currencies, part of the proceeds may, at times, be used to finance trade. For the plant expansion that the Italian company is financing, it might have to import some equipment from abroad. It may be advantageous not to convert into local currency that portion needed to finance imports, and thus avoid the necessity of several foreign exchange transactions. If such imports are also invoiced in dollars, any related exchange risk is also covered.

Eurodollars swapped into local currency may also be a useful financing tool for various types of governmental units. Assume, for instance, that a British local authority needs some money to finance a new sewage plant, with repayment to be made over a period of five years from general tax revenues. One way of arranging the financing may be to borrow Eurodollars and swap them into sterling.

Financing Balance of Payments Deficits

A government may, during one or more years, have a deficit in its balance of payments. While there are several ways of financing a deficit, such as drawing from the IMF, one possibility is to borrow in the Eurocurrencies market. In the past banks were willing only to finance a balance of payments deficit if they considered it to be of a temporary nature. Recently, in the case of third-world countries this policy has been abandoned. Nevertheless, fundamental disequilibria must be taken care of by devaluation or strong deflationary economic measures.

Indirectly, but most importantly, the financing of a temporary balance of payments deficit contributes to the financing of trade. The existence of the Eurocurrencies market adds an important source of international liquidity that may be drawn on to offset temporary swings in a country's balance of payments. Take, for instance, a relatively small country, such as Austria, which at one time had ample reserves of gold and hard currencies. If, in any one year, heavy overseas investment by Austrian companies and unusually heavy imports contributed to a current payments deficit, the government simply borrowed in the Eurodollar market for one or several years, until automatic or government-induced forces started working to correct the imbalance. The purely mechanical transaction was that the amount of the Eurodollar loan became available in the form of credit balances in New York—to be used as a means of payment for Austrian imports, additional foreign direct investment, repayment of previously accumulated commercial debts, or investments in dollar-denominated assets, such as bonds or Treasury bills.

Often, the financial needs of governments and international agencies are of a long-term nature. Austria may wish to finance massive capital investments in its nationalized industries. The construction phase of such large-scale programs may take several years. Generation of enough profits to repay a loan plus interest may be possible only over 10 to 15 years. Similarly, an international organization, such as the World Bank, may wish to raise money for 10 to 15 years in the Eurodollar market to finance its long-term loans for large superstructure and industrial projects in developing countries. Again, Eurocurrency borrowings—this time, in the form of a long-term bond issue—might be most useful.

Large-scale industrial development projects usually require a substantial amount of imports. To the extent that Eurocurrencies are used to finance such projects, the financing of international trade is given a most important assistance at the same time.

Repatriation to Home Country

When money gets extremely tight in the home country of a particular Eurocurrency, banks may wish to repatriate funds from the offshore market to use in domestic lending operations. The classic example of this occurred during the U.S. credit crunch in 1967 and again in 1969 when U.S. banks borrowed billions of Eurodollars to meet the loan demand of domestic companies. Much of this loan demand was probably to carry inventory, accounts receivable, and to finance plant expansion. Some of the money was certainly also used to allow U.S. companies to build on inventories for export, carry foreign receivables, and finance imports.

The repatriation of Eurodollars, to some extent, helped frustrate the tight monetary policies pursued by the Federal Reserve. As a result, to discourage further inflow, the Federal Reserve imposed reserve requirements on any Eurodollar borrowings by U.S.-based banks. This illustrates an accusation frequently made against the offshore market: Since it is an almost completely free international money market, Eurocurrencies move into and out of a country very rapidly in response to credit demands, changing interest rates, and speculative pressures. This free international money market may help to frustrate domestic monetary policies of individual countries. To counteract this, a number of nations, including the United States, Germany, Japan, and others, have put restrictions on the inflow of foreign currencies. While further restrictions may well be possible, nations have generally also been aware of the beneficial effects of the growth of Eurocurrency markets. It is hoped that existing and potential new restrictions will serve only to regulate offshore markets (including the deterrence of money laundering) and their impact on national economies, and will not have the aim of destroying them.

Covering and Hedging

In Chapter 7, it is pointed out that importers who are invoiced in a revaluation-prone currency should cover themselves by buying forward the needed currency. If the forward premium is too high (as indeed it might be if the currency is expected to revalue shortly), a cheaper alternative might be to buy the currency in the spot market and lend out the proceeds in the Eurocurrencies market until needed.

Exporters who invoice in a devaluation-prone currency would normally cover themselves by selling the expected proceeds in the forward market. Again, an alternative means of covering can be arranged by borrowing the devaluation-prone currency in the offshore market or locally and selling the proceeds spot for dollars. Then, when the actual receipts for the export come in, they can be used to repay the loan.

Since the offshore market is relatively free from national restrictions and money can be placed or taken with relatively few formalities, it represents a useful vehicle for businesspeople and bankers to use in covering their exchange risks. It has already been pointed out that exporters and importers are advised to borrow in the same currency as the one in which they will ultimately be paid after selling their goods. Again, the required funds in the required currency may be most readily available in the offshore markets.

Comply with Exchange Regulations

As indicated in the discussion on intercompany debt, some U.S. companies had to sell receivables due from foreign affiliates against Eurodollars to meet OFDI regulations. In other instances, to prevent an excessive outflow of U.S. dollars, companies were also forced to borrow in the offshore market when they wished to increase their investment in overseas subsidiaries and affiliates.

While OFDI regulations have now been discontinued, other countries, still have, or may impose in the future, regulations that prohibit or limit the use of domestic currencies for foreign investment. The United Kingdom, for instance, limits the amount of sterling that may be used for investments in other countries. Hence, U.K. companies that wish to expand abroad must raise a substantial proportion of the needed funds in the offshore market and/or financial markets of host countries.

Versatility

The many services that can be provided through the Eurocurrencies market and worldwide banking networks may perhaps best be illustrated by citing some typical problems brought before international bankers by their customers.

> A British company needs financing for expansion on the continent. The guidance and financial services of a multinational bank are needed because U.K. exchange restrictions limit the amount of sterling that is available for foreign investments. The amount required will have to be borrowed offshore.
>
> The French government expects a substantial balance of payments deficit, due to skyrocketing prices for petroleum imports. It goes to the Eurocurrencies market to borrow several billion dollars for a number of years, until other energy sources can be developed.

A Belgian exporter wishes to sell to Romania. This exporter can only obtain orders, however, if he can also come up with a five-year financing package. The exporter is not financially willing or able to take an Eastern European risk for five years. He, therefore, seeks nonrecourse financing from a Eurobanker.

A major oil company requires several hundred million dollars for drilling and developing a North Sea oil field. It decides that such an enormous amount of money can best be raised in the offshore market, due to the ability of London-based consortium banks to put together a lending syndicate. Moreover, since no reserve requirements are imposed against banks' holding of Eurodollars, this avenue of financing is cheaper than raising the money in the United States.

TIME MARKETS FOR EUROCURRENCY LOANS

In the previous section, we outline the general uses of Eurocurrencies, with special emphasis on their utility in financing trade between nations. The duration of Eurocurrency loans may vary from overnight up to 15 to 20 years, depending on the nature of the borrowers' needs. To service these needs, three distinct markets for short-, medium-, and long-term Eurocurrencies, have developed. A discussion of each of these markets follows.

Short Term—from Banks

Eurocurrency loans with a final maturity of one year or less are usually considered to be short term. Such short-term loans from banks may arise under the following situations:

"One shot" financing of a specific trade or other transaction

Borrowings and repayments under a short-term credit facility to provide general working capital

Credit Facility. The most typical way to borrow is under a credit facility that may be available for one year. While such a credit facility imposes no legal lending obligation on the bank granting it, it does establish that the bank has reviewed the borrower's credit standing and has set a maximum amount it is willing to lend to him. Under normal circumstances—and barring any adverse developments in the borrower's financial position—the facility will be available for one year. Of course, after one year, the facility may be renewed, provided that the borrower's financial condition remains satisfactory.

Since a short-term credit facility is not a legal obligation, banks generally do not charge a commitment fee.

Takedown. A takedown or drawing under the credit can occur anytime during the year, and is usually for a preestablished period, such as one or three months. Once the prearranged period is over, the credit may be rolled over if the borrower requires it.

Rate. The rate is established at each takedown or rollover date for a pre-established period. Usually, it is tied to the interbank offered rate on the day of takedown or rollover. (Eurocurrency transactions are usually executed for value, called takedown, in two business days.) Depending on the credit-worthiness of the customer and other market considerations, the rate may be ¼ of 1% per annum to 1% per annum above the interbank rate.

Uses. The most typical uses of short-term Eurocurrency credits are the financing of self-liquidating trade transactions, providing local currency working capital, and interim financing pending takeout through a medium- or long-term loan or bond equity issue.

Short Term—Other

Commercial Paper. In addition to Euromoney supplied by banks, a still modest market in Eurocurrency commercial paper has developed. This means that a few companies are sidestepping the use of banks as intermediaries and going directly to the market to raise short-term Eurocurrencies by issuing their own promissory notes to lenders and investors.

Eurocurrency commercial paper is usually issued in maturities of three or six months. To provide a fallback facility in case the paper cannot be rolled over, issuers generally arrange for some kind of stand-by credit facility with a commercial bank, for which they pay a commitment fee. In this, as well as in other respects, the Euromarket in commercial paper is similar to the U.S. market.

Issuers of Eurcommercial paper have chosen this vehicle because it adds another source of funds. Occasionally, borrowing via the commercial paper market may be cheaper than a short-term bank loan. Lenders and investors have been attracted to the buying of Eurocommercial paper because it may yield more than Eurodollar certificates of deposit.

Bankers' Acceptances. Another short-term financing vehicle that has been tried are bankers' acceptances denominated in Eurocurrencies. The company requiring financing merely draws a draft in the Eurocurrency desired (usually dollars) on a Eurobank. The latter accepts the draft and discounts it. The fact that the draft is drawn by a company and accepted by a bank makes it two-name paper with ready marketability. The accepting bank, if it so wishes, may, therefore, sell the acceptance in the London discount market.

Euroacceptances are similar to commercial paper. They have, however, the added advantage of carrying the obligation to pay as would a major bank. This feature gives the instrument added marketability and often a lower rate.

Medium Term—from Banks

Over the past few years, banks have become increasingly willing to extend Eurocurrency credit for periods of one to ten years. Occasionally, the term can go as long as 12 years. Some medium-term consortium banks that were formed in Europe specialize particularly in granting medium-term credits going out beyond five years.

Types. Depending on the needs of the borrower, a medium-term credit arrangement may take any of the following forms:

Term loan with periodic amortization.

Term loan with, perhaps, some amortization and a balloon payment at the end of the period.

Revolving credit.

Revolving credit with the option of turning it into an amortizing term loan.

Term Loan. Under a term loan with periodic amortization, the full amount of the credit may be taken down at once, or there may be a schedule of takedowns, depending on need. In the latter case, the bank will usually charge a commitment fee (most typically at ½ of 1% per annum) on any unused portion of the credit. Repayment of the loan usually occurs in equal, semiannual, or quarterly installments over the life of the credits. Sometimes, it may be desirable to schedule repayments exactly in accordance with expected cash generation of the project or trade transaction that is being financed. Thus, for instance, installments payable in the early years of the credit may be lower, and those payable in the later years correspondingly higher.

Balloon Payment. A borrower frequently may know in advance that the underlying project or import cannot throw off sufficient cash to repay the credit over the maximum term available. In such instances, a banker may be willing to accept relatively low amortization over the life of the credit, with a large portion payable at the expiration date in the form of a balloon payment. In such cases, it is usually the intention of both the borrower and banker to refinance the balloon payment with amortization over an additional number of years. The banker, however, undertakes no legal obligation to such refinancing. If, at the expiration of the first credit, he wishes full repayment, he is entitled to it and the borrower will have to find the required funds elsewhere. The banker will generally only ask for full repayment if the borrower's financial condition has deteriorated significantly or the banker's own liquidity position has changed making it more difficult for him to supply the needed funds.

Revolving Credit. A revolving credit is also a medium-term arrangement. The borrower may, however, borrow and repay as required by his fluctuating needs. The bank will set a maximum amount up to which the customer may borrow for a stated number of years (usually three to five years). When the money is no longer needed, the borrower may repay any amounts previously taken down. Usually, a commitment fee of, say, ½ of 1% per annum is charged on the unused portion of a revolving credit.

A revolving credit is most appropriate for growing companies with steadily increasing working capital needs. Sometimes, a company may be planning a major plant expansion but is not certain as to timing; to assure itself of money availability when needed, it may enter into a revolving credit agreement with a bank.

Revolving Credit Turned into Term Loan. As working capital needs grow or as a planned construction program gets under way, increasing amounts of the revolving credit will probably be drawn down. Sufficient earnings to repay the credit will be generated only after a few years. To provide for eventual amortization, most revolving credit agreements allow the outstanding loan balance to be converted into a term loan. The latter will then be amortized in, say, semiannual installments.

Credit Agreement. Medium-term offshore loans are generally covered by a credit agreement between the lender and borrower. The agreement spells out details concerning the interest rate, commitment fee, takedown, repayment, and so on. Sometimes, it also contains covenants that the borrower is expected to obey while any amount on the credit is still outstanding. Typical covenants might restrict the borrower from certain mergers, acquisitions, and additional borrowing; they may require the maintenance of minimum net worth, working capital, and so on. In contrast to U.S. domestic term loans, however, Eurocurrency credit agreements are often written with no or only few restrictive covenants. Part of the reason for this is that most borrowers in the offshore markets are prime companies of undoubted credit standing. A long, restrictive agreement is, therefore, often deemed unnecessary and unduly burdensome to the borrower. Another reason for having few restrictive covenants is the intense competition that exists among Eurocurrency lenders. This has sometimes led to not imposing covenants on borrowers when, in fact, such restrictions would have been warranted under prudent banking practices. Restrictive covenants will almost always appear unduly burdensome to the borrower. In the long run, however, they enforce good financial discipline, which can be beneficial to both borrower and lender.

Multicurrency Clause. Sometimes, Eurodollar term loan agreements contain a multicurrency clause. This allows the client to borrow not only Eurodollars, but also any other available currencies. If, on a particular rollover date, some other Eurocurrency is cheaper than dollars (after duly considering the swap out of dollars into that other currency), it will be advantageous for the borrower to take down the other currency.

A variation of the multicurrency clause may also be useful for companies that have needs in several currencies. One instance could be a multinational company with subsidiaries in London, Paris, Frankfurt, Zurich, and Milan. A bank with branches in these same cities might be able to provide a credit line or revolving credit available in Eurodollars, and, depending on availability, in any other Eurocurrencies or domestic currencies of the respective countries. This greatly resembles one-stop banking. A multicurrency credit may, perhaps, be arranged through the bank's head office. It will be available, however, at bank branches in various countries and in various currencies as needed.

Rates. Rates in the Eurocurrency market are subject to substantial fluctuations. Therefore, most banks are not willing to fix a rate of interest for the entire duration of term loans or revolving credits. Eurocurrency deposits and certificates of deposit, which, in fact, finance the loans, are most typically for three- or six-month periods. Consequently, it is wise to also fix the rate on Eurocurrency loans each three or six months when corresponding deposits must be rolled over at new rates. Rates on term loans and revolving credits are, therefore, generally established each three or six months at a fixed spread over the interbank offered rate prevailing on the day of the rollover. The spread will vary depending on market conditions and the financial standing of the obligor. Rates of ½ of 1% per annum up to and in excess of 2% per annum over the interank offered rate are common.

Occasionally, a bank may be willing to quote a fixed rate for the entire period of a term loan. It will do this most readily when it can generate a matching long-term deposit for exactly the same maturity as the loan. If no such matching deposit can be generated, the bank takes a substantial risk in making a loan for several years at a fixed rate, while having to finance itself each three or six months at prevailing market rates for Eurocurrency deposits. To compensate for this additional risk, fixed-rate term loans will usually be more expensive than the more commonly used fluctuating rate.

When agreeing to a fluctuating rate, it is actually the borrower who takes the risk of a substantial increase in interest rates over the term of the credit. This is certainly a real risk of which the borrower should be aware. In the past, Eurodollar rates for three to six months' borrowings have gone as high as 18 to 20% per annum! The risk to the customer is mitigated, however, since most Eurodollar agreements have no prepayment penalty, as long as such prepayment is made at a regular rollover date. Thus, if Eurocurrency rates rise steeply, the borrower may be able to repay the loan entirely and borrow in a (perhaps) less-expensive, national credit market. Moreover, even though Eurodollar rates may rise steeply for a short period, medium-termed borrowers hope that, over the life of the loan, the rate paid will average out to something more reasonable.

Uses. As has been suggested, medium-term Eurocurrency loans are used for financing imports of such large capital items as machinery, transportation equipment, and turnkey industrial plants. Medium-term Eurocurrency loans are also frequently used for large local projects, such as the building of roads, oil refineries, airports, factories, and so on. Any project that is economically sound and will eventually throw off money to pay for itself may be suitable for financing via offshore currencies.

In addition to economic projects, some governments occasionally use the offshore markets to borrow large amounts of medium-term funds to cover a temporary balance of payments deficit.

Why use the offshore market instead of national money and capital markets for the financing of medium-term needs? The answer to this question is sometimes one of availability,sometimes one of cost, and sometimes a combination of the two. For large projects, the massive amounts of capital that are required may simply not be available through national credit markets. Companies located in smaller countries or countries where capital markets are not very developed may have to look for outside financing sources. In the past, such countries have borrowed in the United States, where the capital market was and is very broadly based and developed. World capital requirements have become so enormous, however, that even the U.S. market is not broad enough to supply all the needed funds.

Certain other government restrictions may force companies to turn to the offshore markets for some of their financing needs. In the United States, for instance, previous OFDI regulations severely limited the ability of U.S. companies to export capital for direct investment overseas. Their only resort, in many cases, was the offshore markets.

Sometimes, cost is also a factor. Credit in domestic capital markets may be available only at a prohibitive cost. Again, the offshore market may present a viable alternative for obtaining the needed funds at a more reasonable price, after taking into consideration the cost of covering the exchange risk.

Special Credits. Often the amount of money required by a multinational company is so large that no single bank can supply all of it. Banks are under restrictions concerning the maximum amount they can lend to any one obligor. Moreover, even for prime companies, banks like to diversity their credit risks. For these reasons, the practice of syndicating large Eurocurrency loans among a number of Eurobanks has grown.

The normal practice in syndication credits is for one bank to take a leading role. This involves making a fairly large amount of the credit for its own account and placing the remainder with one or more other banks. The lead bank also takes care of administrative details, such as preparing and policing the credit agreement, arranging for a disbursement schedule, and allocating payments of interest and principal among the syndicate members according to their respective percentage of participation in the total credit.

For its agency services, the lead bank obtains a special fee from the borrower. Usually, this fee is computed as a flat percentage (most typically ¼ to ½ of 1%) of the total amount of the credit.

Except for the fact that syndication credits involve a number of banks, they are structured in a fashion similar to Eurocurrency term loans or revolving credits. The rates for syndication credits are usually also tied to the three or six months' interbank rate.

Medium Term—Other

To cover their medium-term funds requirements, some companies have issued floating rate notes in different Eurocurrencies. These are, in essence, medium-term notes whose interest rates fluctuate according to market conditions. Companies issuing such paper enjoy the advantage of having needed funds available for several years. Hence, floating rate notes constitute another financing vehicle to supplement credit available through bank loans.

Long Term

Simultaneous with the development of the short- and medium-term Eurocurrencies market has grown the market for Eurobonds. These are, in fact, bearer bonds issued by major multinational companies that have long-term financing needs in one or more of the currencies for which Eurobonds enjoy a market. Their maturity is usually 15 to 20 years and the largest proportion is issued in Eurodollars. There also have been issues in German marks, Swiss francs, units of account, European currency units (ECU), and other currencies.

A unit of account is a composite currency unit based on 17 European currencies. It has special appeal to investors because it protects them against devaluation of any currencies. The gold value of a unit of account does not change unless all 17 currencies have changed. Even then, the change in the unit of account's value is limited to the smallest change that occurred in the direction in which the majority of currencies have moved. Borrowers are, therefore, also protected against upvaluation of any currencies in which a bond obligation is denominated.

An ECU is equal to a fixed amount of each of the currencies of the members of the European Economic Community (EEC). It is based on the prevailing U.S. dollar parities at the time the bond is issued. Subscriptions to ECU-denominated bonds may be made at the option of the investor in any one of the six currencies. The bondholder also has the option to receive payment of principal and interest in any one of the six currencies. The ECU offers substantial inducements to the investor since he can, in fact, purchase in the weakest currency and receive interest and principal in the strongest currency. The borrower, of course, takes a substantial risk. This may, however, be counterbalanced by the lower interest rate the borrower probably will have to pay if he denominates the bonds in ECUs.

Eurobonds may be senior or subordinated straight-debt issues or they may be convertible into common shares of the borrowing company or its parent. Sometimes, to make the issue more attractive to investors, warrants permitting the purchase of shares of the borrower or his parent at a fixed price may also be attached to the bonds. Frequently, when the borrower is a subsidiary of a large multinational corporation, the issue is guaranteed by the parent company.

Money borrowed for 15 or more years is usually used for major industrial or infrastructural projects. Such projects often require the importation of substantial amounts of capital equipment. Thus, the long-term loan may indirectly be financing international trade.

A company wishing to issue Eurocurrency bonds will want to get the advice and assistance of a competent international investment banker. Foreign banks, unlike U.S. domestic banks, are generally permitted to engage in underwriting activities. Foreign subsidiaries of U.S. banks may also engage in underwriting certain types of issues on behalf of foreign obligors. A number of banks, in fact, have subsidiaries located in Europe (primarily London) that are active in this field. An international bank may also be able to help a borrower in arranging for a private placement of the debt issue.

ADVANTAGES AND RISKS

Funds Availability

It has probably become clear that the offshore markets offer substantial advantages to the foreign trader and investor who needs additional funds for expansion. Before the emergence of offshore markets, the availability of money depended to a large extent on national monetary policy, particularly that of the United States and the United Kingdom, whose currencies were used for the vast bulk of international trade financing.

Credit restrictions, in both the United States and the United Kingdom, however, limited the amount of the respective currencies that were available. These restrictions gave a direct boost to the development of Eurodollar and Eurosterling markets. Conversely, the development of the offshore markets substantially reduced the dependence of foreign trade financing on the monetary policies of one or two countries. At the same time, the offshore markets provided a vast new source of world liquidity with enormous versatility as to its utilization: It can be used to finance short- or medium-term trade transactions, investment projects, working capital needs, and even temporary imbalances in a nation's external payments. It should be of some comfort to borrowers that despite recurring crises in international currency markets, Eurodollars have always been available.

Ease of Access

Prime borrowers of Eurocurrencies usually find access to funds easily. In contrast to lending practice in the United States, where complicated and restrictive term loan agreements are usually drawn up, prime companies, governments, and banks can often borrow Eurocurrencies through a mere telephone call. Very little, if any, documentation is usually required to take down an offshore loan.

European companies urgently requiring dollars may also find it advantageous (i.e., faster) to borrow them locally because of time differences between Europe and the United States.

National Monetary Policies

A charge frequently made against Eurocurrencies is that the relative freedom with which they move into and out of a country, due to changes in interest rates or speculation, tends to frustrate national economic policy. This has certainly been true in several instances in the past and has resulted in some national restrictions on Eurocurrency movements. At the same time, governments and central banks have been able to use the Eurocurrency markets as positive tools of their monetary policies. The central banks of both Germany and Italy, for instance, have, in the past, offered favorable swap rates to banks and commercial firms to channel unwanted domestic liquidity out of the country and into the Eurocurrencies market. Local banks were encouraged to take up local currency deposits and convert them into dollars for deposit in London. At the same time, the local currency had to be bought for forward delivery, timed with the maturity of the deposit. By allowing a low premium or even a discount on the forward purchase, central banks can encourage this type of transaction.

The converse has been true in other nations. When faced with temporary payments deficits, these countries have encouraged their banks and commercial firms to borrow offshore currencies for their financing needs.

Diversified Deposit Sources

Another advantage of the offshore market is the wide range of sources from which deposits can be gathered. Individuals, corporations, and governments from practically all over the world have found it useful to place some or all of their money into offshore markets. With such a diversity of sources, a "drying up" of the Eurocurrency market seems most unlikely.

Risks of Borrower

From the individual borrower's point of view, there are some potential risks. Probably the most important one is the volatility of Eurocurrency rates. Another danger to the borrower who swaps Eurocurrencies into his own exchange is the possibility of government restrictions or taxation on this type of activity. If such restrictions are imposed, a borrower, or his bank, may find himself with an expensive tax or reserve requirement that was not counted on when the loan was originally put on the books. Even though taxes or restrictions may be levied against banks, loan agreements usually allow them to pass on to the customer any unexpected charges. Thus, in most cases, it is, in fact, the borrower who must bear the major cost. He can, of course, repay the Eurocurrency loan—provided financing is available from domestic sources.

Risks of Lender

From the bank's point of view, there are also some risks in Eurocurrency lending. In contrast to the domestic market, a borrower of offshore currencies often does not fully inform the banker of the purpose for which the money was borrowed. When trade is being financed in Eurocurrencies, it is not customary to require the surrender of negotiable shipping documents or warehouse receipts. Hence, the bank has no collateral security, nor can it be certain that it is financing a bona fide, self-liquidating trade transaction. The practice of not requiring the usual protective covenants when granting term loans has already been discussed in Chapter 10. Generally, due to the strong competition that prevails, the offshore market has helped to develop some rather unsound lending practices. As long as only class A companies are being financed, there is probably no danger. But offshore currency loans are increasingly also made to second tier companies and developing nations. The risks of making such loans can be substantially greater, unless banks revert to sound lending policies.

The European Monetary System

The European Monetary System (EMS) was created by the major Western European trading nations because of the free float of individual currencies against one another. Since the creation of the EEC, each currency was allowed to float 2¼% above or below the agreed-on exchange rate. But, during the fall of 1993 when the French franc was under constant pressure, the French government headed by Prime Minister Edouard Balladur convinced the authorities in Brussels and in other central European nations to expand the band to 15% for European currencies above or below the agreed-on exchange rate. When a particular currency reached the allowed limit, central banks were to begin intervening in order to maintain the currency within the agreed spread.

The ECU was created by the EEC member countries to be used among them as an official monetary unit. Each country may also use it internally as a reserve currency. The value of the ECU is based on a weighted basket of currencies, that as of February 1, 1995, consisted of the following:

ECU Specifications as of February 1, 1995

The ECU is defined as the sum of the following percentages of each currency:

Component currencies	Percent in the weighted basket
German mark	30.63
French franc	19.16
British pound	12.30
Italian lira	9.86
Dutch guilder	9.58
Belgian franc	7.85
Luxembourg franc	0.31
Danish krone	2.49
Greek drachma	0.61
Irish punt	1.11
Spanish peseta	5.32
Portuguese escudo	0.78

CHAPTER 12

Foreign Collections

Collection services within a banking institution can be of benefit to the foreign buyer/seller as well as to the domestic seller/buyer. Both parties stand to gain from efficient collection, transfer, and processing of documents relating to foreign trade. But automation and cost cutting endeavors by banks are making this product sometimes unavailable within many banking institutions worldwide. Furthermore, the cost of compliance to various government regulations is becoming a heavy burden in the collection services of most countries.

TYPES OF COLLECTION

Documentary-Export Collections

Frequently, exporters ship goods on a documentary-collection basis. When such payment terms are used, the exporter obtains the usual shipping documents, such as a bill of lading, insurance papers, commercial invoice, consular invoice, inspection certificate, and so on. Simultaneously, he draws a draft on the importer for the total amount due, including the cost of the draft on the importer for the total amount due, including the cost of the merchandise and any charges involved, such as for freight, insurance, and bank fees, which were previously agreed in the sales contract as being for the account of the importer. After the draft and all documents are properly assembled, the exporter attaches the documents to the draft and submits everything to his bank, accompanied by detailed instructions as to how the bank is to proceed in obtaining payment from the importer. The bank, acting as agent for the exporter, checks to make sure all the documents are in order and are complete as stated in the instructions. While the bank does not make as thorough an investigation of the documents as it would under a letter of credit, it does look for internal consistency and sees that the bill of lading and insurance documents are properly endorsed. Then, based on the customer's instruction, the bank types its own collection letter and sends it, together with the drafts and documents, to one of its foreign correspondents who is, preferably, in the same city as the importer.

The foreign correspondent, again acting as agent, notifies the importer that it has title documents available for him to be picked up provided he either pays the draft if it is a sight or arrival instrument or accepts it if it is a time draft.

After a sight or arrival draft has been paid, the money is remitted back to the exporter's bank. The latter either credits the exporter's account or sends him a check for the proceeds. An accepted time draft, that is a trade acceptance, generally remains with the overseas correspondent, who will present it to the acceptor for payment at maturity.

Other Documentary Collections

As can be seen from the previous explanation, the main advantage of a documentary collection is that documents of value are not turned over to the buyer before he has either made payment or has acknowledged a real liability by accepting a draft drawn on him. While this procedure is most frequently used for trade transactions, it can also be employed in other instances; the most typical being the sale of securities, either domestically or abroad. A foreigner may, for instance, have bought securities from a U.S. brokerage house. The broker, to obtain payment, may draw a dollar draft on the buyer and, together with the securities, forward it through banking channels to the buyer for collection. The collecting bank will then turn over the securities to the buyer only against payment (or in some cases acceptance) of the draft.

While trade transactions and the sale of securities are the most typical examples of documentary collections, there occasionally may be other uses. The procedure of turning over documents against payment or acceptance of a draft can be used in any instance where the drawer wishes to maintain control of the documents until the recipient has made payment or has performed some other obligation.

Clean Collections

So far, we have described what is commonly called a "documentary collection" because the draft has title documents attached (thus, a documentary draft). This contrasts to a clean collection or a clean draft. In the latter case, only the draft and, if necessary, an instruction letter are sent out for collection. The documents are sent directly to the importer or the exporter's foreign agent. Hence, the exporter is, in fact, shipping on open-account terms. Clean drafts may also be used when goods are shipped to agents overseas on consignment.

A clean draft may represent an underlying trade transaction or a purely financial transaction involving no movement of merchandise and, therefore, no documents. Typical clean items that may be handled on a collection basis are checks, dividend warrants drawn on foreign banks, promissory notes, clean drafts, acceptances, certificates of deposit issued by foreign banks, savings passbooks issued by foreign banks, governments, and post offices, and drafts drawn under a traveler's letter of credit from a foreign bank.

Basically, any time a foreign resident has a financial obligation to a U.S. resident, and if this obligation is evidenced by a negotiable or nonnegotiable money instrument, collection can be made via bank channels on either a documentary or clean basis. In its broadest sense, therefore, a foreign collection is merely a receivable due from a foreigner to a U.S. resident. A foreign collection may be denominated in either dollars or foreign currency depending on the nature of the underlying obligation.

Inward Collections

What we have described are all outward collections—a U.S. resident endeavors to collect an obligation due him. The converse of this is commonly called an "inward collection." In the reverse manner from that previously outlined, U.S. banks receive from foreign correspondents and other foreign residents clean and documentary collection items payable in the United States. Incoming collections are sorted and checked. If they are drawn on a person in the same city as the receiving bank, they are turned over to the drawee against payment or acceptance. If the drawee is in a different city, the item is presented through another correspondent located in the same city or locality as the drawee. Payment received on sight drafts is directly remitted to the beneficiary. Time drafts that have been accepted by the drawee are usually held in safekeeping to be presented for payment at maturity.

LEGAL CONSIDERATIONS

Duties of Collecting Bank

In the United States, the process of collecting negotiable and nonnegotiable money paper is covered by Article 4 of the UCC, entitled "Bank Deposits—Collections." Basically, the UCC provides that the bank becomes the agent of the customer submitting the paper for collection. Hence, the paper still belongs to the customer and, except for negligence on the part of the collecting bank, is handled at his own risk. The duties of the collecting bank include presentation of the item for payment, remittance of the proceeds, and notification of dishonor and protest where applicable. When the bank forwards the paper to a foreign correspondent in the locality of the importer, the domestic bank is not liable for any error or other act of the foreign collecting agent. The domestic bank is merely responsible for following the depositor's instructions after it has received the collection item (UCC 4-20-2, 4-20-3).

Bank Liability for Negligence

It is the duty of the agent-collecting bank to follow the instructions of the drawer correctly. Failure to do so may result in an unwilling breach of the sales contract by the seller and consequent refusal by the buyer to accept or pay the draft. If it can be shown that the bank is at fault for such nonpayment or nonacceptance, the seller might be able to sue for damages. Actually, the foreign collecting bank should never release the bill of lading and other documents without acceptance or payment of the draft by the importer unless specifically authorized to do so by the drawer.

Uniform Rules

Different foreign countries have their own laws governing collections. A number of countries, including the United Kingdom, have agreed to accept the "Uniform Rules for the Collection of Commercial Paper," drawn up by the International Chamber of Commerce. This latter publication outlines, in detail, the rights and responsibilities of the various parties to foreign collection, including the proper procedure to be followed for advice of nonpayment and protest. Basically, these uniform rules correspond to general commercial and banking usage and are not in conflict with provisions of the UCC.

Determining Applicable Law

Since different rules prevail in various countries, it becomes valid to ask which law should be followed when preparing and submitting an item for collection in a foreign country.

Law of Drawer's Country. As a general rule, the drawer should make sure that the laws of his own country are followed scrupulously. Usually, if a collection instrument meets the legal requirements of the drawer's country, it is also recognized in the country of the drawee. Moreover, the drawee does not become legally bound under the draft until he has formally accepted it. Prior to acceptance, any conflict will have to be resolved, based on provisions of the underlying sales contract.

If financing is involved, any litigation that arises is much more likely to be between the drawer and the bank that negotiated the draft and/or any endorsers. Only after the draft has been accepted and is subsequently dishonored, will litigation take place in the drawee's country.

Law of Drawee's Country. To caution an exporter/drawer to follow carefully the legal requirements of his own country does not mean that he should ignore legal and business practices in the drawee's country. In some South American countries, for example, title documents may be turned over to drawees without payment of the draft. To safeguard himself the exporter

It is understood and agreed that: for the purpose of presenting and/or collecting any item, you may forward the same to any branch of your bank or agent of your own selection, who may collect the item through one or more sub-agents selected by it or by any sub-agent; and your liability is limited to due diligence in selecting those to whom the items are forwarded by you. You may, however, without liability on your part, forward any item for presentation and/or collection directly to the bank where it is payable; and you, or any collecting agent or sub-agent, may accept a bank draft in payment of any item. You shall not be responsible for loss of any kind due to the acts or negligence of any such agents or sub-agents, or for loss in or through the mails, or for any failure to present, demand or collect, or protest or give notice of protest or dishonor of any item; and you are authorized to charge back the amount of any items (whether or not the items themselves can be returned) for which payment in cash has not actually been received by you in New York. In cases where any items are collected and the proceeds are credited to your account in a bank in a foreign country, you shall not be responsible for any proceeds of collection except to the extent that you shall have effected a conversion of the same into United States currency in your hands in New York.

Unless we instruct you to the contrary, the following standing instructions to your correspondents will be applicable to the above mentioned collection: Your correspondents will, in case of dishonor, where it appears necessary or advisable, insure the merchandise, if any, against the usual risks and communicate with you immediately by air mail, unless otherwise instructed. The cost of the insurance plus any other necessary disbursements will be for our account. Furthermore, it is understood and agreed that neither you nor any of your correspondents assume any responsibility for failure to procure any insurance or for the sufficiency or adequacy of any insurance obtained or for any delay in, or prohibition of, the conversion of the proceeds of any claims recovered under such insurance, if losses are payable in a currency other than U.S. dollars, or for the failure to recover any loss which may be payable in U.S. dollars because of lack of exchange.

It is further understood and agreed that wherever by reason of general custom, or by reason of the correspondents having deemed it advisable, the correspondents shall have cleared the merchandise, advanced any duties thereon and/or paid storage and/or any other charges, the disbursements thus made by the correspondents shall be for our account to the extent by which they are not paid upon request by the drawee.

SPECIMEN

Whenever we instruct you to collect "with exchange" or "all charges for account of drawee" you will ask your correspondents to do so. In any case where non-payment of the draft is threatened because of the drawee's unwillingness to pay, you will authorize your correspondents to waive such charges, unless we instruct you to the contrary.

Figure 12-1. Collection agreement with bank.

may, therefore, have to consign the goods to a local bank rather than the importer, or have to insist on receiving an irrevocable letter of credit. For his own protection, therefore, an exporter has to know and take into consideration the laws and regulations of the importer's country.

Contact with Bank. Banks acting as collection agents generally ask the drawer to agree to certain stipulations that are primarily intended to limit the liability of the bank. Usually, these provisions are printed on the reverse side of the bank's form that exporters use as their collection letter. A typical bank disclaimer clause is shown in Figure 12-1. The following provisions should be noted:

1 The bank acts as agent for the drawer and it may appoint one or more subagents (e.g., foreign correspondent banks) in collecting the item. If the bank exercises reasonable care in selecting a subagent, it is not liable for any loss resulting from an error or other acts of the subagent.

2 If the drawer's account has been credited in anticipation of receiving the proceeds from the collection, it has the right to charge back any amounts for which final payment is not received.
3 If the drawee dishonors the draft, the subagent is authorized to insure the merchandise, if this appears necessary and advisable. Insurance and all other charges are for the account of the drawer to the extent that reimbursement is not received from the drawee. The collecting bank or its subagents, however, assume no liability for any failure to obtain insurance or for inadequacy of insurance.
4 When payment of the draft is threatened because of the drawee's unwillingness to pay bank charges, the collecting agents are authorized to waive payment of such charges by the drawee, but have the right to collect them from the drawer.

DRAWER'S INSTRUCTIONS

The drawer's instructions is, in fact, a letter written and signed by an exporter to the drawer's bank, instructing it to send out the drawer's documentary or clean draft for collection. The letter defines what should be done with any documents attached to the draft, and what action to take in case the drawee refuses to honor it. Since banks act only as agents, they do only what the drawer specifically instructs. Therefore, the letter of instructions must be complete and clear in every way in order to avoid having to go back to the drawer for clarification or further instructions, thereby causing unnecessary time delays and expenses. Banks usually prefer the drawer's instructions to be submitted on their own preprinted form. This has the advantage of forcing the drawer to consider all pertinent points. The form also spells out the agency agreement between the drawer and the collection bank as illustrated in Figure 12-1.

A typical collection letter form is reprinted in Figure 12-2. An explanation of the key instructions and information that should be supplied by the exporter is useful.

Tenure and Delivery of Documents

Tenure. The draft may be payable at sight, a stated number of days after sight, or a stated number of days after the date of the draft. The tenure placed on the draft should, of course, agree with the stipulation in the underlying sales contract.

Delivery of Documents. Depending on the tenure, the exporter instructs the collecting bank to release the title documents to the importer against payment of a sight draft or acceptance of a time draft. In common banking usage, when documents are to be handed over against payment, it is abbrevi-

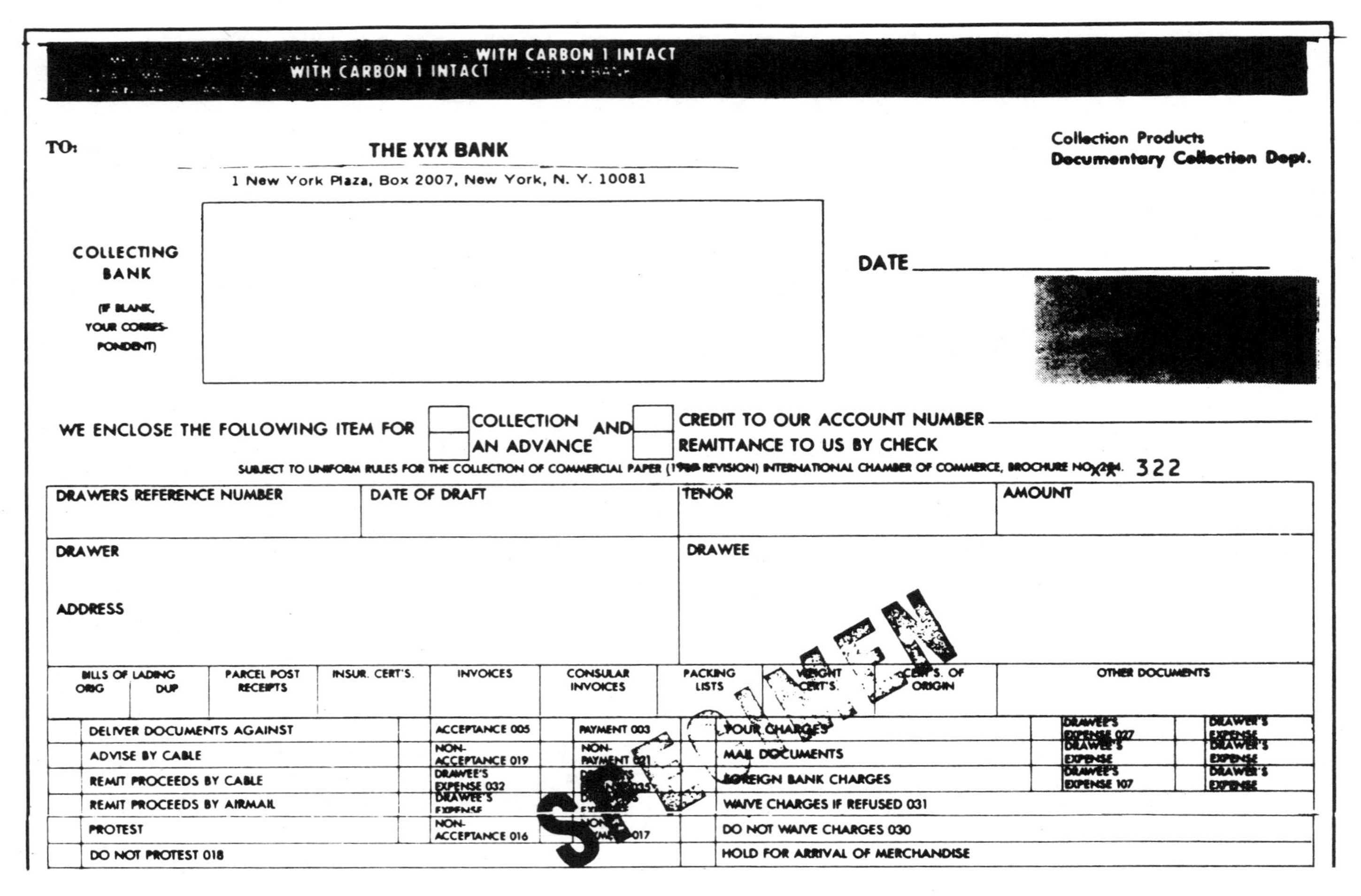

WITH CARBON 1 INTACT
WITH CARBON 1 INTACT

TO: **THE XYX BANK**
1 New York Plaza, Box 2007, New York, N. Y. 10081

Collection Products
Documentary Collection Dept.

COLLECTING BANK
(IF BLANK, YOUR CORRESPONDENT)

DATE ____________

WE ENCLOSE THE FOLLOWING ITEM FOR ☐ COLLECTION ☐ AN ADVANCE AND ☐ CREDIT TO OUR ACCOUNT NUMBER ____________ ☐ REMITTANCE TO US BY CHECK

SUBJECT TO UNIFORM RULES FOR THE COLLECTION OF COMMERCIAL PAPER ([illegible] REVISION) INTERNATIONAL CHAMBER OF COMMERCE, BROCHURE NO. 322

DRAWERS REFERENCE NUMBER	DATE OF DRAFT	TENOR	AMOUNT

DRAWER	DRAWEE
ADDRESS	

BILLS OF LADING ORIG	BILLS OF LADING DUP	PARCEL POST RECEIPTS	INSUR. CERT'S.	INVOICES	CONSULAR INVOICES	PACKING LISTS	WEIGHT CERT'S.	CERT'S. OF ORIGIN	OTHER DOCUMENTS

DELIVER DOCUMENTS AGAINST	ACCEPTANCE 005	PAYMENT 003	YOUR CHARGES	DRAWEE'S EXPENSE 027		DRAWER'S EXPENSE	
ADVISE BY CABLE	NON-ACCEPTANCE 019	NON-PAYMENT 021	MAIL DOCUMENTS	DRAWEE'S EXPENSE		DRAWER'S EXPENSE	
REMIT PROCEEDS BY CABLE	DRAWEE'S EXPENSE 032	[illegible]	FOREIGN BANK CHARGES	DRAWEE'S EXPENSE 107		DRAWER'S EXPENSE	
REMIT PROCEEDS BY AIRMAIL	DRAWEE'S EXPENSE	[illegible]	WAIVE CHARGES IF REFUSED 031				
PROTEST	NON-ACCEPTANCE 016	NON-PAYMENT 017	DO NOT WAIVE CHARGES 030				
DO NOT PROTEST 018			HOLD FOR ARRIVAL OF MERCHANDISE				

SPECIMEN

IF DOLLAR EXCHANGE IS NOT IMMEDIATELY AVAILABLE AT MATURITY (OR ON PRESENTATION IF DRAWN AT SIGHT) AND IT IS NECESSARY TO PROVISIONALLY ACCEPT LOCAL CURRENCY PENDING AVAILABILITY OF DOLLAR EXCHANGE, IT MUST BE DISTINCTLY UNDERSTOOD THAT THE DRAWEE SHALL REMAIN LIABLE FOR ALL EXCHANGE DIFFERENCES. AT TIME OF DEPOSIT OF LOCAL CURRENCY OBTAIN FROM DRAWEES THEIR WRITTEN UNDERTAKING TO BE RESPONSIBLE FOR ANY EXCHANGE DIFFERENCES. THE DRAFT MUST NOT BE SURRENDERED TO DRAWEES UNTIL FINAL PAYMENT FOR FACE AMOUNT IN U.S. DOLLAR EXCHANGE.

ALLOW A DISCOUNT OF ______ IF PAID ______

COLLECT INTEREST AT THE RATE OF ______ % FROM ______

IN CASE OF NEED REFER TO			WHO IS EMPOWERED BY US: TO ACT FULLY ON OUR BEHALF I. E. AUTHORIZE REDUCTIONS, EXTENSIONS, FREE DELIVERY, WAIVING OF PROTESTS ETC.		WHO MAY ASSIST IN OBTAINING ACCEPTANCE OR PAYMENT OF DRAFT, AS DRAWN, BUT IS NOT TO ALTER ITS TERMS IN ANY WAY.

OTHER INSTRUCTIONS

____
AUTHORIZED SIGNATURE

FX50 REV 12-80

SOLE BILL OF EXCHANGE

$ ______________ DATE ______________ NO. ______

DAYS AFTER of this SOLE BILL OF EXCHANGE

pay to the order of ______ THE XYX BANK ______

Value received and charge the same to account of

To ______________

____

Figure 12-2. Collection letter.

ated as "D/P," and documents against acceptances are abbreviated as "D/A."

An exporter rarely may stipulate that title documents are to be released only on payment of an accepted time draft. If the importer wishes to obtain the goods before maturity of the draft, he is thereby forced to prepay the trade acceptance. If documents are released only against payment of a time draft, the foreign collecting bank is forced to store the goods until payment for the trade acceptance is received. This is, at best, a cumbersome procedure and, therefore, is not very popular with collecting banks.

Arrival Draft. Sometimes, the draft may be neither a sight nor a time instrument, but what is called an "arrival draft." In this case, the draft and/or the exporter's instruction letter state that the draft need not be presented before arrival of the vessel carrying the merchandise at its port destination. The collecting bank, however, is not responsible for watching for arrival of the vessel before making presentment. The exporter must, therefore, make sure that the foreign collecting bank is notified, perhaps through the steamship company, when the vessel arrives. Since an arrival draft is theoretically not a negotiable instrument, it is wise to use a sight draft and separately instruct the collecting bank to defer presentation until the goods have actually arrived.

Trade Acceptance. Whenever a trade acceptance is created, it may be held in safekeeping by the collecting bank to be presented for payment when due. Prime trade acceptances can often be discounted for immediate cash. Whether an exporter wishes the accepted draft held until maturity, returned to him, or discounted must be specified in the collection letter.

Documentation

Each collection letter provides space for the exporter to indicate exactly which documents accompany the draft. There may, for instance, be an original bill of lading, as well as one or more duplicate copies. If the bank is extending an advance on the collection, it will, of course, want control over all signed, negotiable copies of little documents.

When determining the kind and number of documents to accompany a collection, the exporter should be guided by stipulations made by the importer in the sales contract, as well as legal requirements of the exporting and importing countries. If certain required documents are missing, the importer may not be able to pass the goods through customs or may have to pay penalties. Under these circumstances, if the missing documents were stipulated in the sales contract, the importer would be justified in refusing to accept the shipment.

Interest and Collection Charges

While bank charges for collections are usually modest, some provisions must be made concerning who is responsible for their payment. Hence, the collection letter should contain instructions as to whether charges of the domestic and foreign collecting banks, as well as mailing charges, are for the account of the drawer or the drawee.

Occasionally, a dispute will arise when a drawee is prepared to pay the amount on the draft but is not willing to pick up bank charges. Such a disagreement usually arises out of an ambiguity in or misunderstanding of the underlying sales contract. To protect himself against nonpayment of a draft merely because of a dispute over bank charges, it is advisable for the drawer to waive charges if they are refused by the drawee. In this case, the drawer will, of course, have to pay the bank. This is, however, still the best procedure, since it does not jeopardize payment of the face amount of the draft.

If interest is to be collected from the drawee (particularly in the case of a time draft), the rate should be indicated in the instruction letter. Sometimes, when payment is delayed, the drawer may wish to charge interest at a higher rate for the period of the delay. Space for this latter instruction is usually also provided on the collection letter.

Payment and Remittance

The amount and currency of payment are indicated on the collection letter. If the currency of payment is U.S. dollars, it should be made payable in New York. If made payable at a foreign point, the exporter will incur time delays and banking charges by remitting the money to the United States. Sometimes, U.S. dollar exchange is not immediately available and the drawer may, therefore, indicate on the collection letter whether, in this case, local currency may be accepted. The drawee then agrees to assume all exchange risks, if there is a devaluation of the local currency between the time payment is made and U.S. dollar exchange becomes again available.

If the draft is in foreign currency, exchange regulations of the importer's country may prevent immediate conversion into dollars. The importer may be required to deposit local currency, which, after the expiration of an appropriate waiting period, can be converted. In countries where the local currency is fully convertible, the foreign collecting bank will usually credit the *nostro* account that the domestic bank maintains with it. The domestic bank will then make the conversion and pay the net proceeds to the exporter.

The manner in which proceeds are to be remitted, and at whose expense, must be indicated in the drawer's instructions. If the amount of the draft is relatively large, it will be advantageous to the exporter to request cable remittance. This way, he incurs some cable charges but has the advantage of receiving his money much earlier. Space is provided on the collection letter for the drawer to indicate whether collection proceeds are to be credited to his or her account or remitted by check.

Dishonor and Protest

Should the foreign drawee refuse to honor the draft, the exporter should give clear instructions as to actions to be taken by the collecting bank.

Notice of Dishonor. Under the UCC, collecting banks are required to give prompt notice of dishonor to all endorsers, as well as to the drawer. It is to the drawer's advantage to have dishonor communicated by cable so that he can take any immediate action required to protect his interest. The sooner the exporter knows of an act of dishonor of a sight draft by nonpayment, the sooner he can arrange for alternative disposition of the goods before they become out of season, deteriorate, and/or incur demurrage charges at the pier.

Protest. In cases where a trade acceptance is dishonored by nonpayment, it will be to the advantage of the drawer to ask the foreign collecting bank to go through the legal procedure of protesting such nonpayment. This usually makes it easier to prove dishonor of the instrument, in court in cases where legal proceedings must be instituted.

Safeguarding the Goods. When a draft is dishonored, often some immediate action is required to preserve the goods after their arrival at the destination. Since demurrage charges are extremely high, the foreign collecting bank should be authorized to store the goods in a warehouse under its own name. The agent bank should also be instructed to insure the goods for their landed cost, including freight and import and ocean marine insurance charges. In some cases, the exporter may wish to extend the original ocean marine insurance to also cover the goods while they are in storage. As indicated, in the absence of specific instructions regarding insurance, collecting banks reserve the right to store and insure nonaccepted goods for the account of the exporter.

Miscellaneous Items. In case of difficulty, such as dishonor by the drawee, it is usually cumbersome and costly for the foreign collecting bank to correspond with the drawer to obtain further instructions. A good way of avoiding unnecessary correspondence is for the exporter to give full instructions in the collection letter. For situations not covered by instructions, it may be useful to give to the collecting bank the name and address of the exporter's agent located close to the importer; in case of need, the foreign collecting bank can then refer to the agent for further instructions. It is important for the exporter to indicate the extent of his local agent's authority in obtaining the honoring of the draft as drawn and/or in disposing of the merchandise if the draft is not honored. Space for giving the name and address of the agent, as well as the extent of his authority, is provided in the collection letter.

In addition to the items already described, it is also customary to include on the collection letter the draft number, date of the draft, exact names and addresses of the drawer and drawee, and the name of the foreign collecting bank that is to be used. If the exporter has no preference as to the foreign collecting bank, the domestic bank will route the item to one of its correspondents in the locality of the importer. Usually, however, importers wish to have collections routed through their own banks and will so stipulate this requirement in the sales contract. It is worth mentioning here that foreign banks find collection business very desirable because of the high fee schedules that generally prevail and because it may also bring them some foreign exchange business. Moreover, if the drawee is not yet a customer of the foreign collecting bank, the latter has a chance to demonstrate its services and perhaps, solicit an account relationship. Foreign banks, therefore, usually request customers (importers) to stipulate in their sales contracts that collections are to be sent through their own bank.

Collection letters generally provide a space wherein exporters can place special instructions to be observed. Instructions concerning insurance, warehousing, and alternative disposition of the merchandise if not accepted by the drawee may be included in this section.

If a rebate is allowed in those cases where a time draft is paid before maturity, the details can be stipulated under special instructions.

If the exporter wishes the bank to give him an advance using the foreign receivable as collateral, he would indicate this on the collection letter, giving the amount of the advance desired. Before being able to receive a loan, the exporter must, of course, have established a special credit relationship with his bank.

It is important to note that the collection letter addressed to the bank must be signed by an authorized officer or other employee of the exporter. Sometimes, as illustrated in Figure 12-2, banks will furnish a draft with their collection letter form, which can be used for the convenience of the exporter.

COLLECTION PROCEDURE

U.S. Collecting Bank

After the domestic collecting bank receives the draft, documents, and drawer's instruction, it will first check to make sure all items listed in the collection letter were indeed enclosed. This involves a cursory examination of the documents to ascertain internal consistency and notice any missing endorsements. While the bank specifically disclaims responsibility for accuracy or genuineness of any documents, a spot-check by an experienced clerk can often turn up inaccuracies or inconsistencies that may cause problems later in getting the importer to honor the draft. It is, of course, desirable to have errors corrected before documents are sent overseas for collection.

Bank Collection Letter. After the initial check, the domestic bank types up a collection letter addressed to its foreign correspondent. This merely involves a retype of the information and instructions that have already been furnished by the exporter. The draft, documents, and bank collection letter are then mailed to the overseas correspondent for further processing. One copy of the bank's fanfold (a cover letter) is mailed to the drawer as an acknowledgment. Other copies are filed for later use in recording, trading, and finally liquidating the transaction.

Follow-Up. Until final payment is received, the domestic collecting bank will assist the exporter in following up the transaction. If payment or notice of acceptance is not received from the foreign correspondent within a stipulated time, the bank will send out one or more tracers. Further, the bank will keep its customer informed of any communication it receives from overseas regarding the status of the transaction. In case of difficulty, the bank may have to revert to the exporter for further instructions.

Foreign Collecting Bank

The foreign collecting bank follows basically the same procedure as would a U.S. bank with an inward collection. At first, receipt of the collection letter, draft, and documents is acknowledged. The drawee is then contacted to inform him that the documents will be turned over on his payment or acceptance of the draft, as the case may be. The collecting bank may send out a messenger with instructions to turn over the documents to the importer only against payment. Alternatively, it may inform the importer that the documents are available for inspection at the offices of the bank. If the importer is also the collecting bank's valued and trusted customer, it may, on occasion, turn over the documents against a trust receipt. In this case, the collecting bank becomes responsible for payment if funds are not received from the importer.

Final Payment

Once final payment has been received from overseas, the exporter is paid either by sending him a check or crediting his account. Any bank fees, interest charges, or advance payments are subtracted from the gross amount received before payment is made to the beneficiary.

PROCEDURES IN DISHONOR AND PROTEST

Occasionally, for whatever reason, a drawee will refuse to honor a draft. There is a significant difference between his refusal to pay or accept a time draft, on the one hand, and refusal to pay a draft he had previously accepted, on the other.

An obligation to pay a sight draft or accept a time draft can only be traced back to the underlying sales contract between the exporter and importer. Any lawsuit by the exporter will thus have to be based on that contract. A trade acceptance, on the other hand, represents an acknowledged financial obligation of the drawee and, if the acceptance is held by a holder in due course, the acceptor can be sued for payment with only the accepted instrument as evidence.

Action by Collecting Bank. In case a draft is dishonored, the foreign collecting bank gives the necessary notices and, if required, arranges for a formal protest by a notary public. If the bank still has possession of the goods, it takes immediate action to the warehouse and insures them on arrival at the port. It then contacts either the exporter (through the domestic collecting bank) or agent to be notified in case of need, to obtain further instructions concerning the disposition of the goods.

Notice of Dishonor

Whenever a negotiable instrument is dishonored, prompt notice thereof must be given to each endorser liable on the paper. Any endorser who does not receive prompt notice cannot be held to his secondary liability unless he has specifically waived this condition (UCC 3-501). Delays in giving notice of dishonor may, however, be excused if caused by circumstances beyond the control of the holder and not the result of his own fault or negligence. When the cause of the delay is removed, notice must be given within reasonable time (UCC 3-511).

The only requirement regarding the form of the dishonor notice itself is for it to bring the dishonor to the attention of the secondarily liable parties. It may be written or oral. Usually, the notice should identify the instrument and the nature of the dishonor, such as nonacceptance or nonpayment (UCC3-508(d)). If the instrument is also protested, a copy of the protest is generally sufficient to give notice of dishonor.

Protest

"Protest" is a written statement made under seal of a notary public or similarly qualified person, attached to the dishonored instrument or containing a copy of it. The statement of protest must mention the fact that presentment was made, the time and place thereof, the nature of the demand made, and the answer given by the drawee, if any (UCC 3-509).

When to Protest. Generally, nonpayment of an accepted time draft should be protested, since this offers the holder some advantages in certain countries. In most countries, the protest enables the holder to base his lawsuit on the accepted draft and certificate of protest, with no reference needed to the underlying sales contract.

In most cases, it makes little sense to protest the nonpayment of a sight draft or nonacceptance of a time draft. Whether the drawee had any obligation to pay or accept can only be established by reference to the sales contract, and little is added by a statement of protest. Moreover, in some foreign countries the names of drawees of protested drafts have to be published, and this has an adverse influence on the drawee's credit standing. In these cases, local banks are understandably reluctant to protest when they cannot be sure whether the drawee had any obligation to pay or accept, under a sales contract to which they have no access. Protest, in some foreign countries, can be an expensive process and thus, it is in the interest of the drawer not to ask his bank to protest unless it serves a useful purpose.

Unless excused or specifically waived, however, protest of dishonor is necessary to retain recourse to the drawer and endorsers of any draft that is drawn or payable outside the United States and its territories (UCC 3-501(3)). When banks act merely as collecting agents, this provision creates no problem, since the collecting bank acts on behalf of and for the risk of the drawer. If a collecting bank negotiates a draft with recourse to the drawer, however, it becomes most important to properly protest a dishonor in order to retain the right of recourse. Whenever banks grant an advance and/or negotiate or discount a negotiable instrument, they generally ask the drawer to execute a loan and collateral agreement in which he specifically waives protest.

For collection items payable in the United States (i.e., incoming collections), prompt protest is especially important. In the state of New York, for protest to be effective, it must be performed within 24 hours of the time when the instrument was dishonored. In most states the maximum permitted time is also 24 hours. Drawers of drafts payable in the United States are, therefore, especially advised to include clear instructions as to when the agent bank should protest. The prevailing limits often do not permit sufficient time to go back to the drawer for clarification when the original instructions are not clear.

Similar to the notice of dishonor, a delay in protesting is excused if it is caused by circumstance beyond the control of the holder, but it must be made promptly after the cause of delay has been removed. The purpose of protesting is to establish the actual fact of dishonor by a disinterested party, namely, the notary public. A protest may also serve as a vehicle for giving notice of dishonor to all interested parties.

Noting a Dishonored Draft. In the United States, under the UCC (3-509), as well as in the United Kingdom, a draft may be "noted" before protesting. Noting is considered a preliminary form of protest and provides a less expensive legal proof of presentation. Once noted, a draft can be protested at a subsequent time if this is required.

COLLECTION-RELATED BANK SERVICES

In addition to collecting items payable abroad, banks offer a number of related services that can be of substantial assistance to exporters and importers.

Completion of Documents

An exporter located inland—say, the Midwest—may wish to ship on a collection basis. To obtain an ocean bill of lading, however, he must first ship the goods by rail or truck to the nearest port. Only after the goods have been loaded onto the vessel can an on-board bill of lading be issued and mailed back to the importer. To eliminate the time delay in mailing the bill of lading back to the Midwest and then sending all the documents to a bank in New York for collection, the exporter instructs his freight forwarder in New York to send the bill of lading and other documents obtained by him—such as the ocean marine insurance policy—directly to the collecting bank. In the meantime, the exporter mails to the bank his instruction letter, blank signed draft, and invoice, as well as a copy of his instructions to the freight forwarder. Once the forwarder has his part of the documents completed, he submits them to the bank. The latter can now determine the amount of additional charges, such as insurance and freight that should be added to the invoice. The bank, thereupon completes the invoice and fills in the total amount due, as well as the date, on the previously received blank signed draft. All the documents are now completed and can be sent out for collection in the usual manner. Since bills of lading are usually consigned to the shipper, the bank endorses them on his behalf, as agent.

The service of completing documents can be most valuable for the exporter, not only in doing work that would otherwise have to be done by his export department, but also by saving time. The exporter, therefore, can expect to get the proceeds of the collection earlier than he would otherwise. The bank's work on a collection involving completion of documents is greater and its commission for this type of service is, therefore, higher than for ordinary collections.

Direct Collections

Occasionally, an exporter shipping out of a port other than New York (say, New Orleans) may wish to send his collections directly to the foreign collecting bank but still make use of the follow-up services of a bank in New York. To facilitate this transaction, the bank in New York supplies the exporter with direct collection forms that enable him to send his draft and documents directly, but for the account of the bank in New York. Several copies of the direct collection form are sent to the domestic collecting bank for information and follow-up.

By using this service, the exporter foregoes the chance of having the bank examine his documents before they are mailed out. The exporter benefits, however, from the bank's follow-up services. Moreover, since the collection is sent out for account of a bank, the foreign collecting bank will usually charge the same collection fee that it would apply when a bank sends in the item directly. Many banks abroad charge lower collection fees to other banks than they do to commercial firms.

Consignments

Occasionally, a foreign shipper may wish to export merchandise to a particular market without having a definite buyer. To be of assistance, banks may be willing to have the merchandise consigned to themselves. The consignee bank arranges for customs entry, storage of the goods in a bonded or free warehouse, and insurance. The shipper probably has potential buyers in mind who may wish to examine the merchandise at the warehouse. Once a sale has been made, the bank arranges for delivery against payment in accordance with instructions received from the exporter or his bank. Usually, consignments are stored against a nonnegotiable warehouse receipt. Hence, partial sales can be released against a delivery order signed by the bank.

Occasionally, goods coming into the United States on consignment have to be examined and cleared through government agencies, such as the Pure Food and Drug Administration or the Department of Health, Education, and Welfare. Release of merchandise for inspection against trust receipt and subsequent placement in a warehouse can also be arranged through commercial banks.

Indemnities

Since documents are sent by airmail while goods move on ships, title papers usually arrive before the goods. Thus, under normal circumstances, the importer will have sufficient time to obtain the bill of lading from the bank to be able to pick up the goods from the pier when they arrive.

Perhaps due to delays in the mail, goods sometimes arrive before the documents. To induce the shipping company to release the goods without a negotiable bill of lading, banks may issue indemnities on behalf of importers. Through the indemnity, the bank agrees to see to it that the bill of lading is duly turned over after it arrives. Moreover, if anyone—including an innocent holder in due course—turns up with the bill of lading and demands the goods, the bank agrees to hold the shipping company harmless.

Banks also issue indemnities to procure payment of drafts sent for collection or under letters of credit when related documents are missing or contain discrepancies. Of course, in all these cases, the bank retains recourse to its customer, if it receives a claim under an indemnity agreement. An indemnity is, therefore, issued by a bank at the request of and based on the credit strength of a customer, that is, the importer in the case of a steamship indemnity and the exporter in the case of documentary discrepancies.

Domiciliations

Companies in the United States selling abroad often offer extended terms evidenced by a series of promissory notes or usance drafts on the buyer. Whenever one or more of these notes or drafts mature, collection must be made from the primary obligor. Before maturity, these instruments may be domiciled with a bank for safekeeping. If the foreign buyer has an account with the bank of domiciliation, it may be possible to set up an arrangement whereby his account is automatically charged at maturity. Alternatively, the account of a foreign correspondent bank may be charged on behalf of the obligor. Payment may also be received from another bank or the note or draft may have to be presented to the obligor at maturity. In the last case, the item may be sent out as a clean collection. Domiciliation with a bank has the advantage of providing safekeeping for the negotiable instruments. At the same time, the exporter is also relieved of having to initiate the collection of each of the instruments at the appropriate time.

ADVANTAGES AND RISKS OF FOREIGN COLLECTION TERMS

At first glance, the use of foreign collection terms seems to be a most satisfactory procedure from the points of view of both the exporter and importer; unfortunately, this is not always the case.

Advantages

The exporter is assured that the importer will not be able to get hold of the merchandise until he has either accepted a time draft or has paid a sight or arrival draft. The importer, on the other hand, gets partial financing in the case of a sight draft (i.e., the time it takes for the exporter and his bank to assemble and mail out the documentary draft, plus mailing time), and complete financing in the case of an arrival or time draft.

Risks for Exporter

Closer examination of collection practices shows, however, that there are a number of risks, especially for the seller but also for the buyer. In a bank, risk management expertise should be welcomed to evaluate and mitigate in all unusual and complicated collection services.

Nonacceptance of Merchandise. One common danger is that the importer may refuse to accept the merchandise. This refusal may be based on some small, inadvertent infraction of the sales contract by the exporter, while the real reason is that between the time the order was placed and the draft received, there has been a significant drop in the market price. When this happens, the exporter is stuck with his merchandise in a foreign port, probably incurring heavy storage charges and a market at a greatly reduced price. Taking court action against the importer is, in most cases, not a satisfactory solution due to the expense and time delay involved.

Usually, the foreign collecting bank will offer its assistance in arranging for storage and insurance at the port of destination. Often the bank can help in finding an alternate buyer for the merchandise, although a substantial discount is still required in most cases.

Nonpayment of Trade Acceptance. Generally, shipping on a time-draft basis is more risky for the seller than a sight draft. In the latter case, at least the seller maintains control over the merchandise until he is paid. Otherwise, the exporter takes not only the risk that the time draft will not be accepted, but that the trade acceptance will not be paid at maturity. If the acceptance is not paid, the importer has control over the merchandise, thus preventing the exporter from selling it elsewhere.

Possession of Goods without Payment. Another danger an exporter might face is that the importer, due to local regulations, can get possession of the merchandise without paying or accepting the draft. Certain governments, for instance, may demand that the buyer show them the shipping documents before they allocate the needed foreign exchange. In this and similar cases, the document may have to be released to the importer on trust receipt. Thus, the exporter and his agent bank lose control over the merchandise before payment.

Exchange Restrictions. It may occur that the importer is perfectly willing to pay, but that local exchange regulations do not permit him to obtain the necessary foreign exchange. The merchandise in question may not be approved for importation and, in this case, exchange will never be made available. Alternatively, those requiring foreign exchange may have to go on a waiting list that may extend several months or even years. If that should happen, the importer usually deposits the local currency counterpart of the amount due with a local commercial or central bank for account of the exporter. The exporter cannot, however, make use of the funds until foreign exchange is made available by the authorities.

Minimizing the Risks

This last potential problem highlights the need by the exporter to keep current on the foreign exchange regulations and conditions prevailing in the countries to which he ships.

Keeping Informed. Many large commercial banks issue periodic reports on import and foreign exchange regulations, as well as the banks' own collection experiences in the various countries. Bank officials who travel overseas frequently are also a good source of information on current conditions. Additionally, the Foreign Credit Interchange Bureau publishes periodic reports on collection experience of commercial firms with various countries.

An exporter can, to some extent, guard himself against refusal to accept merchandise by knowing the reputation and financial strength of the importer and being familiar with the market for his merchandise. If an exporter, for instance, gets a sudden surge of orders from a market that he knows is limited, he may become suspicious and hypothesize that importers are ordering on the basis of a temporary shortage that has driven up prices but that may be back to normal again by the time the draft is presented to the importer. Whenever the exporter has any reason to be suspicious, it is probably a good idea to ask for an irrevocable letter of credit.

Adequate Insurance. When shipping on a foreign collection basis, it is wise for the exporter to insist on using his own underwriter for ocean marine coverage and extending the coverage while goods are at the port or warehouse of destination. This way, if the importer refuses to accept the shipment, the exporter is at least assured of having adequate insurance.

Cash Deposit. The risk to the seller may also be minimized if he requires a cash deposit or irrevocable letter of credit for a percentage of the total amount, with the remainder payable on a collection basis on surrender of title documents. If the importer refuses to accept the goods, the initial payment should be large enough to cover any cost of reshipment or sale of the goods at a discount in the local market.

Risks for the Importer

A transaction based on collection terms is not entirely without risk for the importer. He must rely primarily on the exporter's good reputation, honesty, and ability to deliver merchandise of the grade, quality, and quantity ordered. On sight or arrival draft terms, the importer generally cannot inspect the merchandise before making payment. On time draft terms, he can inspect, but only after obligating himself—at least against holders in due course—by accepting the draft. The importer may be able to protect himself against faulty merchandise by requiring an inspection certificate as part of the documentation.

Justified Refusal to Accept Goods

Often, the importer will be entirely justified in refusing a shipment due to a mistake of the exporter. Very common, for instance, are shipments by the exporter that are later than the date agreed on in the contract. A late shipment, especially of seasonal merchandise, may cause the importer to lose his market. Other common infractions by exporters that may result in nonacceptance of the shipment include

Increase in the product price from the previous agreement without first obtaining the importer's consent.

Quality of the merchandise not as previously agreed on (this may be determined by the importer if he is given the right to inspect the merchandise before accepting it).

Insistence by the exporter that the importer pay certain charges on which there was no previous agreement.

Neglect in carrying out packing and marking instructions supplied by the importer.

Whenever a buyer refuses a shipment, the first thing the exporter should do is make an investigation of the real cause. If the seller is at fault, or if there is valid justification in the importer's complaint, the exporter should, for the sake of good will and further business, make prompt and reasonable adjustment. If the buyer is at fault, due to financial embarrassment, there may be reason for an extension in the credit time. With some luck this may result only in ultimate payment, but might also further cement a lasting customer relationship.

Conclusion

It may be concluded that collection terms are very useful in certain circumstances, but they should never be entered into unless the following conditions are present:

Complete confidence between buyer and seller in each other's honesty, reputation, financial strength, and, in the case of the seller, his ability to deliver the merchandise.

Knowledge by the exporter of local exchange regulations—that is, shipment on a collection basis is not recommended if there is a local exchange shortage that makes it questionable whether exchange will be allocated or whether the exporter may have to go on a waiting list.

Complete understanding and agreement between buyer and seller as to what each other's rights and responsibilities are under the sales contract.

If there is doubt concerning any of the previously outlined points, it would probably be to the benefit of both the seller and the buyer to request letter of credit terms.

FINANCING FOREIGN RECEIVABLES

So far, we have considered foreign collections without the benefit of outside financing. This means that the exporter, in the case of a time or arrival draft, and the exporter and importer jointly, in the case of a sight draft, are themselves providing the financing for the shipment. Of course, to the extent that the exporter and importer have unused lines of credit with their banks, they are in a position to borrow the needed money without necessarily tying the financing to the trade transaction.

A more interesting and challenging situation arises when the exporter's and/or importer's regular lines are used up for other, perhaps domestic, transactions. This means that, to finance their foreign trade, they must ask their bankers to rely on the underlying merchandise being shipped as security.

There are several phases during the movement of goods from exporter to importer, when outside financing may be required.

The exporter may require financing to buy and store the commodities prior to shipment. He can potentially be accommodated with warehouse receipt financing, as discussed in Chapter 10.

The importer may need financing between the time that he has to pay the exporter and the time he gets the proceeds from, in turn, selling the merchandise in question. He can be accommodated by trust receipt or warehouse rereceipt financing or a combination of the two (this was also described in Chapter 10).

The exporter may need financing to carry his foreign receivables. This is commonly done by advances against outward collections, discounting of trade acceptances, factoring, or acceptance financing. It is primarily to these methods of financing foreign collections that this section is devoted.

Advances against Foreign Collections

A manufacturer or merchant doing a purely domestic business can often get a loan from a bank, finance company, or factor by using his accounts receivable. The same general type of financing vehicle is open to exporters.

Pool Basis. The most common method for financing foreign receivables is for the exporter to submit all his outward collections to his bank as security. The bank regards these collections as a pool of collateral and the exporter may then borrow up to a stated maximum percentage of the total amount of receivables in the pool at any one time. When a particular collection is paid, it is remitted by the foreign collecting bank to the domestic bank that has given the advance. The latter uses the proceeds of the collection to credit, that is, to reduce the customer's loan account.

Individual Transaction Basis. Some exporters have no need for a continuous financing arrangement, such as the collateral pool method, as previously outlined. Nevertheless, they would like occasionally to obtain financing on only one foreign collection, perhaps, a very large one that they might have difficulty financing themselves. In these cases, the bank may be willing to give an advance with only this one receivable security. Again, the bank will determine a maximum percentage of the amount of the draft that it is willing to advance. When payment for the financed foreign receivable is received, the bank will first use the proceeds to liquidate the loan and then credit any excess to the exporter.

Determining Percentage of Advance. How does a bank determine what percentage of a collateral pool or individual collection it is willing to advance? Since the bank usually retains recourse to the exporter, the latter's credit strength and reputation is of prime importance. Other factors, however, also often play a significant part. If the foreign importers are prime companies with undoubted reputation and financial strength, the bank is likely to advance a larger percentage on collections directed to them. The countries to which the collections are directed are also carefully weighed. Importers in some countries invariably pay drafts drawn on them promptly. Thus, if a collateral pool contains many drafts drawn on importers in such countries, the percentage advanced will be higher. In other countries, payment is generally slow, perhaps because importers are financially weaker or because currency restrictions make U.S. dollar exchange hard to obtain. If collections are to these countries, the bank will be willing to advance only a lower percentage. Indeed, certain collections to habitually slow-paying importers and/or countries may be entirely ineligible from financing and the bank may insist that they be withdrawn from the collateral pool.

A final factor that banks frequently consider is the nature of the merchandise being financed. If it represents marketable commodities that can be readily sold with no or only a small discount, in the event that the importer refuses to pay or accept the draft, a higher percentage can be advanced. If the goods are perishable, seasonal, or subject to unpredictable changes in fashions, they may be impossible to sell to anyone else if the drawee refuses to accept the shipment. In this case, the bank will be willing to advance only a small percentage. Generally, the percentage of a pool or individual collection that a bank is willing to lend varies between 50 and 100%, depending on its evaluation of the previously discussed factors.

Title Documents. Usually, when a bank makes advances against foreign collections, it will pay particular attention to the documents submitted. Since the financing institution wishes to maintain control of the merchandise, the bill of lading should be either to the order of the shipper and blank endorsed, or to the order of the bank. In no case should the bill of lading be consigned to the buyer, since this gives him control over the goods. Banks generally also insist that shipments they finance are covered by adequate insurance.

Acceptance Financing

An alternate method of financing foreign collections, which may be preferred by banks during periods of tight money, is to use bankers' acceptances. As with all types of acceptance financing, the exporter first executes and submits to his bank an acceptance agreement.

To obtain acceptance financing for his foreign receivables, the exporter has to draw two drafts. One of them is a time draft drawn on the foreign buyer, which, together with the necessary documents, is sent out for collection in the usual manner. The other draft, which may be for the same or a smaller amount as agreed on by the bank and the exporter, is drawn by the exporter on his bank and has the same tenure as the draft addressed to the importer. The bank accepts this latter draft and at the same time discounts it, crediting the net amount to the exporter's account. The bank thus creates a banker's acceptance that, if the bank is large and well known, enjoys a wide market in which it can be sold, if the bank finds itself short of loanable funds.

When payment is received from the importer, the bank uses the proceeds to pay its own acceptance that, if it were sold in the market, would be presented for payment on the same day. Of course, if payment from the drawee is not received, the bank will make use of its right of recourse on the drawer and will demand payment from him.

Discounting Trade Acceptances

Once a draft has been accepted by the foreign buyer, it becomes a trade acceptance carrying the full credit obligation of the importer.

The acceptance, in fact, becomes the property of the exporter, who will ask the collecting bank to present it to the acceptor for payment at maturity. The exporter is, in this instance, providing the financing.

It may be possible that the exporter needs the money before maturity of the trade acceptance. In this case, he may be able to ask his bank or commercial finance company to discount the draft with or without recourse to him. If the primary obligor (acceptor) is a well-known company of top-credit standing, the bank or finance company may be willing to discount the draft without recourse to the exporter. More typically, however, the lender will look to the exporter for recourse if the primary obligor does not pay the amount when due.

When discounting a trade acceptance, the bank advances to the exporter the face amount of the draft minus discount charges until the date of maturity. The lender actually is buying the trade acceptance for value. It, therefore, becomes a holder in due course of a negotiable instrument with all the benefits this status offers when demanding payment from the primary obligor. The same, incidentally, is also true whenever a bank or other financial institution makes an advance against a collection or pool of collections. As far as any intermediary collecting bank is concerned, if it has a financial interest in a collection, it enjoys all the rights of a holder in due course (UCC 4-201).

Factoring

A factor is in the business of buying accounts receivable without recourse. In the past, factoring has been primarily oriented toward domestic trade in certain industries, such as textiles. During the last few years, however, factoring has gone international. Several factoring firms have set up or have invested in foreign affiliates. A number of large commercial banks have also gone into factoring, primarily by buying established firms. To the extent that these commercial banks finance foreign trade, their factoring affiliates have also become more active.

A factor's ability to buy receivables without recourse depends on his ability to make credit judgments on buyers. The factor, therefore, replaces the credit and, in part, the bookkeeping departments of sellers. Credit information is much more easy to obtain on domestic buyers than on those located overseas. However, with the establishment of foreign affiliates, factors have greatly increased their ability to pass on the credit of foreign importers. The factoring for foreign receivables has, therefore, become more popular over recent years, and this trend is likely to continue into the future.

Procedurally, a factor who buys a foreign receivable must give his approval of the specific foreign obligor before the sales contract is concluded. If the factor does not approve the credit risk of a specific foreign buyer, however, the exporter may still go ahead and make the shipment at his own risk. If shipment to approved importers is made on a documentary collection basis, the draft and documents are submitted to the factor who, in fact, purchases them without recourse. He thus pays the money to the exporter, either at the average maturity date, when actually received, or, if financing is also required, immediately. Thereafter, the draft and documents are routed through commercial banks for collection in the usual manner. Since the factor now owns the draft and documents, the collection process is undertaken for his account.

Exporters may also sell abroad on an open-account basis, thus consigning shipping documents directly to the importer. This is more risky, since the exporter and financing institution lose control over the merchandise. Open-account shipments should, therefore, not be undertaken except to the most reputable and trusted foreign buyers. A factor buying foreign accounts receivables that were created through open-account shipments follows in essence the same procedure as he would if he were buying domestic receivables.

Automation and Accounting

Automation has helped in recording collections items and in periodically tracing them. It is customary for the collecting banks to send tracers or reminders every 21 days (from the date of the mailing of the document) to the collecting banks. Without the assistance of automation and system enhancement, these tracers would have to be individually researched and prepared for each correspondent bank. Such a procedure is time consuming and not cost effective.

An automated system generates all the required tracers/reminders for all unpaid items. Once the items are paid, the tracers/reminders, are, of course, stopped.

Automation also makes for an efficient retrieval system that is particularly useful when a bank employee gets a call from a customer inquiring about the state of a collection. The system should be able to show instantly on the screen whether the item is paid or is pending. The information is usually made accessible by a collection number or simply by the name of the customer. A similar advantage of automation is instant access to account totals, such as the total of all items sent for collection to a particular correspondent bank.

CHAPTER 13

Letters of Credit—Procedures

International trade promotes economic development among nations and establishes the necessary ingredients for political and social stability. And as trade is important, so also is the necessary financial means by which the trades can be accomplished. In these last two chapters we examine what is probably the single most important vehicle of all international trade, the letter of credit.

NEED FOR LETTERS OF CREDIT

Frequently, in international trade an exporter will, for some reason, not be entirely satisfied with the credit or reputation of a foreign buyer. Foreign credit reports are often sketchy and do not give sufficient information for the seller to assess his chances of ultimate payment. This applies particularly to the vast majority of foreign companies that are small- or medium-sized and, therefore, not internationally known. Additionally, the country in which the foreign importer is located may be in a weak financial position with limited hard exchange to meet foreign exchange requirements. Thus, even if the importer is financially strong and reputable, conditions beyond his control may prevent him from discharging his foreign obligations.

Even an importer with a good credit standing may be tempted not to accept a shipment that he receives on a collection basis if, in the interim, there has been a significant drop in the price of the merchandise involved. He may try to find some kind of minor noncompliance technicality on which basis the shipment can legitimately be refused. Recourse to the courts in cases of a refused shipment is usually time consuming and expensive. Moreover, a legal battle may result in the loss of a customer.

To solve these and similar problems, letters of credit may be used by exporters and importers, as well as companies that wish either to guarantee performance of an obligation or make certain that all obligations will be properly discharged. Specifically, letters of credit may be useful to the following types of firms:

Sellers who wish to ship on a cash basis—that is, under terms that provide payment to the seller at the time of shipment.

Exporters who sell to companies abroad that are either not well known internationally or not considered to be prime credit risks.

Companies who sell to customers in countries with limited foreign exchange reserves and who, therefore, have found it necessary to impose import and exchange controls.

Sellers of specially manufactured machinery and other merchandise.

Engineering and other service-type firms that use letters of credit to assure payment for services as they are performed.

Companies who sell on a nonrepetitive basis to domestic customers whom they don't know well.

Companies who have overseas subsidiaries requiring borrowings from foreign financial institutions that have to be guaranteed by a reputable domestic bank.

Contractors and others requiring bid and/or performance guarantees.

Most letters of credit issued today cover commercial trade transactions; consequently, these types of credits will receive first attention. In Chapter 14 we also briefly discuss letters of credit used for purposes other than facilitating trade.

Definition

To make sure that an obligation will be met, a seller or other beneficiary may wish the superior credit standing of a large financial institution to stand between him and a buyer or other party who is expected to perform. This can often be done by means of a commercial letter of credit. The credit is, in essence, a letter addressed to the seller, written and signed by a bank acting on behalf of the buyer. In it, the bank promises that it will pay or accept drafts drawn on itself if the seller conforms exactly to the conditions set forth in the letter of credit. In most commercial transactions, these conditions will state that the seller is to submit, together with the draft, certain documents, such as a negotiable bill of lading, insurance papers, invoices, and so on. Only if the documentation submitted is precisely as specified will the bank pay or accept the exporter's draft.

Through the letter of credit, a bank substitutes its own commitment to pay for that of its customer, that is, the buyer. While a letter of credit is not really a guarantee (federally chartered banks are prohibited by law from issuing guarantees), it serves almost the same purpose in that the bank assures payment to the seller as long as he complies with stated conditions.

Advantages to the Seller

To have a letter of credit opened in his favor may be of substantial advantage to a seller of goods and services.

Eliminates Credit Risk. When payment is assured by a prime commercial bank, the exporter no longer needs to rely on the willingness or capability of the importer to make payment. If the bank that opens or confirms the credit is of undoubted standing, the seller can be sure that all amounts due him will be paid on time.

Reduces or Eliminates Exchange and Political Risks. When an exporter ships on a collection, open account, or consignment basis, there is always the danger that payment is delayed or withheld entirely due to political causes. The government of the importing country may cancel or withhold an import license. War or some similar disturbance may prevent payment. The importing country may get into financial difficulties and put a moratorium on all external payments; the importer may deposit payment in local currency with a bank but transfer into hard exchange may be delayed several months or even years.

If a letter of credit is opened by a local bank in the importer's country, the political and exchange risks are reduced, but not eliminated. Most probably, the opening bank would not issue hard currency credit unless it was absolutely assured that the particular import had the blessing of its government and that exchange would be made available by the central bank or other authority when payment was due. Even if a country imposes new exchange restrictions, open letters of credit of its commercial banks would probably be exempted. A country's international credit standing and credibility might be severely damaged if it failed to do this.

While a credit opened by a reputable local bank gives considerable protection, certain political risks are still present. The opening bank may be unable to meet its obligations, due to war, insurrection, or similar causes. The local government may be taken over by a coup d'état and the new regime may not recognize external debts incurred under the old government. To guard himself against these risks, the exporter may wish a prime bank in his own country to also put its name and credit standing behind that of the foreign opening bank. Such a confirmed credit eliminates practically all political and credit risks.

Reduces Need for Credit Checking. An exporter who is assured payment by a bank of international repute needs to devote only minimal time and money to checking up on the credit standing of the foreign importer. As long as the exporter complies with all the conditions of the credit, he is assured payment, regardless of the ability or inclination to pay on the part of the buyer. The major job of checking on the importer's creditworthiness and integrity, as well as all risks connected therewith, is, in fact, taken over by the opening bank. The latter, since it is usually in the same locality of the importer and speaks the same language, has a much easier task in evaluating his creditworthiness than a more geographically and culturally distant exporter. However, it remains good business practice for the exporter at least to seek information about the financial strength and reputation of the foreign buyer and vice versa.

Exporter Knows All Requirements for Payment. The letter of credit will stipulate exactly which requirements the seller must meet to get payment. When he receives a credit in his favor, an exporter has a clear and unambiguous description of all the terms with which he must comply. The exporter can then take steps to meet all the documentary requirements with full confidence that, in due course, he will receive payment.

Protection on Preshipment Risks. A manufacturer who is under contract to produce a specialized piece of equipment or render a special service runs the risk of cancellation of contract before shipment. For specialized equipment, the manufacturing period may take many months and even years, involving substantial out-of-pocket expenditures to the exporter. If the buyer reneges on the contract before shipment, substantial losses may result.

A letter of credit, if opened at the time a contract is signed, can give complete protection during the manufacturing period. The exporter is assured by a reliable bank that if he manufactures and ships the product within the time period and follows other terms stipulated in the credit, he will receive payment. The importer is, therefore, not in a position to renege on the contract during the manufacturing period.

To obtain complete protection, it is important for the exporter to insist that a credit be opened in his favor at the same time the contract is signed or at least no later than the start of the manufacturing process. Also, most importantly, the credit should not expire prior to the contracted shipment date.

Facilitates Financing. Funds to finance a shipment may be supplied by the exporter, importer, or their respective banks. Regardless of who supplies the funds, it is the importer's credit line at his bank that is being used to open the letter of credit. The exporter will look to the bank for payment. The bank will, in turn, look to the importer for immediate or eventual reimbursement, based entirely on the credit facility it holds at the exporter's disposal.

When shipments are made under a letter of credit it becomes especially easy to create bankers' acceptances. Moreover, a specific transaction with a sound credit backing and clear-cut source of payout is identified. This makes commercial banks and others particularly ready to provide needed financing.

In addition to financing the actual shipment, a manufacturer or exporter may require a loan to finance the production process or buy the goods that are to be exported. Having a letter of credit in his favor assures the exporter a ready and willing buyer, provided the exporter can come up with the desired product. Since a letter of credit in favor of the exporter is, in fact, a purchase order with payment guaranteed by a bank (provided the goods are shipped), it may make it a lot easier for the exporter to obtain a loan to finance the purchasing and/or manufacturing of the product to be sold.

Immediate Payment. Whether the letter of credit calls for sight or time drafts to be drawn on the opening or confirming bank, the exporter is virtually assured payment immediately after he ships in conformity with the credit. A sight draft is paid on presentation to the opening or paying bank. A time draft, on the other hand, is accepted by the bank. Since this creates a prime banker's acceptance, the exporter can usually find a financial institution willing to discount the draft prior to maturity—thus again providing the exporter with immediate cash.

Advantages to Buyer

A letter of credit offers most of its advantages to the seller. It is, therefore, usually the seller who insists on letter of credit terms during contract negotiations. A buyer would generally prefer shipments on an open account or collection basis.

Despite the fact that a letter of credit offers its overwhelming value to a seller, it also contains a number of advantages for the buyer.

Payment Only after Compliance. The importer can be confident that payment to the exporter will only be made after the latter has complied with all the conditions stipulated in the credit. Consequently, the importer is able to ascertain that goods are actually shipped on or before a certain date by requiring an on-board bill of lading. If the importer doubts the exporter's ability to perform, he may include an inspection certificate as part of the required documentation. Similarly, the importer may require other documents under the credit to give him assurance of full compliance with governmental regulations and provisions of the sales contract by the exporter.

Expert Examination of Documents. Once the exporter has submitted the required papers to the bank, they are examined by clerks with many years of experience. The importer can, therefore, be assured that each document is carefully inspected for compliance with the letter of credit. Moreover, if, due to its own oversight, the bank misses an important discrepancy, it must take full responsibility for any resulting loss to the importer.

Expanded Sources of Supply. Some exporters are willing to sell only against cash in advance or letters of credit as a matter of policy. An importer who can offer a letter of credit may, therefore, be able to expand the number of suppliers who are willing to ship to him.

Easier Financing. It has already been mentioned that a letter of credit makes it particularly easy to create a banker's acceptance. An importer may therefore find financing under a letter of credit less expensive and more easily obtainable than under other methods of payment. If his bank or other financing institution can follow a transaction from beginning to end, it will be more willing to extend advances to the importer.

No Tie-Up of Cash. When a letter of credit is used as an alternative to cash in advance, the importer is required to pay only after shipment. He thereby avoids the unnecessary tying up of his cash resources. Bank commission charges for opening a letter of credit may be less than the interest forgone by having to pay to the importer at an earlier date.

PARTIES TO LETTER OF CREDIT TRANSACTIONS

Beneficiary

If a letter of credit is required, this must be stipulated in the sales contract between the importer and exporter. Since a letter of credit generally benefits the exporter, such payment terms are usually included in the contract at his request. The party in whose favor the instrument is issued—that is, the exporter—is called the "beneficiary."

Account Party

It is up to the importer to find a commercial bank or other financial institution that is willing to open a letter of credit on his behalf. In banking circles, the applicant for a letter of credit, that is, the importer, is referred to as the "account party."

Opening Bank

The bank that opens the letter of credit on behalf of the importer is called the "opening" or "issuing bank." By issuing a credit, it assumes full responsibility for payment after the proper drafts and documents have been presented. The credit of the opening bank is thus substituted for that of the account party.

Advising Bank

The letter of credit may be mailed directly to the beneficiary, who may then present his draft and documents to any local bank willing to negotiate the draft. Alternatively, the issuing bank may send the letter of credit to one of its correspondents who is usually located in the same locality as the exporter. This correspondent is called the "notifying" or "advising bank." It has the task of informing the beneficiary that a letter of credit has been opened in his favor.

The notifying bank advises the letter of credit to the beneficiary without responsibility on its part. In some instances, it may, however, still be held liable for such things as erroneous notification of letter of credit terms if this results in a loss to the beneficiary.

Paying Bank

In addition to notifying the exporter of the establishment of the credit, the advising bank may also be authorized to pay the exporter's local currency drafts when presented and accompanied by the proper documentation. In this case, the notifying bank also becomes the paying bank. The latter, after having paid the beneficiary, gets reimbursed by the opening bank. Legally, the paying bank acts as agent for the opening bank.

Negotiating Bank

A bank that, by its own choice, buys an exporter's drafts submitted to it under a letter of credit is called a "negotiating bank." Sometimes, a letter of credit may be addressed and mailed directly to the beneficiary without going through the intermediary of an advising bank. The exporter may then present his draft and documents to any local bank willing to buy his drafts drawn under the credit. If all letter of credit conditions are met, the negotiating bank buys the exporter's drafts with or without recourse. It then forwards the draft and documents to the opening bank for reimbursement. The opening bank itself examines the documents. If everything is in order, it, in turn, reimburses the negotiating bank.

The negotiating bank actually becomes a purchaser in due course of the exporter's draft and documents. Therefore, unless otherwise specified on the draft, it retains recourse to the drawer. Of course, if all documents are in order, the opening bank must ultimately pay. Recourse to the drawer is, therefore, only of theoretical significance in most cases. The negotiating bank warrants that it has acquired the draft and documents in good faith. As a holder in due course, it is entitled to have its draft honored by the opening bank—provided all the documentary requirements have been met.

When a negotiating bank makes payment to an exporter, it is really extending an advance against foreign collections. The bank is thus entitled to charge interest until it receives reimbursement from the opening bank.

Confirming Bank

Frequently, an advising or paying bank is requested to add its own commitment to the letter of credit. In this case, it is called the "confirming bank." For adding its own name to the credit, the confirming bank charges a fee that is usually paid by the opening bank and thus indirectly by the importer.

Such a confirmed letter of credit is considered very safe from the exporter's point of view, since it contains the obligation to pay on the part of two banks.

Combined Bank Roles

A bank may, for any particular transaction, perform more than one of these functions. An opening bank that sends the letter of credit directly to the beneficiary acts also as an advising bank. Moreover, if drafts are payable at the opening bank's office, it also acts as a paying bank. Similarly, the advising and paying bank may be the same institution. If an advising or paying bank adds its own obligation to the credit, it also becomes a confirming bank.

A hypothetical illustration may be useful to define more clearly the roles of various banks. Assume that a Dutch company imports from Japan and invoices in U.S. dollars. The importer requests the Amsterdam-Rotterdam Bank to open a letter of credit in favor of the Japanese exporter. Since payment is in U.S. dollars, the paying bank must be located in the United States. Assume the paying bank to be Chase Manhattan. The Amsterdam-Rotterdam Bank asks Chase Manhattan to notify the beneficiary in Japan. This is done by forwarding the credit to the Chase branch in Tokyo. The latter, as advising bank, forwards the instrument to the beneficiary.

The beneficiary may prefer to do business with his local Japanese bank. He, therefore, submits his draft and documents for negotiation to, say, Mitsubishi Bank. If everything is in order after Mitsubishi's examination, it pays the exporter the yen equivalent amount of the credit. It then applies to the paying bank for reimbursement in U.S. dollars. The latter, in turn, reimburses itself by debiting the dollar account maintained on its books by the Amsterdam-Rotterdam Bank. Finally, the Dutch importer has to pay the opening bank the guilder equivalent at the current rate of exchange.

Usually, a letter of credit transaction does not involve as many banks as does the previously outlined example. The Amsterdam-Rotterdam Bank could, for instance, have sent the credit directly to Mitsubishi Bank with a request that it reimburse itself on Chase. Most letter of credit transactions minimally require two banks, one in the country of the importer, the other in the country of the exporter.

LEGAL CONSIDERATIONS

It is not our purpose to give a detailed legal description of the letter of credit. Whenever exporters or bankers have specific legal problems, they should obtain competent counsel. Our purpose here is limited to giving a general description of the legal framework within which the letter of credit operates as a business tool.

Case Law

In the United Kingdom and the United States, as well as in many other countries, the letter of credit developed as an instrument for facilitating international trade. Its legal foundation can, therefore, be found in the customary practices of merchants and bankers and in court decisions passed down to resolve disputes that arose from business transactions.

Codified Law

In almost all states in the United States the law for letters of credit was codified through the adoption of Article 5 of the UCC, which deals with the letter of credit. The UCC represents a broad outline of the law governing letters of credit. However, it specifically permits the parties to a commercial transaction to establish their own rules and regulations in contract form. Moreover, since the UCC is the law for most of the United States, it has meaning only in cases where the jurisdiction of a code-state court is clearly established. Letter of credit laws of other countries may be different from those of the United States. Hence, Article 5 applies to letter of credit transactions only if and when the parties have not established their respective rights and duties in the form of a contract and if the transaction comes under the jurisdiction of the courts of a state that has adopted the UCC.

Contractual Law

In addition to case law and codified law, letter of credit procedure is governed by the Uniform Custom and Practices for Commercial Documentary Credits (UCP) adopted originally in 1930 by the International Chamber of Commerce and last revised in 1993. The UCP is not actually a law, but represents a formalization of customary rules followed by banks all over the world when dealing in letters of credit.

Practically all banks in the United States as well as the banks of most other countries have adopted the UCP as the basic set of ground rules for their letter of credit dealings. Whenever a letter of credit is subject to the UCP, it is specifically stated in the credit by a phrase, such as: "This Credit is subject to the Uniform Customs and Practices for Documentary Credits (1993 Revision), International Chamber of Commerce Brochure No. 500."

The UCP is, in fact, a contractual formulation between bankers and their customers outlining what they feel their respective rights and responsibilities should be.

The UCP does not cover all situations under which conflicts involving letters of credit might arise. Moreover, provisions of the UCP might occasionally be in conflict with statutory or decision law of the various states and countries. For instance, in the State of New York, Article 5 of the UCC applies when a particular letter of credit is not in whole or any part subject to the UCP. Most other states adopted the UCC without such a qualification; in case of conflict, courts may draw from codified law, decision law, and/or the UCP in reaching decisions. If litigation should occur, a court may feel that the UCP favors the position of banks. Therefore, a national code of law may be applied in specific instances because a court thinks this will result in a more just adjudication.

Banks Deal Only in Documents

When banks are parties to a letter of credit transaction, they are not concerned at all with the underlying sales contract, nor do they usually wish to know its provisions. Banks deal only in documents. The opening and paying banks make payment after the proper documents have been presented; whether the actual merchandise shipped complies with the sales contract is immaterial to them. The seller, in complete disregard of the sales contract, may ship cases full of bricks or sawdust, claiming that they actually contain the merchandise for which the buyer and seller have contracted. Banks do not assume any liability or responsibility for the description, quantity, weight, quality, condition, packing, delivery, value, or existence of the goods represented thereby, or for the good faith or acts and/or omissions, solvency, performance, or standing of the consignor, the carriers, or the insurers of the goods, or any other person whomsoever. If the documents are presented exactly as stipulated in the letter of credit, the issuing bank will make payment and will, furthermore, have the right to demand payment from the account party.

The account party may, however, have legal recourse directly to the seller if the latter does not live up to provisions of the sales contract. This then becomes a legal action between buyer and seller in which the banks are not involved. Banks, when issuing or making payments under letters of credit, deal at a level of abstraction that is completely separated from the underlying sales contract. A buyer under a letter of credit must either have complete confidence in the integrity of the exporter or he must demand, as part of the documentation against which payment is to be made, an inspection certificate by a reputable third party.

Banks Not Responsible for Fraudulent Documents

Banks are charged with the responsibility of examining all documents with reasonable care and ascertaining that they appear on their face to be in accordance with the terms and conditions of the credit. The important phrase here is "on their face." Obviously, banks cannot be expected to submit each document to a complete legal scrutiny to make sure it has been correctly issued, properly signed by an authorized person, and meets all other legal requirements. Banks are, therefore, satisfied if documents appear to be genuine on the surface and in accordance with the terms of the credit. Banks assume no liability or responsibility for the form, sufficiency, accuracy, genuineness, falsification, or legal effect of any documents and for the general and/or particular conditions stipulated in the documents or superimposed thereon.

If fraudulent documents are discovered by the buyer, he may take direct legal action against the exporter. Again, any banks involved in the letter of credit transaction would not be drawn into the legal action.

OPENING OF A LETTER OF CREDIT

A letter of credit may be opened anytime after signing the sales contract but before shipment. It is to the advantage of the exporter to have the importer arrange for the opening of a credit as soon after the signing of the sales contract as possible.

If there is a price decline prior to issuance of the credit, or some other subsequent development that would make it difficult for the importer to accept the shipment, he may be tempted to renege on the contract. Losses to the exporter in this case may be especially heavy if he has, in the interim, manufactured a specialized product that cannot be sold elsewhere. The exporter, of course, has recourse for damages to the importer. The long legal process required, however, will usually be expensive in terms of time and legal fees. Moreover, a favorable judgment is not always assured.

The danger of a unilateral cancellation of an order by the importer can be minimized by requiring an irrevocable letter of credit immediately after signing the sales contract.

Credit Factors

A letter of credit is a contract involving the account party, the opening bank, and the beneficiary. The opening bank, by issuing a credit, obligates itself to make payment to the beneficiary at a future time whenever proper documentation is presented. Such payment must be made regardless of whether or not the account party will, at that time, be in a position to reimburse the opening bank. Hence, the issuing of a letter of credit requires an analysis of the creditworthiness of the account party by the opening bank.

Unsecured Credit. If the financial strength and integrity of the importer is sufficient to warrant the extension of unsecured credit, the bank can open the letter of credit without having to pay too much attention to the nature and marketability of the underlying merchandise and without requiring any special collateral.

A letter of credit is unsecured, from a bank's point of view, if it holds no collateral and the bill of lading is consigned directly to the importer. The bank, in this case, cannot obtain possession of the underlying merchandise to serve as security. Similarly, if the letter of credit permits payment against an invoice or a nonnegotiable copy of a bill of lading, the bank cannot use the underlying goods being shipped as security.

Secured Credit. If, on the other hand, the account party's reputation and financial strength leave something to be desired, the bank will require some form of collateral. This security may take a number of different forms.

Cash-Commercial Credit. At one extreme, the bank may require a cash deposit for the entire amount of the letter of credit. In this case, it is usually called cash-commercial credit.

Merchandise As Collateral. At the other extreme, the bank may rely only on the value of the underlying merchandise as security. In this case, it must also evaluate a number of additional factors:

The beneficiary—that is, the exporter—must be creditworthy and reliable in order for the bank to be certain that the goods it counts on as collateral will be shipped as provided for in the contract.

The bank must have confidence in the value and salability of the merchandise being shipped. If the importer is unable to pay for the shipment, the bank may have to sell the goods to some other party to cover the amount due under the letter of credit. If the goods are readily marketable commodities that enjoy relative price stability, the bank can probably dispose of them at little or no loss; if the goods are seasonal, perishable, or subject to the whims of changing fashions, a sale on the open market may be possible only at a substantial discount.

The adequacy of insurance coverage while the goods are in transit becomes particularly important. The insurance policy or certificate must be in negotiable form so that the bank may make claims in case of a loss.

If the account party intends to sell the imported merchandise to a third party, the creditworthiness and reputation of this ultimate buyer should be considered. If he is of doubtful financial strength, the possibility of a loss suffered by the account party is substantially enhanced. In some instances, the bank may even wish to see the sales contract between the ultimate buyer and importer to make sure that the firm arrangements for the sale have been made.

Cash Collateral Credit. An "in between" alternative that provides the bank with more security than pure reliance on the underlying merchandise is the requirement of a cash deposit of only a percentage of the total amount of the credit. The percentage required will vary depending on the financial standing of the account party and nature of the merchandise. Bankers may require *no* cash deposit for the amount at which the merchandise could be sold at a fair sale price. The remaining percentage may then be covered by a cash deposit. A letter of credit so secured is generally called a "cash collateral credit."

It must again be stressed that security of any type is only required in those cases where the account party does not have sufficient financial strength to merit an unsecured credit line or when unsecured lines are all used up. In most cases, banks rely primarily on the importer's general financial strength and reputation, but also obtain negotiable bills of lading to their order or endorsed over to them as added protection in case of need.

Requirements for the Account Party

When requesting its bank to open a letter of credit, the account party must submit a completed and signed application as well as a signed letter of credit agreement.

When a credit is opened or advised for the account of a foreign correspondent bank, that bank must have an agreement with the opening/advising bank that includes approval of the foreign bank's institutional credit officer. In case the risk is not approved, notice of such refusal must be given to the foreign correspondent bank by the credit officer of the advising bank. Any credit agreement must clearly indicate the manner by which reimbursement will be made, whether by debit of the foreign correspondent bank's Demand Deposit Account (DDA) with the advising bank, or whether through a third party bank.

Application. A typical application is shown in Figure 13-1. Through it, the account party gives the bank exact instructions concerning the type of credit to be opened, manner of notification to the beneficiary, amount, tenure, required documents, expiration dates, and so forth. It is important that instructions given to the bank are complete and in conformity with the underlying sales contract so that the credit will be opened exactly as required. It must, for instance, be specified what type of insurance coverage is required; if this remains unspecified, the bank is free to accept whatever coverage is tendered. All terms used in filling out the application should be as concrete and specific as possible. Vague or ambiguous terms, such as "usual documents" or "if possible," should be avoided.

The application shown in Figure 13-1 indicates that the bank may, at its option, waive the presentation of drafts. In some countries, stamp taxes are levied on drafts and similar negotiable instruments. Hence, if payment is made against receipt of other required documents but no draft, it is sometimes possible to save these taxes.

The application calls for a general description of the merchandise to be shipped. Occasionally, an account party may wish to insist on the inclusion of a detailed description in the letter of credit. Such a request is usually resisted by the opening bank for the following reasons:

1 Since banks deal only in documents, a detailed description of the merchandise will give no additional protection to an importer. The insertion of unnecessary details does not prevent a dishonest seller from invoicing

the goods as called for in the sales contract, but actually shipping something different.

2 The inclusion of unnecessary details increases the possibility that the checking bank will overlook small documentary discrepancies and may, therefore, cause disputes concerning the bank's responsibility for payment.

3 If too much detail is included, an unscrupulous importer may be provided with a pretext for refusing payment due to superficial discrepancies, when his real reason for not wishing to accept the merchandise may be a drop in the market price or other considertions that are outside the terms of the letter of credit.

Letter of Credit Agreement. The letter of credit agreement is a bank form executed by the account party. It may be a separate continuing agreement between a bank and its client or may be printed on the reverse side of each letter of credit application.

In the agreement, the buyer states that he will provide the bank with funds to pay for sight drafts as they are submitted under the credit agreement or for acceptances as they mature. The buyer also agrees to pay bank fees, commissions, and interest charges. According to the agreement, title to the underlying merchandise remains with the bank until payment is received. The buyer agrees to keep the goods properly insured for the entire duration of the transaction. The Uniform Customs and Practices for Documentary Credits (1993 Revision) are specifically integrated into the letter of credit agreement unless otherwise provided.

Requirements for Opening Bank

Receipt of Application. The application for opening of a credit is generally received by a so-called opening section of the bank's letter of credit department. Most generally, the credits opened are import credits—that is, they are issued on behalf of domestic customers who need a letter of credit in favor of a foreign exporter. Occasionally, however, a letter will also be opened on behalf of a foreign correspondent bank. This may be an export credit or may involve a trade transaction between third countries. In either case, the basic procedure of issuing the credit is the same. The opening clerk reviews the application to make sure that all the conditions are clear and technically satisfactory.

Advice to Beneficiary. After checking, the credit is typed and sent to the beneficiary, either directly or through the advising bank. When there is a degree of urgency, the credit may be advised by cable or telex. A letter of credit may be transmitted by authenticated cable or telex and thus does not have to be mailed. In the absence of specific instructions to the contrary, the bank may notify the beneficiary, either by wire or mail at its option (UCC 5-104).

TO: The Chase Manhattan Bank, N.A.
Letter of Credit Division
1 New York Plaza
New York, New York 10081

Date ____________

APPLICATION FOR COMMERCIAL CREDIT

IN FAVOR OF:

TO BE ADVISED THRU:

Please issue an Irrevocable Letter of Credit by ☐ Airmail ☐ Full Cable ☐ Brief Cable
by order of
and for account of

up to an aggregate amount of

Available by drafts at ____________ for ______ % of invoice value
Drawn at your option on you or any of your correspondents
accompanied by

☐ COMMERCIAL INVOICE
☐ SPECIAL CUSTOMS INVOICE
☐ MARINE/AIR WAR Insurance Policy or Certificate ☐ Insurance covered by Buyer
☐ PACKING LIST ____________
☐ INSPECTION CERTIFICATE
☐ AIRWAY BILL ☐ RAILROAD ☐ TRUCK
☐ FULL SET OF ON-BOARD CLEAN OCEAN BILLS OF LADING relating to shipment

From ____________ To ____________

Drawn to the order of ____________ marked notify ____________

Indicating Freight: ☐ Prepaid ☐ Collect-dated no later than ____________

evidencing shipment of: ____________

TERMS: ☐ FAS ☐ FOB ☐ C&F ☐ CIF ☐ C&I ☐ Other ____________
☐ Partial Shipment Prohibited ☐ Transhipment Prohibited

Drafts and Documents must be dated and negotiated not later than ____________

Unless otherwise stated herein, you may authorize the negotiating/paying bank to send all documents to you in one airmail or courier service, if available.

☐ SPECIAL INSTRUCTIONS For continuation of other documents or special instruction be guided by enclosed sheet which forms an integral part of this credit.

DEMAND DEPOSIT A/C # ____________

The Security Agreement on the reverse hereof is hereby accepted and made applicable to this Application and the Credit.

We warrant that no shipment involved in this Application is in violation of U.S. Treasury Foreign Assets Control or Cuban Assets Control Regulations.

We further warrant that the Agreement below has been duly and validly executed by or on behalf of the Account Party.

____________ (APPLICANT)

____________ (ADDRESS)

____________ (AUTHORIZED SIGNATURE) (TITLE)

(THE FOLLOWING IS TO BE EXECUTED IF THE APPLICANT IS NOT ALSO THE ACCOUNT PARTY)

AUTHORIZATION AND AGREEMENT OF ACCOUNT PARTY

To: THE CHASE MANHATTAN BANK, N.A.

We join in the request to you to issue the above-described Credit, naming us as Account Party and, in consideration thereof, we irrevocably agree that (i) the above Applicant has sole right to give instructions and make agreements with respect to the Application, the Credit and the disposition of documents and we have no right or claim against you or your correspondent in respect of any matter arising in connection with any of the foregoing and (ii) if the Applicant fails to pay when due any amount or amounts owing to you in respect of the Credit or payments or acceptances thereunder, we will forthwith pay the same to you on demand. The Applicant is authorized to assign or transfer to you all or any part of any security held by the Applicant for our obligations arising in connection with this transaction and, upon any such assignment or transfer, you will be vested with all powers and rights in respect of the security transferred or assigned to you.

L.C. #
C. of LIAB.
L.C.O
Comm.
Approval

____________ (NAME)

____________ (ADDRESS)

____________ (AUTHORIZED SIGNATURE) (TITLE)

FX 612 REV. 1-80 PTG. 3-84

Figure 13-1. Application for commercial credit.

If similar credits for the same account party and beneficiary have been issued in the past, time and expense can be saved by merely cabling a request to the advising bank to issue a credit similar to the last one and giving only items that are changed, such as the amount, quantity, and the shipping and expiration dates. If the previous credit has been subject to amendments, the new credit based on the old one will be advised to the beneficiary without the amendments, unless instructions specify clearly any amendments that are to apply.

Once the beneficiary receives the irrevocable letter of credit, the liability of the issuing bank to pay when the proper documents are submitted is established.

Amendments

Frequently, changed or unanticipated circumstances may require a letter of credit to be amended. The seller may, for instance, not be able to ship within a specific time limit and will require an extension. The buyer may require a larger shipment, due to unanticipated demand, and, therefore, have to increase the amount of the credit. If the letter of credit is irrevocable, an amendment can be made only with the consent of all parties—the buyer, opening bank, and seller. (Note that if the credit is confirmed, the agreement of the confirming bank is also required.)

An amendment is processed in the same manner as the opening of a new credit. If the underlying credit has been mailed directly to the beneficiary, any amendment that is restrictive to the rights of the beneficiary must be sent through a local bank, that is, a correspondent of the issuing bank. The local bank will then contact the beneficiary to obtain his agreement and ask him to submit the original letter of credit so that the amendment can be entered on the reverse side of the instrument.

When processing an amendment, a bank has to make sure that it is clear and unambiguous when looked at in the context of the original letter of credit. A request to increase the amount of a credit may, for instance, mean that more goods should be shipped at the same prices, fewer goods at higher prices or even entirely different kinds or grades of goods. In ambiguous cases, the opening bank has an obligation to its customer to make sure that instructions are clear.

Opening Credits for Smaller Banks

Since the purpose of a letter of credit is to substitute the name of the well-known international bank for that of a relatively unknown importer, a credit opened by a small- or medium-sized bank not internationally well known is usually unsatisfactory to the beneficiary. Smaller banks can overcome this obstacle by opening their customers' credits with a large city bank correspondent. A smaller bank can either apply directly to its city correspondent for the opening of a credit or request that the city bank open the credit on behalf of the local customer under its guarantee.

Generally, large banks supply their correspondents with two-part application forms to be used when requesting the opening of credits on behalf of local customers. One part of the form is completed and signed by the customer and addressed to the local bank. It constitutes a regular application and letter of credit agreement that gives the usual detailed instructions needed for the opening of a credit. The other part is signed by the local bank and is addressed to its city correspondent. It requests the latter to act as its agent in opening the credit and also authorizes the city bank to look to the local bank for payment after proper documents under the credit have been submitted.

The city bank then opens the credit in its own name, thereby substituting the name of a well-known international bank for that of the local importer.

LETTER OF CREDIT CONTENTS

To be valid, a letter of credit must be written and signed by an authorized person of the opening bank. Frequently, however, a credit is transmitted to the notifying bank by telex or cable. In this case, it is still a valid and binding commitment as long as it contains the cable authentication of the opening bank. When the opening of a letter of credit is advised by cable or telex, it is usually confirmed in writing.

The information most typically found in a letter of credit is as follows:

1. Place and date of issuance.
2. Names of the account party and the beneficiary.
3. A general description of the merchandise. Since banks deal only in documents and never in terms of the underlying merchandise, a detailed description of the goods should be avoided. The quantity of merchandise to be shipped is usually indicated. When the words "about" or "circa" are used in connection with the quantity, a variance of 3% is permitted.
4. The tenure of the draft: This indicates whether the exporter is to draw a sight or a time draft for a stated number of days on the opening or paying bank.
5. The name of the bank on whom drafts may be drawn.
6. The percentage of the invoice amount for which drafts are to be drawn: In many cases, drafts are drawn for 100% of the invoice amount; sometimes, however, only a partial payment is required. In this case, the seller and buyer have probably made a separate arrangement for payment of the remainder over a period of time.
7. The ports of origin and destination.
8. A listing of the exact documents that must be attached to the draft. Usually, a commercial letter of credit covering the movement of goods requires the presentation of a negotiable, on-board, clean bill of lading that conveys title to the goods being shipped. Additional documents

often required include insurance policy or certificate, commercial invoice, consular invoice, inspection certificate, and others depending on the particular transaction.

9 The maximum amount up to which drawings may be made by the beneficiary: Sometimes, words like "about" or "circa" are used in connection with the amount of the credit. In this case, a variance of 10% either above or below is permitted.

10 An expiration date of the credit: Actually two dates are usually stated to clarify the latest time at which certain actions must have been taken. The latest shipping date is the time on or before which the on-board bill of lading must be dated. The final expiration date gives the time by which the draft and documents must be presented to the paying bank for payment or acceptance. Usually, the final expiration date is a few days after the last permissible shipping date to give the exporter a chance to present his documents to the negotiating or paying bank.

11 A commitment by the issuing bank stating that the drafts drawn on it by the exporter will be honored provided all the conditions of the letter of credit are met.

12 Whether the letter of credit is revocable or irrevocable.

13 When several drawings are allowed under the same credit, the paying or negotiating bank records each drawing on the reverse side of the instrument. This allows any subsequent (different) negotiating banks to determine what amount of the credit is still available. The reverse side of most letter of credit instruments provides space where negotiating banks may list the amounts and dates of any partial drawings that are made.

Several typical letters of credit are illustrated in Chapter 14.

PAYMENTS

Action by Beneficiary

As soon as the beneficiary receives a letter of credit, he should check all its stipulations to see that

They agree with the underlying sales contract.
He will be able to meet all the requirements.

The beneficiary will want to make sure that the amount of the credit is sufficient after all required transportation and insurance charges are added to the basic cost of the merchandise. He should also check the latest permissible dates for shipping and submission of documents to ascertain whether these allow him sufficient time to manufacture and/or purchase the merchandise, place it on board the steamer, and obtain necessary documentation for submission to the bank. All the required documentation should be carefully reviewed for obtainability. The requirements for insurance coverage particularly have to be checked for agreement with the sales contract and availability. The description of the goods should contain no cumbersome technical terms in representing the merchandise; such unnecessary details may give the importer an excuse to refuse payment based on mere technicality.

If there is any discrepancy between the underlying sales contract and the letter of credit, or if the beneficiary is not able to comply with all the conditions, he should take immediate action to contact the importer with a request for the necessary amendment. An amendment can be requested either by contacting the importer directly or by passing the request through banking channels, that is, through the advising and opening banks.

The beneficiary should remember that compliance with the terms of the letter of credit must be complete in every detail before he can obtain payment. If there is any discrepancy or misunderstanding, it is important that it be cleared up immediately.

Checking of Documents

After the exporter has shipped the merchandise and has obtained all necessary documents, he submits these as soon as possible to the negotiating or paying bank. The documentary section of the bank's letter of credit department examines the documents in detail to make sure that they comply with all the terms of the credit. The different documents that may be required have been discussed in Chapter 8. It is, however, worth repeating that, unless otherwise stated, only clean, on-board bills of lading are acceptable. Moreover, no bill of lading showing that the merchandise is stowed on deck is permitted, unless specifically stipulated in the credit.

While insurance documentation must be exactly as specified in the credit, when general terms such as "usual insurance" or "usual risk" are used, the bank may accept the insurance documentation as rendered. The currency of the insurance coverage must be the same as the currency of the letter of credit. Banks may also refuse any insurance document that bears a date later than the date of shipment as stated in the bill of lading.

The commercial invoice should be made out in the name of the customer and its total amount may not be in excess of what is allowed under the letter of credit. The description of the goods on the invoice should be exactly the same as it is in the credit. On other shipping documents, the goods may be described in general terms.

Common Discrepancies

Unfortunately, the submission of documents that do not meet all the specifications of the credit occurs often. Sometimes, documentation required is difficult or impossible to obtain and the exporter may realize this when it is no longer possible to amend the credit. More typically, however, discrepancies are due to clerical errors, delays at the office, and failure to understand or follow instructions of the letter of credit. It may, therefore, be useful to list some common discrepancies that often cause additional work and delays in getting payment to the beneficiary:

1 Presentation of documents to the bank after expiration date of the credit.
2 Documents presented before the expiration date of the credit but with a stale bill of lading. A bill of lading becomes stale when the time between shipment of the goods and the time it is delivered to the bank is unduly long. Determination of whether a bill of lading is stale is up to the bank. When making this judgment, banks consider the shipping time required from port of departure to port of destination. The documents, after being processed by the paying bank and airmailed to the opening bank abroad, should arrive before the merchandise. If an exporter delays submitting the documents to the bank, there is a danger that they will not arrive overseas before the merchandise, and, consequently, payment will probably be refused.
3 The exporter may be making partial shipments when the credit allows only one shipment to be made for the full amount. Even when partial shipments are permitted, the draft for one particular shipment may be in excess of the pro rata value allocated to the partial shipment.
4 The invoice value may exceed the amount available under the letter of credit. Often this means that the exporter has shipped a larger quantity of merchandise than is permitted.
5 A beneficiary of two letters of credit from the same opener may be tempted to combine the shipment and present only one set of documents. This is not permitted. Each credit is considered a separate transaction and, unless specifically authorized, no combined shipments are allowed.
6 The documents submitted may not be internally consistent. The amount, quantity, description, and so on, may not be the same on all of the documents.
7 Insurance coverage may not be as prescribed in the credit. The amount of insurance may be inadequate—the exporter may submit a certificate or cover note when the credit actually calls for a policy.
8 The bill of lading may not be in order. Unless specifically allowed, banks may not accept foul or on-deck bills of lading. If the bill of lading is consigned to the shipper, it must be endorsed before being turned over to the bank.

DOCUMENTARY LETTER OF CREDIT EXAMINATION PROCEDURES

These procedures will, to a large extent, eliminate problems arising from the checking and examination of both letters of credit and their required supporting documents.

Schedule Including the Drawing and the Documents

1 The schedule must contain instructions as to how to pay the beneficiary of the letter of credit (payment can be made by check or wire transfer). If payment is to be made to a party other than the beneficiary, then an Assignment of Proceeds form must be submitted to the bank.

2 The required documents under the letter of credit must be attached, and if additional documents are presented, they should not be retained by the bank but returned to the presenter. It may seem odd that a bank would not want to keep supplementary materials, but such documents may contain clauses or caveats (sometimes in the language of the originating country) that may be poorly understood by the bank but for which the bank would assume liability if it accepted them.

The Letter of Credit and the Drawing

1 Ascertain that the letter of credit is valid and operative, that it covers the amount of the drawing, and that it relates to the documents presented.

2 All figures, headings, terms, amounts, and labels appearing on the drawings must agree with the invoice. Drawings that are accepted should contain no restrictive endorsements or alterations. All drawings should be endorsed and dated.

Commercial Invoice

1 Ascertain that the name and address of the beneficiary and applicant are exactly as indicated in the letter of credit.

2 The description of the merchandise is exactly as required in the credit, including the unit price, and that the CIF (Cost Insurance and Freight), CFR (Cost and Freight), FOB (Free on Board), FAS (Free Along Side) terms are as stipulated in the letter of credit.

3 If the credit requires a signed or visaed invoice, ascertain that it complies.

4 Shipping marks must be consistent in all presented documents, including the quantity of the merchandise, weights, measurements, and so forth. No charges should be included unrelated to this shipment, nor should there be an indication of an unauthorized combined shipment.

5 No overshipment should be indicated, and there should be no storage or demurrage charges.

6 If prohibited, discounts can not be allowed. If the credit is silent, 5% can be deducted from the ex-factory value, provided the value of the shipment does not exceed the credit amount.

7 If the credit allows partial shipment, the value of the invoice is proportionate to the partial quantity shipped.

Ocean/Marine Bill of Lading

1 As per requirements of the letter of credit, ascertain that a full set of originals are presented; this function can be verified by the number of originals indicated at the bottom of the bill of lading.

2 Ports of loading and unloading must comply with the credit terms. Bills of lading are consigned to "order of shipper blank endorsed" or straight consigned to a named consignee or to the order of a named consignee as required in the credit. The bills of lading can not be issued "straight consigned" if the credit requires "order" bills of lading.

3 All shipping marks and number of packages must agree with those appearing in all other documents. No superimposed clauses should appear on the face of the bill of lading that declare a defective condition of the goods or packaging. Such clauses are not acceptable unless authorized in the credit.

4 "Shipped on Board" or "On Board" notation must appear on the face of the bill of lading. If the credit requires a "Clean On Board" bill of lading, then the bill of lading must contain the notation "Clean On Board."

5 If the terms of the credit are CIF or CFR then the words "Freight Prepaid" or "Freight Paid" must appear on the face of the bill of lading. "Freight to be Paid" or "Freight Prepayable" are not acceptable.

6 If the bill of lading shows additional charges to be paid, such charges are not acceptable if not allowed in the credit unless they represent minor miscellaneous expenses connected with loading and unloading charges.

7 The description of the merchandise must not be inconsistent with that shown in the credit. If transshipment has taken place, the bill of lading must ensure the safe arrival of the merchandise at the final port of destination and must be issued by the same carrier for the entire voyage.

8 Unless authorized by the terms of the credit, bills of lading governed by Charter Party Agreement are not acceptable. Statements such as "Shippers Load and Count" are acceptable if not prohibited. Also "Shipment in Containers" is acceptable unless prohibited by the terms of the credit. "Goods Loaded on Deck" is not acceptable unless authorized by the terms of the credit.

9 Always ascertain that the bill of lading is within the latest date for shipment allowed in the credit, and that it is properly endorsed. Bills of lading are usually presented within 21 days from the "On Board" date or within the limitation of the credit for presentation of documents.

10 Any and all alterations are authenticated and bear the stamp of the issuer. The bill of lading does not cover any other merchandise not called for in the credit.

11 "Notify Party's" name, address, and telephone numbers must be as indicated in the credit.

Insurance Policy or Certificate

1 Always confirm the insurance requirements of the credit and ensure that a certificate is not presented instead of a policy. Cover notes are not acceptable unless authorized in the credit.

2 If the document is presented in duplicate, verify that both the original and duplicate are presented. Check to see if an endorsement is needed.

3 Check that the document is dated not later than the transport document, and verify that the insurance coverage is effective from the shipment date.

4 The policy or certificate must be denominated in the proper currency for at least 110% of the amount of the shipment and, unless otherwise stipulated in the credit, it should not include a statement that the cover is subject to a franchise or an excess (deductible) if the credit requires the cover to be irrespective of percentage.

5 Check that the loading and unloading ports, including the name of the vessels indicated in the document, are not inconsistent with those in the bill of lading. Also, the description of the merchandise, quantity, and the shipping marks must be consistent with the credit.

6 The document must be consistent with the credit terms and must cover the following as the case may be: transshipment, shipment on deck, specific risks, all risks, war risks, TPND (theft, pilferage, and nondelivery), riots, civil commotions, and so on.

7 The document should contain all riders cross-referenced, stamped, or signed. Also, marine extension clauses should be manifested in the form stated in the credit, that is, French clauses, Indian clauses, and so on.

Other Documents

In many letters of credit there are multiple documents required. It is not feasible to classify these documents or enumerate steps for their examination. However, the practice in the marketplace is to require the issuer of the credit to stipulate by whom such documents are to be issued, their wording, and data content. If the credit is silent, banks will accept such documents as tendered. For example, if the requirement in the credit is: "Inspection Certificate" without giving any additional information, then the bank will be satisfied, if such "Inspection Certificate" is issued by the beneficiary with any data content not inconsistent with the credit.

Consular Invoice

1 The process of the "Visa System" is the application of the Official Seal by the consul of the buyer's country (the importing country), and the examiner must verify the requirements of the credit unless the credit allows the visa process to be executed by another country. If the credit requires a consular invoice in duplicate, both copies must be issued on the official form as photocopies are usually not acceptable.

2 Ascertain that the CIF, CFR, or FOB value together with the merchandise description marks and numbers, quantities, import license numbers, and the name of the vessel agree with the details appearing on the commercial invoices and transport document.
3 Alterations on the forms are prohibited.

Packing List

1 This document lists the contents of each package, bale, carton, or container.
2 It relates to the other documents required by the letter of credit and must not be inconsistent with those documents.
3 The number of cases indicated on the invoices should be the same as on the packing list.

Weight List

This document lists the individual weight of each package, bale, carton, or container shipped. Many technicians confuse it with a "Weight Note" or "Weight Certificate" and it is neither.

Certification of Analysis

1 This document is a certificate, and as such must be signed. It must comply with the analysis specifications required in the credit and be issued by the party designated in the credit.
2 It must cover the goods shipped under the credit and should not be inconsistent with any of the other documents presented under the credit.
3 The merchandise description must be exactly as stipulated in the credit.

Certificate of Origin

This document is a certificate and as such must be signed. It must comply with the requirement of the credit. If the credit stipulates that it must be issued by the Chamber of Commerce, then such document should evidence that it was printed on the stationery of the Chamber of Commerce. A mere visa is not enough.

Inspection Certificate

1 This document is a certificate and as such must be signed. It must cover the goods that were shipped and must bear a certification of compliance to the specifications, if required in the letter of credit.
2 It must be issued by the party required in the credit.

3 The details must be consistent with all other documents presented in the credit.

Action in Cases of Documentary Discrepancies

When a negotiating or paying bank discovers some documentary discrepancies, it will withhold payment from the beneficiary. If this happens, the exporter can follow one of several courses of action.

Correction of Discrepancies. If still possible, the best course is for the beneficiary to promptly get the discrepancy corrected and to resubmit his draft and documents for payment. This can be done, however, only if time permits and if the discrepancy is of such a nature that corrective action is still possible. If, for instance, the discrepancy is a foul on-board bill of lading, no corrective action is possible, since the defectively packaged goods are already on the high seas.

Waiver by Importer. Another possible alternative is for the beneficiary to request a waiver of the discrepancy from the importer. The normal procedure is for the paying bank to contact the importer and the opening bank by telex to get their waiver for specific discrepancies if they do not impair the quality and quantity of merchandise to be received.

In times of falling prices or a business recession, however, the buyer may well insist that his instructions be followed exactly before payment can be made. Sometimes, an importer will request a reduction in price before accepting a shipment with documentary discrepancies.

Indemnity. In case of incomplete documentation, the beneficiary's bank (i.e., the negotiating bank) may issue a letter of indemnity to the paying bank. This holds the paying bank harmless in case it does not receive payment from the opening bank and importer as a result of the discrepancies. Consequently, the indemnity is made under the assumption that, while the exporter's performance has been deficient in some way, this deficiency will not result in a loss.

An indemnity is a convenient way of getting payment to the exporter if it is too late to correct any documentary discrepancies. Of course, any bank issuing a letter of indemnity retains recourse to the exporter in case a payment must be made. The exporter, therefore, loses one of the key advantages of a letter of credit opened in his favor; that is, the payment of his draft without recourse, provided all stipulations of the credit are met.

Collection Basis. As a last resort, the seller may request the opening bank to present the documents to the importer against payment or acceptance of the draft, that is, on a collection basis. In this case, the exporter is entirely at the mercy of the importer, who may or may not accept the shipment. He may, for instance, desire to accept delivery only if he receives a cut in price to make up for the documentary discrepancies. If the importer refuses to accept the goods, some other buyer will usually have to be found, often at substantial losses to the exporter.

Letters of Credit Risk Manager

As we have seen, the letter of credit is a complex and sophisticated instrument, and the slightest error at any point in its execution can lead to considerable problems and/or delays. It is, therefore, standard practice for each credit over $500,000 to be individually reviewed and approved by a letter of credit risk officer. It is his job to avoid any inconsistencies or errors that could lead to future difficulties in the interpretation of the various clauses in the body of the instrument.

Obviously, all the individuals dealing with a letter of credit cannot know all the legal and cultural differences between the buyer's bank and the seller's bank or their respective countries. It is advisable, therefore, that the credit risk officer have broad international banking experience and that he be seasoned in all aspects of money market instruments. Also desirable, of course, is complete knowledge of foreign exchange and exchange control regulations.

CHAPTER 14

Letters of Credit—Types and Uses

Chapter 13 outlines the basic procedure that is applicable to practically all commercial letters of credit. The specific needs and desires of exporters and importers will, however, often differ. There are a host of factors that play a part in the exact type of credit that may be suitable for a particular transaction. A few of the most important considerations are:

Nature of the merchandise.

Degree of closeness and mutual trust existing between the exporter and importer.

Financial strength and reputation of the exporter and importer.

Financial standing and international reputation of the opening bank.

Repetitiveness of the underlying transaction, that is, is it a one-shot export or do the exporter and importer have periodic shipments?

Financing needs of the exporter and importer.

Relative availability and cost of financing in different countries.

In this chapter, we explore the major types of letters of credit and show how some of these may be used as effective financing vehicles.

COMMERCIAL CREDITS

Letters of credit may be classified according to whether they arise as the result of a commercial trade transaction or for the purpose of meeting some other nontrade related need. Since commercial credits account for the greatest bulk of letters of credit opened, these major types are discussed first.

Certainty of Commitment

Letters of credit may be classified according to the certainty of the commitment to pay made by the account party and opening bank. If this commitment can be revoked at any time without notice, we have a revocable credit. If the commitment cannot be revoked without the specific permission of all parties concerned, we have an irrevocable credit.

Irrevocable Letters of Credit. An irrevocable credit is one that cannot be modified or rescinded by the opening bank or account party without express permission of all parties, including the exporter, importer, and intermediary banks. The opening bank is irrevocably committed to honor the exporter's drafts provided all the stipulations of the credit are met. The credit cannot be altered in any way without the exporter's consent.

Most credits are of the irrevocable type. Indeed, one of the main advantages of a letter of credit is that it represents a commitment by a bank to honor drafts when presented. If the importer could, at will, change his mind and alter the instructions, this advantage would be lost. The exporter may, based on a letter of credit, go through considerable trouble and expense to manufacture and prepare a shipment. His losses could be substantial if the credit were revoked halfway through the manufacturing process or just before shipment.

Revocable Letters of Credit. A revocable letter of credit may be altered or rescinded at the will of the account party. It is, therefore, not a very useful instrument for an exporter who must make a substantial financial commitment before he or she can ship the goods. He may manufacture and load on board a vessel the order covered by the credit, only to find out when the documents are presented at the bank that the instrument has been revoked. By that time the goods are usually somewhere on the high seas, and can probably be disposed of at the overseas location at only a sizable loss. Indeed, the essential characteristic of a letter of credit—the substitution of a bank's name for that of a merchant's—is absent with a revocable credit.

Despite its shortcomings, a revocable credit may still be useful in certain instances. First, the mere fact that a bank is willing to open a credit for an importer means that it has confidence in his ability to make payment. Hence, at the minimum, a revocable credit may be considered a favorable credit report, on the part of the bank. Second, if the goods in question have a large international market, it might be possible to sell them to someone else at little or no loss if the credit is revoked. The exporter can also minimize his risk by calling the bank just before he is ready to ship the goods, to make sure no revocation notice has come in. Then the exporter should present his documents and draft for payment as soon as possible after shipment.

Once the beneficiary of a revocable credit has received payment, the paying bank has no recourse to him if a subsequent revocation notice comes in. Moreover, if the paying and opening banks are not the same institution, and the paying bank honors the beneficiary's draft before it receives the cancellation notice, the opening bank *must* reimburse the paying bank.

A revocable letter of credit is, from the exporter's point of view, safer than sending goods on a collection basis. If no revocation has been received prior to shipment, the risk lasts for only a few days after shipment to allow for assembly of all documents and their presentation to the bank. Moreover, on a foreign collection basis, the exporter actually finances the goods for all or part of the transit time; on a (revocable) sight letter of credit basis, the financing of the shipment becomes the responsibility of the buyer.

A revocable letter of credit is never sent directly to the exporter but is always channeled through the intermediary of a local bank. This is important because any subsequent revocation notice must also be sent through the same bank. If it were sent directly to the beneficiary, a negotiating bank would not know that the credit had been revoked. Hence, both the original credit and any changes or revocations must be advised through a bank.

Due to the shortcomings previously outlined, revocable letters of credit are not used very frequently. They are, however, used effectively for shipments between affiliated companies and in other instances when there is no doubt concerning creditworthiness and mutual trust between the parties. Even in such instances, a letter of credit may still be required to satisfy local exchange regulations or make sure that the central bank has allocated the necessary exchange. When this is the case, a revocable credit may be preferred to save on bank fees, which may occasionally be less for this type of instrument.

Authority to Pay or Accept. This instrument allows drafts to be drawn on a correspondent or branch of the opening bank in the exporter's locality. Depending on the nature of the authority, it may provide for the payment of a sight draft or the acceptance of a time draft.

An authority to pay or accept contains no obligations on either the issuing bank or its correspondent or branch. Hence, the authority may be amended or canceled at any time without notice. An authority to pay or accept is, therefore, similar to a revocable letter of credit.

Negotiability

Credits may be classified as negotiation or straight credits, depending on whether or not they specifically authorize third parties to negotiate the beneficiary's drafts.

Straight Credits. Under a straight credit, the obligations of the opening bank extend only to the named beneficiary. Banks and other financial intermediaries may elect to negotiate (buy) the beneficiary's drafts. Any negotiating party, however, acts as agent for the beneficiary. The letter of credit conveys no legal undertaking to protect such intermediaries. It is important to note that a straight credit does not deter any financial intermediary from negotiating the beneficiary's drafts. It merely states that any negotiating bank acts at its own risk, relying on possible recourse to the beneficiary in case payment is refused by the paying or opening banks.

Negotiation Credits. This type of instrument contains a phrase, such as:

> We hereby engage with the drawer, endorsers, and bona fide holders that each draft drawn under, and in compliance with, the terms of said credit, and accompanied by the above-specified documents will be duly honored on or before January 23, 19--.

A negotiation credit assures anyone who negotiates drafts under the instrument that these will be honored by the opening bank, provided they comply with all the terms. Hence, a negotiating bank is not merely an agent of the beneficiary. It is a legally recognized party to the instrument with clearly defined rights if it presents a draft and documents in compliance with the credit.

The beneficiary of a negotiation credit may negotiate his drafts with any bank in his locality that has a record of the official signatures of the bank signing the credit and is willing to buy drafts on the opening or paying bank. When a bank negotiates the exporter's draft, it is actually buying the draft from the exporter for local currency. The negotiating bank buys the instrument for value, in good faith and without notice of dishonor, and thereby becomes a holder in due course of a negotiable instrument. It, in fact, relies on the promise made by the opening bank to honor drafts drawn in compliance with the credit. Should the opening bank not honor the draft due to a documentary noncompliance, the negotiating bank usually retains recourse to the beneficiary. Sometimes, a letter of credit may provide that the beneficiary draws his drafts without recourse. In this case, the negotiating bank looks entirely to the paying and opening banks for ultimate payment. If such payment is refused, the negotiating bank no longer has recourse to the beneficiary.

Currency. The currency in which a credit is denominated may be that of the exporter, the importer, or a third country. When drafts are denominated in the currency of the importer or third country, they have to be bought or negotiated by a bank in the exporter's locality. The negotiating bank, in fact, buys the draft drawn by the exporter on the opening bank as foreign exchange. If, on the other hand, the credit is denominated in the exporter's own currency, drafts have to be drawn on a bank in his locality. If all conditions of the credit are met, the local paying bank will honor the draft and reimburse itself by charging a *nostro* account that the opening bank maintains with it.

When selling against a foreign currency letter of credit, the exporter has an exchange risk if the currency depreciates relative to his own before payment is received. This risk can usually be covered, however, by merely selling the exchange forward at the time of signing the sales contract. The foreign currency draft, when presented to the bank, will then be in cover of the forward sale.

If the letter of credit is denominated in the exporter's or third country's currency, the importer runs an exchange risk that he may wish to cover.

(For instance, letter of credit agreements of U.S. banks usually state: "If any drafts are payable in other than lawful money of the United States, they are payable at the rate of exchange current when payment is demanded.") Customarily, all charges—including those of the paying bank—are for the account of the importer.

Commitments by Different Banks

An irrevocable letter of credit carries the commitment of the opening bank. When an additional commitment of a second bank in the exporter's locality is added, the credit becomes irrevocable confirmed.

Irrevocable Unconfirmed Credit. When the opening bank is a financial institution of undoubted reputation and financial strength, a confirmation by a bank in the exporter's country is not necessary. The instrument, in this case, is called an irrevocable unconfirmed credit. The advising bank acts merely as an intermediary and does not assume any responsibility.

Irrevocable Confirmed Credit. An irrevocable confirmed credit represents not only the obligation of the opening bank, but also the undertaking of a bank in the exporter's locality, usually the advising/paying bank. An exporter may find this valuable when he has little confidence in or does not know the financial strength of the foreign opening bank. In this case, the exporter requests in the sales contract that the importer, through the opening bank, obtain the confirmation of a prime bank in the exporter's country. Such a confirmation usually reads: "We confirm the credit and thereby undertake that all drafts drawn and presented as above specified will be duly honored by us."

When to Request a Confirmed Credit. How does an exporter know when to ask for the confirmation by a U.S. bank? There are a number of factors to consider. One of the most important is the reputation and financial standing of the foreign opening bank. If it is a large institution with an undoubted international reputation, probably no confirmation will be needed. On the other hand, even if the bank is prime in its own market but, due to its small size, is not well known abroad, the exporter may not have enough information to judge its creditworthiness. In this case, it will probably be wise to obtain the confirmation of a better-known bank, unless the exporter has the facility to investigate and evaluate the foreign "local" bank's credit. Of course, if the foreign bank's reputation is questionable, a confirmation by a prime bank becomes increasingly important.

Of at least equal importance as the reputation of the opening bank is the country in which it is located. As pointed out in Chapter 7, many countries have exchange restrictions that may prevent local banks from honoring certain external payments. Moreover, some countries enjoy a better credit standing than others. If a country's foreign exchange resources are skimpy, external debt large, balance of payments persistently negative, or if it has a record of having defaulted on its international obligations, it is probably wise not to put too much trust in its commercial banks. Exporters would, in these cases, be advised to insist on a letter of credit that is confirmed by a prime bank in their own country.

The confirming bank, in fact, adds its name to that of the opening bank. This, therefore, becomes an extension of credit by the confirming bank to the opening bank. The confirming bank may be in a position to extend such credit because it knows the financial position of the opening bank better than the exporter. In some cases, the opening bank may also have lodged collateral, such as cash or precious metals, with the confirming bank.

Revolving Credits

Frequently, in international trade a buyer will purchase continually from a foreign supplier. To facilitate such repeat shipments between the same buyer and seller, a revolving letter of credit may be used. This eliminates the need to establish a new credit for each shipment. Instead of issuing several letters of credit, the bank issues only one, with a fixed amount available for each defined calendar period. When a drawing is made by the beneficiary, the amount becomes again available for the next period.

Many revolving letters of credit cover regular and periodic sales between affiliated companies, such as a parent and its subsidiaries. For this reason, revolving credits may sometimes be in revocable form.

Cumulative versus Noncumulative. A revolving letter of credit may be cumulative or noncumulative. Article 45 of the UCP stipulates that a credit is noncumulative unless its terms provide that shipments and/or amounts may be cumulative. When cumulative, any amount of the credit available for a fixed calendar period that is not used during that time may be used by the exporter in a subsequent period. Thus, if the credit allows for 12 monthly shipments of $100,000 each for a total of $1.2 million, and the exporter ships only $50,000 worth in month one, the unused $50,000 may be employed in a subsequent month.

When a credit is noncumulative, any amount not used during a given period is automatically canceled at the end of that period. In the previous example, the $50,000 not shipped in month one is permanently lost to the exporter and may not be added to the allowed shipments of any of the subsequent months.

Nonautomatic Reinstatement. A bank may be willing to open monthly credits of $100,000 each for an importer, but the latter's credit strength may not be sufficient to allow for, say, 12 such credits for a total of $1.2 million. In this case, the bank will not be prepared to provide for automatic reinstatement of the amounts available each month. The clause that is then included in the credit may read as follows: "The amounts paid under this credit become available to you again on your receiving advice from us to this effect."

As each shipment is received by the importer and as he pays the opening bank, the beneficiary is so informed and the original amount of the credit is again made available. This type of clause gives the importer a chance to periodically reevaluate whether he wishes to continue the revolving credit. It also limits the maximum exposure of the bank and allows the latter, in turn, to periodically reevaluate the importer's creditworthiness.

Expiration Date. Of course, even a revolving letter of credit must have a final expiration date. This may, however, be extended by amendment. Often banks are reluctant to open credits with a final expiration date beyond one year. The reason for this is that banks generally wish to reevaluate a customer's (importer's) credit condition at least once a year before incurring any additional letter of credit liabilities on his behalf.

Authority to Purchase

Under a letter of credit, drafts are normally drawn on the opening or paying bank. Under an authority to purchase, in contrast, drafts are drawn on the buyer.

This practice has its origin in practices of Asia. Instead of issuing letters of credit, banks in Asia sometimes issue authorities to purchase. The opening bank thereby authorizes its correspondent bank in the locality of the exporter to negotiate, that is, to purchase the draft for the former's account.

Authority to Purchase with Recourse. Originally, most authorities to purchase were with recourse. This meant that if the buyer in Asia did not honor the draft drawn on him, the opening bank had recourse to the negotiation bank which, in turn, could recover the previously made payment from the exporter. The presumption could be made by the exporter that if the Asian bank had any doubts whether the importer would honor drafts drawn on him, it would not have opened the authority to purchase in the first place. Thus, an authority to purchase with recourse is not much better protection for the exporter than a favorable credit report on the importer by his bank.

Authority to Purchase without Recourse. The inadequate protection offered by an authority with recourse caused a gradual shift toward issuing such instruments without recourse. Now, many authorities to purchase state that the opening bank irrevocably agrees to honor the drafts drawn on the importer. This allows the negotiating bank, in turn, to buy the exporter's drafts without recourse. When submitting his draft and documents, the exporter should, in this case, clearly indicate, on the face of the draft, the words "without recourse." Under these circumstances, an authority to purchase becomes identical with an irrevocable letter of credit as far as protection for the exporter is concerned.

Confirmed Authority to Purchase. An irrevocable authority to purchase without recourse may additionally be confirmed by the negotiating bank in the exporter's locality. In this case, the instrument becomes practically identical to an irrevocable confirmed letter of credit.

Interest Paid by Importer. Regardless of whether an authority to purchase is with or without recourse, the negotiating bank will make payment to the exporter well before the drafts and documents can be presented to the importer for ultimate reimbursement. Since the beneficiary usually wishes to receive the full face amount of the draft, any interest charges for the interim between payment and ultimate collection is borne by the importer. Drafts drawn on the buyer, therefore, usually bear a so-called "Far Eastern clause" that obligates the buyer to pay interest at a stipulated rate covering the period between payment to the exporter and reimbursement from the importer. A typical Far Eastern clause may read: "Payable at the current rate of exchange for demand drafts on Seattle with all collection charges and interest at 7% per annum from date hereof to approximate due date of arrival of return remittance in Seattle."

The rate allowed under a Far Eastern clause may, however, not be the same as the rate at which the negotiating bank is prepared to advance funds. If, for instance, the authority to purchase allows only 7% per annum in the Far Eastern clause while the negotiating bank charges 9% per annum, the exporter must absorb the difference.

FINANCING UNDER COMMERCIAL CREDITS

The opening of a letter of credit is based on a creditor-debtor relationship between the opening bank and the account party. The bank, before opening a credit, has to determine whether its customer—the buyer—is good for the amount of money involved. When the bank is called on to make payment under the credit, it looks to the importer for reimbursement. The act of opening a credit is thus counted against the credit line the importer enjoys with the opening bank.

Who Should Finance a Transaction?

While the credit backing for the transaction is furnished by the importer, the actual financing of the goods while they are in the channels of trade may be furnished by any one or a combination of the different parties to the transaction. Whether the buyer, seller, or either of their respective banks furnishes the financing depends on a number of factors.

Money Availability. One important consideration may be money availability. If, for instance, the seller has sufficient funds to finance the transaction to its completion, he may agree to the opening of a time credit and hold the banker's acceptance in his portfolio until maturity. If money is tight in the importer's country, it may be easier to arrange financing through the exporter or his bank. Alternatively, if the money is hard to get in the exporter's country, it may be easier to arrange financing in the importer's country.

Cost. A second consideration, which parallels that of availability, is cost. Often the financing will be arranged where it can be done most cheaply. The cost of credit may be cheaper in the exporter's currency, the importer's currency, or a third currency, such as the Eurocurrencies market.

Relative Bargaining Strength. A third factor is the bargaining strength of the two parties. The buyer may be willing to arrange for a letter of credit, but insists on financing arranged by the exporter. In this case, the bank will open a time credit calling for the exporter to draw usance drafts on the bank, which will accept them when accompanied by the proper documentation. The exporter, unless he discounts the acceptance at his bank, will not get paid until maturity of the time credit. Alternatively, if the exporter is strong enough to insist on immediate payment, the letter of credit will call for sight drafts. In this case, any financing that may be arranged will be for the account of the importer.

Need. A final consideration that is often important is relative need. It may be impossible for the importer to pay for the goods immediately without some kind of credit. This is often true in developing countries where foreign exchange is scarce and every opportunity is taken to obtain hard currency credits. On the other side of the coin, the exporter may be so financially weak that, even though he may be the beneficiary of a letter of credit, he may find it impossible to buy the goods to be shipped for his own account. Consequently, such tools as a transferable, back-to-back, or red clause letter of credit may be helpful.

Time Letters of Credit

A time letter of credit calls for usance drafts to be drawn on and accepted by the opening or paying bank. A typical import credit calling for time drafts is shown in Figure 14-1. If the letter of credit is denominated in the importer's currency, the time draft is usually drawn on the opening bank.

Creation of the Acceptance. If the credit is denominated in the exporter's currency, the time draft is drawn on a paying bank. If all the documents are in order, the drawee bank accepts the draft. Since the exporter has the promise of a reputable accepting bank, he can be confident that he will be paid at the maturity of the acceptance. The creation of the acceptance is based on the strength of the promise of the opening bank, which, in turn, relies on the importer for ultimate reimbursement.

XYZ Bank

1 York Street
New York

Beneficiary:

Indian Export Co.,
1, Main Lane,
Calcutta, India.

Date ....

IRREVOCABLE CREDIT

All drafts must be marked
drawn under credit No. 1234.

Dear Sirs,

We hereby authorize you to draw on XYZ Bank,

for account of: ABC Importer
17, Seaview Street,
New York, NY

up to an aggregate amount of $18,000.00 (Eighteen Thousand US Dollars)

Available by your drafts at 90 days sight for 100% invoice value, to be accompanied by the following documents:

1.– Signed Commercial Invoice in duplicate

2.– Special Customs Invoice.

3.– Insurance Policy or Certificate covering marine and war risks for 110% of invoice value.

4.– Full set clean on board Ocean Bills of Lading, evidencing shipped on board (name of the vessel), from Calcutta to New York, drawn to the order of ABC Importer, notify same, and showing Freight Prepaid.

Covering: Shipment of about 10,000 Lbs. of Tea
Partial shipment allowed and transhipment prohibited.

Ocean Bills of Lading must be dated not later than Sept. 6, 19––.

Drafts and documents must be negotiated not later than Sept. 27, 19––.

This credit is subject to the Uniform Customs and Practice for Documentary Credits (1983 Revision) ICC Pub No. 400.

We hereby agree with the drawers, endorsers and bona fide holders of drafts drawn under and in compliance with the terms of this credit, that such drafts will be duly honored on due presentation to the drawee.

Sincerely,

(Signature)

Figure 14-1. Irrevocable time letter of credit.

Discounting the Acceptance. Often the exporter is not willing or able to wait until the maturity of the acceptance before receiving payment. He will, therefore, generally ask the accepting bank to discount the acceptance, thus giving him the net proceeds (face amount minus discount charges) immediately. Since there is an active market for bankers' acceptances, a bank is generally willing to discount its own acceptances at prevailing market rates.

Discount Charges for Account of Seller. When the exporter discounts the acceptance, receiving only the net proceeds, he is actually paying for the financing of the shipment. He does so, however, without using up any of his own bank credit lines; this, therefore, may still be a desirable method for the exporter.

Discount Charges for Account of Buyer. In many instances, it may be previously agreed in the sales contract that while financing should be in the currency of the exporter's country, the actual cost thereof is to be borne by the importer. In these cases, the time letter of credit will stipulate that finance charges are for the account of the importer. The exporter then gets the full face amount of the draft. Discount and any other bank charges are debited to the account of the opening bank and thus indirectly to the account of the importer.

Acceptance in Foreign Currency. If the letter of credit is denominated in the importer's currency, drafts are drawn on and accepted by the opening bank. In this case, the exporter is taking the exchange risk that the currency in question may depreciate before maturity of the acceptance. This risk can generally be covered as outlined in Chapter 7. It may also be possible to sell the foreign currency acceptance immediately against the exporter's own currency.

Maturity. At maturity of an acceptance, the bank looks to its customer for reimbursement. In actual practice, the customer or correspondent is expected to supply the accepting bank with sufficient funds one day prior to maturity.

Deferred Payment Credits. Somewhat similar to a time letter of credit is a deferred payment credit. Rather than calling for a time draft drawn on and accepted by the paying or opening bank, a deferred payment credit provides for payment at a specified period of time after presentation of the necessary documents.

Documentary Credits. After the exporter has submitted all the required documents, he may receive a letter from the bank indicating that it has received the documents and has found them to be in compliance with the letter of credit. The effect is the same as with acceptance credits in that it gives the importer some extra time before making payment. A deferred payment letter of credit may be used when the payment period extends beyond six months, that is, when the transaction would not be eligible for acceptance financing. Deferred payment credits may also be issued by banks in countries where exchange restrictions do not permit the issuance of acceptance credits.

The task of arranging financing under a deferred payment credit is usually placed on the exporter. Since the latter has no acceptance instrument that he can discount, he has to wait until the stipulated time has expired before drawing a sight draft on the paying or opening bank.

Clean Credit. Sometimes, a deferred payment credit may be of the "guarantee" type and will call for future payment against simple receipt without documents evidencing an underlying trade transaction.

Loans. Beneficiaries of deferred payment credits (whether documentary or clean) may, on occasion, wish to use the credit as a basis for a loan. Then, whenever the date occurs on which the beneficiary is permitted to draw at sight on the opening or paying bank, the proceeds of the sight payment are used to liquidate the loan. A bank that extends an advance against a deferred payment credit will probably wish an assignment of the letter of credited proceeds as collateral.

Refinancing of Sight Credits

When a letter of credit calls for sight drafts on the opening or paying bank, the beneficiary receives payment as soon as he has presented the necessary documents. (A typical letter of credit drawn at sight is shown in Figure 14-2.) To provide financing while the goods are in the channels of trade, the importer may wish to arrange for acceptance financing. Importers in lesser developed countries are often encouraged to arrange for short-term financing in hard currency markets to supplement the local availability of foreign exchange. Moreover, credit may be less expensive and easier to obtain in the exporter's or a third market.

Illustration. To illustrate how a sight payment may be refinanced, assume that a U.S. exporter is the beneficiary of an irrevocable sight credit advised or confirmed through a U.S. bank. The exporter, therefore, receives payment as soon as he draws a sight draft on the confirming bank and submits with it the documents stipulated in the credit. Now, the foreign opening bank—and, therefore, the importer—may not wish to immediately reimburse the U.S. paying bank. If the latter has a credit line available in favor of the opening bank, a refinancing of the sight payment can easily be arranged, either through a direct loan or through the creation of an acceptance.

Refinancing through Loan. If the loan vehicle is chosen, the paying bank merely debits the opening bank's loan account for the amount of the sight payment that it makes to the exporter. Thus, the opening bank receives a U.S. dollar loan, usually for a period of 90 to 180 days. At maturity of the loan, the paying bank charges the current account of the opening bank for the amount due plus interest.

Refinancing through Banker's Acceptance. If, due to tightness of money or some other reason, it is desirable to do the refinancing on an acceptance basis, it becomes necessary to create a time draft covering the period for which financing is desired. This can be done by the drawing of a time draft signed and endorsed by the opening bank on the paying bank for the amount of the underlying transaction and desired tenure. The paying bank accepts the draft, discounts it, and uses the proceeds to make the required sight payment.

1 York Street
New York

Beneficiary:

Indian Export Co.,
1, Main Lane,
Calcutta, India.

Date ....

IRREVOCABLE CREDIT

All drafts must be marked
drawn under credit No. 1234.

Dear Sirs,

We hereby authorize you to draw on XYZ Bank,

for account of: ABC Importer
17, Seaview Street,
New York, NY

up to an aggregate amount of $18,000.00 (Eighteen Thousand US Dollars)

Available by your drafts at sight for 100% invoice value, to be accompanied by the following documents:

1.– Signed Commercial Invoice in duplicate

2.– Special Customs Invoice

3.– Insurance Policy or Certificate covering marine and war risks for 110% of invoice value.

4.– Full set clean on board Ocean Bills of Lading, evidencing shipped on board (name of the vessel), from Calcutta to New York, drawn to the order of ABC Importer, notify same, and showing Freight Prepaid.

Covering: Shipment of about 10,000 Lbs. of Tea
Partial shipment allowed and transhipment prohibited.

Ocean Bills of Lading must be dated not later than Sept. 6, 19––.

Drafts and documents must be negotiated not later than Sept. 27, 19––.

This credit is subject to the Uniform Customs and Practice for Documentary Credits (1983 Revision) ICC Pub. No. 400.

We hereby agree with the drawers, endorsers and bona fide holders of drafts drawn under and in compliance with the terms of this credit, that such drafts will be duly honored on due presentation to the drawee.

Sincerely,

(Signature)

Figure 14-2. Irrevocable sight letter of credit.

In actual practice, the confirming bank will pay the exporter immediately after he submits the necessary documents. It then writes or cables the opening bank requesting the necessary time draft. During the mailing time required to request and receive the draft, the amount is debited to a temporary loan account sometimes called "advances pending refinance on an acceptance basis." After the draft has been received, accepted, and discounted, the temporary loan account is liquidated.

Often, when an opening bank has many customers who wish refinancing of sight payments, it may, for the sake of efficiency, supply the confirming or paying bank with a number of blank, presigned, preendorsed drafts. The paying bank agrees to keep these drafts in its vault, using them only when specifically authorized. Then, when an authorized sight payment has to be made and refinanced on an acceptance basis, the bank merely pulls one of those presigned and preendorsed drafts from its vaults, fills in the desired amount and date, accepts it, and discounts it. This procedure avoids lengthy correspondence and the need for a temporary advance account.

Discount charges are always for the account of the opening bank and, therefore, the exporter receives the face amount of his sight draft. At maturity of the acceptance, it is liquidated in the usual manner by a debit to the account of the opener.

Financing Third-Country Transactions. A similar procedure can be used for refinancing sight payments covering trade transactions between third countries. An export from Japan to Romania may, for instance, be payable in U.S. dollars. The U.S. paying or confirming bank would pay the sight draft when it is presented together with the required documents. Actually, the documents would probably be checked and payment made by the Tokyo branch or correspondent of the U.S. bank. On telex advice that documents had been presented in Tokyo and payment effected, the U.S. bank would create an acceptance as previously described. The net U.S. dollar proceeds from discounting the acceptance would be credited to the account of the Japanese branch or correspondent in cover of the yen that were paid to the exporter. One day prior to the maturity of the acceptance, the Romanian opening bank would supply the U.S. paying bank with sufficient dollars for payment.

U.S. Imports. Imports into the United States under sight letters of credit can also be refinanced by using the acceptance vehicle. The U.S. opening bank will, of course, make payment immediately after the proper documentation and sight draft have been presented. The importer who wishes further extension of credit may simply draw a time draft on his bank. The latter will accept this time draft and discount it in the usual manner. At maturity of the acceptance, the importer's account is debited for the amount due.

After the goods arrive, the importer probably wishes to take possession of them before making final payment. The importer's bank is generally willing to turn over the documents to him against his signing of a trust receipt (described in Chapter 10). This procedure applies regardless of whether imports are financed by means of a time letter of credit or whether refinancing of a sight credit on a loan or acceptance basis takes place.

Once an exporter has sold the goods to his own customer and has received the proceeds, the exporter is required to liquidate any loans or acceptances that were made to finance the specific transaction. If he receives the proceeds of the sale before maturity of the acceptance, he is generally expected to prepay the acceptance. In case of such prepayment, the bank makes an allowance by rebating to the customer any unearned discount charges.

Transfers and Assignments

Sometimes, an exporter who acts primarily as a middleman will have a letter of credit opened in his favor. He may, however, still have to buy the goods required from a manufacturer. The latter may wish some kind of assurance of payment before releasing goods. If the exporter does not have adequate financial substance himself, some other means must be found to assure the manufacturer of timely payment.

To give some assurance of payment, the exporter may be able to transfer a letter of credit that is in transferable form to the manufacturer. Alternatively, the proceeds of the credit may be assigned to the manufacturer.

A transfer of a letter of credit or the assignment of its proceeds may be arranged by a primary beneficiary who does not himself have sufficient financial strength to arrange independently for the opening of a credit in favor of his suppliers or to give some other assurance of payment. The exporter (primary beneficiary) thus uses the fact that a letter of credit has been opened in his favor to induce his own supplier to ship the goods in question.

Transfers. A transferable letter of credit is one under which the beneficiary has the right to instruct the paying or opening bank to make the credit available to one or more secondary beneficiaries. No letter of credit is transferable unless specifically authorized in the credit. Moreover, the secondary beneficiary must be domiciled in the same country as the original beneficiary unless specifically permitted otherwise (UCP, Article 48; UCC 5-116).

When a credit is transferred, all conditions must remain as in the original credit except the following:

1. The amount of the credit and quantity of goods called for may be reduced. This is to allow the transferrer his own profit margin and to allow transfer to several secondary beneficiaries where this may be required.
2. The unit price may be reduced, again to allow for the primary beneficiary's profit margin.
3. The period of validity and/or shipment may be shortened. This is to allow time for the primary beneficiary to substitute his own invoices for those of his supplier.

When documents covering a transferred portion of a credit are received by the bank, it generally notifies the primary beneficiary. The latter may then substitute his own invoice for that of the secondary beneficiary. He also draws a draft on the bank for the remainder of the credit representing his profit. The documents with the new invoice are then sent to the opening bank for reimbursement.

When part of a credit is transferred, the rights as well as the duties go to the secondary beneficiary. The latter is obligated to present his draft and certain clearly defined documents to the bank before he will receive payment.

The documents required are those stipulated in the credit; however, the primary beneficiary may substitute his own invoice and draw for the amount remaining under the credit.

Assignments. An assignment, in contrast to a transfer, assigns part or all of the proceeds of the credit to another party without, however, transferring to him the corresponding duties of submitting documents to the bank. The assignee, therefore, has no control over whether or not proper documentation as required by the credit will be submitted by the primary beneficiary. An assignment is, therefore, not as safe for the assignee as a transfer. The beneficiary of an assignment usually has to turn control of the merchandise and shipping documents over to the primary beneficiary. Payment under the credit is only received after the primary beneficiary meets all the stipulations. If the documents do not conform to the stipulations, no payment is made. Moreover, a dishonest primary beneficiary may choose not to ship the goods under the primary letter of credit but instead to sell them to a third party. Thus, an assignee who is a seller of merchandise to the primary beneficiary (exporter) should have complete confidence in the latter's honesty before making shipment.

An assignment of proceeds may be requested by the primary beneficiary when a credit is not transferable but some confidence of payment must still be given to the assignee. The latter should, however, not put too much faith in such an assignment. As pointed out, the primary beneficiary is responsible for performance under the letter of credit—a responsibility he may or may not wish to exercise. Moreover, the assignee cannot be sure that no previous assignments of the credit have been made that conflict with his own rights. Since assignments are only marginally safer than selling on open-account terms to the exporter, the vehicle is little used. Banks also generally shy away from assignments because of the possible risks and conflicts.

An assignment of a letter of credit is not necessarily always to a supplier of goods and services. The assignment may simply serve to pay an obligation owed by the primary beneficiary to the assignee.

Back-to-Back Credits

Another vehicle through which the beneficiary of a letter of credit can take advantage of the creditworthiness of the importer is the back-to-back credit. The fact that an exporter has an irrevocable letter of credit in his favor may induce his bank to open a second, similar credit on behalf of the exporter with the ultimate supplier or manufacturer as the beneficiary.

Procedure. The exporter, in this case, assigns the primary credit to the bank as collateral and fills out a regular letter of credit application. The second credit is similar to the first except that the amount may be lower and it will have a shorter validity to allow time for substitution of invoices and other contingencies.

Risks. This arrangement gives maximum protection to the supplier, since he has a letter of credit in his favor that guarantees payment provided he meets with all the stipulations. Unless some precautions are taken, however, the opening of a secondary credit based solely on the existence of a primary credit may involve considerable risks to the opening bank.

Generally, to avoid undue risk, the bank opening the secondary credit should strive to have exactly the same documentary requirements as under the primary credit. In the ideal situation, all the documents are the same. Compliance with the secondary credit will then also constitute compliance with the original credit, thus involving no risk to the bank. Typically, the primary beneficiary will wish to substitute his own invoice for that of the supplier. The opening bank may, in fact, request the invoice to be lodged with it already before issuing the secondary credit. Thus, when a drawing is made, the bank already has the invoice on hand for ready substitution.

A more serious risk arises when the secondary beneficiary ships from an inland point and thus is not able to get the on-board bill of lading. In this case, the expiration and shipping dates of the back-to-back credit should be shortened to allow for the arranging of shipping space and an on-board bill of lading *before* expiration of the main credit. But even then, there is no assurance that the primary beneficiary can comply with the conditions of the credit. There may, for instance, be an unanticipated delay in inland transportation, or a dock strike at the port of shipment may prevent the obtaining of an on-board bill of lading. If the primary credit expires before compliance with its terms can be arranged, the bank is stuck with the merchandise, which may or may not be salable. If the goods involved are readily marketable commodities whose price is not subject to great fluctuations, the risk of opening a secondary credit is minimized.

Some U.S. banks do not, as a matter of policy, open back-to-back credits on behalf of an exporter for whom they would not independently issue a letter of credit for a like amount. As pointed out, the risks of opening such a credit may be substantial. There are also, however, precautions that can be taken to reduce or entirely eliminate the risk of opening the second credit. If, for instance, the bank that is requested to open the second credit is also the opener of the first credit, and if all the documentation required is the same, additional risk of opening the second credit is practically nonexistent.

Red Clause Credits

Another vehicle by which the credit standing of the importer may be used by the beneficiary is the red clause letter of credit. This instrument is similar to a normal letter of credit except that it contains a clause (originally typed or printed in red) authorizing the negotiating bank to make clean advances to the exporter.

A typical red clause reads:

> The negotiating bank is hereby authorized to make advances to the beneficiary up to an aggregate amount of ______ or the remaining unused balance of this

letter of credit, whichever is less, against the beneficiary's receipt stating that such advances are used to buy the merchandise for which the credit is opened. Such advances must be deducted from the first shipment, even if the first shipment equals the value that was advanced and the shipper does not receive any payment. If the first shipment is lower than the value advanced, then the shipper's second shipment amount should be deducted by the remaining balance of the unreimbursed advance.

Origin. The red clause letter of credit originated in connection with the China fur trade. Chinese exporters (or agents of Western firms) first had to buy furs from the inland provinces against cash. To give them the necessary means to buy the furs, the negotiating bank was allowed to grant the exporter a loan under the guarantee of the importer and the opening bank. When documents were finally submitted under the letter of credit, any proceeds were first used to liquidate the loan. Once the loan had been repaid, the remainder was turned over to the beneficiary.

Today red clause credits are used primarily in situations where the buying company (importer) has an agent in the exporting country. The agent's role is to purchase merchandise to be exported. To finance these purchases, the importer may arrange for the opening of a red clause letter of credit.

Risk to Importer. Since the clean advances are based on the responsibility of the opening bank and its customer, the importer, the latter is liable for repayment in cases where no shipment is made under the letter of credit or when the loan is not repaid by the exporter. The importer is thus giving an unsecured loan to the exporter to allow the latter to buy the needed merchandise. Before permitting red clause advances, the importer must have a considerable amount of confidence in the capacity and integrity of the beneficiary. In addition to assuming a credit risk, the importer also takes on an exchange risk, since red clause advances are usually in the local currency. However, the exchange risk can be eliminated if the clean advances are given directly by the opening bank in the currency of the importer (called "anticipatory drawings").

GOVERNMENT LETTERS OF COMMITMENT

Many U.S. exports are financed by various governmental and international agencies, such as the Agency for International Development (AID), Commodity Credit Corporation (CCC), Eximbank, the World Bank, and so on. The exportation of goods thus financed is often covered by an ordinary letter of credit advised, issued, or confirmed by a U.S. bank. Rather than looking to the foreign importer or his bank for payment, however, the opening bank receives reimbursement from one of the governmental or international agencies.

The usual procedure for AID and CCC is to issue a letter of commitment whereby it undertakes to reimburse the opening bank for payments effected under letters of credit up to a total dollar limitation. The exact documentation required by the bank before it may make payment to the exporter is spelled out in the letter of commitment and is also included in the actual credit.

Agency for International Development

Normally, a cooperating country wishing financing for a development project or specified imports applies directly to AID. If AID finds the project acceptable, it issues a procurement authorization or enters into a loan agreement with the cooperating country.

AID Commitment. The latter then requests AID to issue letters of commitment to U.S. banks chosen by the particular country. The commitment letters specify the type of merchandise that may be shipped, its value, the time period within which it may be shipped, and the required origin of the goods. Through the letters of commitment, U.S. commercial banks are authorized to issue letters of credit at the request of specified banks or agencies of the cooperating country. Reimbursement for payments made by the U.S. bank under such letter of credit may then be obtained from AID.

Review of Commitment Letter. Once a U.S. bank receives an AID letter of commitment, it reviews it for workability. Each letter of commitment names an approved applicant—the foreign bank or government agency authorized to give the U.S. bank instructions to open and advise letters of credit under the commitment. This approved applicant must be satisfactory to the U.S. bank since it has recourse to it in case of nonpayment by AID.

Letter of Agreement. Usually, the U.S. bank asks the approved applicant for a letter of agreement. In it, the approved applicant states that if, for any reason, AID does not reimburse the U.S. bank, it has recourse to it.

Opening a Letter of Credit. Once a letter of commitment has been received, it could lie dormant until the approved applicant furnishes the U.S. bank with instructions to open a letter of credit thereunder. Once instructions for opening a credit are received, the U.S. bank reviews the request for workability and ensures that it meets the conditions outlined in the AID letter of commitment. Specifically, the following key items are checked:

Are instructions to open the letter of credit really from the approved applicant?

Is the amount of money stated in the letter of commitment sufficient to cover the letter of credit request?

Are the goods in question eligible under the letter of commitment?

Is delivery to be effected within the time limit in the commitment letter?

Once the U.S. bank has satisfied itself that the credit is reimbursable from AID, the letter of credit is prepared and sent to the beneficiary (i.e., the U.S. exporter) in the usual fashion.

Payment. The beneficiary, in the normal course of events, will ship the goods and present his documents to the bank for payment. The documents are checked to make sure they comply with the terms of credit as well as with the AID commitment. Documents usually required by AID include a commercial invoice, certificate of origin, nonnegotiable copy of the bill of lading, and the AID supplier's certificate.

If everything is in order, the beneficiary gets paid. The U.S. bank then mails the shipping documents to the overseas applicant and sends other required documents and its reimbursement claim to AID. Reimbursement is usually received within one week. In the meantime, the U.S. bank debits a special advance account with interest being paid by the approved applicant, or as otherwise provided in the commitment.

Commodity Credit

Manner of Financing. Under the so-called GSM-4 program, CCC finances the export of U.S. agricultural commodities for periods up to three years. Repayment is usually made by the foreign country in equal annual installments. Such financing is available only for specified commodities that happen to be in surplus at any particular time. Approved lists of eligible commodities are published once a month and additions or deletions are made from time to time.

At first the foreign importer and U.S. exporter negotiate a sales contract covering commodities eligible for financing. When required conditions are met, CCC buys the exporter's account receivable without recourse.

Standby Letter of Credit. One of CCC's requirements is an irrevocable standby letter of credit from an acceptable bank guaranteeing payment by the importer to CCC. While the bank may be either a U.S. or a non-U.S. bank, CCC has the following requirements:

1. At least 10% of the financed amount must be confirmed (i.e., guaranteed) by a U.S. bank for commercial credit risks.
2. The total value of the credit must be advised through a U.S. bank.

If the buyer—for credit reasons—does not pay when due, CCC has the right to draw under the standby letter of credit.

Preferred Interest Rate. For any portion of the standby letter of credit that is opened or confirmed by a U.S. bank, CCC reduces the foreign buyer's borrowing rate by one percentage point per annum. Hence, in practice, foreign buyers try to get U.S. bank confirmation for 100% of the required standby letter of credit. As long as the U.S. bank charges somewhat less than 1% per annum for opening or confirming the standby credit, the foreign buyer benefits from cheaper financing.

Interest rates currently charged by CCC are announced each month. They may be obtained directly from CCC or through U.S. embassies.

Eximbank of the United States

Eximbank finances U.S. exports for which private funds are difficult or impossible to obtain. A prospective foreign borrower approaches Eximbank with a request for financing of a specific project involving U.S. exports.

Credit Agreement. Once a project is approved, Eximbank enters into a credit agreement with the foreign borrower. At the same time, the borrower is requested to designate one or more U.S. commercial banks to act as intermediaries.

Agency Agreement. The U.S. bank designated by the foreign borrower receives an agency agreement from Eximbank stating

1. that Eximbank has entered into a line of credit with the named borrower.
2. the amount of the line.
3. that, under the line, the named bank has been designated to issue one or more letter of credit.
4. that any payments made under such a letter of credit with previous Eximbank approval will be reimbursed.

Opening the Letter of Credit. At the request of an overseas correspondent, the U.S. bank draws up a pro forma letter of credit and sends it to Eximbank for approval. If Eximbank approves, the credit is formally opened and the beneficiary advises in the usual manner.

Payment. After the exporter ships the required goods, he submits his draft and documents to the opening bank. If everything is in order, the beneficiary is paid. The offsetting debit goes to a temporary advance account. Once a month, the opening bank claims reimbursement for payments plus interest from Eximbank.

Other Institutions

The procedure for reimbursement from other institutions such as the World Bank and the Inter American Development Bank is similar to the one outlined for Eximbank.

The World Bank, for instance, requires the U.S. commercial bank to draw up a pro forma letter of credit. This credit is compared to the loan agreement that the World Bank has entered into with the foreign borrower. If everything is in order, a formal guarantee of reimbursement is issued to the opening bank. The commercial bank opens the letter of credit in the usual manner. Once the beneficiary submits the required documents, he receives payment and the commercial bank claims reimbursement from the World Bank.

TRAVELER'S LETTERS OF CREDIT

The credits discussed so far all cover the movement of merchandise. They were, therefore, referred to as commercial letters of credit. A traveler's letter of credit, in contrast, provides funds for businesspeople and others who travel abroad for relatively long periods of time.

A traveler's letter of credit is a letter addressed by a bank to its branches and correspondents authorizing them to pay the drafts of a designated individual up to a certain maximum amount. Actually, the traveler's letter of credit comes in two parts:

1. The actual credit
2. A letter of identification bearing the beneficiary's signature

Both parts are needed to draw money under the credit and when traveling, it is wise to keep the two parts separate for security reasons.

Issuance

The bank issuing a traveler's letter of credit may do so based on the good credit standing of the applicant-beneficiary, with payment for individual drawings made by debiting the applicant's checking account at the bank after each specific disbursement. Alternatively, the bank may require an advance deposit for the full amount of the credit before it is issued.

Drawings

When a traveler requires money, he presents the two parts of his instrument to a correspondent of the opening bank in the locality where he happens to be. Payments are usually made in local currencies against the beneficiary's clean sight draft drawn on the opening bank.

Whenever a drawing is made, the amount and date are entered on the back of the letter of credit. This is to enable banks at which subsequent drawings are made to know how much of the total amount is still available.

Uses

Traveler's letters of credit may be useful for businesspeople who are on prolonged trips and require large amounts of money that would be inconvenient to carry in the form of traveler's checks. Sometimes, in addition to travel expenses, businesspeople have to pay for entertainment, fees for trade fairs, temporary secretarial help, purchasing of goods, and so on. In these cases, traveler's letters of credit come in handy not only because they are less bulky than checks, but also because they provide an exact record of amounts spent.

There are also some disadvantages, the most important of which probably is that drawings under a traveler's letter of credit can only be made at designated correspondents or branches of the opening bank during business hours. Moreover, bank personnel at overseas correspondents away from major commercial centers are often not very familiar with the traveler's letter of credit instrument. More than one traveler has experienced substantial delays before someone at an overseas bank could be found who knew what to do and was willing to make payment. To overcome these shortcomings, it is useful for the businessperson to carry a few traveler's checks so that money can be readily obtained in case of urgent need.

SPECIAL CREDITS

So far, with the exception of the traveler's letter of credit, all the different instruments we have discussed facilitate international trade in some kind of goods. There is, however, another broad category of letters of credit that can be most useful to the international businessperson, although the underlying need for the credit does not arise directly from a trade transaction. These instruments are commonly called "special" or "clean" letters of credit.

Broadly speaking, a special credit may be used when an account party wishes to give assurance through a bank to the beneficiary that the latter will receive due compensation in case of nonperformance or default by the account party or by a third party. Alternatively, special credits may be used to assure progress payments to a contractor after he has completed certain clearly defined stages of a project. Just as with a commercial letter of credit, the name and credit of the bank is substituted for that of the account party. The beneficiary may be sure that if he complies with the terms of the special credit, payment from the bank will be forthcoming.

Documentation Required for Payment

For payment to be made under a special credit, the only requirement may be a draft drawn on the opening bank. Alternatively, the draft may have to be accompanied by some kind of documents, such as a certificate of completion or a third party inspection certificate. For instance, if the beneficiary is a contractor who gets paid after he has completed certain clearly defined stages of a particular project, payment may be provided through a special letter of credit. This credit would typically authorize the contractor to draw on the bank for a fixed amount of money after having attested to the completion of a certain stage. The draft might have to be accompanied by the contractor's signed certification that he has completed that particular stage of construction. Alternatively, a signed certification by an independent third party, such as an inspector or architect, may be required.

As another example, if an account party or a third party is to perform some kind of obligation, the remedy for nonperformance may be to allow a drawing under a special credit. Thus, a draft on the opening bank together with a signed statement by the beneficiary or by an independent third party certifying to the nonperformance will usually be sufficient to draw under such a special credit.

The variety of usage to which special credits may be put is limited only by the needs of individuals and businesses and the imagination of their bankers. There are three general kinds of special credits: the bid, performance, and guarantee types.

Bid Type

Frequently, a merchant, manufacturer, or builder has to engage in competitive bidding in order to obtain a specific contract. To show good faith when submitting a bid, the potential supplier or contractor is often asked to submit a bid bond or bid type letter of credit. If he is awarded and signs the contract or if he does not get the contract, no drawing is made under the credit. If, however, after submitting the low bid, the supplier or contractor refuses to sign the sales (i.e., performance) contract, he presumably did not bid in good faith and a drawing may be made under the credit.

A sample bid type letter of credit is shown in Figure 14-3. It allows the beneficiary (foreign buyer) to draw on the bank, provided the draft is accompanied by a signed statement indicating that the account party's (the seller's) bid was accepted, but that he did not sign the contract as required. The bid-type letter of credit illustrated is, therefore, a special credit allowing the beneficiary to draw on the bank if the account party does not sign the contract on which he was the low bidder.

Performance Type

Let us assume that, in the previous illustration involving the bid type of special credit, the seller/contractor actually signed the contract. If the buyer still has some uncertainty as to the seller's ability to deliver, he may request a performance bond or a performance letter of credit. If the seller does not deliver the goods as contracted or the project being built by the supplier is performance defective, the buyer is allowed to draw under the credit.

A sample performance credit is shown in Figure 14-4. Note that it allows the beneficiary to draw on the bank on the basis of his signed statement that the account party did not fulfill his obligations under a specific contract. Sometimes the statement of an independent third party, such as an expert arbitrator, may also be required.

Another type of performance credit allows drawings to be made if and

XYZ Bank

1 York Street
New York

Date......................................

IRREVOCABLE COMMERCIAL
LETTER OF CREDIT

"BID" TYPE

All drafts must be marked
drawn under credit No. 1234.

Beneficiary:

(Overseas buyer)

This credit advised through:

(Overseas correspondent)

Gentlemen:

We hereby authorize you to draw on XYZ Bank,

by order of: (Customer) or (Correspondent)

for account of: (Customer, the seller)

up to an aggregate amount of .... US Dollars.

Available by your drafts at sight

Accompanied by:

– Your signed statement that the bid of (Customer) under invitation No. .... relating to the supply of (brief description of the merchandise) was accepted and (Customer) failed to sign the corresponding contract as required.

Drafts must be drawn and negotiated not later than ....

The amounts hereof must be endorsed on this letter of credit. We hereby agree with the drawers, endorsers and bona fide holders of all drafts drawn under and in compliance with the terms of this credit, that such drafts will be duly honored upon presentation to the drawees.

This credit is subject to the Uniform Customs and Practice for Documentary Credits (1983 Revision) ICC Pub No. 400.

Sincerely,

(Signature)

Figure 14-3. Bid type letter of credit.

when certain well-defined stages of a project have been satisfactorily completed. For instance, if a U. S. manufacturer agrees to put up a plant in a foreign country, progress payments can be arranged after completion of certain well-defined stages. The manufacturer thus may be allowed to draw on the bank if he furnishes a statement signed by him or an independent third party certifying that a certain stage of the project has been completed.

Guarantee Type

Often a foreign subsidiary or affiliate of a domestic company will require a local currency loan. Sometimes, perhaps due to newness of the operation, the local company's financial standing is not strong enough to get bank

XYZ Bank

1 York Street
New York

Date ....

IRREVOCABLE COMMERCIAL
LETTER OF CREDIT

All drafts must be marked
drawn under credit No. 1234.

"PERFORMANCE" TYPE

Beneficiary:

(Overseas buyer)

This credit advises through:

(Overseas correspondent)

Gentlemen,

We hereby authorize you to draw on XYZ Bank,
by order of: (Customer) or (Correspondent)
and for account of (Customer the seller)
up to an aggregate amount of .... US Dollars.

Available by your drafts at sight

Accompanied by:

– Your signed statement that the amount drawn is due you because (Customer) failed to fulfill their obligations under their Contract with you No. .... dated .... relating to the supply of (description of merchandise)

Drafts must be drawn and negotiated not later than ....

The amount hereof must be endorsed on this letter of credit. We hereby agree with the drawers, endorsers and bona fide holders of all drafts drawn under and in compliance with the terms of this credit, that such drafts will be duly honored upon presentation to the drawees.

This credit is subject to the Uniform Customs and Practice for Documentary Credits (1983 Revision) ICC Pub No. 400.

Sincerely,

(Signature)

Figure 14-4. Performance type letter of credit.

credit. Nevertheless, a loan may be obtained either under the direct guarantee of the parent company or through the intermediary of a bank.

In most countries, banks may extend guarantees on behalf of their customers. Thus, if a Latin American subsidiary of a Dutch company requires a local currency loan, a Dutch bank might directly guarantee repayment to the local bank on behalf of the parent company. Banks in the United States are, however, prohibited by law from extending their guarantee in such circumstances. American banks may, however, issue letters of credit, and

XYZ Bank

1 York Street
New York

Date ....

IRREVOCABLE LETTER OF CREDIT

All drafts must be marked drawn under credit No. 1234.

"STAND-BY" TYPE

This credit is advised through, and refers to our telex of today through:

(Advising Bank)

Beneficiary

Gentlemen,

By order and for account of (Our Customer)
we hereby agree to pay up to US$5,000,000.00 (Five Million US Dollars) available upon receipt by us of your statement that the amount of your availment represents the amount due to you in settlement of loan made by you to (borrower) which was not paid when due, plus accrued interest.

Partial drawings are permitted.

This credit expires ....

This credit is subject to the Uniform Customs and Practice for Documentary Credits (1983 Revision) ICC Pub No. 400

Sincerely,

(Signature)

Figure 14-5. Guarantee type letter of credit.

these may be worded so that the effect is approximately the same as the issuance of a direct guarantee.

Generally, the procedure is for the U.S. bank to open a special credit in favor of the foreign bank that is extending the loan. If the obligor defaults in repaying the loan, the foreign bank is permitted to draw on the U.S. bank for reimbursement.

Figure 14-5 shows a typical "guarantee" type of credit. Note that the foreign bank is allowed to draw on the opening bank together with its signed statement that the amount of the draft represents the amount due in settlement of an unpaid loan to the borrower plus interest.

Guarantee type letters of credit may also be used in instances when it is desired that payment by a specific party has to be guaranteed by a bank. Figure 14-5, for instance, shows how a guarantee letter of credit may be used to assure payment by an importer. The standby credit required by the CCC to assure payment by importers of surplus U.S. agricultural commodities may also be broadly defined as a guarantee type letter of credit. Guarantee

XYZ Bank

1 York Street

New York

Date ....

Omdurman Exporting Co.,
Khartoum, Sudan.

Gentlemen,

By order of Messrs. . . . of the Arabic Gum Importing Co., New York, we hereby issue our Clean Irrevocable Letter of Credit No. 1234, in your favor for an amount of US $150,000.00 (One Hundred and Fifty Thousand Dollars) effective immediately and expiring at our counters on Oct. 28, 19--; relative to the exportation through yourselves only of:

80,000 Kgs Arabic Gum

Funds under this credit are available against your sight draft drawn on us, mentioning our ref. Credit No. 1234, accompanied by your signed commercial invoice, and statement to the effect that the amount of your draft represents the amount due you which remained unpaid 60 days after the date of shipment of the above merchandise.

Partial drawings are not allowed.

This credit is subject to the Uniform Customs and Practice for Documentary Credits (1983 Revision) ICC Pub No. 400.

Sincerely,

(Signature)

Figure 14-6. Clean irrevocable letter of credit.

type letters of credit are also called "standby" letters of credit, as shown in Figure 14-6.

The previous examples of bid, performance, and guarantee types of credits are meant only to be illustrative. The vehicle of the special letter of credit is extremely versatile and can be applied to many different situations that may arise in international and domestic commerce. In all cases, however, the bank's obligation to pay is conditional on the receipt of either a clean draft or a draft accompanied by some documentation. Thus, the bank's liability depends only on the presentation of documents, and it is *not* concerned with underlying facts of the particular situation. Special credits—like all other letters of credit—must be limited to a maximum amount and have a definite expiration date. Generally, the fees that banks charge for opening special credits are higher than those for regular commercial letters of credit.

CHAPTER 15

Recent Innovations

COFINANCING

Debt reimbursement and liability reduction are viable alternatives to creating new financings for banks that have suffered heavily in international financing. However, Less Developed Countries (LDCs) are in need of both debt relief and fresh influx of funds.

Traditional lenders, for their part, may be overburdened if called upon to act as the sole source of new financing. Therefore, cofinancing may not be exactly the miracle cure that is obviously needed; yet in its more innovative methods it can become a healthy alternative.

What Is Cofinancing?

Cofinancing is the multifaceted source of financing where the funding of a large project is provided by more than one lender, such as:

1 Multilateral agencies (MLAs) such as the World Bank, the International Finance Corporation (IFC), the Asian Development Bank (ADB), the Inter American Development Bank (IDB), the African Development Bank (AFDB), and any other financial institution capable of lending its support
2 Export credit agencies advancing or financing funds to cover the country's risk exposure
3 Commercial banks or other multilateral financial agencies

These funds are often injected in the form of loans, or they may be invested in the form of equities provided all parties agree. Commercial banks may become the vehicle of aid packages for a strongly backed project in an acceptable country at the lender's own risk or ultimately underwritten by an export credit agency, eliminating all or part of the country's risk exposure.

Table 15.1. World Bank Cofinancing Operations, Fiscal 1980–1989 (by source of financing, in U.S. $ millions)

Fiscal	*No. of Projects Cofinanced and Amounts from All Sources*		*Source of Cofinancing*						*World Bank Contribution*		*Total Costs of Cofinanced Projects*
			Official		*Export CR*		*Private*				
Year	*No.*	*Amount*	*No.*	*Amount*	*No.*	*Amount*	*No.*	*Amount*	*IBRD*	*IDA*	
1980	88	5724	70	3103	20	1461	18	1159	3438	1605	20252
1981	75	3564	69	1813	9	881	9	870	2910	1532	16297
1982	100	5060	80	2320	25	1985	13	756	4046	1231	18291
1983	86	5718	82	2393	12	2330	11	995	3071	1164	19355
1984	102	5204	86	2011	18	1226	11	1967	4906	1568	22411
1985	108	5964	89	2664	23	1838	11	1463	4978	1660	24132
1986	117	3958	103	2639	14	470	5	849	4359	1480	24832
1987	111	5311	100	2697	18	2081	5	534	5009	1604	21628
1988	100	6407	85	3237	17	2518	8	652	3755	2366	18295
1989	131	9943	120	5686	21	3197	3	1060	9247	2504	35816
Total	1018	56853	884	28563	177	17987	94	10305	45719	16714	221309

Source: World Bank's Annual Report, 1989.

Procedures and Actual Practices

Multilateral agencies focus on project support for the benefit of developing countries. The initial feasibility study concentrates on project development with parties in the borrowing country responsible for implementation such as a Ministry of Industrial Output, Planning, or Finance, and the borrowing government entity such as health administration, water resources, energy generating authority, and the like.

The assessment and the feasibility study to finance an individual project or an investment program is part of a continuing process that starts early, prior to introducing the procurement process for the project and the technical equipment requirements.

As a matter of risk management and the credit exposure evaluation process, commercial banks initially examine the project risk, its feasibility, and their own country's risk exposure when assessing any potential lending activity. One other essential factor in difficult markets is the priority treatment for funds allocations under a commercial bank's country ceilings where cofinancing has been granted to the bank's best performing borrowers.

However, this situation may be difficult to achieve when a financing commitment from a commercial bank is requested at a stage when the procurement process for an attractive project has probably not even been sought. The ultimate goal of a commercial bank's involvement in cofinancing is to cater satisfactorily to the needs and requirements of the multilateral agencies involved and at the same time serve its client borrower base. This is again not easy to achieve and involves sophisticated information gathering with regard to the project work undertaken by the multilateral agencies on the one hand and knowledge of the ability and competitiveness of a bank's client as project director on the other.

Methods of Financing

Cofinancing involving commercial banks as lenders is not just one specific financing procedure. In fact, there is a wide range of possible agreements that eventually combine various forms and exposure elements for the commercial bank. The following three types of cofinancing agreements can be distinguished:

1 *Subparticipation.* Under this form of cofinancing, the entire loan is handled by a multilateral agency, which arranges all terms directly with the borrower on the basis of its own documentation. The multinational agency itself is thus "lender of record" for the full amount over the entire duration of the loan. Before committing itself to a formal loan agreement, though, the MLA, acting as agent, broadens the lending base by offering loan participations to commercial banks willing to consider attractive projects in developing countries. It is understood that the purchase of a participation includes all risks and benefits "at initial terms

and conditions." The leading MLA continues to act as lender, one of its duties being to collect from the borrower all principal and interest due for the entire loan on behalf of the participating financial institutions. Subparticipations for commercial lenders are also offered by the IFC and in a different manner by the Inter-American Bank and the Asian Development Bank.

2 *Participation in B-Loans.* A number of years ago the World Bank launched its B-loan program for projects targeted for cofinancing. Under this scheme, total financing for a specific project is divided into A-loans and B-loans. The first part of the project cost, if funded by an A-loan, is provided solely by the World Bank while a consortium of commercial banks acts as lender for the "B" tranche. The World Bank's participation in the B-loan often runs to 10% and never exceeds 20%. In some cases the World Bank may guarantee or assume a contingent obligation on a portion of a loan, or else agree to underwrite the longest maturities, encouraging other banks to extend the terms of their own participation in a B-loan. Take, for example, the commercial bank willing to lend up to six years to a developing country in the form of plain finance credit; the same lender might be willing to lengthen its commitment to eight years if and when the World Bank underwrites that portion of the facility with maturities of nine to ten years.

3 *Parallel Financing.* This type of financing is considered outside but "parallel" to the package offered by an MLA for a specific project. Agreement on the loan documentation has to be reached through a direct dialogue between borrower and lender. This dialogue may be coordinated by the MLA, but the MLA may not become a party to it. However, project assessment may be handled by the MLA. For example, the lender of a parallel loan may agree to a simple double check of the data relating to project risks without additional in-depth evaluation or investigation. Parallel financing is normally tied to goods or services delivered by an individual supplier and often benefits from ECA cover.

Is Cofinancing Important?

In the commercial world, the importance of a given initiative is frequently measured in terms of "How much?" If we apply this to cofinancing, the answer to the question may understate the true significance of this type of procedure. The reason behind this supposition is that such projects—cofinanced by several categories of lenders together with MLAs—are often high on the priority list, well evaluated, researched, and supervised. And the few available figures are also respectable ones. The World Bank alone, as the most important MLA offering cofinancing possibilities, reports that, since FY 1980, 1,018 projects of 2,354 World Bank projects with a total value of U.S.$221.3 billion have been cofinanced; and about one-fifth (U.S.$10.3 billion) of the total amount put up by cofinanciers (U.S.$56.8 billion) has come from private sources, mainly the commercial banks. (See Table 15.1.) U.S.$10 billion over ten years does not by itself sound like very much. However, at a time when commercial lenders are actually seeking to reduce their exposures to LDCs, it represents quite an achievement, and one that may hold considerable promise for the future. Opportunities for financing are ample.

The World Bank is often the sole lender of hard currency to finance infrastructure projects. Nevertheless, cofinancing does matter in this respect, too: Projects with a large equipment-financing component may be cofinanced by both official lenders and—to a lesser extent—by commercial banks.

The International Finance Corporation (IFC) relies substantially on cofinancing inasmuch as it seeks to leverage the financing package by including commercial banks active in this market. The banks are invited to accept subparticipations in IFC loans and, if they are willing to do so, to take a stake in the equity.

Regional development banks (IDB, ADB) have in recent years been improving their cofinancing programs and soliciting additional funds from commercial and official sources on a more regular basis. Attractive projects in the private or semiprivate sector qualify ideally for cofinancing between development banks, ECAs, and commercial banks.

Cofinancing and the Debt Issue

What happens if a country where projects were cofinanced has trouble servicing a heavy external debt? For the commercial bank as lender, there is doubtless a risk that cofinancing will not be treated any differently from plain finance credits that may some day form part of a restructuring package. This package might include a simple lengthening of the maturities or a more radical debt reduction program, possibly combined with forced lending in the form of new money exercises.

In the past, loans made by MLAs themselves have not been included in such restructuring agreements, these loans being, as a rule, repaid at the terms originally agreed. And certainly, as declarations from time to time seek to underline, any deviation from this rule is staunchly resisted as this would put the preferred creditor status of the MLAs at risk.

The aim for any cofinancing lender is, of course, to benefit as much as possible from the priority status of an MLA (and hence to get paid at the original terms). However, the impact of an MLA with regard to protecting cofinanciers differs depending on its form of participation.

The lender of record of a parallel loan is the commercial bank. If this loan is additionally covered by an ECA, then, in the event of restructuring, it is subject to the terms of the Paris Club. Parallel loans can also be arranged without ECA cover, in which case the terms of the restructuring agreement for commercial lenders will be applied.

Subparticipations, on the other hand, do form part of an MLA loan since the lender of record is the MLA. In restructurings, they have up to now been considered as "exempted debt" and serviced at original terms. Subparticipations thus offer substantial "protection" as they are usually not part of a restructuring package.

The lender of record of a World Bank-sponsored B-loan is the participating commercial bank. Since no B-loan has been restructured to date, it remains an open question whether participations in such a loan would be treated any differently from ordinary commitments.

The limited success of the B-loan program has, however, provoked second thought at the World Bank, which recently brought the following new instruments to the market.

Expanded Cofinancing Operations (ECOs). This new initiative by the World Bank was authorized in July 1989 as a pilot program to be reviewed after one year's trial. The program is intended to help countries that have not recently restructured their external debt to gain or broaden their access to private sources of financing. The main focus lies on the international capital markets in the form of public bond offerings and private placements, but commercial bank loans are suitable too. Support through the ECOs program is to be provided most frequently by partial guarantees, options, or other contingent liabilities supplied or assumed by the World Bank. ECOs' support may even be available for risk coverage in the context of limited-recourse project finance.

Therefore, ECOs' lendings by commercial banks or other private lenders consist of both a guaranteed (or otherwise backed) portion and a nonguaranteed portion, both of which should, as a rule, qualify as "expected debt" under a restructuring program.

Export Credit Enhanced Leverage Program (EXCEL). This program focuses on partial financing through export credits with ECA cover to countries where an ECA is currently either restricted or unavailable. EXCEL initially looks at private sector borrowers whose projects have to be approved by a World Bank-assisted "financial intermediary" (e.g., a development bank in the borrower's country).

Outlook

The unfriendly environment with regard to the debt situation in developing countries places severe constraints on any lending activity, cofinancing included. In addition to the risk aspect and the problem of receiving an adequate compensation for accepting both project and country risk exposure, the bank regulators require lending banks to finance all lendings to overexposed debtor countries partially out of an equity-funded provision account. For Swiss banks, for instance, this means that 50% of all medium- and long-term exposure has to be set aside in the form of provisions. Since the additional cost of provision funding can hardly be charged to the borrower, banks are unable to focus their cofinancing activities on those projects and on countries where such assistance is arguably needed most.

But even aside from this consideration, cofinancing is a rather demanding technique: On the part of the lending bank it requires truly professional service that, moreover, has to be maintained over the entire procurement process. This may perhaps be another reason why only a relatively small number of projects are in fact cofinanced by private commercial banks.

However, in spite of the constraints and the limitations imposed by a rather unfriendly environment and the inherent difficulties involved, it appears that cofinancing programs—particularly the new World Bank ECOs and EXCEL schemes, as well as the successful syndication of IFC participations—will continue to support valuable projects in developing countries, enhance prospects of supply by the banks' exporting clients, and add lending possibilities with acceptable risks and adequate returns to bank loan portfolios. The combination of project know-how and financial engineering seems to be a promising way to look beyond the immediate, still bleak, future of the debt problem in developing countries.

Worldwide Safekeeping Services

The steady growth of trade and investment worldwide has prompted many money center banks to recognize their cross-border investment facilities in ways that serve the money management needs not only of local businesses but of exporters and importers as well. To meet the increased demand for securities services, many banks have enhanced the domestic securities-handling capabilities in their overseas locations to bring international investment opportunities to local investors wishing to reallocate their funds overseas.

These banks provide services in which the bank acts as custodian, settles trades, safekeeps securities, services securities, collects coupons, and provides technical and financial information to its clients. Such an expansion of bank operations offers a variety of advantages to the exporter/importer. Various money centers can oversee the accommodations at every level offered by the bank for safekeeping in that region, and offer securities transactions appropriate for investors seeking to increase their global market or simply in need of foreign safekeeping.

Safekeeping and Servicing. Safekeeping securities depends entirely on the market involved. Some markets are largely automated and the "safekeeping" is of an electronic type. Other markets use the physical securities. These markets may have a central depository that keeps share certificates. In this case, the custodian's job is to keep track of what is registered in a client's name. A final possibility is a market with physical securities and no central depository. In this case, the custodian must actually "safekeep" the certificates in a secure vault, as well as maintain records of what is held in a client's name.

Servicing of securities held in safekeeping consists of dividend collection, tax reclamation, and corporate actions. Although in the United States dividends are issued four times a year, foreign dividends are normally issued biannually. In most markets, taxes are withheld from dividend and interest payments *prior* to disbursement to shareholders. The bank should make an effort to minimize or eliminate the withholding taxes assessed against its client. In markets where tax is withheld, or withheld excessively, the bank should file for the returns. The returns should be monitored until the funds are actually received. The bank is also responsible for ensuring that all corporate actions are communicated to the client and that appropriate action is taken including actions on rights, bonuses, splits, takeovers, tender offers, and so on.

Because securities transactions may not be the primary activity of the exporter/importer and foreign securities operations may be nonstandard, the company should exercise care in these transactions. The following safeguards are suggested:

Adequate documentation should accompany every transaction.

Proper authorization should accompany every instruction. Check the accuracy of backlog of reconciliations.

Do not settle two trades together since this can create an overdraft.

Check fees for consistency with the bank's manuals.

Check that dividends and interests are credited immediately to your account and are not delayed by postings to internal bank accounts.

Avoid bulk settlements to your bank. Require detailed settlements.

Check that stock statements and tax reclaims are received promptly.

Foreign Export/Import Trade Commissions

Sometimes, it is necessary for importers to be familiar with the financing options available to suppliers within their home countries. While a survey of the Export/Import Bank facilities of the major exporting countries is beyond the scope of this book, the example of the Australian Trade Commission will suffice for illustration. While not all the information is directly relevant to the U.S. importer, it will give an overview of the types of support that may be available to a supplier seeking markets in the United States.

AUSTRADE

The Australian Trade Commission (AUSTRADE) was formed by the Commonwealth government to improve Australia's export performance of goods and services by working for an improved environment for exports, stimulating industry to be export-oriented, and facilitating export marketing. It is a statutory authority replacing and incorporating the Export Development Grants Board, the Export Finance and Insurance Corporation, the Australian

Overseas Project Corporation, the Trade Commissioner Service, and the marketing and promotion elements of the Department of Trade. In addition to the services that follow, AUSTRADE can be of indirect benefit to Australian exporters by advising as to the export opportunities available through the Asian Development Bank and the World Bank.

Export Market Development Grants. These grants aim to encourage Australian exporters to seek out and develop overseas markets for goods, services, industrial property rights, and know-how that are substantially of Australian origin. Financial incentives are provided in the form of taxable cash grants for overseas activities. Examples of eligible expenditures are:

Market research.
Fares for overseas travel.
Advertising outside Australia.
Overseas representation (such as a sales office).
Communication costs.
Preparation of tenders and quotations.
Provision of free samples to induce sales.
Training overseas agents/buyers in Australia to promote sales.
Subscriptions to "approved" bodies that carry out export promotional activities for members.
Expenses related to the registration and protection of property rights.
Language training for export executives.

Grants are based on 70% of eligible expenditures in excess of $100,000 with a maximum of $200,000 in any one year. For a ninth annual grant the maximum is reduced to $150,000, and for a tenth grant the maximum is $100,000.

After receiving grants for two or more years, claimants are subject to an export earnings test for the third and subsequent grants, but approved bodies are exempt from this test. Grants are not payable to claimants with export earnings in excess of $20 million in a grant year. A corporate test applies under which a corporation and all its wholly owned companies that are claimants are treated as a single company (for the purpose of the $20 million export earnings ceiling). Any expenditure tied to sales is not eligible, and if any financial assistance is received toward the cost of promoting exports, it has to be deducted from the expenditure claimed.

Strategies have been implemented or developed for a range of industries including automotive, computer hardware and software, education services, horticulture, medical and hospital services, railway equipment, and scientific and medical equipment.

Eligibility criteria are:

1. Grants are payable to Australian residents, companies, and partnerships except that companies with more than 50% beneficial South African ownership are excluded.
2. Australian content is required. Goods manufactured, produced, assembled, or processed in Australia must have non-Australian parts less than 50% of their total value. For goods manufactured, produced, or assembled outside Australia, the Australian parts and materials must be at least 75% of the value of all parts and materials.
3. Generally, whoever submits the claim must have incurred the expenditures and be the intended exporter.
4. Claimants must submit export market plans as a test of commitment to export.

Claims must be submitted within five months of the conclusion of the grant year (i.e., by November 30) and any grants are paid only for expenditures made in that grant year.

Export Finance and Insurance. AUSTRADE offers a range of insurance, guarantee, and finance facilities through its Export Credits Division, which operates under the trading name Export Finance and Insurance Corporation (EFIC).

The main function is, through export payments insurance, to encourage trade with overseas countries by protecting Australian exporters of goods and services against risks not normally covered by commercial insurers. The risks cover commercial causes (e.g., buyer's insolvency or default) and political/economic causes (e.g., exchange transfer delays, import restrictions). The maximum percentage of indemnity depends on the risk and ranges from 90 to 100%. Premium rates are available on application, but as an example for short-term business they average less than 0.5%. The advantages of taking out cover are to protect accounts receivable and prevent working capital from being tied up in bad debts and overdue accounts. It should be noted that losses due directly to trade disputes or exchange rates fluctuations are not covered.

A brief summary of AUSTRADE's insurance/finance facilities is as follows:

Shipments and contracts policies on a comprehensive or specific basis: Cover commences from the date of shipment or date of contract, comprehensive policies being appropriate for exports like raw materials, primary products, and consumer goods, and specific policies for large individual contracts of capital goods. A variation of the comprehensive policy is the extended terms policy for sales on credit terms over six months.

Unconditional guarantees to banks and other financial institutions to facilitate the financing of extended terms transactions covered under specific shipment or specific contract policies: There is cover for banks confirming letters of credit, and irrevocable letter of credit cover to exporters for unconfirmed letters of credit.

Preshipment finance guarantees issued to financiers as a partial security for amounts disbursed during the manufacturing period of firm orders.

Cover for stocks held overseas or commodities processed overseas.

Cover for services performed for overseas clients and payments under royalty agreements or patent fees.

Protection to lessors of Australian equipment against nonpayment.

Cover for foreign goods shipped from the country of origin to an overseas buyer, provided such goods are not competitive with Australian-made goods.

Construction works policy cover against nonpayment in respect of constructional works contracts.

Cover for export business transacted by confirmers/financiers, provided they pay the Australian supplier without recourse.

A buyer credit guarantee to an Australian lending institution, which finances an overseas buyer's purchase of Australian capital goods/services: An extension of this is the line of credit to cover a range of sales.

An agreement to guarantee, which is a commitment to an overseas agency to insure contracts placed with Australian exporters up to an agreed amount for bulk purchases and a supporting guarantee to the Australian institutions financing the exports.

The direct lending (export financing) facility providing finance at concessional rates for the purchase of Australian capital goods and services, and establishing general and project lines of credit, especially to developing countries and state trading organizations.

Protection against noncommercial risks for Australian equity investment overseas.

Various innovative schemes are introduced from time to time, such as the High Technology Scheme for Exports (concluded in 1989) and the Innovative Agricultural Marketing Program (concluded in 1991), aimed at stimulating innovation in the marketing of agricultural products. The latter offered grants of up to $250,000 each year. These programs do not provide working capital for businesses. They are for the promotion of new products and new processes.

International Business Services. Some of AUSTRADE's services are free and others are provided on a partial cost recovery basis, especially those provided by AUSTRADE's overseas posts. Among the free services is export counseling for the development of an export plan. Information is also provided on overseas trade controls such as tariffs and quotas.

State offices help eligible firms identify markets and countries offering the best prospects. They can arrange to provide off-the-shelf lists of potential agents and importers. Researched lists, which are even more valuable, can also be provided. These contain the names of contacts in firms identified as being interested in hearing from the client Australian firm. Specific market research can be undertaken to provide a comprehensive export market entry strategy plan for a firm and its products. Credit status reports on overseas importers and notification of trade and tender opportunities are also available.

AUSTRADE's overseas display program matches identified products to key markets. Some Trade Commissioner Posts have showrooms that are suitable for displaying Australian products and assistance can be given with publicity and advertising. Posts can also arrange store promotions. Exhibitors contribute toward defraying the costs of these activities. Trade missions are organized so that participants can make sales contacts, and arrangements can be made for visits to Australia of importers, distributors, and others who can influence the purchase of Australian goods or services.

In-market support includes appointments with post staff to discuss the market. In addition, a Trade Commissioner or Marketing Officer may be able to accompany a company representative on calls and arrange appointment schedules. Posts can arrange commercial services, such as translations, and limited use may be made of a post's office facilities. Apart from the first example, these services are chargeable.

Australian Export Awards. The Australian Export Awards were established in 1963 and recognize outstanding export achievement. They are jointly organized by AUSTRADE and the Confederation of Australian Industry (CAI). In 1987 cash prizes were awarded for the first time. The seven categories are:

New Exporter (less than three years' export experience).
Services Exporter (e.g., transportation, consultancy, tourism, banking).
Small Manufacturer (less than $A10 million sales PA).
Medium Manufacturer ($A10 million to $A30 million sales PA).
Large Manufacturer (over $A30 million sales PA).
Commodities Exporter (e.g., minerals, fuels, bulk foodstuffs, industrial raw materials).
Individual Achievement in Export.

APPENDIX 1

The Export Trading Company Act of 1982

An Act

To encourage exports by facilitating the formation and operation of export trading companies, export trade associations, and the expansion of export trade services generally.

Be it enacted by the Senate and House of Representatives of the United States of America in Congress assembled.

TITLE 1—GENERAL PROVISIONS

Short Title

SEC. 101. This title may be cited as the "Export Trading Company Act of 1982."

Findings; Declaration of Purpose

SEC. 102. (a) The Congress finds that:

(1) United States exports are responsible for creating and maintaining one out of every nine manufacturing jobs in the United States and for generating one out of every seven dollars of total United States goods produced;

(2) the rapidly growing service-related industries are vital to the wellbeing of the United States economy inasmuch as they provide jobs for seven out of every ten Americans, provide 65 per centum of the nation's gross national prod-

uct, and offer the greatest potential for significantly increased industrial trade involving finished products;

(3) trade deficits contribute to the decline of the dollar on international currency markets and have an inflationary impact on the United States economy;

(4) tens of thousands of small- and medium-sized United States businesses produce exportable goods or services but do not engage in exporting;

(5) although the United States is the world's leading agricultural exporting nation, many farm products are not marketed as widely and effectively abroad as they could be through export trading companies;

(6) export trade services in the United States are fragmented into a multitude of separate functions, and companies attempting to offer export trade services lack financial leverage to reach a significant number of potential United States exporters;

(7) the United States needs well-developed export trade intermediaries which can achieve economies of scale and acquire expertise enabling them to export goods and services profitably, at low per unit cost to producers;

(8) the development of export trading companies in the United States has been hampered by business attitudes and by government regulations;

(9) those activities of state and local governmental authorities which initiate, facilitate, or expand exports of goods and services can be an important source for expansion of total United States exports, as well as for experimentation in the development of innovative export programs keyed to local, state, and regional economic needs;

(10) if United States trading companies are to be successful in promoting United States exports and in competing with foreign trading companies, they should be able to draw on the resources, expertise, and knowledge of the United States banking system, both in the United States and abroad; and

(11) the Department of Commerce is responsible for the development and promotion of United States exports, and especially for facilitating the export of finished products by United States manufacturers.

(b) It is the purpose of this act to increase United States exports of products and services by encouraging more efficient provision of export trade services to United States producers and suppliers, in particular by establishing an office within the Department of Commerce to promote the formation of export trade associations and export trading companies, by permitting bank holding companies, bankers' banks, and Edge Act corporations and agreement corporations that are subsidiaries of bank holding companies to invest in export trading companies, by reducing restrictions on trade financing provided by financial institutions, and by modifying the application of the antitrust laws to certain export trade.

Definitions

SEC. 103. (a) For purposes of this title:

(1) the term "export trade" means trade or commerce in goods or services produced in the United States which are exported, or in the course of being exported, from the United States to any other country;

(2) the term "services" includes, but is not limited to, accounting, amusement, architectural, automatic data processing, business, communications, construction franchising and licensing, consulting, engineering, financial, insurance, legal, management, repair, tourism, training, and transportation services;

(3) the term "export trade services" includes, but is not limited to, consulting, international market research, advertising, marketing, insurance, product research and design, legal assistance, transportation, including trade documentation and freight forwarding, communication and processing of foreign orders to and for exporters and foreign purchasers, warehousing, foreign exchange, financing, and taking title to goods, when provided in order to facilitate the export of goods or services produced in the United States;

(4) the term "export trading company" means a person, partnership, association, or similar organization, whether operated for profit or as a nonprofit organization, which does business under the laws of the United States or any state and which is organized and operated principally for purposes of—

(A) exporting goods or services produced in the United States; or

(B) facilitating the exportation of goods or services produced in the United States by unaffiliated persons by providing one or more export trade services;

(5) the term "state" means any of the several states of the United States, the District of Columbia, the Commonwealth of Puerto Rico, the Virgin Islands, American Samoa, Guam, the Commonwealth of the Northern Mariana Islands, and the Trust Territory of the Pacific Islands; and

(6) the term "United States" means the several states of the United States, the District of Columbia, thte Commonwealth of Puerto Rico, the Virgin Islands, American Samoa, Guam, the Commonwealth of the Northern Mariana Islands, and the Trust Territory of the Pacific Islands; and

(7) the term "antitrust laws" means the antitrust laws as defined in subsection (a) of the first section of the Clayton Act (15 U.S.C.12(a)), section 5 of the Federal Trade Commission Act (15 U.S.C.45) to the extent that section 5 applies to unfair methods of competition, and any state antitrust or unfair competition law.

(b) The Secretary of Commerce may by regulation further define any term defined in subsection (a), in order to carry out this title.

Office of Export Trade in Department of Commerce

SEC. 104. The Secretary of Commerce shall establish within the Department of Commerce an office to promote and encourage to the greatest extent feasible the formation of export trade associations and export trading companies. Such office shall provide a referral service to facilitate contact between producers of exportable goods and services and firms offering export trade services.

TITLE II—BANK EXPORT SERVICES

Short Title

SEC. 201. This title may be cited as the "Bank Export Services Act."

SEC. 202. The Congress hereby declares that it is the purpose of this title to provide for meaningful and effective participation by bank holding companies, bankers' banks, and Edge Act corporations, in the financing and development of export trading companies in the United States. In furtherance of such purpose, the Congress intends that, in implementing its authority under section 4(c)(14) of the Bank Holding Company Act of 1956, the Board of Governors of the Federal Reserve System should pursue regulatory policies that:

(1) provide for the establishment of export trading companies with powers sufficiently broad to enable them to compete with similar foreign-owned institutions in the United States and abroad;

(2) afford to United States commerce, industry, and agriculture, especially small- and medium-size firms, a means of exporting at all times;

(3) foster the participation by regional and smaller banks in the development of export trading companies; and

(4) facilitate the formation of joint venture export trading companies between bank holding companies and nonbank firms that provide for the efficient combinations of complementary trade and financing services designed to create export trading companies that can handle all of an exporting company's needs.

Investments in Export Trading Companies

SEC. 203. Section 4(c) of the Bank Holding Company Act of 1956 (12 U.S.C. 1843(c)) is amended:

(1) in paragraph (12)(B), by striking out "or" at the end thereof;

(2) in paragraph (13), by striking out the period at the end thereof and inserting in lieu thereof "or"; and

(3) by inserting after paragraph (13) the following:

"(14) shares of any company which is an export trading company whose acquisition (including each acquisition of shares) or formation by a bank holding company has not been disapproved by the Board pursuant to this paragraph, except that such investments, whether direct or indirect, in such shares shall not exceed 5 per centum of the bank holding company's consolidated capital and surplus.

"(A) (i) No bank holding company shall invest in an export trading company under this paragraph unless the Board has been given 60 days' prior written notice of such proposed investment and within such period has not issued a notice disapproving the proposed investment or extending for up to another 30 days the period during which such disapproval may be issued.

"(ii) The period for disapproval may be extended for such additional 30-day period only if the Board determines that a bank holding company proposing to invest in an export trading company has not furnished all the information required to be submitted or that in the Board's judgment any material information submitted is substantially inaccurate.

"(iii) The notice required to be filed by a bank holding company shall contain such relevant information as the Board shall require by regulation or by specific request in connection with any particular notice.

"(iv) The Board may disapprove any proposed investment only if:

"(I) such disapproval is necessary to prevent unsafe or unsound banking practices, undue concentration of resources, decreased or unfair competition, or conflicts of interest;

"(II) the Board finds that such investment would affect the financial or managerial resources of a bank holding company to an extent which is likely to have a materially adverse effect on the safety and soundness of any subsidiary bank of such bank holding company, or

"(III) the bank holding company fails to furnish the information required under clause (iii).

"(v) Within three days after a decision to disapprove an investment, the Board shall notify the bank holding company in writing of the disapproval and shall provide a written statement of the basis for the disapproval.

"(vi) A proposed investment may be made prior to the expiration of the disapproval period if the Board issues written notice of its intent not to disapprove the investment.

"(B) (i) The total amount of extensions of credit by a bank holding company which invests in an export trading company, when combined with all such extensions of credit by all the subsidiaries of such bank holding company, to an export trading company shall not exceed at any one time 10 per centum of the bank holding company's consolidated capital and surplus. For purposes of the preceding sentence, an extension of credit shall not be deemed to include any amount invested by a bank holding company in the shares of an export trading company.

"(ii) No provision of any other federal law in effect on October 1, 1982, relating specifically to collateral requirements shall apply with respect to any such extension of credit.

"(iii) No bank holding company or subsidiary of such company which invests in an export trading company may extend credit to such export trading company or to customers of such export trading company on terms more favorable than those afforded similar borrowers in similar circumstances, and such extension of credit shall not involve more than the normal risk of repayment or present other unfavorable features.

"(C) For purposes of this paragraph, an export trading company:

"(i) may engage in or hold shares of a company engaged in the business of underwriting, selling, or distributing securities in the United States only to the extent that any bank holding company which invests in such export trading company may do so under applicable federal and state banking laws and regulations; and

"(ii) may not engage in agricultural production activities or in manufacturing, except for such incidental product modification including repackaging, reassembling, or extracting byproducts, as is necessary to enable United States goods or services to conform with requirements of a foreign country and to facilitate their sale in foreign countries.

"(D) A bank holding company which invests in an export trading company may be required, by the Board, to terminate its investment or may be made subject to such limitations or conditions as may be imposed by the Board, if the Board determines that the export trading company has taken positions in commodities or commodity contracts, in securities, or in foreign exchange, other than as may be necessary in the course of the export trading company's business operations.

"(E) Notwithstanding any other provisions of law, an Edge Act corporation, organized under section 25(a) of the Federal Reserve Act (12 U.S.C. 611–631), which is a subsidiary of a bank holding company, or an agreement corporation, operating subject to section 25 of the Federal Reserve Act (12 U.S.C. 601–604(a)), which is a subsidiary of a bank holding company, may invest directly and indirectly in the aggregate up to 5 per centum of its consolidated capital and surplus (25 per centum in the case of a corporation not engaged in banking) in the voting stock of other evidences of ownership in one or more export trading companies.

"(F) For purposes of this paragraph:

"(i) the term 'export trading company' means a company which does business under the laws of the United States or any state, which is exclusively engaged in activities related to international trade, and which is organized and operated principally for purposes of exporting goods or services produced in the United States or for purposes of facilitating the exportation of goods and services produced in the United States by unaffiliated persons by providing one or more export trade services.

"(ii) the term 'export trade services' includes, but is not limited to, consulting, international market research, advertising, marketing, insurance (other than acting as principal, agent, or broker in the sale of insurance on risks resident or located, or activities performed, in the United States, except for insurance covering the transportation of cargo from any point of origin in the United States to a point of final destination outside the United States), product research and design, legal assistance, transportation, including trade documentation and freight forwarding communication and processing of foreign orders to and for exporters and foreign purchasers, warehousing, foreign exchange, financing, and taking title to goods, when provided in order to facilitate the export of goods or services produced in the United States;

"(iii) the term 'bank holding company' shall include a bank which (I) is organized solely to do business with other banks and their officers, directors, or employees; (II) is owned primarily by the banks with which it does business; and (III) does not do business with the general public. No other such bank, owning stock in a bank described in this clause that invests in an export trading company, shall extend credit to an export trading company in an amount exceeding at any one time 10 per centum of such other bank's capital and surplus; and

"(iv) the term 'extension of credit' shall have the same meaning given such term in the fourth paragraph of section 23A of the Federal Reserve Act."

SEC. 205. On or before two years after the date of the enactment of this Act, the Federal Reserve Board shall report to the Committee on Banking,

Housing, and Urban Affairs of the Senate and the Committee on Banking, Finance and Urban Affairs of the House of Representatives the Board's recommendations with respect to the implementation of this section, the Board's recommendations on any changes in United States law to facilitate the financing of United States exports, especially by small, medium-sized, and minority business concerns, and the Board's recommendations on the effects of ownership of United States banks by foreign banking organizations affiliated with trading companies doing business in the United States.

Guarantees for Export Accounts Receivable and Inventory

SEC. 206. The Export-Import Bank of the United States is authorized and directed to establish a program to provide guarantees for loans extended by financial institutions or other public or private creditors to export trading companies as defined in section 4(c)(14)(F)(i) of the Bank Holding Company Act of 1956, or to other exporters, when such loans are secured by export accounts receivable or inventories of exportable goods, and when in the judgment of the Board of Directors:

(1) the private credit market is not providing adequate financing to enable otherwise creditworthy export trading companies or exporters to consummate export transactions; and

(2) such guarantees would facilitate expansion of exports which would not otherwise occur.

The Board of Directors shall attempt to insure that a major share of any loan guarantees ultimately serves to promote exports from small, medium-sized, and minority businesses or agricultural concerns. Guarantees provided under the authority of this section shall be subject to limitations contained in annual appropriations Acts.

Bankers Acceptances

SEC. 207. The seventh paragraph of section 13 of the Federal Reserve Act (12 U.S.C. 372) is amended to read as follows:

"(7) (A) Any member bank and any federal or state branch or agency of a foreign bank subject to reserve requirements under section 7 of the International Banking Act of 1978 (hereinafter in this paragraph referred to as 'institutions'), may accept drafts or bills of exchange drawn upon it having not more than six months' sight to run, exclusive of day's grace:

"(i) which grow out of transaction involving the importation or exportation of goods;

"(ii) which grow out of transactions involving the domestic shipment of goods; or "(iii) which are secured at the time of acceptance by a warehouse receipt or other such document conveying or securing title covering readily marketable staples.

"(B) Except as provided in subparagraph (C), no institution shall accept such bills, or be obligated for a participation share in such bills, in an amount equal at any time in the aggregate to more than 150 per centum of its paid up and unimpaired capital stock and surplus or, in the case of a United States branch or agency of a foreign bank, its dollar equivalent as determined by the Board under subparagraph (H).

"(C) The Board, under such conditions as it may prescribe, may authorize, by regulation or order, any institution to accept such bills, or be obligated for a participation share in such bills, in an amount not exceeding at any time in the aggregate 200 per centum of its paid up and unimpaired capital stock and surplus or, in the case of a United States branch or agency of a foreign bank, its dollar equivalent as determined by the Board under subparagraph (H).

"(D) Notwithstanding subparagraphs (B) and (C), with respect to any institutions, the aggregate acceptances, including obligations for a participation share in such acceptances, growing out of domestic transactions shall not exceed 50 per centum of the aggregate of all acceptances, including obligations for a participation share in such acceptances, authorized for such institution under this paragraph.

"(E) No institution shall accept bills, or be obligated for a participation share in such bills, whether in a foreign or domestic transaction, for any one person, partnership, corporation, association, or other entity in an amount equal at any time in the aggregate to more than 10 per centum of its paid up and unimpaired capital stock, and surplus, or in the case of a United States branch or agency of a foreign bank, its dollar equivalent as determined by the Board under subparagraph (H), unless the institution is secured either by attached documents or by some other actual security growing out of the same transaction as the acceptance.

"(F) With respect to an institution which issues an acceptance, the limitations contained in this paragraph shall not apply to that portion of an acceptance which is issued by such institution and which is covered by a participation agreement sold to another institution.

"(G) In order to carry out the purposes of this paragraph,

the Board may define any of the terms used in this paragraph, and, with respect to institutions which do not have capital or capital stock, the Board shall define an equivalent measure to which the limitations contained in this paragraph shall apply.

"(H) Any limitation or restriction in this paragraph based on paid-up and unimpaired capital stock and surplus of an institution shall be needed to refer, with respect to a United States branch or agency of a foreign bank, to the dollar equivalent of the paid-up capital stock and surplus of the foreign bank, as determined by the Board, and if the foreign bank has more than one United States branch or agency, the business transacted by all such branches and agencies shall be aggregated in determining compliance with the limitation or restriction."

TITLE III—EXPORT TRADE CERTIFICATES OF REVIEW

Export Trade Promotion Duties of Secretary of Commerce

SEC. 301. To promote and encourage export trade, the Secretary may issue certificates of review and advise and assist any person with respect to applying for certificates of review.

Application for Issuance of Certificate of Review

SEC. 302. (a) To apply for a certificate of review, a person shall submit to the Secretary a written application which

(1) specifies conduct limited to export trade, and

(2) is in a form and contains any information, including information pertaining to the overall market in which the applicant operates, required by rule or regulation promulgated under section 310.

(b) (1) Within 10 days after an application submitted under subsection (a) is received by the Secretary, the Secretary shall publish in the Federal Register a notice that announces that an application for a certificate of review has been submitted, identifies each person submitting the application and describes the conduct for which the application is submitted.

(2) Not later than seven days after an application submitted under subsection (a) is received by the Secretary, the Secretary shall transmit to the Attorney General:

(A) a copy of the application,

(B) any information submitted to the Secretary in connection with the application, and

(C) any other relevant information (as determined by the Secretary) in the possession of the Secretary, including information regarding the market share of the applicant in the line of commerce to which the conduct specified in the application relates.

Issuance of Certificate

SEC. 303. (a) A certificate of review shall be issued to any applicant that establishes that its specified export trade, export trade activities, and methods of operation will:

(1) result in neither a substantial lessening of competition or restraint of trade within the United States nor a substantial restraint of the export trade of any competitor of the applicant,

(2) not unreasonably enhance, stabilize, or depress prices within the United States of the goods, wares, merchandise, or services of the class exported by the applicant,

(3) not constitute unfair methods of competition against competitors engaged in the export of goods, wares, merchandise, or services of the class exported by the applicant, and

(4) not include any act that may reasonably be expected to result in the sale for consumption or resale within the United States of the goods, wares, merchandise, or services exported by the applicant.

(b) Within 90 days after the Secretary receives an application of a certificate of review, the Secretary shall determine whether the applicant's export trade, export trade activities, and methods of operation meet the standards of subsection (a). If the Secretary, with the concurrence of the Attorney General, determines that such standards are met, the Secretary shall issue to the applicant a certificate of review. The certificate of review shall specify:

(1) the export trade, export trade activities, and methods of operation to which the certificate applies

(2) the person to whom the certificate of review is issued, and

(3) any terms and conditions the Secretary or the Attor-

ney General deems necessary to assure compliance with the standards of subsection (a).

(c) If the applicant indicates a special need for prompt disposition, the Secretary and the Attorney General may expedite action on the application, except that no certificate of review may be issued within 30 days of publication of notice in the Federal Register under section 302(b)(1).

(d) (1) If the Secretary denies in whole or in part an application for a certificate, he shall notify the applicant of his determination and the reasons for it.

(2) An applicant may, within 30 days of receipt of notification that the application has been denied in whole or in part, request the Secretary to reconsider the determination. The Secretary, with the concurrence of the Attorney General, shall notify the applicant of the determination upon reconsideration within 30 days of receipt of the request.

(e) If the Secretary denies an application for the issuance of a certificate of review and thereafter receives from the applicant a request for the return of documents submitted by the applicant in connection with the application for the certificate, the Secretary and the Attorney General shall return to the applicant, not later than 30 days after receipt of the request, the documents and all copies of the documents available to the Secretary and the Attorney General, except to the extent that the information contained in a document has been made available to the public.

(f) A certificate shall be void ab initio with respect to any export trade, export trade activities, or methods of operation for which a certificate was procured by fraud.

Reporting Requirement; Amendment of Certificate; Revocation of Certificate

SEC. 304. (a) (1) Any applicant who receives a certificate of review:

(A) shall promptly report to the Secretary any change relevant to the matters specified in the certificate, and

(B) may submit to the Secretary an application to amend the certificate to reflect the effect of the change on the conduct specified in the certificate.

(2) An application for an amendment to a certificate of review shall be treated as an application for the issuance of a certificate. The effective date of an amendment is submitted to the Secretary.

(b) (1) If the Secretary of the Attorney General has reason to believe that the export trade, export trade activities, or methods of operation of a person holding a certificate of review, no longer comply with the standards of section 303(a), the Secretary shall request such information from such person as the Secretary or the Attorney General deems necessary to resolve the matter of compliance. Failure to comply with such request shall be grounds for revocation of the certificate under paragraph (2).

(2) If the Secretary or the Attorney General determines that the export trade, export trade activities, or methods of operation of a person holding a certificate no longer comply with the standards of section 303(a), or that such person has failed to comply with a request made under paragraph (1), the Secretary shall give written notice of the determination to such person. The notice shall include a statement of the circumstances underlying, and the reasons in support of, the determination. In the 60-day period beginning 30 days after the notice is given, the Secretary shall revoke the certificate or modify it as the Secretary or the Attorney General deems necessary to cause the certificate to apply only to the export trade, export trade activities, or methods of operation which are in compliance with the standards of section 303(a).

(3) For purposes of carrying out this subsection, the Attorney General, and the Assistant Attorney General in charge of the antitrust division of the Department of Justice, may conduct investigations in the same manner as the Attorney General and the Assistant Attorney General conduct investigations under section (3) of the Antitrust Civil Process Act, except that no civil investigative demand may be issued to a person to whom a certificate of review is issued if such person is the target of such investigation.

Judicial Review; Admissibility

SEC. 305. (a) If the Secretary grants or denies in whole or in part, an application for a certificate of review or for an amendment to a certificate, or revokes or modifies a certificate pursuant to section 304(b), any persons aggrieved by such determination may, within 30 days of the determination, bring an action in any appropriate district court of the United States to set aside the determination on the ground that such determination is erroneous.

(b) Except as provided in subsection (a), no action by the Secretary or the Attorney General pursuant to this title shall be subject to judicial review.

(c) If the Secretary denies, in whole or in part, an application for a certificate, or revokes or amends a certificate, neither the negative determination nor the statement of reasons therefore shall be admissible in evidence, in any administrative or judicial proceeding, in support of any claim under the antitrust laws.

Protection Conferred by Certificate of Review

SEC. 306. (a) Except as provided in subsection (b), no criminal or civil action may be brought under the antitrust laws against a person to whom a certificate of review is issued which is based on conduct which is specified in, and complies with the terms of, a certificate issued under section 303 which certificate was in effect when the conduct occurred.

(b) (1) Any person who has been injured as a result of conduct engaged in under a certificate of review may bring a civil action for injunctive relief, actual damages, the loss of interest on actual damages, and the cost of suit (including a reasonable attorney's fee) for the failure to comply with the standards of section 303(a). Any action commenced under this title shall proceed as if it were an action commenced under section 4 or section 16 of the Clayton Act, except that the standards of section 303(a) of this title and the remedies provided in this paragraph shall be the exclusive standards and remedies applicable to such action.

(2) Any action brought under paragraph (1) shall be filed within two years of the date the plaintiff has notice of the failure to comply with the standards of section 303(a) but in any event within four years after the cause of action accrues.

(3) In any action brought under paragraph (1), there shall be a presumption that conduct which is specified and complies with a certificate of review does comply with the standards of section 303(a).

(4) In any action brought under paragraph (1), if the court finds that the conduct does comply with the standards of section 303(a), the court shall award to the person against whom the claim is brought the cost of suit attributable to defending against the claim (including a reasonable attorney's fee).

(5) The Attorney General may file suit pursuant to section 15 of the Clayton Act (15 U.S.C. 25) to enjoin conduct threatening clear and irreparable harm to the national interest.

Guidelines

SEC. 307. (a) To promote greater certainty regarding the application of the antitrust laws to export trade, the Secretary, with the concurrency of the Attorney General, may issue guidelines:

(1) describing specific types of conduct with respect to which the Secretary, with the concurrence of the Attorney General, has made or would make, determinations under sections 303 and 304, and

(2) summarizing the factual and legal bases in support of the determinations.

(b) Section 553 of title 5, United States Code, shall not apply to the issuance of guidelines under subsection (a).

Annual Reports

SEC. 308. Every person to whom a certificate of review is issued shall submit to the Secretary an annual report, in such form and at such time as the Secretary may require, that updates where necessary the information required by section 302(a).

Disclosure of Information

SEC. 309. (a) Information submitted by any person in connection with the issuance, amendment, or revocation of a certificate of review shall be exempt from disclosure under section 552 of title 5, United States Code.

(b) (1) Except as provided in paragraph (2), no officer or employee of the United States shall disclose commercial or financial information submitted in connection with the issuance, amendment, or revocation of a certificate of review if the information is privileged or confidential and if disclosure of the information is privileged or confidential and if disclosure of the information would cause harm to the person who submitted the information.

(2) Paragraph (1) shall not apply with respect to information disclosed.

(A) upon request made by the Congress or any committee of the Congress,

(B) in a judicial or administrative proceeding, subject to appropriate protective orders,

(C) with the consent of the person who submitted the information,

(D) in the course of making a determination with respect to the issuance, amendment, or revocation of a certificate of review, if the Secretary deems disclosure of the information to be necessary in connection with making the determination, promulgated under section 310 permitting the disclosure of the information to an agency of the United States or of a state on the condition that the agency will disclose the information only under the circumstances specified in subparagraphs (A) through (E).

Rules and Regulation

SEC. 310. The Secretary, with the concurrence of the Attorney General, shall promulgate such rules and regulations as are necessary to carry out the purposes of this Act.

Definitions

SEC. 311. As used in this title:

(1) the term "export trade" means trade or commerce in goods, wares, merchandise, or services exported, or in the course of being exported, from the United States or any territory thereof to any foreign nation,

(2) the term "service" means intangible economic output, including, but not limited to:

(A) business, repair, and amusement services,

(B) management, legal, engineering, architectural, and other data-based services, and communication services,

(C) financial, insurance, transportation, informational, and any other data-based services, and communication services,

(3) the term "export trade activities" means activities or agreements in the course of export trades.

(4) the term "methods of operation" means any method by which a person conducts or proposes to conduct export trade,

(5) the term "person" means an individual who is a resident of the United States; a partnership that is created under and exists pursuant to the laws of any state or of the United States; a state or local government entity; a corporation, whether organized as a profit or nonprofit corporation, that is created under and exists pursuant to the laws of any state or of the United States; or any association or combination, by contract or other arrangement, between or among such person,

(6) the term "antitrust laws" means the antitrust laws, as such term is defined in the first section of the Clayton Act (15 U.S.C. 12), and section 5 of the Federal Trade Commission Act (15 U.S.C. 45) (to the extent that section 5 prohibits unfair methods of competition), and any state antitrust or unfair competition law.

Effective Dates

SEC. 312. (a) Except as provided in subsection (b), this title shall take effect on the date of the enactment of this Act.

(b) Section 302 and section 303 shall take effect 90 days after the effective date of the rules and regulations first promulgated under section 310.

TITLE IV—FOREIGN TRADE ANTITRUST IMPROVEMENTS

Short Title

SEC. 401. This title may be cited as the "Foreign Trade Antitrust Improvements Act of 1982."

Amendment to Sherman Act

SEC. 403. Section 5(a) of the Federal Trade Commission Act (15 U.S.C. 45(a)) is amended by adding at the end thereof the following new paragraph:

"(A) such methods of competition have a direct substantial, and reasonably foreseeable effect.

"(i) on commerce which is not commerce with foreign nations, or on import commerce with foreign nations; or

"(ii) on export commerce with foreign nations, or a person engaged in such commerce in the United States; and

"(B) such effect gives rise to a claim under the provisions of this subsection, other than this paragraph."

If this subsection applies to such methods of competition only because of the operation of subparagraph (A)(ii), this subsection shall apply to such conduct only for injury to export business in the United States.

Approved, October 8, 1982.

APPENDIX 2

Export Credit Insurers of Major Countries

	ARGENTINA
(CASC)	Compania Argentina de Seguros de Credito, SA, Calle San Martin No, 440 Capital federal.
	AUSTRALIA
(Epic)	Export Payments Insurance Corporation, PO Box 2595, 2 Castlereagh Street, Sydney, New South Wales.
	AUSTRIA
(Garant)	(a) 'Garant' Versicherungs, A/G Wohllebengasse 4, Vienna 4.
(OKB)	(b) Öesterreichische Kontrollbank, A/G, Am Hof 4, 1010 Vienna.
	BELGIUM
(CBAC)	(a) Cie. Belge d'Assurance-Credit SA, 15 Rue Montoyer, Bruxelles 4.
(AC)	(b) Les Assurances du Credit, SA Avenue Prince de Liege, Jambes-Namur.
(OND)	(c) Office National de Ducroire, 40 Square de Meeûs, Bruxelles 4.
	BRAZIL
(IRB)	Instituto de Resseguros do Brasil, Avenida Marechal Camara, 171. Rio de Janeiro, GB Brazil.

CANADA

(ECIC) Export Credits Insurance Corporation, PO Box 655, Ottawa 4, Ontario.

CZECHOSLOVAKIA

(Statni) Statni Pojistovna, Insurance and Reinsurance Corporation, Prague 1, Spalena 16.

DENMARK

(EKR) Eksportkreditradet (Export Credit Council) Codanhus, G1. Kongevej 60, Copenhagen V.

FINLAND

(VTL) Vientitakuulaitos (Export Guarantee Board) Eteläranta 6, Helsinki 13.

FRANCE

(COFACE) Compagnie Française d'Assurance pour le Commerce Extérieur, 32 Rue Marbeuf, 75-Paris 8eme.

GERMANY

(Hermes) (a) Hermes Kreditversicherungs, A/G, 2000 Hamburg 13, Hallerstr. 1.

(GKS) (b) Gerling-Konzern Speziale Kreditversicherungs, A/G, 5000 Köln, Gerling-Hochhaus.

HONG KONG

(HKECIC) Hong Kong Export Credit Insurance Corporation, International Building, 141 Des Voeux Road, Central, Hong Kong.

HUNGARY

(ALLAMI) Allami Biztosito (Insurance Enterprise of the State), Budapest IX, Ü11öi ut. 1, Hungary.

INDIA

(ECGC) Export Credit & Guarantee Corporation Ltd., 4 Ramtart Row, PO Box 1932, Fort, Bombay 1.

IRELAND

(a) The Insurance Corporation of Ireland Ltd., 3336 Dame Street, Dublin 2.
(b) The Hibernian Insurance Co., Ltd., Hawkins House, Hawkins Street, Dublin 2.

ISRAEL

(IFTRIC) The Israel Foreign Trade Risks Insurance Corporation Ltd., 74 Petah Tikva Road, Tel-Aviv.

ITALY

(INA) (a) Instituto Nazionale delle Assicurazioni, Via Sallustiana 51, 00100 Roma.

(SIAC) (b) Comitato Assicurazione Crediti all'Esportazione, c/o The Italian Institute for Foreign Trade, Via Liszt 21, 00144 Roma.

(SIC) (c) Societa-Italiana Cauzioni (Cia. di Assicurazioni e Riassicurazioni), Via Crescenzio, 12, 00193 Roma.

JAPAN

(MITI) Export Insurance Section, International Trade Bureau, Ministry of International Trade & Industry, 1, 3-Chome Kasumigaseki, Chiyoda-ku, Tokyo.

LUXEMBOURG

(ODL) Office du Ducroire Luxembourgeois, 8 Avenue de l'Arsenal, Luxembourg.

MEXICO

(Fondo) Banco de Mexico, SA, Fondo para el Fomento de las Exportaciones de Productos Manufacturados, Av. 5 de Mayo No. 2, Mexico DF.

NETHERLANDS

(NCM) Nederlandsche Credietverzekering Maatschappij, N.V., Keisersgracht 271, PO Box 473, Amsterdam-C.

NEW ZEALAND

(Exgo) Export Guarantee Office, PO Box 5037, Lambton Quay, Wellington.

NORWAY

(GIEK) Garanti-Instituttet for Eksportkreditt (Export Credit Guarantee Institute), Fr. Nansens Plass 2, Oslo.

PAKISTAN

(ECGS) Pakistan Insurance Corporation, Export Credit Guarantee Scheme, Pakistan Insurance Building, Bunder Road, PO Box 4777, Karachi 2.

POLAND

(Warta) 'Warta' Insurance and Reinsurance Company Ltd., Warszawa 51, 12, Swietokrzyska Str.

PORTUGAL

(CCSCEN) (a) Comissao de Creditos e de Seguro de Creditos a Exportacao Nacional, Fundo de Fomento de Exportacao, Rua Camilo Castelo Branco 2, Lisbon.

SOUTH AFRICA

(CGIC) Credit Guarantee Insurance Corporation of Africa Ltd., Avril Malan Building, 57–59 Commissioner Street, Johannesburg, PO Box 9244.

SPAIN

(CESCC) (a) Cia, Española de Seguros de Crédito y Caución, SA, R. F. Villaverde, 61, Madrid.

(b) Cosorcio de Compensación de Sequros, Ministerio de Hacienda, Serrano, 69, Madrid—1.

SWEDEN

(EKN) (a) Exportkreditnämnden (Export Credits Guarantee Board), Box 16015, S-103 21 Stockholm 16.

(Svenskakredit) (b) Svenska Kreditfórsäkrings AB, Box 7073, S-103 82 Stockholm 7.

SWITZERLAND

(a) Geschaftsstelle fur die Exportrisikogarantie, Kirchenweg 4, 8032 Zurich.

(The Federal) (b) The Federal Insurance Co. Ltd. (Eidegenossische Versicherungs, A/G), Flossergasse 3, 8001 Zurich.

	TAIWAN
(Central Trust)	Central Trust of China, Purchasing Department, 49 Wu Chang Street, Sec. 1, Taipei, Taiwan.
	UNITED KINGDOM
(ECGD)	Export Credits Guarantee Department, Aldermanbury House, Aldermanbury, London, EC2P 2EL.
	UNITED STATES
(Eximbank)	(a) Export-Import Bank of the United States, 811 Vermont Avenue, NW, Washington, DC 20571.
(FCIA)	(b) Foreign Credit Insurance Association, 1 World Trade Center, New York, NY 10047.
	YUGOSLAVIA
(Yugoslavia)	(a) 'Yugoslavia' Insurance & Reinsurance Company, Knez Milhailova 6, PO Box 250, Belgrade. (b) Export Credits Finance & Insurance Fund, Knez Milhailova 14, Belgrade.

APPENDIX 3

Revised American Foreign Trade Definitions

Adopted 1990 by a Joint Committee representing the
Chamber of Commerce of the United States of America
National Council of American Importers, Inc.
National Foreign Trade Council, Inc.

FOREWORD

Since the issuance of *American Foreign Trade Definitions* in 1919 many changes in practice have occurred. The 1919 Definitions did much to clarify and simplify foreign trade practice, and received wide recognition and use by buyers and sellers throughout the world. At the Twenty-Seventh National Foreign Trade Convention, 1940, further revision and clarification of these Definitions was urged as necessary to assist the foreign trader in the handling of his transactions.

The following *Revised American Foreign Trade Definitions—1990* are recommended for general use by both exporters and importers. These revised definitions have no status at law unless there is specific legislation providing for them, or unless they are confirmed by court decisions. Hence, it is suggested that sellers and buyers agree to their acceptance as part of the contract of sale. These revised definitions will then become legally binding upon all parties.

In view of changes in practice and procedure since 1941, certain new responsibilities for sellers and buyers are included in these revised definitions. Also, in many instances, the old responsibilities are more clearly defined than in the 1941 Definitions, and the changes should be beneficial both to sellers and buyers. Widespread acceptance will lead to a greater standardization of foreign trade procedure, and to the avoidance of much misunderstanding.

Adoption by exporters and importers of these revised terms will impress on all parties concerned their respective responsibilities and rights.

General Notes of Caution

1. As foreign trade definitions have been issued by organizations in various parts of the world, and as the courts of countries have interpreted these definitions in different ways, it is important that sellers and buyers agree that their contracts are subject to the *Revised American Foreign Trade Definitions—1990* and that the various points listed are accepted by both parties.

2. In addition to the foreign trade terms listed herein, there are terms that are at times used, such as Free Harbor, C.I.F. & C. (Cost, Insurance, Freight, and Commission), C.I.F.C. & I. (Cost, Insurance, Freight, Commission, and Interest), C.I.F. Landed (Cost, Insurance, Freight, Landed), and others. None of these should be used unless there has first been a definite understanding as to the exact meaning thereof. It is unwise to attempt to interpret other terms in the light of the terms given herein. Hence, whenever possible, one of the terms defined herein should be used.

3. It is unwise to use abbreviations in quotations or in contracts which might be subject to misunderstanding.

4. When making quotations, the familiar terms "hundredweight" or "ton" should be avoided. A hundredweight can be 100 pounds of the short ton, or 112 pounds of the long ton. A ton can be a short ton of 2,000 pounds, or a metric ton of 2,204.6 pounds, or a long ton of 2,240 pounds. Hence, the type of hundredweight or ton should be clearly stated in quotations and in sales confirmations. Also, all terms referring to quantity, weight, volume, length, or surface should be clearly defined and agreed upon.

5. If inspection, or certificate of inspection, is required, it should be agreed, in advance, whether the cost thereof is for account of seller or buyer.

6. Unless otherwise agreed upon, all expenses are for the account of seller up to the point at which the buyer must handle the subsequent movement of goods.

7. There are a number of elements in a contract that do not fall within the scope of these foreign trade definitions. Hence, no mention of these is made herein. Seller and buyer should agree to these separately when negotiating contracts. This particularly applies to so-called "customary" practices.

Definitions of Quotations

(I) EXW (Ex Works—Named Place)

"EX FACTORY", "EX MILL", "EX MINE",
"EX PLANTATION", "EX WAREHOUSE", etc. (named point of origin)

Under this term, the price quoted applies only at the point of origin, and the seller agrees to place the goods at the disposal of the buyer at the agreed place on the date or within the period fixed.

Under this quotation:

Seller must

(1) bear all costs and risks of the goods until such time as the buyer is obliged to take delivery thereof;

(2) render the buyer, at the buyer's request and expense, assistance in obtaining the documents issued in the country of origin, or

of shipment, or of both, which the buyer may require either for purposes of exportation, or of importation at destination.

Buyer must

(1) take delivery fo the goods as soon as they have been placed at his disposal at the agreed place on the date or within the period fixed;

(2) pay export taxes, or other fees or charges, if any, levied because of exportation;

(3) bear all costs and risks of the goods from the time when he is obligated to take delivery thereof;

(4) pay all costs and charges incurred in obtaining the documents issued in the country of origin, or of shipment, or of both, which may be required either for purposes of exportation or of importation at destination.

(II) F.O.B. (Free on Board)

Note: *Seller and buyer should consider not only the definitions but also the "Comments on all F.O.B. Terms" given at the end of this section* (page 435), *in order to understand fully their respective responsibilities and rights under the several classes of "F.O.B." terms.*

*(II-A) "F.O.B. (named inland carrier at named inland point of departure)"**

Under this term, the price quoted applies only at inland shipping point, and the seller arranges for loading of the goods on, or in, railway cars, trucks, lighters, barges, aircraft, or other conveyance furnished for transportation.

Under this quotation:

Seller must

(1) place goods on, or in, conveyance, or deliver to inland carrier for loading;

(2) provide clean bill of lading or other transportation receipt, freight collect;

(3) be responsible for any loss or damage, or both, until goods have been placed in, or on, conveyance at loading point, and clean bill of lading or other transportation receipt has been furnished by the carrier;

(4) render the buyer, at the buyer's request and expense, assistance in obtaining the documents issued in the country of origin, or of shipment, or of both, which the buyer may require either for purposes of exportation, or of importation at destination.

Buyer must

(1) be responsible for all movement of the goods from inland point of loading and pay all transportation costs;

(2) pay export taxes, or other fees or charges, if any, levied because of exportation;

(3) be responsible for any loss or damage, or both, incurred after loading at named inland point of departure;

*See Note (this page) and Comments on all F.O.B. Terms (page 435).

(4) pay all costs and charges incurred in obtaining the documents issued in the country of origin, or of shipment, or of both, which may be required either for purposes of exportation, or of importation at destination.

*(II-B) "F.O.B. (named inland carrier at named inland point of departure) FREIGHT PREPAID TO (named point of exportation)"**

Under this term, the seller quotes a price includeing transportation charges to the named point of exportation and prepays freight to named point of exportation, without assuming responsibility for the goods after obtaining a clean bill of lading or other transportation receipt at named inland point of departure.

Under this quotation:

Seller must

(1) assume the seller's obligations as under II-a (page 431), except that under (2) he must provide clean bill of lading or other transportation receipt, freight prepaid to named point of exportation.

Buyer must

(1) assume the same buyer's obligations as under II-A (page 431), except that he does not pay freight from loading point to named point of exportation.

*(II-C) "F.O.B. (named inland carrier at named inland point of departure) FREIGHT ALLOWED TO (named point)"**

Under this term, the seller quotes a price including the transportation charges to the named point, shipping freight collect and deducting the cost of transportation, without assuming responsibility for the goods after obtaining a clean bill of lading or other transportation receipt at named inland point of departure.

Under this quotation:

Seller must

(1) assume the same seller's obligations as under II-A (page 431), but deducts from his invoice the transportation cost to named point.

Buyer must

(1) assume the same buyer's obligations as under II-A (page 431), including payment of freight from inland loading point to named point, for which seller has made deduction.

*(II-D) "F.O.B. (named inland carrier at named point of exportation)"**

Under this term, the seller quotes a price including the costs of transportation of the goods to named point of exportation, bearing any loss or damage, or both, incurred up to that point.

Under this quotation:

Seller must

(1) place goods on, or in, conveyance, or deliver to inland carrier for loading;

*See Note (page 431) and Comments on all F.O.B. Terms (page 435).

(2) provide clean bill of lading or other transportation receipt, paying all transportation costs from loading point to named point of exportation;
(3) be responsible for any loss or damage, or both, until goods have arrived in, or on, inland conveyance at the named point of exportation;
(4) render the buyer, at the buyer's request and expense, assistance in obtaining the documents issued in the country of origin, or of shipment, or of both, which the buyer may require either for purposes of exportation, or of importation at destination.

Buyer must
(1) be responsible for all movement of the goods from inland conveyance at named point of exportation;
(2) pay export taxes, or other fees or charges, if any, levied because of exportation;
(3) be responsible for any loss or damage, or both, incurred after goods have arrived in, or on, inland conveyance at the named point of exportation;
(4) pay all costs and charges incurred in obtaining the documents issued in the country of origin, or of shipment, or of both, which may be required either for purposes of exportation, or of importation at destination.

(*II-E*) "*F.O.B. VESSEL* (*named port of shipment*)"*

Under this term, the seller quotes a price covering all expenses up to, and including, delivery of the goods upon the overseas vessel provided by, or for, the buyer at the named port of shipment.

Under this quotation:

Seller must
(1) pay all charges incurred in placing goods actually on board the vessel designated and provided by, or for, the buyer on the date or within the period fixed;
(2) provide clean ship's receipt or on-board bill of lading;
(3) be responsible for any loss or damage, or both, until goods have been placed on board the vessel on the date or within the period fixed;
(4) render the buyer, at the buyer's request and expense, assistance in obtaining the documents issued in the country of origin, or of shipment, or of both, which the buyer may require either for purposes of exportation, or of importation at destination.

Buyer must
(1) give seller adequate notice of name, sailing date, loading berth of, and delivery time to, the vessel;
(2) bear the additional costs incurred and all risks of the goods from the time when the seller has placed them at his disposal if the vessel named by him fails to arrive or to load within the designated time;

*See Note (page 431) and Comments on all F.O.B. Terms (page 435).

(3) handle all subsequent movement of the goods to destination:
  (a) provide and pay for insurance;
  (b) provide and pay for ocean and other transportation;
(4) pay export taxes, or other fees or charges, if any, levied because of exportation;
(5) be responsible for any loss or damage, or both, after goods have been loaded on board the vessel;
(6) pay all costs and charges incurred in obtaining the documents, other than ocean ship's receipt or bill of lading, issued in the country of origin, or of shipment, or of both, which may be required either for purposes of exportation, or of importation at destination.

*(II-F) "F.O.B. (named inland point in country of importation)"**

Under this term, the seller quotes a price including the cost of the merchandise and all costs of transportation to the named inland point in the country of importation.

Under this quotation:

Seller must

(1) provide and pay for all transportation to the named inland point in the country of importation;
(2) pay export taxes, or other fees or charges, if any, levied because of exportation;
(3) provide and pay for marine insurance;
(4) provide and pay for war risk insurance, unless otherwise agreed upon between the seller and buyer;
(5) be responsible for any loss or damage, or both, until arrival of goods on conveyance at the named inland point in the country of importation;
(6) pay the costs of certificates of origin, consular invoices, or any other documents issued in the country of origin, or of shipment, or of both, which the buyer may require for the importation of goods into the country of destination and, where necessary, for their passage in transit through another country;
(7) pay all costs of landing, including wharfage, landing charges, and taxes, if any;
(8) pay all costs of customs entry in the country of importation;
(9) pay customs duties and all taxes applicable to imports, if any, in the country of importation.

NOTE: *The seller under this quotation must realize that he is accepting important responsibilities, costs, and risks, and should therefore be certain to obtain adequate insurance. On the other hand, the importer or buyer may desire such quotations to relieve him of the risks of the voyage and to assure him of his landed costs at inland point in country of importation. When competition is keen, or the buyer is accustomed to such quotations from other sellers, seller may quote such terms, being careful to protect himself in an appropriate manner.*

*See Note (page 431) and Comments on all F.O.B. Terms (page 435).

Buyer must
(1) take prompt delivery of goods from conveyance upon arrival at destination;
(2) bear any costs and be responsible for all loss or damage, or both, after arrival at destination.

Comments On All F.O.B. Terms

In connection with F.O.B. terms, the following points of caution are recommended:

1. The method of inland transportation, such as trucks, railroad cars, lighters, barges, or aircraft should be specified.

2. If any switching charges are involved during the inland transportation, it should be agreed, in advance, whether these charges are for account of the seller or the buyer.

3. The term "F.O.B. (named port)", without designating the exact point at which the liability of the seller terminates and the liability of the buyer begins, should be avoided. The use of this term gives rise to disputes as to the liability of the seller or the buyer in the event of loss or damage arising while the goods are in port, and before delivery to or on board the ocean carrier. Misunderstandings may be avoided by naming the specific point of delivery.

4. If lighterage or trucking is required in the transfer of goods from the inland conveyance to ship's side, and there is a cost therefor, it should be understood, in advance, whether this cost is for account of the seller or the buyer.

5. The seller should be certain to notify the buyer of the minimum quantity required to obtain a carload, a truckload, or a barge-load freight rate.

6. Under F.O.B. terms, excepting "F.O.B. (named inland point in country of importation)", the obligation to obtain ocean freight space, and marine and war risk insurance, rests with the buyer. Despite this obligation on the part of the buyer, in many trades the seller obtains the ocean freight space, and marine and war risk insurance, and provides for shipment on behalf of the buyer. Hence, seller and buyer must have an understanding as to whether the buyer will obtain the ocean freight space, marine and war risk insurance, as is his obligation, or whether the seller agrees to do this for the buyer.

7. For the seller's protection, he should provide in his contract of sale that marine insurance obtained by the buyer include standard warehouse to warehouse coverage.

(III) F.A.S. (Free Along Side)

Note: *Seller and buyer should consider not only the definitions but also the "Comments" given at the end of this section (page 436), in order to understand fully their respective responsibilities and rights under "F.A.S." terms.*

"F.A.S. VESSEL (named port of shipment)"

Under this term, the seller quotes a price including delivery of the goods along side overseas vessel and within reach of its loading tackle.

Under this quotation:

Seller must

(1) place goods alongside vessel or on dock designated and provided by, or for, buyer on the date or within the period fixed; pay any heavy lift charges, where necessary, up to this point;
(2) provide clean dock or ship's receipt;
(3) be responsible for any loss or damage, or both, until goods have been delivered alongside the vessel or on the dock;
(4) render the buyer, at the buyer's request and expense, assistance in obtaining the documents issued in the country of origin, or of shipment, or of both, which the buyer may require either for purposes of exportation, or of importation at destinations.

Buyer must

(1) give seller adequate notice of name, sailing date, loading berth of, and delivery time to, the vessel;
(2) handle all subsequent movement of the goods from along side the vessel:
    (a) arrange and pay for demurrage or storage charges, or both, in warehouse or on wharf, where necessary;
    (b) provide and pay for insurance;
    (c) provide and pay for ocean and other transportation;
(3) pay export taces, or other fees or charges, if any, levied because of exportation;
(4) be responsible for any loss or damage, or both, while the goods are on a lighter or other conveyance alongside vessel within reach of its loading tackle, or on the dock awaiting loading, or until actually loaded on board the vessel, and subsequent thereto;
(5) pay all costs and charges incurred in obtaining the documents, other than clean dock or ship's receipt, issued in the country of origin, or of shipment, or of both, which may be required either for purposes of exportation, or of importation at destination.

F.A.S. Comments

1. Under F.A.S. terms, the obligation to obtain ocean freight space, and marine and war risk insurance, rests with the buyer. Despite this obligation on the part of the buyer, in many trades the seller obtains ocean freight space, and marine and war risk insurance, and provides for shipment on behalf of the buyer. In others, the buyer notifies the seller to make delivery alongside a vessel designated by the buyer and the buyer provides his own marine and war risk insurance. Hence, seller and buyer must have an understanding as to whether the buyer will obtain the ocean freight space, and marine and war risk insurance, as is his obligation, or whether the seller agrees to do this for the buyer.

2. For the seller's protection, he should provide in his contract of sale that marine insurance obtained by the buyer include standard warehouse to warehouse coverage.

(IV) CFR

NOTE: *Seller and buyer should consider not only the definitions but also the "CFR Comments" (below) and the "CFR and C.I.F. Comments" (page 439), in order to understand fully their respective responsibilities and rights under CFR terms.*

"CFR (named point of destination)"

Under this term, the seller quotes a price including the cost of transportation to the named point of destination.

Under this quotation:

Seller must

(1) provide and pay for transportation to named point of destination;
(2) pay export taxes, or other fees or charges, if any, levied because of exportation;
(3) obtain and dispatch promptly to buyer, or his agent, clean bill of lading to named point of destination;
(4) where received-for-shipment ocean bill of lading may be tendered, be responsible for any loss or damage, or both, until the goods have been delivered into the custody of the ocean carrier;
(5) where on-board ocean bill of lading is required, be responsible for any loss or damage, or both, until the goods have been delivered on board the vessel;
(6) provide, at the buyer's request and expense, certificates of origin, consular invoices, or any other documents issued in the country of origin, or of shipment, or of both, which the buyer may require for importation of goods into country of destination and, where necessary, for their passage in transit through another country.

Buyer must

(1) accept the documents when presented;
(2) receive goods upon arrival, handle and pay for all subsequent movement of the goods, including taking delivery from vessel in accordance with bill of lading clauses and terms; pay all costs of landing, including any duties, taxes, and other expenses at named point of destination;
(3) provide and pay for insurance;
(4) be responsible for loss of or damage to goods, or both, from time and place at which seller's obligations under (4) or (5) above have ceased;
(5) pay the costs of certificates of origin, consular invoices, or any other documents issued in the country of origin, or of shipment, or of both, which may be required for the importation of goods into the country of destination and, where necessary, for their passage in transit through another country.

CFR COMMENTS

1. For the seller's protection, he should provide in his contract of sale that marine insurance obtained by the buyer include standard warehouse to warehouse coverage.

2. The comments listed under the following C.I.F. terms in many cases apply to CFR terms as well, and should be read and understood by the CFR seller and buyer.

(V) C.I.F. (Cost, Insurance, Freight)

Note: *Seller and buyer should consider not only the definitions but also the "Comments" (page 439), at the end of this section, in order to understand fully their respective responsibilities and rights under "C.I.F." terms.*

"C.I.F. (named point of destination)"

Under this term, the seller quotes a price including the cost of the goods, the marine insurance, and all transportation charges to the named point of destination.

Under this quotation:

Seller must

(1) provide and pay for transportation to named point of destination;
(2) pay export taxes, or other fees or charges, if any, levied because of exportation;
(3) provide and pay for marine insurance;
(4) provide war risk insurance as obtainable in seller's market at time of shipment at buyer's expense, unless seller has agreed that buyer provide for war risk coverage (See Comment 10 (c), page 440);
(5) obtain and dispatch promptly to buyer, or his agent, clean bill of lading to named point of destination, and also insurance policy or negotiable insurance certificate;
(6) where received-for-shipment ocean bill of lading may be tendered, be responsible for any loss or damage, or both, until the goods have been delivered into the custody of the ocean carrier;
(7) where on-board ocean bill of lading is required, be responsible for any loss or damage, or both, until the goods have been delivered on board the vessel;
(8) provide, at the buyer's request and expense, certificates of origin, consular invoices, or any other documents issued in the country of origin, or of shipment, or both, which the buyer may require for importation of goods into country of destination and, where necessary, for their passage in transit through another country.

Buyer must

(1) accept the documents when presented;
(2) receive the goods upon arrival, handle and pay for all subsequent movements of the goods, including taking delivery from vessel in accordance with bill of lading clauses and terms; pay all costs of landing, including any duties, taxes, and other expenses at named point of destination;
(3) pay for war risk insurance provided by seller;
(4) be responsible for loss of or damage to goods, or both, from time and place at which seller's obligations under (6) or (7) above have ceased;
(5) pay the cost of certificates of origin, consular invoices, or any

other documents issued in the country of origin, or of shipment, or both, which may be required for importation of the goods into the country of destination and, where necessary, for their passage in transit through another country.

CFR and C.I.F. Comments

Under CFR and C.I.F. contracts there are the following points on which the seller and the buyer should be in complete agreement at the time that the contract is concluded:

1. It should be agreed upon, in advance, who is to pay for miscellaneous expenses, such as weighing or inspection charges.
2. The quantity to be shipped on any one vessel should be agreed upon, in advance, with a view to the buyer's capacity to take delivery upon arrival and discharge of the vessel; within the free time allowed at the port of importation.
3. Although the terms CFR and C.I.F. are generally interpreted to provide that charges for consular invoices and certificates of origin are for the account of the buyer, and are charged separately, in many trades these charges are included by the seller in his price. Hence, seller and buyer should agree, in advance, whether these charges are part of the selling price, or will be invoiced separately.
4. The point of final destination should be definitely known in the event the vessel discharges at a port other than the actual destination of the goods.
5. When ocean freight space is difficult to obtain, or forward freight contracts cannot be made at firm rates, it is advisable that sales contracts, as an exception to regular CFR or C.I.F. terms, should provide that shipment within the contract period be subject to ocean freight space being available to the seller, and should also provide that changes in the cost of ocean transportation between the time of the sale and the time of shipment be for account of the buyer.
6. Normally, the seller is obligated to prepay the ocean freight. In some instances, shipments are made freight collect and the amount of the freight is deducted from the invoice rendered by the seller. It is necessary to be in agreement on this, in advance, in order to avoid misunderstanding which arises from foreign exchange fluctuations which might affect the actual cost of transportation, and from interest charges which might accrue under letter of credit financing. Hence, the seller should always prepay the ocean freight unless he has a specific agreement with the buyer, in advance, that goods can be shipped freight collect.
7. The buyer should recognize that he does not have the right to insist on inspection of goods prior to accepting the documents. The buyer should not refuse to take delivery of goods on account of delay in the receipt of documents, provided the seller has used due diligence in their dispatch through the regular channels.
8. Sellers and buyers are advised against including in a C.I.F. contract any indefinite clause at variance with the obligations of a C.I.F. contract as specified in these Definitions. There have been numerous court decisions in the United States and other countries invalidating C.I.F. contracts because of the inclusion of indefinite clauses.

9. Interest charges should be included in cost computations and should not be charged as a separate item in C.I.F. contracts, unless otherwise agreed upon, in advance, between the seller and buyer; in which case, however, the term C.I.F. and I. (Cost, Insurance, Freight, and Interest) should be used.

10. In connection with insurance under C.I.F. sales, it is necessary that seller and buyer be definitely in accord upon the following points:

(a) The character of the marine insurance should be agreed upon in so far as being W.A. (With Average) or F.P.A. (Free of Particular Average), as well as any other special risks that are covered in specific trades, or against which the buyer may wish individual protection. Among the special risks that should be considered and agreed upon between seller and buyer are theft, pilferage, leakage, breakage, sweat, contact with other cargoes, and others peculiar to any particular trade. It is important that contingent or collect freight and customs duty should be insured to cover Particular Average losses, as well as total loss after arrival and entry but before delivery.

(b) The seller is obligated to exercise ordinary care and diligence in selecting an underwriter that is in good financial standing. However, the risk of obtaining settlement of insurance claims rests with the buyer.

(c) War risk insurance under this term is to be obtained by the seller at the expense and risk of the buyer. It is important that the seller be in definite accord with the buyer on this point, particularly as to the cost. It is desirable that the goods be insured against both marine and war risk with the same underwriter, so that there can be no difficulty arising from the determination of the cause of the loss.

(d) Seller should make certain that in his marine or war risk insurance, there be included the standard protection against strikes, riots and civil commotions.

(e) Seller and buyer should be in accord as to the insured valuation, bearing in mind that merchandise contributes in General Average on certain bases of valuation which differ in various trades. It is desirable that a competent insurance broker be consulted, in order that full value be covered and trouble avoided.

(VI) DEQ Delivered

Ex Quay (Duty Paid)

Note: *Seller and buyer should consider not only the definitions but also the "DEQ Comments" at the end of this section (page 441), in order to understand fully their respective responsibilities and rights under "DEQ" terms.*

Under this term, seller quotes a price including the cost of the goods and all additional costs necessary to place the goods on the dock at the named port of importation, duty paid, if any.

Under this quotation:

Seller must

(1) provide and pay for transportation to named port of importation;
(2) pay export taxes, or other fees or charges, if any, levied because of exportation;
(3) provide and pay for marine insurance;

(4) provide and pay for war risk insurance, unless otherwise agreed upon between the buyer and seller;
(5) be responsible for any loss or damage, or both, until the expiration of the free time allowed on the dock at the named port of importation;
(6) pay the costs of certificates of origin, consular invoices, legalization of bill of lading, or any other documents issued in the country of origin, or of shipment, or of both, which the buyer may require for the importation of goods into the country of destination and, where necessary, for their passage in transit through another country;
(7) pay all costs of landing, including wharfage, landing charges and taxes, if any;
(8) pay all costs of customs entry in the country of importation;
(9) pay customs duties and all taxes applicable to imports, if any, in the country of importation, unless otherwise agreed upon.

Buyer must
(1) take delivery of the goods on the dock at the named port of importation within the free time allowed;
(2) bear the cost and risk of the goods if delivery is not taken within the free time allowed.

DEQ Comments

This term is used principally in United States import trade. It has various modifications, such as "Ex Quay", "Ex Pier", etc., but it is seldom, if ever, used in American export practice. Its use in quotations for export is not recommended.

APPENDIX 4

Programs of the Export-Import Bank of the United States

The Export-Import Bank of the United States is the U.S. government agency that helps finance export sales of U.S. goods and services. In its fifty-four years of operation, Eximbank has used loan, guarantee, and insurance programs to support more than $152 billion in U.S. exports.

Eximbank has an agency and reinsurance agreement with the Foreign Credit Insurance Association (FCIA), a group of U.S. property, casualty, and marine insurance companies, that sells and services its export credit insurance policies.

The following chart summarizes the major features of Eximbank's export finance and insurance programs. It was designed so that you can easily determine the program most appropriate for specific export transactions.

The information presented gives a general overview of each program. Eximbank should be contacted for complete program details and application instructions. The appropriate address is Marketing Department, Eximbank, 811 Vermont Avenue, NW, Washington, DC 20571.

COUNTRY CATEGORIES

The interest rates on Eximbank's Direct Loan Program, Engineering Multiplier Program, Medium-Term Credit Program, and Small Business Credit Program are determined by the classification of the country to which the export will be shipped. Eximbank uses the following country classification adopted in the OECD Arrangement on Officially Supported Export Credits:

Rich Countries

Andorra; Australia; Austria; Bahrain; Belgium; Bermuda; Brunei; Canada; Czechoslovakia; Denmark; Finland; France; Germany; Greece; Iceland; Ireland; Israel; Italy; Japan; Kuwait; Liechtenstein; Luxembourg; Libya; Monaco; Netherlands; New Zealand; Norway; Qatar; San Marino; Saudi Arabia; Spain; Sweden; Switzerland; United Arab Emirates; United Kingdom; United States; United Soviet Socialist Republic; Vatican City.

Intermediate Countries

Albania; Algeria; Antigua; Argentina; Bahamas; Barbados; Belize; Botswana; Brazil; Bulgaria; Colombia; Chile; Costa Rica; Cuba; Cyprus; Dominican Republic; Ecuador; Fiji; Gabon; Gibraltar; Guatemala; Hong Kong; Hungary; iran; Iraq; Ivory Coast; Jamaica; Jordan; Kiribati; Korea, North; Korea, South; Lebanon; Macao; Malaysia; Malta; Mauritius; Mexico; Montserrat; Morocco; Namibia; Nauru; Netherlands Antilles; Nigeria; Oman; Panama; Papua New Guinea; Paraguay; Peru; Poland; Portugal; Romania; St. Kitts-Nevis; St. Lucia; Seychelles; Singapore; South Africa; Suriname; Syria; Taiwan; Trinidad & Tobago; Tunisia; Uruguay; Venezuela; Yugoslavia.

Developing Countries

Angola; Bangladesh; Benin; Bolivia; Burkina; Burma; Burundi; Cameroon; Central African Republic; Chad; China; Congo, People's Republic; Egypt; El Salvador; Ethiopia; Gambia; Ghana; Guinea-Bissau; Haiti; Honduras; India; Indonesia; Kenya; Lesotho; Liberia; Madagascar; Malawi; Mali; Mauritania; Mozambique; Nepal; Nicaragua; Niger; Pakistan; Philippines; Rwanda; Senegal; Sierra Leone; Somalia; Sri Lanka; Sudan; Tanzania; Thailand; Togo; Uganda; Yemen Arab Republic; Yemen, People's Democratic Republic; Zaire; Zambia; Zimbabwe.

(Note: Not all the countries listed are eligible for Eximbank financing.)

Eximbank Programs

Program	Eligible Nonmilitary U.S. Products and Services	Description	Eligible Applicants
Eximbank Working Capital Guarantee Program	All products and services.	Loan guarantee program designed to provide eligible exporters with access to working capital loans from commercial lenders.	Commercial lenders financing export-related working capital loans principally for creditworthy small- to medium-sized businesses.
FCIA New-To-Export Insurance Policy	Consumables, raw materials, spare parts, agricultural commodities, consumer durables and services.	One-year blanket policy insuring all eligible short-term export credit sales.	Companies that are just beginning to export or have an average annual export sales volume of less than $750,000 for past 2 years. Exporters must not have used FCIA in the past 2 years.
FCIA Umbrella Insurance Policy	Consumables, raw materials, spare parts, agricultural commodities, consumer durables and services.	One-year blanket policy insuring all eligible short-term export credit sales of exporters with average annual export credit sales of less than $2 million for the past 2 years and who have not used FCIA in the past 2 years.	Any entity capable of administering a policy on behalf of multiple exporters.
FCIA Short-Term Insurance Policy	Consumables, raw materials, spare parts, agricultural commodities, consumer durables and services.	One-year blanket policy insuring all eligible short-term export credit sales.	Exporters of U.S. goods and services or financial institutions in the United States.
FCIA Medium-Term Insurance Policy	Capital equipment and services including automobiles/trucks, general aviation aircraft, mining, construction and agricultural equipment, processing and communications equipment, and planning/feasibility studies.	Single buyer policy insuring individual medium-term export credit sales.	Exporters of U.S. goods and services or financial institutions in the United States.

Eximbank Programs *(Continued)*

Program	Eligible Nonmilitary U.S. Products and Services	Description	Eligible Applicants
FCIA Combined Short-Term/ Medium-Term Insurance Policy	Capital equipment including automobiles/ trucks, construction, mining and agricultural equipment, and general aviation aircraft.	Single buyer policy for repetitive export sales to a dealer or distributor. Policy provides insurance for short-term inventory financing followed by medium-term coverage for receivables financing.	Exporters of U.S. goods or financial institutions in the United States.
FCIA Master Insurance Policy	All products eligible for short-term or medium-term insurance.	One-year blanket policy insuring all eligible short- and medium-term export credit sales.	Exporters of U.S. goods who conduct a sizable export business, particularly those selling to an extensive dealer network overseas.
Eximbank Medium-Term Bank Guarantee Program	Capital equipment and services including automobiles/trucks, general aviation aircraft, mining, construction and agricultural equipment, processing and communications equipment, and planning/feasibility studies.	Guarantee by Eximbank of export financing extended to individual foreign buyers. Covers either single or repetitive sales to single buyer.	Approved commercial banking institutions in the United States.
Eximbank Small Business Credit Program	Capital equipment and services produced by eligible small businesses.	Eximbank funding commitment to enable U.S. banks to offer medium-term fixed rate export loans at the lowest rates permitted under the internationally agreed export credit guidelines.	Approved commercial banking institutions in the U.S. financing exports produced by small businesses (as defined by the Small Business Administration).
Eximbank Medium-Term Credit Program	Capital equipment and services including automobiles/truck, general aviation aircraft, mining, construction and agricultural	Same as Small Business Credit Program except (a) the exporter need not be a small business, (b) the exporter must face officially	Approved commercial banking institutions in the United States.

Eximbank Programs *(Continued)*

Program	Eligible Nonmilitary U.S. Products and Services	Description	Eligible Applicants
	equipment, processing and communications equipment, and planning/feasibility studies.	supported subsidized foreign competition.	
Eximbank Preliminary Commitment	Major projects or major procurement including power generation/transmission projects, mining and industrial projects, project-related services, commercial jet aircraft, and locomotives.	Offer from Eximbank detailing, in advance of a particular transaction, the terms and conditions for direct loan/financial guarantee support.	Prospective borrower, exporter, or financial institution.
Engineering Multiplier Program	Project-related feasibility studies and preconstruction design and engineering services.	Medium-term, fixed interest rate direct loans to support up to $10 million of services for projects with potential for procurement of U.S. equipment and services worth $10 million or twice the amount of the original contract, whichever is greater.	Creditworthy foreign buyers. (Exporter may apply for Preliminary Commitment).
Eximbank Direct Loan	Major projects or major procurement including power generation/transmission projects, mining and industrial projects, project-related services, commercial jet aircraft, and locomotives.	Long-term, fixed interest rate loan program for export sales facing officially-supported foreign competition.	Creditworthy foreign buyers.
Eximbank Financial Guarantee	Major projects or major procurement including power generation/transmission projects, mining and industrial projects, project-related services, commercial jet aircraft, and locomotives.	Guarantee by Eximbank of export financing extended to foreign buyers.	Domestic or foreign financial institutions.

Eximbank Programs *(Continued)*

Program	Eligible Nonmilitary U.S. Products and Services	Description	Eligible Applicants
Private Export Funding Corporation (PEFCO)	Major projects or major procurement including power generation/transmission projects, mining and industrial projects, project-related services, commercial jet aircraft, and locomotives.	Medium- and long-term fixed interest rate loans guaranteed by Eximbank.	Financial institutions, U.S. exporters, or creditworthy foreign buyers.

Program	Maximum Coverage	Maximum Repayment Period	Fees and Premiums
Eximbank Working Capital Guarantee Program	Guarantee applies to 90% of the principal amount of the loan and interest up to the U.S. Treasury rate plus 1%.	Generally up to 12 months.	One percent of the loan amount up to 6 months; 0.5% for each additional 6 months or portion thereof.
FCIA New-To-Export Insurance Policy	100% Political Risk Protection. 95% Commercial Risk Protection (98% for bulk agricultural sales). Interest up to U.S. Treasury rate plus 1%.	180 days (360 days for bulk agricultural commodities and consumer durables).	Varies with each sale but is usually priced 0.25 to 1.00% of sales value. Minimum annual premium of $500.
FCIA Umbrella Insurance Policy	100% Political Risk Protection. 90% Commercial Risk Protection (98% for bulk agricultural sales). Interest up to U.S. Treasury rate plus 1%.	180 days (360 days for bulk agricultural commodities and consumer durables).	Same fee rates as FCIA New-to-Export Policy. $500 minimum annual premium is paid by the Umbrella Policyholder/Administrator in advance.
FCIA Short-Term Insurance Policy	100% Political Risk Protection. 90% Commercial Risk Protection (98% for bulk agricultural sales) after annual first-loss deductible. Interest up to U.S. Treasury rate plus 1%.	180 days (360 days for bulk agricultural commodities and consumer durables).	Premium rate is determined by factors such as insured's sales profile, history of export credit losses, average term of repayment, and size of first-loss commercial deductible.

Eximbank Programs *(Continued)*

Program	Maximum Coverage	Maximum Repayment Period	Fees and Premiums
FCIA Medium-Term Insurance Policy	100% Political Risk Protection. 90% Commercial Risk Protection. Interest up to U.S. Treasury rate plus 1%.	Contract Value / Maximum Term (yrs.): Up to $50,000 — 2; $50,000 to $100,000 — 3; $100,000 to $200,000 — 4; Over $200,000 — 5 (Exceptionally up to 7 years).	Varies from 1 to 6.5% of export receivable depending on term and nature of buyer.
FCIA Combined Short-Term/ Medium-Term Insurance Policy	100% Political Risk Protection. 90% Commercial Risk Protection. Interest up to U.S. Treasury rate plus 1%.	Up to 270 days for inventory phase followed by up to 3 years for receivables financing (exceptionally 5 years).	Varies from 1.25 to 6.5% of export receivable depending on term and nature of buyer.
FCIA Master Insurance Policy	100% Political Risk Protection. 90% Commercial Risk Protection after annual first-loss deductible. Interest up to U.S. Treasury rate plus 1%.	Same as FCIA Short-Term Policy for short-term sales. Same as FCIA Medium-Term Policy for medium-term sales.	Same as FCIA Short-Term Policy.
Eximbank Medium-Term Bank Guarantee Program	100% Political Risk Protection. For commercial risk, after the exporter retains a 10% participation, the financing bank assumes 5 or 15% participation and Eximbank covers the balance. Interest up to U.S. Treasury rate plus 1%.	Same as FCIA Medium-Term Policy.	Same as FCIA Medium-Term Policy.
Eximbank Small Business Credit Program	The outstanding balance of the export loan.	Same as FCIA Medium-Term Policy.	Eximbank charges financial institution a one-time commitment fee at beginning of transaction of 0.15 to 0.75%, depending on term of loan.
Eximbank Medium-Term Credit Program	The outstanding balance of the export loan.	Same as FCIA Medium-Term Policy.	Same as Small Business Credit Program.

Eximbank Programs *(Continued)*

Program	Maximum Coverage	Maximum Repayment Period	Fees and Premiums
Eximbank Preliminary Commitment	Not applicable.	Not applicable.	None.
Engineering Multiplier Program	Loan for 85% of U.S. costs. Financial guarantee for local costs up to 15% of the eligible U.S. costs.	Same as FCIA Medium-Term Policy.	Same as Eximbank Direct Loan and Financial Guarantee.
Eximbank Direct Loan	Loan up to 65% of the export value, or up to 75% when supplier extends 10% credit to buyer at same interest rate as Eximbank.	5 to 10 years (exceptionally longer for nuclear projects) beginning at delivery or start up.	Eximbank charges borrower a 2% fee when loan is approved and a 0.5% per annum commitment fee on the undisbursed balance.
Eximbank Financial Guarantee	100% Political and Commercial Risk Protection. Interest up to the U.S. Treasury rate plus 1%.	Same as Eximbank Direct Loan.	Eximbank charges the lender a financial guarantee fee of 0.5% per annum on the outstanding balance and a commitment fee of 0.125% per annum on the undisbursed balance.
Private Export Funding Corporation (PEFCO)	Loan up to 85% of the export value.	Usually 5 to 10 years.	Commitment Fee: 0.5% per annum of undisbursed balance. Interest rate to borrower usually averages 1% to 2% over comparable rate for U.S. Treasury obligation.

Eximbank Programs *(Continued)*

Program	Minimum Buyer Cash Payment	Financing Characteristics	Special Features
Eximbank Working Capital Guarantee Program	Not Applicable.	Guarantee is made with recourse to exporter. The exporter must provide the lender with sufficient collateral so that the loan balance does not exceed 90% of the collateral value.	The guarantee can be for either a single export-related loan or for a revolving line of credit.
FCIA New-To-Export Insurance Policy	None.	Policy proceeds are assignable for financing purposes. Under special assignment, financial institutions are assured of repayment up to policy limits in event of default.	Political risk only coverage also available. Initially no annual commercial risk deductible required.
FCIA Umbrella Insurance Policy	None.	Same as FCIA New-to-Export Policy.	Policy Administrator relieves exporter of administrative responsibilities by providing for all required reporting to/from FCIA, including premium payment. No exporter commercial risk deductible or minimum annual premium required of exporters.
FCIA Short-Term Insurance Policy	None.	Same as FCIA New-To-Export Policy.	Political risk only coverage also available. Exporter has some discretionary authority to sell on insured basis without FCIA buyer clearance.
FCIA Medium-Term Insurance Policy	15% at shipment.	Policy proceeds are assignable for financing purposes. Medium-Term obligations are in the form of notes which usually carry a floating market rate	Political risk only coverage also available. No annual commercial risk deductible required. Covers either single or repetitive sales to a single buyer. 95%

Eximbank Programs *(Continued)*

Program	Minimum Buyer Cash Payment	Financing Characteristics	Special Features
		of interest, paid at least semi-annually.	commercial risk protection for small businesses.
FCIA Combined Short-Term/ Medium-Term Insurance Policy	None for short-term financing. 15% when rolled over to medium-term.	Dealers can purchase inventory for resale without making a cash payment for up to 270 days (360 days if no rollover to medium-term).	Usually issued to cover a one-year revolving sales plan. No annual commercial risk deductible required.
FCIA Master Insurance Policy	None for short-term sales. 15% for medium-term sales.	Policy proceeds are assignable for financing purposes.	Political risk only coverage is also available. Reduced premium rate due to blanket policy and commercial risk deductible requirement. Exporter can insure most sales without clearing buyers through FCIA.
Eximbank Medium-Term Bank Guarantee Program	15% at shipment.	Except for specified exporter's commercial risk participation, the financing must be provided without recourse to the exporter. Medium-Term obligations are in the form of notes which usually carry a floating market rate of interest, paid at least semi-annually.	Political risk only coverage also available. Qualified banks can commit Eximbank's Guarantee on a discretionary basis by assuming a 15% commercial risk participation. Small businesses retain only 5% commercial risk participation. Available for loans in selected foreign currencies.
Eximbank Small Business Credit Program	15% at shipment.	The interest rate may be as mutually agreed but must not yield less than the following consensus rates: 13.35% for rich countries, 11.55% for intermediate countries, and 10.7% for poor countries (as of 7/15/84). Eximbank	The repayment risk on the foreign obligation is borne by the financial institution unless that obligation is also insured or guaranteed by Eximbank/FCIA. Maximum contract value is $2.5 million

Eximbank Programs *(Continued)*

Program	Minimum Buyer Cash Payment	Financing Characteristics	Special Features
		will lend or purchase the export loan with recourse to the commercial bank at 1% below the rate charged.	per transaction. Aggregate commitment cannot exceed $10 million per buyer, per year.
Eximbank Medium-Term Credit Program	15% at shipment.	Same as Small Business Credit Program.	The repayment risk on the foreign obligation is borne by the financial institution unless that obligation is also guaranteed or insured by Eximbank/FCIA. Maximum contract value is $10 million per transaction.
Eximbank Preliminary Commitment	Not applicable.	Enables borrower, exporter, and financial institution to establish terms of financing for more effective planning or marketing.	Generally valid for 180 days but may be renewed at discretion of Eximbank. Buyer must apply to Eximbank to convert a preliminary commitment to a loan or a financial guarantee.
Engineering Multiplier Program	15% prior to or concurrently with loan disbursement by Eximbank.	Eximbank's interest rates (as of 7/15/84) for 2–5 year loans are: 13.35% for rich countries, 11.55% for intermediate countries and 10.7% for poor countries. If Eximbank undertakes final project financing, preconstruction lending can be rolled over into long-term financial package.	Contract amounts in excess of $10 million eligible for Eximbank's regular Direct Loan and Financial Guarantee. Preliminary Commitment available for up to 180 days. Available for negotiated contracts if foreign competition would be encountered if given the opportunity to bid.

Eximbank Programs *(Continued)*

Program	Minimum Buyer Cash Payment	Financing Characteristics	Special Features
Eximbank Direct Loan	15% at shipment.	Eximbank's interest rates (as of 7/15/84) are as follows: 13.6% for rich countries, 11.9% for intermediate countries and 10.7% for poor countries.	If Eximbank's loan is blended with commercial bank or PEFCO loan, Eximbank portion will apply to the later maturities.
Eximbank Financial Guarantee	15% at shipment.	Eximbank often blends its direct loan with its financial guarantee to provide a complete financing package. Guarantee may extend up to 85% of the export, depending on the amount of Eximbank's loan, if any.	Financial guarantee also available for loans in select foreign currencies.
Private Export Funding Corporation (PEFCO)	15% at shipment.	PEFCO is often co-lender with commercial banks lending the earlier maturities, PEFCO the middle maturities and Eximbank financing the later maturities. Loan size ranges from $1 million with no upper limit.	Several different options are available to the applicant for determining when PEFCO's interest rate is set.

APPENDIX 5

Guide to Federal Reserve Regulations

This appendix is designed to give the reader a general overview of the regulations issued by the Board of Governors of the Federal Reserve System and not intended to cover each regulation in detail.

The headings (only) are listed below.

A — Loans to Depository Institutions
B — Equal Credit Opportunity
C — Home Mortgage Disclosure
D — Reserve Requirements
E — Electronic Fund Transfers
F — Securities of Member Banks
G — Margin Credit Extended by Parties Other Than Banks, Brokers, and Dealers
H — Membership Requirements for State-Chartered Banks
I — Member Stock in Federal Reserve Banks
J — Check Collection and Funds Transfer
K — International Banking Operations
L — Interlocking Bank Relationships
M — Consumer Leasing
N — Relationships with Foreign Banks
O — Loans to Executive Officers of Member Banks
P — Member Bank Protection Standards
Q — Interest on Deposits
R — Interlocking Relationships between Securities Dealers and Member Banks
S — Reimbursement for Providing Financial Records

T — Margin Credit Extended by Brokers and Dealers
U — Margin Credit Extended by Banks
V — Guarantee of Loans for National Defense Work
W — Extension of Consumer Credit (revoked)
X — Borrowers Who Obtain Margin Credit
Y — Bank Holding Companies
Z — Truth in Lending
AA — Consumer Complaint Procedures
BB — Community Reinvestment

REGULATIONS GROUPED BY SUBJECT

Bank Holding Companies	Regulation Y
Federal Reserve Banks	Regulations A, I, J, N, V, and BB
Foreign Banking Business	Regulations K, M, and N
Interlocking Directorates	Regulation L and R
Other Member Bank Requirements	Regulations F, H, O, P, Q, and U
Consumer Protection	Regulations B, C, E, M, Z and AA
Monetary Policy	Regulations A, D, and Q
Securities Credit	Regulations G, T, U, and X
Financial Privacy	Regulation S

Regulation A governs borrowing by depository institutions at the Federal Reserve discount window.

The Federal Reserve discount window is open to any depository institution that maintains transaction accounts or nonpersonal time deposits. The regulation provides for lending under two basic programs. First, adjustment credit is advanced for brief periods to help borrowers meet short-term needs for funds when their usual sources, including such special industry lenders as the Federal Home Loan Bank Board, are not reasonably available. Second, extended credit is designed to assist depository institutions meet longer-term needs for funds. This category includes seasonal credit to smaller depository institutions lacking access to market funds; asssitance to an individual depository institution that experiences special difficulties arising from exceptional circumstances; and assistance to address liquidity strains affecting a broad range of depository institutions. Emergency credit may also be advanced to entities other than depository institutions where failure to obtain credit would adversely affect the economy.

Regulation B prohibits creditors from discrimination against credit applicants, establishes guidelines for gathering and evaluating credit information, and requires written notification when credit is denied.

The regulation prohibits creditors from discriminating against applicants on the basis of age, race, color, religion, national origin, gender, marital status, or receipt of income from public assistance programs. As a general rule, creditors may not ask on applications the race, color, religion, national origin, or gender of applicants. In addition, if the application is for individual, unsecured credit, the creditor may not ask the applicant's marital status. Exceptions apply in the case of residential mortgage applications, as noted below. Creditors also may not discriminate against applicants who exercise their rights under the Federal Consumer Credit laws.

Model credit application forms are provided in the regulation to facilitate compliance. By properly using these forms, creditors can be assured of being in compliance with the application requirements of the regulation. Creditors may use credit-scoring systems that allocate points or weights to key applicant characteristics. Creditors also may rely on their own judgment of an applicant's creditworthiness.

The regulation also requires creditors to give applicants a written notification of rejection of an application, a statement of the applicant's rights under the Equal Credit Opportunity Act, and a statement either of the reasons for the rejection or of the applicant's right to request the reasons. Creditors who furnish credit information, when reporting information on married borrowers, must report information in the names of each spouse.

The regulation establishes a special residential mortgage credit monitoring system for regulatory agencies by requiring that lenders ask residential mortgage applicants their race/national origin, gender, marital status, and age.

Regulation C requires depository institutions making federally related mortgage loans to make annual public disclosure of the locations of certain residential loans. The regulation carries out the Home Mortgage Disclosure Act of 1975, which seeks to provide citizens and public officials with enough information to determine whether depository institutions are meeting the housing credit needs of their local communities.

The regulation applies to commercial banks, savings banks, savings and loan associations, building and loan associations, homestead associations, and credit unions that make federally related mortgage loans, with the exception of institutions with assets under $10 million and institutions that do not have a home office in an SMSA (Standard Metropolitan Statistical Area). Institutions covered by the regulation must disclose annually, in central locations within their communities, the number and total principal amount of (a) residential mortgage loans originated or purchased and (b) home improvement loans originated or purchased during the most recent calendar year.

The Board of Governors is charged with writing regulations to carry out the Act, while enforcement is left to the appropriate federal financial regulatory agencies. The Board may exempt from Regulation C any institutions complying with substantially similar state or municipal laws or regulations that have adequate provision for enforcement.

Regulation D imposes uniform reserve requirements on all depository institutions with transactions accounts or nonpersonal time deposits; defines such deposits and requires reports of deposits to the Federal Reserve; and sets phase-in schedules for reserve requirements.

Regulation D sets uniform reserve requirements on all depository institutions—including commercial banks, savings banks, savings and loan associations, credit unions, and industrial banks—that have transaction accounts or nonpersonal time deposits.

Transaction accounts are defined to include checking accounts, NOW accounts, share draft accounts, savings that allow automatic transfers or third party payments by automated teller machines, and accounts that permit more than three telephone or preauthorized payments or transfers each month. The Reserve requirement on transactions accounts is 33% of the first $25 million of net transactions balances and 12% of the rest.

Time deposits with original maturities of four years or more presently are subject to a zero percent reserve requirement. Nontransferable time deposits (including personal savings deposits) with maturities of less than four years do not have to be backed by reserves when they are owned by natural persons. Nonpersonal time deposits owned by anyone else and transferable time deposits are subject to a 3% reserve requirement.

Time deposits are deposits or certificates with original maturities of at least 14 days, and savings accounts (including regular share accounts at credit unions and regular accounts at thrifts) that allow the institution to require at least 14 days' notice by the depositor before a withdrawal is made.

Reserves are maintained in the form of cash or a noninterest-bearing balance held with a Federal Reserve Bank on a direct or indirect basis.

Reserves for nonmember depository institutions are being phased in over an eight year period that began in late 1980 and for members over a 3½ year period.

Regulation E establishes the rights, liabilities, and responsibilities of parties in electronic fund transfers and protects consumers using EFT Systems.

Regulation E prescribes rules for the solicitation and issuance of EFT cards; governs consumers' liability for lost or stolen cards; requires institutions to disclose certain terms and conditions of EFT services; provides for documentation of electronic transfers; sets up a resolution procedure for errors on EFT accounts; and covers notice of crediting and stoppage of preauthorized payments to and from a customer's account.

Regulation F requires certain state-chartered member banks to register and file financial statements with the Board of Governors.

The regulation applies to state-chartered member banks that have 500 or more stockholders and at least $1 million in assets, or whose securities are registered on a national securities exchange. Generally, it does not apply to banks whose shares are owned by holding companies since these usually have fewer than 500 stockholders.

In general, these state chartered member banks must file registration statements, periodic financial statements, proxy statements, statements of election contests, and various other disclosures of interest to investors. Officers, directors, and principal stockholders also must file reports on their holdings in the bank.

The regulation also prohibits tender offers for the stock of a bank subject to the regulation unless certain information is filed with the Board at the same time.

Regulations issued by the Board of Governors in this area are substantially similar to those issued by the Securities and Exchange Commission. Information filed under the provisions of Regulation F is available to the public at the offices of the Board of Governors in Washington, D.C., and at the Federal Reserve Bank in the district where the registrant is located.

Regulation G is one of four regulations concerning credit extended to finance securities transactions (see also Regulations T, U, and X). Regulation G governs credit secured by margin securities extended or arranged by parties other than banks, brokers, and dealers.

The regulation applies, with the exceptions noted, to any party who normally extends or arranges credit secured by margin securities of $100,000 or more in a calendar quarter, or who has credit outstanding to $500,000 or more during a quarter. These lenders must register with the Board of Governors within 30 days after the quarter ends.

Margin securities are those listed on national exchanges, securities convertible into margin securities, most mutual funds, and over-the-counter securities identified by the Board of Governors' Over-the-Counter (OTC) list. (The OTC list published periodically by the Board is available from the Board or at Federal Reserve Banks.) The amount of credit a registered lender can extend or arrange for a securities transaction based on margin securities may not exceed the "maximum loan value" of the stock securing the credit. The maximum loan value of stock is a percentage of current market value fixed by the Board from time to time.

The regulation also includes special provisions covering loans to finance purchases of securities under stock option plans.

Regulation H defines the membership requirements for state-chartered banks, describes membership privileges and conditions imposed on these banks, explains financial reporting requirements, and sets out procedures for requesting approval to establish branches and for requesting voluntary withdrawal from membership.

State member banks are prohibited under the regulation from engaging in practices that are unsafe or unsound or that result in violation of law, rule, or regulation.

The regulation also prohibits state-chartered member banks from making or renewing loans secured by improved real estate or mobile homes located or to be located in flood hazard areas not covered by the National Flood Insurance Program.

The Regulation also requires state-chartered member banks acting as securities transfer agents to register with the Board of Governors.

Regulation I requires each bank joining the Federal Reserve System to subscribe to the stock of its District Reserve Bank in an amount equal to 6% of the member bank's capital and surplus. Half the total must be paid on approval. The remainder is subject to call by the Board of Governors.

A 6% dividend is paid on paid-in portions of Reserve Bank stock. The stock is not transferable and cannot be used as collateral.

Whenever a member bank increases or decreases its permanent capitalization, it must adjust its ownership of Reserve Bank stock to maintain the same ratio of stock to capital. Payment for additional shares of Reserve Bank stock, cancellation of shares, as well as semi-annual dividend payments, are made through the member bank's reserve account.

A member bank's ownership of Federal Reserve stock is subject to cancellation on discontinuance of operations, insolvency, or voluntary liquidation, conversion to nonmember status through merger or acquisition, or voluntary or involuntary termination of membership.

Regulation J establishes procedures, duties, and responsibilities among Federal Reserve Banks and (1) the senders and payers of checks and other cash items, and noncash items, and (2) the originators and recipients of transfers of funds.

Regulation J provides a legal framework for depository institutions to collect checks and other cash items, and to settle balances through the Federal Reserve System. It specifies terms and conditions under which Reserve Banks will receive items for collection from depository institutions and present items to depository institutions, and establishes rules under which depository institutions return unpaid items. The regulation also specifies terms and conditions under which Reserve banks will receive and deliver transfers of funds from and to depository institutions.

The regulation is supplemented by operating circulars issued by the Reserve Banks and detailing more specific terms and conditions under which they will handle checks and other cash items, noncash items, and transfer of funds.

Regulation K governs the organization, capitalization, and operations of domestic corporations involved in international banking or finance, and certain operations of foreign banks and banking organizations in the United States.

Corporations organized to engage in international banking or other financial operations are chartered by the Board of Governors under Section 25(a) of the Federal Reserve Act. This section of the Act was introduced as an amendment in 1919 by Senator Walter E. Edge of New Jersey. Thus, these corporations are known as "Edge Corporations."

The regulation permits Edge Corporations to engage in a broad range of international banking and financial activities, subject to supervision, while limiting transactions within the United States to those clearly international in character. It also imposes reserve requirements on certain deposits of these corporations.

As to foreign bank operations, the regulation reflects limitation of the International Banking Act on interstate banking and specific exemptions from nonbanking prohibitions.

Regulation L seeks to avoid restraints on competition among depository organizations by restricting the interlocking relationships that a management official may have with depository organizations.

The regulation prohibits a management official of a state member bank, bank holding company, or nonbank affiliate from serving simultaneously as a management official of another depository organization if both organizations are not affiliated, or are very large, or are located in the same local area.

The regulation provides a ten-year grandfather period for certain interlocks and defines changes in circumstances that will cause interlocks to become prohibited. Exceptions are provided for certain interlocks, including those involving depository organizations in low income or economically depressed areas, organizations owned by women or minority groups, newly chartered organizations and organizations facing disruptive management loss or conditions endangering safety and soundness.

Regulation M implements the consumer leasing provisions of the Truth in Lending Act.

Regulation M applies to leases of personal property for more than four months for personal, family, or household use. It requires leasing companies to disclose in writing the cost of a lease, including security deposit, monthly payments, license, registration, taxes, and maintenance fees and, in the case of an open end lease, whether a "balloon payment" may be applied. It also requires written disclosure of the terms of a lease, including insurance, guarantees, responsibility for servicing the property, standards for wear and tear and any option to buy.

Regulation N is internal to the Federal Reserve System. It governs relationships and transactions among Reserve Banks and foreign banks, bankers, and governments and describes the role of the Board of Governors in these relationships and transactions.

The regulation gives to the Board the responsibility for approving in advance negotiations or agreements by Reserve Banks with any foreign banks, bankers, or governments. Reserve Banks must keep the Board fully advised of all foreign relationships, transactions, and agreements.

Under direction of the Federal Open Market Committee, a Reserve bank maintaining accounts with a foreign bank may undertake negotiations, agreements, or contracts to facilitate open market transactions. Reserve Banks must report to the Board at least quarterly on accounts they maintain with foreign banks.

Regulation O prohibits member banks from extending credit to their own executive officers and prohibits banks that maintain correspondent account relationships with other banks from extending credit on preferential terms to one another's executive officers.

Regulation O also implements the reporting requirements of the Financial Institutions Regulatory and Interest Rate Control Act of 1978.

Each executive officer and principal shareholder of an insured bank is to report annually, to the bank's board of directors, the amount of his or her own indebtedness, and that of "related interests," to each of the insured bank's correspondent banks outstanding ten days before the report is filed. The range of interest rates on such loans and other terms and conditions of the loans must also be reported. A "related interest" is a company controlled by and political or campaign committees controlled by or benefiting bank officials and shareholders.

Each insured bank is to forward an annual, publicly available report to the appropriate banking agency, listing the name of each executive officer or principal shareholder who files a report of indebtedness with the bank's board of directors, and the aggregate amount of indebtedness of these persons and their related interests to the insured bank's correspondent banks.

The regulation also requires that each insured bank file with its appropriate regulator an annual report, available to the public upon request, listing the names of the bank's principal shareholders as of December 31, a list of executive officers and principal shareholders who were indebted or those related interests were indebted to the bank during the year, and the aggregate amount of such debt.

Regulation P Regulation P sets minimum standards for security devices and procedures state-chartered member banks must establish to discourage robberies, burglaries, and larcenies and to assist in identifying and apprehending persons who commit such acts.

A member bank must appoint a security officer to develop and administer a security program at least equal to the requirements of the regulation. The program must be in writing and approved by the bank's directors.

Each state-chartered member bank must annually file with its district reserve bank a signed statement certifying its compliance with the regulation.

Regulation Q prescribes the maximum rates of interest that may be paid by member banks on time and savings deposits.

Under the Depository Institutions Deregulation and Monetary Control Act of 1980, limitations on maximum rates of interest that may be paid on time and savings deposits are to be phased out gradually and eliminated as of 1986. In the interim, rules governing such deposits are prescribed by the Depository Institutions Deregulation Committee, The Secretary of the Treasury, Chairman of the Federal Reserve Board, Chairman of the Board of Directors of the Federal Deposit Insurance Corporation, Chairman of the Federal Home Loan Bank Board and Chairman of the National Credit Union Administration Board are voting members of the committee; the Comptroller of the Currency is a nonvoting member.

Regulation R aims at avoiding interlocking relationships between securities dealers and member banks, and thus any potential conflict of interest, collusion, or undue influence on member bank investment policies or investment advice to customers.

The regulation restates a general statutory prohibition on individuals involved in various phases of securities activities (including issuance, flotation, underwriting, public sale, or distribution) as either a director, officer, partner, or employee from serving simultaneously as a director, officer, or employee of a member bank.

However, the regulation permits member bank directors, officers, and employees to serve simultaneously as directors, officers, partners, or employees of organizations involved only in "government" securities transactions. These securities generally include, for example, those of the United States, the International Bank for Reconstruction and Development, the Tennessee Valley Authority, and the general obligations of states and municipalities.

Regulation S establishes the rates and conditions for reimbursement to financial institutions for providing records to a government authority.

Regulation S implements that section of the Right to Financial Privacy Act of 1978 requiring government authorities to pay a reasonable fee to financial institutions for providing financial records of individuals and small partnerships to federal agencies. Costs for searching for, reproducing or transporting books, papers, records, or other data requested are covered, with exceptions for such information as records furnished in connection with government loan programs or Internal Revenue summons.

Regulation T governs credit extension by securities brokers and dealers, including all members of national securities exchanges.

The regulation limits the amount of credit that may be extended to customers for purchasing or carrying securities based on the amount of cash and margin securities contained in the accounts. Generally, margin securities are those listed on national exchanges or identified as subject to margin requirements by the Board of Governors' Over-the-Counter stock list.

The maximum credit that may be extended to cover a purchase of margin securities is fixed from time to time by the Board. When securities on which credit has been extended are withdrawn from an account, cash or securities of an equivalent loan value usually must be deposited or a portion of the account liquidated to the extent necessary to assure that the proper equity of the account is maintained.

The regulation also prescribes rules governing cash transactions among brokers, dealers, their customers, and other brokers and dealers. It also limits the sources from which lending brokers and dealers may borrow in the ordinary course of their business.

Regulation U governs extension of credit by banks for purchasing and carrying margin securities.

If a loan is to be secured, directly or indirectly, by certain equity securities, a bank must obtain a properly completed Form U-1 in which the borrower must state the purpose of the loan. If the purpose is to purchase or carry any margin stock, the loan is a "purpose credit." If purpose credit is secured by designated equity securities, it is subject to the credit limitations and other restrictions of Regulation U.

Margin stocks include stocks listed on national exchanges, securities convertible into margin stock, most mutual funds, and over-the-counter stocks listed on the Board of Governors' OTC list of securities subject to credit regulations.

At the time a purpose credit to Regulation U is extended, the amount of the loan may not exceed the "maximum loan value" of the collateral. The maximum loan value of stock is a percentage of current market value fixed by the Board from time to time.

Regulation V facilitates and expedites the financing of contractors, subcontractors, and others involved in national defense work.

The Defense Production Act of 1950 and Executive Order 10480, as amended, authorize several federal departments and agencies to guarantee loans by private financing institutions to contractors, subcontractors, and others involved in national defense work. Regulation V spells out the authority granted to reserve banks, as fiscal agents of the United States, to assist federal departments and agencies in making and administering these loan guarantees and sets maximum rates of interest, guarantee fees, and commitment fee.

Regulation W was revoked in 1952.

Regulation W prescribed minimum down payments, maximum maturities, and other terms applicable to extensions of consumer credit. Such action was authorized by Executive Order during World War II, and by Congressional legislation in 1947–1948 and again during the Korean conflict. With the repeal of authorizing legislation in 1952, Regulation W was revoked.

Regulation X extends the provision of regulations G, T, and U (governing extensions of credit for purchasing or carrying securities in the United States) to certain borrowers and to certain types of credit extensions not specifically covered by those regulations.

The regulation currently applies to borrowers who, for purposes of purchasing or carrying securities, obtain credit in the United States and to borrowers who are "United States persons" or foreign persons controlled by, acting in behalf of, or in conjunction with, U.S. persons.

Regulation X requires that regulated borrowers obtaining credit within the United States comply with Regulations G, T, or U—whichever applies to the lenders in the transaction. When credit is obtained outside the United States, regulated borrowers must comply as if the foreign lender were subject to regulations G, T, or U.

Records substantially in conformity with Federal Reserve Form X-1 must be kept by borrowers subject to Regulation X who obtain credit outside the United States.

Regulation Y relates to the bank and nonbank expansion of bank holding companies and to the divestiture of impermissible nonbank interests.

Under the Bank Holding Company Act of 1956, as amended, a bank holding company is a company that directly or indirectly owns or controls a bank. The regulation contains presumptions and procedures the Board uses to determine whether a company controls a bank. The regulation also explains the procedures for obtaining Board approval to become a bank holding company and procedures to be followed by bank holding companies acquiring voting shares in banks or nonbank companies. The Board has specified in the regulation those nonbank activities that are closely related to banking and therefore permissible for bank holding companies.

Regulation Z prescribes uniform methods of computing the cost of credit, disclosure of credit terms, and procedures for resolving billing errors on certain credit accounts.

The credit provisions of the regulation apply to all persons who extend consumer credit more than twenty-five times a year or, in the case of real estate, more than five times a year. Consumer credit is generally defined as credit offered or extended to individuals for personal, family, or household purposes.

The major provisions of the regulation require lenders to:

- Provide borrowers with meaningful, written information on the cost of credit in terms of both the finance charge and the annual percentage rate.
- Respond to consumer complaints of billing errors on certain credit accounts within a specified period.
- Identify credit transactions on periodic statements of open end credit accounts.
- Provide certain rights regarding credit cards.

- Inform customers of the right to rescind certain real property transactions within a specified period.
- Comply with special requirements when advertising credit.

Regulation AA establishes consumer complaint procedures.

Under the regulation, any consumer complaint about an alleged unfair or deceptive act or practice by a state member bank, or an alleged violation of law or regulation, will be investigated. Complaints should be submitted, preferably in writing, to the Director of the Division of Consumer and Community Affairs at the Board of Governors of the Federal Reserve System, Washington, DC 20551, or to the reserve bank for the district in which the institution is located.

The complaint should describe the practice or action objected to an should give the names and addresses of the bank concerned and the person complaining.

The Board will attempt to give a substantive reply within 15 business days, or, if that is not possible, will acknowledge the complaint within 15 business days and set a reasonable time for a substantive reply.

The Board will also receive complaints regarding institutions other than state member banks, and refer them to the appropriate federal agencies.

A person filing a complaint does not have to be a customer of the institution in question, and the acts or practices complained of do not have to be subject to federal regulation. Consumers may complain about acts or practices that may, in fact, be expressly authorized, or not prohibited, by a current federal or state law or regulation.

Regulation BB implements the Community Reinvestment Act and is designed to encourage banks to help meet the credit needs of their communities.

Under Regulation BB, each bank office must make available a statement for public inspection indicating, on a map, the communities served by that office and the type of credit the bank is prepared to extend within the communities served. The regulation requires each bank to maintain a file of public comments relating to its CRA statement. The Federal Reserve Board, in examining a bank, must assess its record in meeting the credit needs of the entire community, including low and moderate income neighborhoods, and must take account of the record in considering certain bank applications.

Index